M

$ 19.99

ZION & BRYCE

JUDY JEWELL & W. C. McRAE

Contents

Although every effort was made to make sure the information in this book was accurate when going to press, research was impacted by the COVID-19 pandemic and things may have changed since the time of writing. Be sure to confirm specific details, like opening hours, closures, and travel guidelines and restrictions, when making your travel plans. For more detailed information, see p. 342.

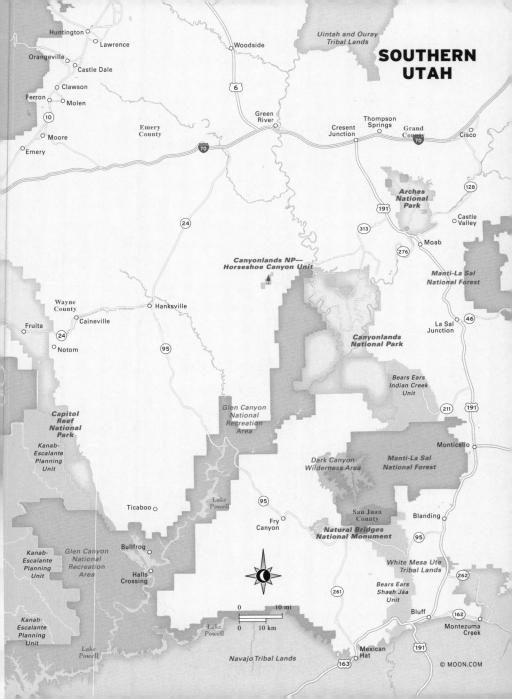

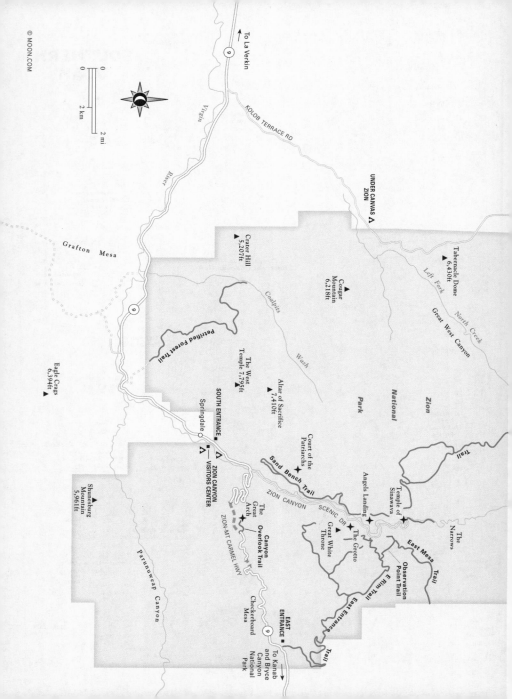

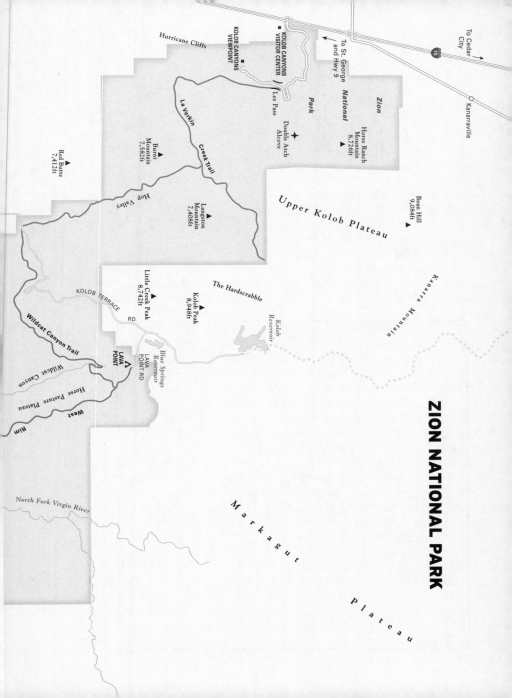

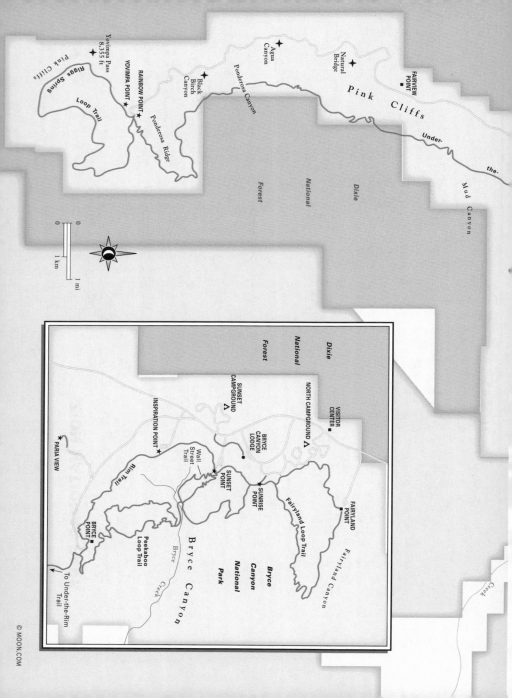

Pink Cliffs

Agua Canyon

Natural Bridge

FAIRVIEW POINT

Under-

the-

Mud Canyon

Yovimpa Pass 8,355 ft

Pink Cliffs

Riggs Spring

YOVIMPA POINT

RAINBOW POINT

Loop Trail

Black Birch Canyon

Ponderosa Canyon

Ponderosa Ridge

Dixie

National

Forest

0

1 km

0

1 mi

Dixie

National

Forest

NORTH CAMPGROUND

VISITOR CENTER

SUNSET CAMPGROUND

BRYCE CANYON LODGE

INSPIRATION POINT

Wall Street Trail

Rim Trail

SUNSET POINT

SUNRISE POINT

FAIRYLAND POINT

Fairyland Loop Trail

Fairyland Canyon

PARIA VIEW

BRYCE POINT

Peekaboo Loop Trail

Bryce Creek

Bryce Canyon

National

Park

To Under-the-Rim Trail

Creek

© MOON.COM

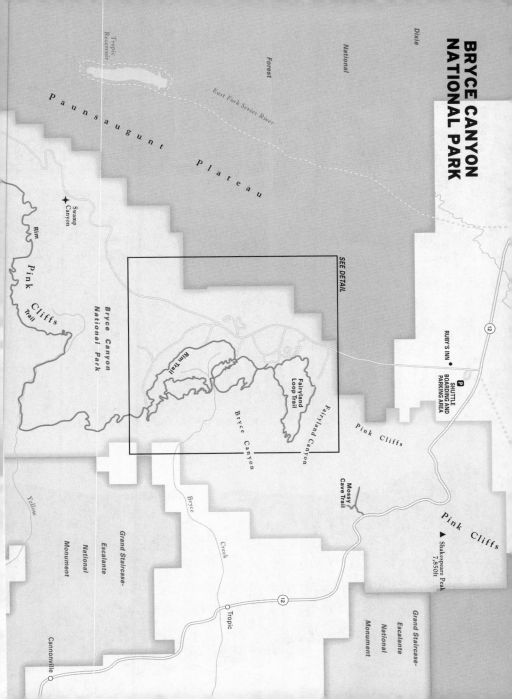

BRYCE CANYON NATIONAL PARK

Dixie

National

Forest

Tropic
Reservoir

East Fork Sevier River

P a u n s a u g u n t   P l a t e a u

Swamp
Canyon

Rim

Pink

Cliffs

Trail

Bryce Canyon
National Park

SEE DETAIL

Rim Trail

Fairyland
Loop Trail

Bryce Canyon

Fairyland Canyon

Pink Cliffs

RUBY'S INN

P
SHUTTLE
BOARDING AND
PARKING AREA

12

Mossy
Cave Trail

Pink Cliffs

▲ Shakespeare Peak
7,850ft

Yellow

Bryce

Creek

Grand Staircase-
Escalante
National
Monument

12

Tropic

Cannonville

Grand Staircase-
Escalante
National
Monument

Zion & Bryce

Filled with staggering beauty, drama, and power, Southern Utah seems like a place of myth. Five spectacular national parks and over a dozen national monuments, recreation areas, and state parks are all within a day's drive of one another. The colorful canyons, arches, and mesas found within this arid, high-elevation region are surprisingly diverse, and each park has its own characteristic landscape.

Zion National Park contains stunning contrasts, with towering rock walls deeply incised by steep canyons containing a verdant oasis of cottonwood trees and wildflowers. Bryce Canyon National Park is famed for its red-and-pink hoodoos, delicate fingers of stone rising from a steep mountainside. At sunrise, the light is magical, the air crisp, and the trails nearly empty.

A large section of the Grand Staircase-Escalante National Monument preserves the dry washes and slot canyons trenched by the Escalante River and its tributaries. Long-distance hikers descend into the deep, narrow river channels here to experience the near-mystical harmony of flowing water and stone. The Grand Staircase and Kaiparowits Plateau units of the monument preserve rock

---

Clockwise from top left: Natural Bridges National Monument; cabins in Escalante; images from the Great Gallery; Wild West scene in Kanab; biking the Slickrock Trail; view from the East Rim Trail in Zion.

arches, jutting promontories, and fossil-rich formations that are best explored on rugged backroad adventures.

The highlight of Capitol Reef National Park is the Waterpocket Fold, an enormous wrinkle of rock rising from the desert. The Fremont River carves a magnificent canyon through the formation, offering a leafy, well-watered sanctuary.

In Canyonlands National Park, the Colorado River carves through deep, red sandstone. From the Island in the Sky District, expansive vistas take in hundreds of miles of canyon country, while rafting the Colorado's Cataract Canyon is the wet and thrilling climax of many a vacation. The beauty is more serene and mystical at Arches National Park, where delicate rock arches provide windows into the region's geology. Short trails draw hikers into an eerily beautiful land of slickrock promontories and stone arches. High-spirited Moab is the recreational mecca of southeastern Utah, known for its mountain biking and comfortable—even sophisticated—dining and lodging.

Southern Utah is more than a showcase of erosion. Its cliffs and canyons have been home to Indigenous peoples for thousands of years, and the haunting beauty of Native American rock art is on display at hundreds of locations. After a glimpse of the magnificence and variety, some latch on to one special place and return year after year, growing to know it intimately.

Clockwise from top left: Delicate Arch with the La Sal Mountains in the background; Bryce Canyon on horseback; Hovenweep National Monument; Riverside Walk along the verdant Virgin River.

10 TOP
EXPERIENCES

1 **Stare at Picture Perfect Arches:** Delicate Arch (page 236), Mesa Arch (page 199), and the Windows Section (page 230) are just some of the stunning rock formations that are endlessly photographed by visitors.

2 **Drive Scenic Routes:** Take in the landscape from the comfort of your vehicle along scenic highways throughout the parks (pages 37, 132, and 168).

3 **Take Day Hikes in the Slot Canyons:** While the main Escalante River Canyon takes multiple days to traverse, side canyons give hearty day-hikers a chance to explore narrow rock channels carved deep into massive sandstone formations (page 143).

>>>

4 **River-Hike The Narrows:** Follow the all-abilities Riverside Walk up the verdant Virgin River canyon in Zion National Park, then plunge into the river and follow the watery trail through The Narrows (page 61).

5 **Admire Ancient Rock Art:** The Colorado Plateau contains a rich tapestry of pictographs and petroglyphs (page 35).

6 **Go Sky-gazing:** Whether painted with fiery sunsets or glowing with countless stars, these are some of the most gorgeous skies you'll ever see (page 96, page 114, and page 298).

>>>

7 **Wander in a Winter Wonderland:** Bryce Canyon is especially beautiful and otherworldly in winter. Snowshoe, ski, and join in the festivities (page 106).

>>>

8 **Go Off-Road Biking:** When it comes to mountain biking, **Moab's Slickrock Trail** may get all the love but Southern Utah offers an abundance of off-road adventures (page 38).

9 **Hike among the Hoodoos:** Bryce Canyon National Park's pink and gold hoodoos are magnificent viewed from a distance, but for a more profound experience follow trails to see the pillars up-close (page 102).

10 **Explore Ancestral Puebloan Villages:** Wander amid the stone structures built around 900 years ago at Edge of the Cedars State Park Museum (page 285) and Hovenweep National Monument (page 289).

<<<

Planning Your Trip

Where to Go

Zion National Park

In Zion National Park, **hiking trails** lead up **narrow canyons** cut into **massive sandstone cliffs,** passing quiet pools of water and **hanging gardens.** The park's main canyon, carved by the Virgin River, is an easy place to find a **day hike;** the rest of the park's canyons are the province of canyoneers and long-distance hikers.

Bryce Canyon National Park

Bryce Canyon has famous vistas across an eroded amphitheater of **pink sandstone hoodoos.** **Short trails** lead down from the canyon edge into a wonderland of fanciful formations and outcrops, and you'll have quite a different experience from the amateur photographers perched

along the rim if you venture into the park's backcountry.

Grand Staircase-Escalante

The Grand Staircase-Escalante region preserves some of the Southwest's best **canyon hiking.** Numerous day hikes and long-distance trails follow the slot canyons of the Escalante River. **Mountain bikers** can travel the jeep paths of **Hole-in-the-Rock Road** or **Burr Trail Road** to visit some of the same landscapes; even cruising **scenic Highway 12** in a car is an eye-popping experience.

Capitol Reef National Park

Capitol Reef preserves a vast wrinkle of rock

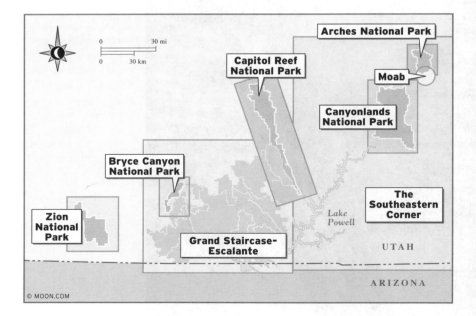

© MOON.COM

If You're Looking for...

rock-climbing at Indian Creek National Monument

- **Backpacking:** Head into the canyons and washes of Escalante Canyons unit.

- **Canyoneering:** Hike through the water of the Virgin River on the Narrows hike in Zion. For something more challenging, plan ahead and go to the Subway, accessible via the less traveled Kolob Terrace area of Zion.

- **Horseback Riding:** Zion and Bryce National Parks and Kodachrome Basin State Park each offer horseback rides into the backcountry.

- **Kid-Friendly Activities:** There's something magical about the sandstone spans and hoodoos in Arches, and exploring these awe-inspiring landmarks doesn't require a lot of stamina from little legs.

- **Mountain Biking:** Moab gets all the press, and serious mountain bikers must visit, but Red Canyon (just outside Bryce) has good biking without the hype.

- **Photography:** Sleep the day away if need be, but be sure to catch sunrise and sunset at Bryce. And don't stop there; the hoodoos are at their most photogenic when you hike down to visit them close-up.

- **Rafting:** The Colorado River offers sensational river rafting, with outfitters in Moab tempting you with everything from tame family excursions to heart-pounding white water.

- **Rock Climbing:** The big walls in Zion Canyon attract climbers, but the true hot spot is just east of Canyonlands' Needles District, in the new Indian Creek National Monument.

- **Scenic Driving:** Head east from Bryce and follow Highway 12 all the way to Capitol Reef. It's only a little over 100 miles (161 km), but it's best to allow at least half a day for the drive.

- **Solitude:** It's true—the marquee parks like Arches and Bryce are busy places. Plan a backcountry trek in Natural Bridges National Monument to have the wilderness to yourself.

- **Winter Sports:** Cross-country skiers can enjoy the quiet (and cheap) season at Bryce, when snow makes the hoodoos especially lovely.

- **Accessible Views:** It's hard to beat the views from the 0.5-mile (0.8-km) stretch of the paved Rim Trail between Bryce's Sunrise and Sunset Points.

Mesa Arch, Island in the Sky District of Canyonlands National Park

called the **Waterpocket Fold,** which buckles up into a vertical barricade across more than 100 miles (161 km) of southeast Utah. Of the few canyons that penetrate Waterpocket Fold, the Fremont River Canyon is most accessible along Highway 24. **Ancient petroglyphs,** pioneer farms and orchards, and soaring rock formations extend the length of the canyon. A **paved scenic drive** explores more canyons along the fold's western face. The rest of the park is **remote backcountry**—just the way hikers and backpackers like it.

Canyonlands National Park

Canyonlands National Park is made up of four sections: the **River District,** containing the canyons of the Colorado and Green Rivers; the **Needles District,** with **hiking trails** and backcountry roads through a standing-rock desert; the **Maze District,** a remote area filled with **geologic curiosities** and labyrinthine canyons; and the **Island in the Sky District,** a flat-topped mesa that overlooks the rest. A

separate area, the **Horseshoe Canyon Unit,** lies to the west and contains a significant cache of **prehistoric rock art.**

Arches National Park

Just up the road from Moab is Arches National Park, with its **famous natural bridges.** Arches is a **great family park:** It's not too large and there are lots of accessible hikes to explore. Unlike other Utah national parks, there's plenty to see even if you can't get out of the car and hike. Be sure to hike the **Windows Section,** a series of arches and rock fins at the center of the park, and to **Delicate Arch,** overlooking the Colorado River.

Moab

At the heart of Utah's slickrock country, Moab is the recreation capital of southeastern Utah. Although **mountain biking** put Moab on the map, old mining roads make **four-wheel-driving** an increasingly popular alternative. Arches National Park is just minutes from downtown, and Canyonlands' districts are an easy drive from Moab. But Moab is a destination in itself: a youthful, high-energy town that offers good **restaurants and brewpubs.**

The Southeastern Corner

Although Arches and Canyonlands National Parks get most of the attention from first-time visitors, veterans of the area know that southeastern Utah has abundant other wonders in **national recreation areas, national monuments,** and **state parks.** After you have explored the national parks, take time to visit such fascinating destinations as **Natural Bridges** and **Hovenweep National Monuments,** and the lovely alpine glades of **Manti-La Sal National Forest.**

When to Go

High Season
(APRIL-SEPTEMBER)
The parks are all open year-round, although **spring** (Apr.-early June) and **early fall** (Sept.-Oct.) are the most pleasant times to visit. They are also the busiest seasons, and travelers may find that popular campgrounds and hotels are booked well in advance.

Spring rain can dampen trails, and late winter-early spring storms can play havoc with backcountry roads. **Bryce Canyon,** at elevations ranging 6,600-9,100 feet (2,012-2,774 m), can be snowy well into the spring, but it is pleasant during the summer when other areas of Southern Utah bake.

Thunderstorms are fairly common in **summer** (late July-early Sept.) and bring the threat of flash flooding, especially in slot canyons. In **Canyonlands, Arches,** and **Moab,** summer temperatures can exceed 100°F.

Low Season
(OCTOBER-MARCH)
A few highways close for the winter (Nov.-Mar.), most notably the roads around Cedar Breaks National Monument. However, **winter** can be a great time to visit the high country around **Bryce,** where cross-country skiers take to the park roads. Around **Escalante,** the canyons can be quite nice in the winter during the day, but nights are freezing. In **Canyonlands** and **Arches,** winter days tend to be bright and sunny, but nighttime temperatures can dip into the teens or lower.

Before You Go

Park Fees and Passes
If you're planning on making the rounds of the national parks, buy an **America the Beautiful—National Parks and Federal Recreational Lands Pass** (valid for one year, $80) at your first stop to cover entrance to all national parks. Senior passes (lifetime pass $80) and free passes for residents with permanent disabilities are also available. Paid fees are good for seven days.

- **Zion, Bryce:** $35 per vehicle
- **Canyonlands, Arches:** $30 per vehicle
- **Capitol Reef, Natural Bridges:** $20 per vehicle
- **Cedar Breaks:** $10 per person
- **Grand Staircase-Escalante:** no entrance fee; backcountry permit required

Cedar Breaks National Monument

Many areas outside Utah's national parks are often less crowded but equally compelling.

- **Cedar Breaks National Monument** (page 114) preserves an area with formations similar to Bryce Canyon, but without the crowds.

- **Red Canyon** (page 112) is immediately west of Bryce Canyon and shares its geology, but because it's not a national park, you can mountain bike amid the red-rock formations. Dogs are allowed on the trails here, too.

- **Kodachrome Basin State Park** (page 127), between Bryce Canyon and Grand Staircase, is ringed by remarkable pink cliffs plus odd rock pillars called sand pipes.

- **Hovenweep National Monument** (page 289) contains the ruins of Ancestral Puebloan stone villages.

- **Natural Bridges National Monument** (page 298) contains rock formations that rival Arches National Park.

- **Dead Horse Point State Park** (page 250), on the road into Canyonlands, provides an eagle's-eye view over the Colorado River canyon.

- **Goblin Valley State Park** (page 307) has trails among goblin-shaped hoodoos.

Reservations

Many national parks now offer **reserved campsites.** If you want to camp in a park, reserve ahead—this is especially important at Arches—or plan to arrive early in the day to get an unreserved site.

ZION

Reservations at **Zion Lodge** (888/297-2757, www.zionlodge.com) can be made up to 13 months in advance. **Watchman and South Campgrounds** (877/444-6777, www.recreation.gov) accept advance reservations for some campsites.

BRYCE

Make reservations at the **Lodge at Bryce Canyon** (877/386-4383, www.brycecanyonforever.com) as far in advance as possible. Reservations are accepted at least two days in advance for all sites at **Sunset Campground** (877/444-6777, www.recreation.gov).

ARCHES

Reservations at **Devils Garden Campground** (www.recreation.gov) must be made no less than 4 days and no more than 240 days in advance.

In the Parks

Visitors Centers

There are more visitors centers than can be listed here, but these will get you started.

- **Zion Canyon Visitor Center** (8am-6pm daily mid-Apr.-late May and Sept.-mid-Oct., 8am-7pm daily late May-Aug., 8am-5pm daily mid-Oct.-mid-Apr.) is located at the south entrance.

- **Bryce Canyon Visitors Center** (8am-8pm daily May-Sept., 8am-6pm daily mid-Mar.-Apr. and Oct., 8am-4:30pm daily Nov.-mid-Mar.) is 4.5 miles (7.2 km) south of the Highway 12 turnoff.

- **Escalante Interagency Visitor Center** (8am-4:30pm daily) is in Escalante.

- **Capitol Reef Visitors Center** (Hwy. 24, 8am-6pm daily mid-May-Sept., 8am-4:30pm daily Oct.-May) is on Highway 24 at the turnoff for Fruita Campground and the Scenic Drive.

- The **Arches Visitor Center** (8am-5pm daily Mar.-Oct., 9am-4pm daily Nov.-mid-Mar.) is just past the park entrance booth.

- The **Moab Information Center** (8am-4pm daily) can handle inquiries about the town and the nearby parks, Arches and Canyonlands.

Where to Stay

If you don't have a reservation, the following are your best options for a **last-minute overnight.**

ZION

Outside the park, **Springdale** offers lodging and private campgrounds.

BRYCE

North Campground (year-round) has 99 sites available on a first-come, first-served basis. There are many motel rooms and a large private campground just outside the park boundary. The nearby towns of **Tropic** and **Panguitch** are also

Outside the Zion Canyon Visitors Center, this relief map offers a bird's eye view.

With a landscape characterized by mountain peaks and deep canyons, Southern Utah is filled with **big views.** And the state's trademark delicate-seeming **arches** and **hoodoos** are jaw-dropping sights as well.

CANYON VIEWS

With a few exceptions, you won't need to hike up-hill for miles to get a bird's-eye view—most of the vista points below are easily reached by a short hike or detour by car.

- **Angels Landing and Court of the Patriarchs:** If you really want views, take the steep hike to Angels Landing in Zion National Park (page 57). For an eyeful without a hike, jump off the shuttle bus at the Court of the Patriarchs (page 45).

- **Hog's Back:** Between Escalante and Boulder, Highway 12, aka the **Million-Dollar Road,** climbs this steep fin of rock to a jaw-dropping 360-degree vista of the slot canyons of the Escalante River and the cliffs of the Aquarius Plateau (page 131).

- **Navajo Knobs:** From this point 1,500 feet (457 m) above the Fremont River Canyon, reached after a 6-mile (9.7-km) climb from the **Hickman Natural Bridge** trailhead, you'll take in most of Southern Utah and the snakelike ridge of the 100-mile-long Waterpocket Fold (page 176).

- **Dead Horse Point State Park and Grand View Point:** From the main access road into the Island in the Sky section of Canyonlands, two road-end vista points provide swallow-your-gum views over the incredible Colorado River canyon. From Dead Horse Point State Park (page 278), a 30-foot-wide neck of land extends into the void over the twisting channels of the river 2,000 feet (610 m) below. Continue to Grand View Point, above the confluence of the Colorado and the Green Rivers, for vistas of canyons, sheer rock walls, pinnacles, and distant mountains (page 196).

ARCHES AND HOODOOS

How do they remain standing? These delicate-seeming stone pinnacles and arches have stood the test of time.

Monument Valley

- **Sunrise and Sunset Points:** Though the name is cliché, the angle of the rising sun really does make Sunrise Point in Bryce special. If you can't quite make it by sunrise, try a sunset view at Sunset Point (page 96).

- **Delicate Arch:** Looking across the Colorado River Canyon to the distant La Sal Mountains through Delicate Arch is a memory-of-a-lifetime experience (page 236).

- **Natural Bridges National Monument:** Often overlooked, the incredible rock spans here are some of the largest and most dramatic in Utah (page 298).

- **Monument Valley:** These towering pinnacles of stone have served as backdrop to innumerable Western movies (page 296).

good bets. **Kodachrome Basin State Park,** about 20 miles (32 km) south of Bryce, has great campsites.

GRAND STAIRCASE-ESCALANTE
Deer Creek Campground (year-round), outside Boulder, and **Calf Creek Campground** (early Apr.-late Oct.), near Escalante, offer primitive first-come, first-served campsites. **Escalante Petrified Forest State Park,** just west of town, has showers. The town of **Escalante** offers a range of accommodations.

CAPITOL REEF
Most sites at the popular **Fruita Campground** are reservable and open year-round. It's a green, well-watered spot, unlike most dusty Utah campgrounds. Stay in nearby **Torrey** if you want a roof over your head.

CANYONLANDS
All campgrounds are open year-round. Reservations can be made at the **Needles Campground** (Mar. 15-June 30 and Sept. 1-Oct. 31) in the Needles District. If Needles Campground is full, head east to the first-come, first-served campgrounds, either at the private **Needles Outpost** or at **Bureau of Land Management** sites along Lockhart Basin Road, east of the park entrance.

ARCHES
In **winter,** sites 1 to 24 at **Devils Garden Campground** are available first come, first served. Nearby **Moab** offers lodging as well as camping, from primitive sites along the Colorado River to shady comfort in town at the private tents-only **Up the Creek** campground.

Getting Around
Although the national parks of Utah are located in a geographically compact area, connecting the dots to visit each of them isn't always straightforward. The rugged topography of the area has made road building difficult, so visiting all of the parks requires **a lot of driving.** Unpaved back roads can serve as shortcuts if you have a high-clearance vehicle, but check locally before setting out to determine current conditions: Rainstorms and snowmelt can render these roads impassable.

PARK SHUTTLES
Early March-November, **Zion's** park road is accessible only via a park shuttle (reservation required). A free shuttle serves **Bryce Canyon** 8am-8pm daily mid-April to mid-October.

The Best of Zion & Bryce

The following itinerary only scratches the surface of what there is to see, but with this sampler, you'll know where to focus your long-weekend adventure.

Day 1

If you fly into Salt Lake City or Las Vegas, you'll probably get to **Zion National Park** in the late afternoon. Settle into your motel in Springdale and head into the park to check out the visitors center and take a ride up Zion Canyon on the park **shuttle bus.** Hop off for views of the **Court of the Patriarchs** and to take an easy hike up the **Riverside Walk.**

Day 2

Hike up the **West Rim Trail** to **Angels Landing,** or, for something a bit easier, hike the **Lower Emerald Pool Trail.** Visit Springdale's galleries in the afternoon. End the day with an early-evening hike up the **Watchman Trail.**

Alternatively, if weather permits and you're an experienced hiker and swimmer, hike the Riverside Trail into **the Narrows.** After a full day of hiking, enjoy dinner in Springdale.

Day 3

Head east out of the park via the Zion-Mt. Carmel Highway (Hwy. 9); turn north onto U.S. 89 and east onto Highway 12 to reach **Bryce Canyon National Park** (84 mi/135 km from Zion). Park the car and spend the day riding the park shuttle to vista points and exploring hoodoos from trailheads along the road. Camp in the park, or stay at the historic park lodge or one of the motels just outside the park entrance.

With More Time

If you're driving from Bryce back to Las Vegas, leave time for a stop in the **Kolob Canyons** section of **Zion National Park.** It's just off I-15 south of Cedar City. This is a little out of the way for Salt Lake City-bound travelers, who may want to take time to visit **Red Canyon,** which is just a few miles outside of Bryce's entrance.

Emerald Pools Trail

the Narrows

the sandstone formations at Devils Garden

Red Rocks Road Trip

Despite their proximity to one another, **visiting all of Utah's national parks** is a bit complicated because of the rugged terrain and lack of roads. You must plan on a lot of driving. So get in a road-trip frame of mind, cue up some good music, and head out.

Day 1

From Bryce Canyon National Park, drive 42 miles (68 km) east on Highway 12 through the town of Escalante to the dramatic **Lower Calf Creek Falls** trail. Cool your toes in the pool under the falls, then continue east to Boulder, where you'll spend the night at the **Boulder Mountain Lodge** (be sure to make reservations for dinner at **Hell's Backbone Grill** when you book your hotel room).

Day 2

Explore more of the Escalante River canyons. Backtrack along Highway 12 about 23 miles (37 km) toward the town of Escalante and turn onto Hole-in-the-Rock Road to traipse around **Devils Garden.** You can also visit the canyons of **Dry Fork of Coyote Gulch,** 26 bumpy dirt-road miles (42 km) south of Highway 12. Return to Boulder for the night.

Day 3

From Boulder, follow Highway 12 north 39 miles (63 km) over Boulder Mountain to Highway 24 and Torrey, your base for exploring **Capitol Reef National Park.** In the park, explore the old pioneer town of Fruita, hike to see petroglyphs, and drive the scenic park road. Add a hike along the **Chimney Rock Loop** or **Grand Wash Trail,** then return to Torrey for dinner and bed.

Day 4

Head to the east side of Capitol Reef and turn south from Highway 24 onto the **Notom-Bullfrog Road.** Follow this well-maintained

Road Trip Stops Between Zion and Bryce

The trip from Zion Canyon to Bryce Canyon is just over 70 miles (113 km)—a little more than an hour's drive along U.S. 89. It's just long enough that you might want some diversions along the way. Here are some worthwhile stops between Zion and Bryce. If you're starting in Bryce and heading to Zion, reverse the order.

- **Rock Shops:** There are lots of rocks in them there hills—get a trunkful the easy way at the **Rock Stop** (385 W. State St., Orderville, 435/648-2747). The friendly owners also make the best coffee in this part of the state.

- **German Bakery:** Dreaming of artisanal bread? Head to **Forscher Bakery** (110 N. State St., Orderville, 435/648-3040, www. forschergermanbakery.com), which makes outstanding naturally leavened breads (go for the rye) and good sandwiches.

- **Zip Line:** Soar on two zip lines (one that'll accommodate an adult and a small child) at **Mystic River Outdoor Adventures** (5000 U.S. 89, 435/648-2823, http:// mysticriveradventures.com). This small family-run park north of Glendale also has a fishing pond.

- **Horseback Rides:** Even if you're not spending the night, pull off at the **Bryce Zion Campground** (5 mi/8 km north of Glendale, 855/333-7263, https://brycezioncampground.net) and saddle

horseback riding in Zion National Park

up for a guided trail ride. The campground makes a good base for visiting both national parks.

- **Red Canyon:** Pause and take a breath before you get to busy Bryce. **Red Canyon** has lots of hiking and biking trails among the red sandstone spires.

(but mostly dirt) road 68 miles (109 km) south to Bullfrog Bay, where a ferry (May-Oct.) crosses Lake Powell. Ride the ferry, and once on the other side, head away from the lake for 40 miles (64 km) on Highway 276 to Highway 95 and **Natural Bridges National Monument.** (If you'd rather stick to pavement, or if the ferry isn't in season, continue east on Highway 24 to Hanksville, then turn south onto Highway 95 to reach Natural Bridges.) Often overlooked, this small park is a gem, with three massive rock bridges and an Ancestral Puebloan cliff dwelling along a 9-mile

(14.5-km) loop highway. A small campground is the only lodging at Natural Bridges, so you'll have to head back to Highway 95 and continue east to U.S. 191 to find a room for the night. The first town you'll come to on U.S. 191 is Blanding, which has plenty of options; however, tiny Bluff, 26 miles (42 km) south, is more charming.

Day 5

Get an early start if you want to explore the **Needles District of Canyonlands National Park.** Head north 46 miles (74 km) from Bluff

BLM Newspaper Rock Historical Monument

and follow well-marked paved roads west and north to **BLM Newspaper Rock Historical Monument,** one of the finest and most accessible petroglyph sites in Utah. From Newspaper Rock, continue west on Highway 211 to the Needles District, where a good short hike is along the **Cave Spring Trail.** Unless you're camping in Canyonlands, head back to U.S. 191 and go north 40 miles (64 km) to spend the night in **Moab.**

Day 6

Moab is just a few miles south of **Arches National Park.** You can tour Arches in half a day if you take only short hikes to viewpoints; if you want to visit all of the sites along the park road and hike to famed **Delicate Arch,** you'll spend all day in the park.

Day 7

Spend your last day exploring **Canyonlands' Island in the Sky District,** taking in the astonishing vista points (particularly **Grand View Point**) and saving time for a hike to the cliff edge. In the evening, enjoy the lively scene in Moab, with its good restaurants and brewpubs.

Best Day Hikes

These hikes through epic canyons, arches, and needles of sandstone invite you to get out of your vehicle and explore.

Zion

Starting from Zion Lodge, hike both the **Upper and Lower Emerald Pools Trails** (page 55) to small ponds, waterfalls, and verdant hanging gardens. If these trails are too tame (and you are up for a stiff climb and sheer drop-offs), the **West Rim Trail to Angels Landing** (page 57) is a classic hike you'll want to try.

Bryce

Given the high elevation and the fact that all of Bryce's best hikes descend from the rim (meaning a climb back up to the rim at the hike's end), it's good to start with the relatively easy 1.5-mile (2.4-km) **Queen's Garden Trail** (page 102). This will get you off the rim and down into the hoodoos and, unless you're acclimated to the 8,000-foot elevation, give you a bit of a workout. You can connect with the **Navajo Loop Trail** (page 103) to bring the total distance to about 3 miles (4.8 km).

Escalante Canyons

The hike up Calf Creek to **Lower Calf Creek Falls** (page 142) is a delectable sampler of the sights that make the slickrock canyon country of Escalante so compelling. From a trailhead right off Highway 12 (15 mi/24 km northeast of Escalante), a trail follows a desert canyon past rock art, ruins of an ancient Native American village, and beaver ponds, and terminates at a delicate 126-foot waterfall. The 5.5-mile (8.9-km) round-trip trail is easy enough for families.

Capitol Reef

Many of the hikes in Capitol Reef involve quite a bit of climbing, but hiking **Grand Wash** (page 177) is easy and scenic. Grand Wash is

West Rim Trail to Angels Landing, Zion National Park

Ancient Rock Art

The Colorado Plateau contains a rich tapestry of **pictographs** (drawings painted on rock using natural dyes) and **petroglyphs** (images carved into stone). Searching out rock-art panels can easily become an obsession, and it's a good one, because it will lead you far off the beaten path and deep into canyons that were once central to the area's ancient inhabitants.

petroglyphs at the Great Gallery

- **Boynton Overlook:** Stop at this overlook between the towns of Escalante and Boulder and scan the cliff face across the river to see a pictograph of many handprints (page 131).

- **Fremont Petroglyphs:** Easily viewed along Highway 24 in Capitol Reef's Fremont River Canyon, these petroglyphs depict horned mountain sheep and humans in headdresses (page 168).

- **BLM Newspaper Rock Historical Monument:** This easily reached showcase of rock art with an astonishing variety of images is located just outside Canyonlands' Needles District (page 204).

- **Great Gallery:** One of the most important rock-art sites in the United States is found at the end of a half-day hike in Canyonlands' Horseshoe Canyon Unit (page 221).

- **Delicate Arch:** On this popular hiking trail in Arches National Park, look for an often-overlooked panel of Ute-style rock-art images (page 232).

- **Holly Ruins:** You'll find many petroglyphs in this portion of Hovenweep National Monument, one of Utah's best-preserved Ancestral Puebloan villages (page 290).

one of only five canyons that cut through the rock reef, with walls up to 800 feet (244 m) high and narrows of just 20 feet (6 m). Pick up the trail from Highway 24, 5 miles (8 km) south of the visitors center, where Grand Wash enters Fremont Canyon. For a view over the wash, continue on the trail and climb to **Cassidy Arch** (3.5 mi/5.6 km round-trip), named after outlaw Butch Cassidy.

Canyonlands

Hiking into **Horseshoe Canyon** (page 191) to view the phenomenal rock art is a near-mystical experience. The **Great Gallery Trail** (page 221, 7 mi/11.3 km round-trip) requires negotiating a steep canyon wall, but these stunning petroglyphs in a verdant canyon are well worth the effort. The trailhead is 30 miles (48 km) east of Highway 24 on gravel roads.

In Canyonlands' **Island in the Sky District**, the landscape is nearly all vertical. The **Grand View Trail** (page 200) traverses more level ground, ending at the southernmost tip of the Island in the Sky peninsula, where you'll have views over much of the park, including the Green and Colorado River gorges.

Utah is famously family friendly, and the national parks all have programs for children (generally Memorial Day-Labor Day). Junior Ranger programs are essentially workbooks that will keep kids occupied.

- **Zion National Park:** The **Zion Nature Center** (page 45) offers daily programs on geology, animals, and ecosystems; short hikes on weekdays may include lessons on using a global positioning system (GPS) unit. **Horseback riding** (page 68) is a hit with kids ages seven and older; trail rides start at the corrals near Zion Lodge.

- **Bryce Canyon National Park:** Fantastically sculpted rocks give even the stodgiest hikers a child's sense of imagination. Wander down the **Queen's Garden Trail** (page 102) and make up your own names for the rock formations.

- **Canyonlands National Park:** The short **Cave Spring Trail** (page 208) in the Needles District gives hikers a chance to scamper across slickrock, scale ladders up cliffs, examine pictographs, and visit an old cowboy line camp. Stop by the visitors center for an Explorer Pack loaded with binoculars, a hand lens, a notebook, and other naturalist tools.

- **Arches National Park:** A ranger-led hike in the **Fiery Furnace** (page 237) requires a bit of hiking experience and agility; children under age five are not permitted, but older kids will enjoy the scenery and the scrambling.

Fiery Furnace hike in Arches National Park

- **Moab:** Cap a visit to canyon country with a raft trip down the Colorado River. Rent rafts and life jackets for the put-in at **Fisher Towers** (page 266), 23 miles (37 km) north of town. With quiet stretches punctuated by white water, it's a good bet for families.

The hike to **Chesler Park** (page 212), in the **Needles District,** begins at the busy four-wheeling Elephant Hill parking area but quickly leads away from the noisy crowds to a lovely meadow, complete with an old cowboy line camp.

Arches

The 3-mile (4.8-km) round-trip hike to **Delicate Arch** (page 236) is a moderately demanding trail up a slickrock formation to the arch and transcendent views over the Colorado River canyon. If you'd prefer a trail without the crowds, go early or late in the day to **Devils Garden** (page 241) at the end of the paved parkway, and hike the 7.2-mile (11.6-km) loop trail past eight arches and the weird formations in Fin Canyon.

Best Scenic Drives

Sometimes you barely need to get out of the car to enjoy southern Utah. These scenic drives are perfectly enjoyable from behind the windshield, but all offer chances to stop and explore.

Zion-Mount Carmel Highway

Starting point: Zion Canyon Visitor Center
Ending point: Mount Carmel Junction (at Hwy 9 and Hwy 89)
Mileage: 24.5 miles (39 km) one-way
Driving time: 2 hours

From Zion Canyon Visitor Center, this road climbs through a series of switchbacks, passes through a crazy long tunnel (or a much shorter alternate), and provides access to the canyons and high plateaus east of Zion Canyon, where you'll find fewer hikers than on the canyon trails. Take the easy 1-mile (1.6-km) round-trip Canyon Overlook Trail to peer down at the Great Arch of Zion, a "blind" arch that's not carved all the way through. Even if you're not up for a hike, be sure to stop and admire Checkerboard Mesa, a huge lump of hatch-marked sandstone right at the road's edge. From the east entrance to the park, the road continues about 13 miles to its junction with Highway 89. From here, head north to Bryce Canyon National Park or south to the Coral Pink Sand Dunes State Park, the town of Kanab, and the southern part of Grand Staircase-Escalante National Monument.

Bryce Scenic Drive

Starting point: Bryce Canyon Visitor Center
Ending point: Rainbow Point
Mileage: 36 miles (58 km) round-trip
Driving time: 3-4 hours

As you head out from the visitors center, don't be immediately tempted by the turnoff for the amphitheater: continue south and climb 18 miles (29 km) and 1,100 feet (335 m) to Rainbow Point.

The Zion-Mount Carmel Highway has views down into Zion Canyon.

Biking Southern Utah

Moab may be the center of mountain biking in southern Utah, but it's by no means the only place that offers great trails and a vibrant infrastructure of bike rental shops and tour operators. Top mountain biking trails and destinations include:

- **MOAB Brand Trails:** This series of interconnected trails north of Moab are great for slickrock beginners, with plenty of loop options to keep the ride interesting (page 262).

- **Slickrock Bike Trail:** This is the trail that put Moab on the map, with 12 miles of trails on often steep sandstone outcrops. Be warned: this is not the place to learn slickrock biking skills; if you're not totally confident, check out other local trails that will prime you to conquer this world-famous route (page 263).

- **Gemini Bridges Trail:** Accessed from the Island in the Sky highway, this trail is one of the most scenic in the Moab area and makes only moderate demands in terms of skill and endurance. If you take a shuttle to the trailhead, most of the ride is downhill (page 263).

- **Burr Trail Road:** Originally a cattle trail, this partly paved and dirt road skirts the north edge of canyons of the Escalante River between Boulder and the Notom-Bullfrog Road. Bikers have the freedom to explore canyon side-roads that may prove too daunting for most SUVs (pages 132 and 147).

biking the Slickrock Trail

- **Red Canyon:** Adjacent to Bryce Canyon National Park, this BLM recreation area offers 17 miles of trails through a similarly vertical landscape of hoodoos and red-rock canyons. Bikes aren't allowed off-road in Bryce Canyon National Park, but are free to explore here (page 113).

Here you'll get an overview of most of the park. A short walk away, Yovimpa Point looks out onto the cliffs and terraces of the Grand Staircase. Turn the car around and take your time coming back. (All sites will now be on the right side of the road, making turns easy since you're not turning against traffic.). Stop to photograph the Natural Bridge and the panorama from Farview Point.

After about 15 miles (24 km), stop to check out the views of the hoodoo-studded amphitheater from Bryce Point and Inspiration Point. Head to the lodge for a bite to eat and the half-mile walk on the Rim Trail to Sunrise and Sunset Points.

For one last view, turn in to Fairyland Point; the access road is just before you leave the park (but after the pay station).

Highway 12

Starting point: Junction of Hwy 89 and Hwy 12, near Panguitch

Ending point: Junction of Hwy 12 and Hwy 24, Torrey

Mileage: 123 miles (198 km) one-way

Driving time: 4 hours-1 week

This "All-American Road" from Highway 89 near Panguitch to Highway 24 in Torrey packs in more parks, monuments, and geology than just about any other road in the country. Pass through red rock arches in Red Canyon, skirt the edge of Bryce Canyon National Park, get within close range of Kodachrome Basin State Park, and continue east through the northern edge of Grand Staircase-Escalante National Monument, crossing the Hell's Backbone Bridge and the narrow Hog's Back to Boulder. The road turns north to cross over Boulder Mountain, with views of the Colorado Plateau, and practically lands in the lap of Capitol Reef National Park. You'll pass cliffs, rock spires, petroglyphs, and views of the Grand Staircase. There are lots of chances to get out and explore.

The Capitol Reef Scenic Drive

Starting point: Capitol Reef Visitor Center
Ending point: Capitol Gorge
Mileage: 21 miles (34 km) round-trip
Driving time: 1.5-2 hours

Head into the heart of the park on this short but absolutely scenic excursion. As you set off from the Capitol Reef visitors center, you'll pass the early settlement of Fruita; stop here coming or going (or both) for pie and ice cream at the century-old Gifford Farmhouse or fruit from the U-pick orchards.. The road climbs out of the Fremont River valley beneath a tall escarpment with tilted layers of rock. Stop to walk into the dry channels of the Grand Wash or continue on to Capitol Gorge (once the area's main highway, now a hiking trail that passes between tall sandstone walls and leads to petroglyphs and early settler signatures carved into the rock walls).

Notom-Bullfrog Road

Starting point: Hwy 24 at eastern edge of Capitol Reef National Park
Ending point: Bullfrog Marina, Lake Powell
Mileage: 70 miles (113 km) one-way
Driving time: 3 hours

The views of the eastern edge of the Waterpocket Fold are a highlight of this drive. The partially paved road goes from the eastern edge of Capitol Reef to Bullfrog Marina in Glen Canyon National Recreation Area. The drive itself is long and slow but beautiful. Consider taking the whole day to explore the relatively uncrowded hikes up dry washes and into slot canyons.

From Bullfrog, take a car ferry across the lake to Halls Landing and follow the easy route to Natural Bridges National Monument, or head back north on a paved road to Hanksville and Goblin Valley State Park.

Zion National Park

Zion is a magnificent park with sheer cliffs and monoliths reaching high into the heavens. Energetic streams and other forces of erosion created this land of finely sculptured rock. Trickles of water, percolating through massive chunks of sandstone over the centuries, have created both dramatic canyons and an incredible variety of niche ecosystems.

The park spreads across 147,000 acres and contains eight geologic formations and four major vegetation zones. Elevations range from 3,666 feet (1,117 m), in lower Coalpits Wash, to 8,726 feet (2,660 m), atop Horse Ranch Mountain.

The canyon's name is credited to Isaac Behunin, a Mormon pioneer who believed this spot to be a refuge from religious persecution. When

Highlights

Look for ★ to find recommended sights, activities, dining, and lodging.

★ **Drop by Zion Canyon Visitor Center:** Outdoor exhibits, an excellent bookstore, and a shuttle bus that will ferry you up the canyon ensure that a stop at the visitors center is always worthwhile (page 44).

★ **Capture a View of the Patriarchs:** It's a challenge to fit these massive sandstone peaks into your camera frame, but even without a photo, you'll remember this view for a lifetime (page 45).

★ **Wander to the Upper Emerald Pool:** The pool, at the base of a 300-foot-high cliff and waterfall, is indeed emerald green and the trail is lined with wildflowers (page 55).

★ **Hike the West Rim Trail to Angels Landing:** On this vigorous day hike, you'll find spectacular views and some tenuous footing—not for acrophobes or children (page 57)!

★ **Explore the Narrows:** Wade into the Virgin River through the high walls of spectacular canyons (page 61).

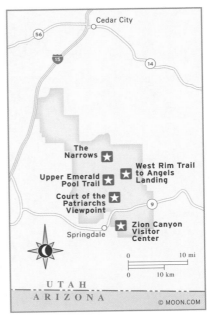

Zion National Park

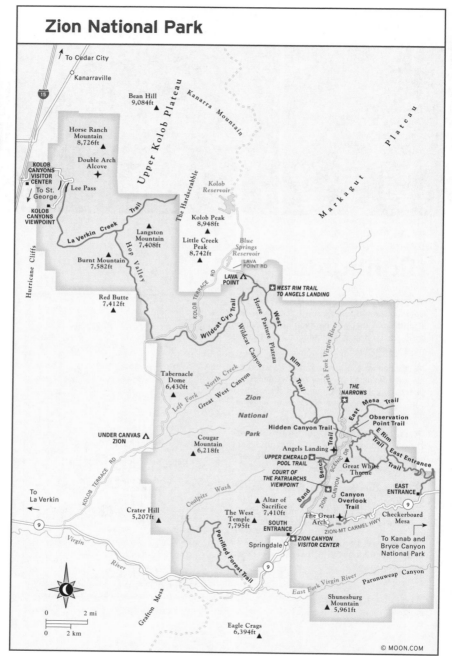

To Cedar City

Kanarraville

15

Bean Hill
9,084ft

Kanarra Mountain

Upper Kolob Plateau

Plateau

Markagunt

Horse Ranch
Mountain
8,726ft ▲

Double Arch
Alcove ✦

KOLOB
CANYONS
VISITOR
CENTER ■
To St.
George ↓

Lee Pass

The Hardscrabble

Kolob Reservoir

KOLOB
CANYONS
VIEWPOINT ■

La Verkin Creek

Hop Valley

Trail

Langston
Mountain
7,408ft ▲

Kolob Peak
8,948ft ▲

Little Creek
Peak
8,742ft ▲

Blue Springs Reservoir

LAVA
POINT RD

LAVA
POINT ⚠

✦ WEST RIM TRAIL
TO ANGELS LANDING

Burnt Mountain
7,582ft ▲

Hurricane Cliffs

Red Butte
7,412ft ▲

KOLOB TERRACE RD

Wildcat Cyn Trail

Wildcat Canyon

Horse Pasture Plateau

West Rim Trail

North Fork Virgin River

THE
NARROWS
✦

East Mesa Trail

Observation
Point Trail

Tabernacle
Dome
6,430ft ▲

North Creek

Left Fork

Great West Canyon

Zion

National

Park

Hidden Canyon Trail

E Rim Trail

East Entrance

UNDER CANVAS ⚠
ZION

Cougar
Mountain
6,218ft ▲

Angels Landing
✦
UPPER EMERALD ✦
POOL TRAIL

COURT OF
THE PATRIARCHS
VIEWPOINT

Bench Trail

Scenic Dr

Great White
Throne ▲

EAST
ENTRANCE ■

To
La Verkin
←

9

KOLOB TERRACE RD

Coalpits Wash

▲ Altar of
Sacrifice
7,410ft

Sand Canyon

Zion Canyon

Canyon
Overlook
Trail ✦

9

Checkerboard
Mesa

Crater Hill
5,207ft ▲

The West
Temple ▲
7,795ft

SOUTH
ENTRANCE

The Great
Arch ✦

ZION-MT CARMEL HWY

To Kanab and
Bryce Canyon
National Park →

Virgin River

Petrified Forest Trail

Springdale

✦ ZION CANYON
VISITOR CENTER

East Fork Virgin River

Parunuweap Canyon

9

Grafton Mesa

Shunesburg
Mountain
5,961ft ▲

0   2 mi
0   2 km

Eagle Crags
6,394ft ▲

© MOON.COM

Zion in One Day

- Park your car at **Zion Canyon Visitor Center.** Enjoy the exhibits, then jump on the **park shuttle.**

- Head to **The Grotto** where you'll hike to the **Upper Emerald Pool** via the **Kayenta Trail.** Explore the pretty green pool, then return the way you came.

- Walk or take a short shuttle ride to **Zion Lodge** and lunch at the **Red Rock Grill.**

- When you're ready for an afternoon activity, ride the shuttle to its final stop, the **Temple of Sinawava,** and stroll the **Riverside Walk.**

- For dinner, remember that **Springdale** is just a short walk or shuttle ride from the park entrance, and it has good restaurants, shops, and galleries.

Brigham Young later visited the canyon, however, he found tobacco and wine in use and declared the place "not Zion"—which some dutiful followers then began calling it.

Zion's grandeur is evident all through the year. Even rainy days can be memorable, as waterfalls plunge from nearly every crevice in the cliffs. Spring and fall are the choice seasons for pleasant temperatures and the best chances of seeing wildlife and wildflowers. From about mid-October through early November, cottonwoods and other trees and plants blaze with color. Summer temperatures in the canyons can be uncomfortably hot, with highs hovering above 100°F. Summer is also the busiest season. In winter, nighttime temperatures drop to near freezing, and the weather tends to be unpredictable, with bright sunshine one day and freezing rain the next. Snow-covered slopes contrast with colorful rocks. Snow may block some of the high-country trails and the road to Lava Point, but the rest of the park is open and accessible year-round.

Exploring the Park

PLANNING YOUR TIME

Visitors short on time should drop in at the Zion Canyon Visitor Center and ride the shuttle along Zion Canyon Scenic Drive, stopping for a short walk on the Riverside Walk Trail. If you have a full day, you can also include an easy hike to the Upper Emerald Pool or a challenging trek up the West Rim Trail to Angels Landing.

It's always worth spending part of a day hiking with a park ranger. If you can join a ranger hike, spend the morning of your second day going wherever the ranger leads you. In the afternoon, depending on your energy, hike the short but steep Watchman Trail or drive to the east entrance of the Zion-Mt. Carmel tunnel and get a bird's-eye view of Zion Canyon from the Canyon Overlook Trail.

After that, it's time for longer hikes: Angels Landing is a classic for those who are in good shape and not afraid of heights. Alternatively, if weather conditions and your own abilities are suitable, the hike up the Virgin River (largely in the river) is a spectacular way to spend another full day.

Beautiful Zion Canyon does get crowded; 2019 saw nearly 4.5 million visitors, and most of them come expecting to see the sights along the 6-mile-long (9.7-km) scenic drive. Escape the crowds by heading to the Kolob sections of the park. Take an extra day to drive Kolob Canyons Road, which begins at I-15 about 17 miles (27 km) south of Cedar City, and hike the less crowded trails. Visitors with more time may also want to drive Kolob Terrace Road and hike from Lava Point for another perspective of the park; this steep drive is about 44 miles (71 km) round-trip from the town of Virgin.

Exploring the Park

Zion National Park (435/772-3256, www.nps.gov/zion, $35 per vehicle, $30 motorcyclists, $20 pedestrians or bicyclists, admission good for 7 days) has four main sections: Zion Canyon, a higher-elevation area east of Zion Canyon, the Kolob Terrace, and Kolob Canyons. The highlight for most visitors is Zion Canyon, which is approximately 2,400 feet (732 m) deep. Zion Canyon Scenic Drive winds through the canyon floor along the North Fork of the Virgin River, past some of the most spectacular scenery in the park. A shuttle bus ferries visitors along this route spring-fall. Hiking trails branch off to lofty viewpoints and narrow side canyons. Waterloving adventurers can continue past the pavement's end and hike up the Virgin River at the Narrows in upper Zion Canyon.

The spectacular Zion-Mt. Carmel Highway, with its switchbacks and tunnels, provides access to the canyons and high plateaus east of Zion Canyon. Two other roads enter the rugged Kolob section northwest of Zion Canyon. Kolob is a Mormon name meaning "the brightest star, next to the seat of God." The Kolob section includes wilderness areas rarely visited by humans.

VISITORS CENTERS
★ Zion Canyon Visitor Center
The park's sprawling **Zion Canyon Visitor Center** (435/772-3256, 8am-6pm daily mid-Apr.-late May and Sept.-early Oct., 8am-7pm daily late May-Aug., 8am-5pm daily early Oct.-mid-Apr.), between Watchman and South Campgrounds, is a hub of activity. The plaza outside the building features good interpretive plaques with enough info to get you going on a hike. Inside, a large area is devoted to backcountry information;

staff members can answer your questions about various trails, give you updates on the weather forecast, and help you arrange a shuttle to remote trailheads. The wilderness desk (435/772-0170) opens at 7am daily late April-late November, an hour earlier than the rest of the visitors center. A Backcountry Shuttle Board allows hikers to coordinate transportation between trailheads.

The busiest part of the visitors center is the bookstore, stocked with an excellent selection of books covering natural history, human history, and regional travel. Topographic and geologic maps, posters, and postcards are also sold here.

Kolob Canyons Visitor Center
Although it is small and has just a handful of exhibits, the **Kolob Canyons Visitor Center** (435/772-3256, 8am-5pm daily mid-Mar.-early Oct., 8am-4:30pm daily mid-Oct.-mid-Mar.) is a good place to stop for information on exploring the Kolob region. Hikers can learn about current trail conditions and obtain the permits required for overnight trips and Zion Narrows day trips. The visitors center and the start of Kolob Canyons Road are just off I-15 exit 40.

TOURS
Except for ranger-led walks, classes, horseback rides from Zion Lodge, and the shuttle bus, Zion is a do-it-yourself park. Outfitters are not permitted to lead trips within the park. If you'd like a guided tour outside park boundaries, where you'll find equally stunning scenery and adventure, several outfitters in Springdale lead cycling, canyoneering, and climbing trips.

The best way to get a feel for Zion's

impressive geology and variety of habitats is to take in a walk with a park ranger. Many nature programs and hikes are offered late March-November; check the posted schedule at the Zion Canyon Visitor Center. Children's programs, including the popular Junior Ranger program, are held intermittently during March and April and daily Memorial Day-mid-August at **Zion Nature Center** near South Campground; ask at the visitors center for details.

The **Zion National Park Forever Project** (435/772-3264, https://zionpark.org) is authorized to run educational programs in the park, which include animal tracking, photography, and archaeology; fees vary.

Sights

ZION NATURE CENTER

At the northern end of South Campground, the **Zion Nature Center** (2pm-6pm daily Memorial Day-Labor Day) houses programs for kids, including Junior Ranger activities for ages 6-12. Although there's no shuttle stop for the Nature Center, it's an easy walk along the **Pa'rus Trail** from the Zion Canyon Visitor Center or the Zion Human History Museum. Check the park newsletter for kids' programs and family hikes. Programs focus on natural history topics such as insects and bats in the park. Many Junior Ranger activities can be done on your own—pick up a booklet ($1) at the visitors center bookstore.

ZION HUMAN HISTORY MUSEUM

The old park visitors center has been retooled as the **Zion Human History Museum** (9am-6pm daily mid-Apr.-late May, 9am-7pm daily late May-early Sept., 9am-6pm daily early Sept.-early Oct., 10am-5pm Sat.-Sun. early Oct.-mid.-Apr., entry included in park admission fee), covering Southern Utah's cultural history with a film introducing the park and bare-bones exhibits focusing on Native American and Mormon history. It's at the first shuttle stop after the visitors center. This is a good place to visit when you're too tired to hike any farther or if the weather forces you to seek shelter. The museum's back patio is a good place to watch the sun rise over the tall peaks of the West

Temple and Altar of Sacrifice, so named because of the red streaks of iron on its face.

ZION CANYON

During the busy seasons (7am-6pm final two weekends in Feb. and first weekend of March, 7am-7:30pm daily early Mar.-mid May, 6am-8:30pm daily mid-May-Sept., 7am-6:30pm daily Oct.), the 6-mile (9.7-km) Zion Canyon Scenic Drive is closed to private cars, and you must travel up and down Zion Canyon in a shuttle bus (90 minutes round-trip, free). Most visitors find the shuttle an easy and enjoyable way to visit Zion Canyon sites. The road follows the North Fork of the Virgin River upstream, passing impressive natural formations along the way, including the Three Patriarchs, Mountain of the Sun, Lady Mountain, Great White Throne, Angels Landing, and Weeping Rock. The bus stops at points of interest along the way; you can get on and off the bus as often as you want at these stops. The road ends at Temple of Sinawava and the beginning of the Riverside Walk Trail. Buses are scheduled to run every 7 to 10 minutes.

★ Court of the Patriarchs Viewpoint

A short trail from the shuttle stop leads to the viewpoint. The Patriarchs, a trio of peaks to the west, overlook Birch Creek; they are, from left to right, Abraham, Isaac, and Jacob. Mount Moroni, the reddish peak on the far right, partially blocks the view of Jacob. Although the official viewpoint is a beautiful

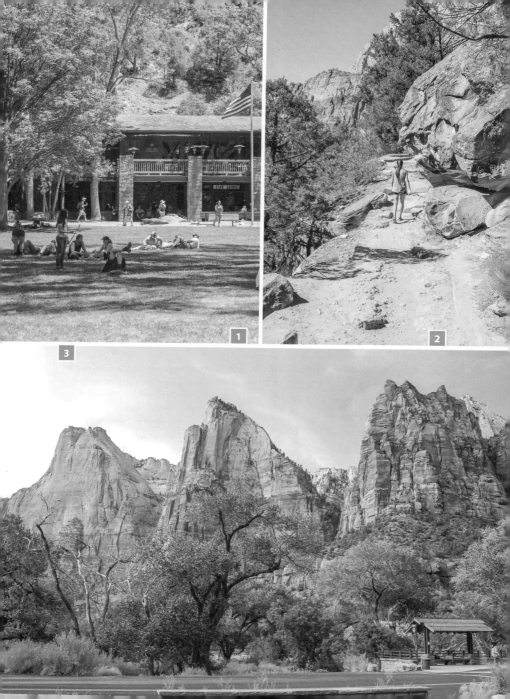

place to relax and enjoy the view, you'll get an even better view if you cross the road and head about 0.5 mile (0.8 km) up **Sand Bench Trail.**

Zion Lodge

Rustic **Zion Lodge** (435/772-7700, www.zionlodge.com), with its big front lawn, spacious lobby, and accessible snack bar, restaurant, and public restrooms, is a natural stop for most park visitors. You don't need to be a guest at the lodge to enjoy the ambience of its public areas, and the snack bar is not a bad place to grab lunch.

From the lodge, cross the road to hike the **Lower Emerald Pool Trail.** Or you can reach the **Upper Emerald Pool** by walking the 0.5 mile (0.8 km) **Grotto Trail** to **The Grotto** picnic area. (The shuttle also make a stop at The Grotto.) From there, you can take the **Kayenta Trail** to the **Upper Emerald Pool Trail.**

The Grotto

The Grotto is a popular place for a picnic. From here, the **Grotto Trail** leads back to the lodge; across the road, the **Kayenta Trail** links to the **Upper Emerald Pool Trail** and the **West Rim Trail** leads to Angels Landing and, eventually, to the Kolob Terrace section of the park.

Visible from several points along Zion Canyon Drive is the **Great White Throne.** Topping out at 6,744 feet (2,056 m), this bulky chunk of Navajo sandstone has become, along with the Three Patriarchs, emblematic of the park. Ride the shuttle in the evening to watch the rock change color in the light of the setting sun.

Weeping Rock

Several hikes including the short and easy **Weeping Rock Trail,** start at Weeping Rock; however, this shuttle stop and trailhead was closed following a huge rockfall in the summer of 2019. The slab of Navajo sandstone

that dropped 3,000 feet from the side of Cable Mountain injured several visitors (they all survived). A Utah Geological Survey report found that the area was susceptible to future large rockfalls, and the park has characterized the closure as being "long term" but in 2020, park staff thought some trail access might be possible by 2021.

Weeping Rock is home to hanging gardens and many moisture-loving plants, including the striking Zion shooting star. The rock "weeps" because this is a boundary between porous Navajo sandstone and denser Kayenta shale. Water trickles down through the sandstone, and when it can't penetrate the shale, it moves laterally to the face of the cliff.

While you're at Weeping Rock, scan the cliffs for the remains of cables and rigging that were used to lower timber from the top of the rim to the canyon floor. During the early 1900s, this wood was used to build pioneer settlements in the area.

Big Bend

Look up: This is where you're likely to see rock climbers on the towering walls or hikers on Angels Landing. These climbers presumably are quite experienced and know what they're doing.

Temple of Sinawava

The last shuttle stop is at this canyon, where 2,000-foot-tall (610-m) rock walls reach up from the sides of the Virgin River. There's not enough room for the road to continue farther up the canyon, but it's spacious enough for a fine paved wheelchair-accessible walking path. Plants sprout from hanging gardens on the cliffs, and birds nest in some of the holes in the cliff walls. The Riverside Walk heads 1 mile (1.6 km) upstream to the Virgin Narrows, a place where the canyon becomes too narrow even for a sidewalk to squeeze through. You may see people hiking up the Narrows, in the river, from the end of the Riverside Walk. Don't join them unless you're properly outfitted.

1: the shady lawns at Zion Lodge **2:** hiking the Kayenta Trail **3:** Court of the Patriarchs

ZION-MOUNT CARMEL HIGHWAY

The east section of the park is a land of sandstone slickrock, hoodoos, and narrow canyons. You can get a good eyeful of the dramatic scenery along the Zion-Mt. Carmel Highway (Hwy. 9) between Zion Canyon Visitor Center and the east entrance station. Highlights on the plateau include a hike on the Canyon Overlook Trail, which begins just east of the long tunnel, and views of the Checkerboard Mesa, near the east entrance station.

Mile 0.0: Zion Canyon Visitor Center

Mile 1.6: Canyon Junction; 3.5 miles from the visitor center. Highway 9 turns east here and begins to climb from the floor of Zion Canyon through a series of six switchbacks to a high plateau. Pullouts allow the non-acrophobic a chance to take a look at the canyon below.

Mile 5.0: Zion-Mt. Carmel Tunnel; This 1.1-mile (1.8-km) tunnel, completed in 1930, is narrow and a little harrowing to drive, though passengers may enjoy glimpses of park scenery through several windows cut into the tunnel wall.

Any vehicle more than 7 feet, 10 inches wide, 11 feet, 4 inches high, or 40 feet (12 m) long (50 ft/15 m with a trailer) must be "escorted" through in one-way traffic; a $15 fee, good for two passages, is charged at the tunnel to do this. Although the park service persists in using the term *escort*, you're really on your own through the tunnel. Park staff will stop oncoming traffic, allowing you enough time to drive down the middle of the tunnel, but you do not follow an escort vehicle.

Hours for large vehicles are limited (8am-6pm daily early to mid-March and late Sept.-Oct., 8am-7pm daily mid-Mar.-late April and early Sept.-late Sept., 8am-8pm daily late April-late Aug., 8am-4:30pm daily Nov.-early Mar.). Bicycles must be carried through the long tunnel on a car or truck; it's too dangerous to ride (hitchhiking is permitted).

A much shorter (530-foot/162-m) tunnel to the east is easy to navigate and requires no special considerations.

Mile 6.1: Canyon Overlook Trail; Just past the eastern end of the tunnel, this 1-mile (1.5-km, round-trip) trail leads to a viewpoint overlooking Zion Canyon.

Mile 10.9: Checkerboard Mesa is visible from the road; Pull off to admire this hulking rock's distinctive pattern, caused by a combination of vertical fractures and horizontal bedding planes, both accentuated by weathering.

Mile 11: East entrance; This is just a pay station with no services.

Mile 24.5: Mt. Carmel Junction; From here, Highway 89 heads north to Bryce Canyon National Park or south to Kanab.

KOLOB TERRACE

The Kolob Terrace section of the park is a high plateau roughly parallel to and west of Zion Canyon. From the town of Virgin (15 mi/24 km west of the south entrance station on Hwy. 9), the steep Kolob Terrace Road—now paved, though still unsuitable for trailers—runs north through ranchland and up a narrow tongue of land with drop-offs on either side, and then onto a high plateau where the land widens out. The Hurricane Cliffs rise from the gorge to the west, and the back sides of Zion Canyon's big walls are to the east. The road passes in and out of the park and terminates at Kolob Reservoir, a popular boating and fishing destination outside the park. This section of the park is much higher than Zion Canyon, so it is a good place to explore when the canyon swelters in the summertime. It's also much less crowded than the busy canyon. Snow usually blocks the way in winter.

Lava Point

The panorama from **Lava Point** (elev. 7,890 ft/2,405 m) takes in the Cedar Breaks area to the north, the Pink Cliffs to the northeast,

1: Kolob Canyons **2:** high plateau east of Zion Canyon

Navajo Sandstone

Take a look anywhere along **Zion Canyon** and you'll see 1,600-2,200-foot (488-671-m) cliffs of Navajo sandstone. According to researchers at the University of Nebraska-Lincoln, these big walls were formed from immense sand dunes deposited during a hot dry period about 200 million years ago, when the landmass on which they sit was located about 15 degrees north of the equator (about the same location as Honduras is today). Shifting winds blew the sand in one direction, then another—a careful inspection of the sandstone layer reveals the diagonal lines resulting from this "cross-bedding." The shift patterns in the sandstone—the slanting striations easily seen in the cliff faces—were caused in part by intense monsoon rains, which compacted and moved the dunes.

Checkerboard Mesa

Eventually, a shallow sea washed over the dunes, leaving shells behind. As the shells dissolved, their lime seeped down into the sand, cementing it into sandstone. After the Colorado Plateau formed, rivers cut deeply through the sandstone layer. As a result, the cliff's lower layers are stained red from iron oxides.

The east side of Zion is a particularly good place to view the warps and striations in the sandstone. Get up close and personal with **Checkerboard Mesa** to see the intricate patterns or check out the **Great White Throne,** which is largely white Navajo sandstone. But really, with the right light and a pair of binoculars, examination along any part of Zion Canyon's big walls will reveal the cross-bedding.

Zion Canyon Narrows and tributaries to the east, the monoliths of Zion Canyon to the southeast, and Mount Trumbull on the Arizona Strip to the south. Signs help identify features. Lava Point, which sits atop a lava flow, is a good place to cool off in summer—temperatures are about 20°F cooler than in Zion Canyon. Aspen, ponderosa pine, Gambel oak, and white fir grow here. A small primitive campground near the point offers sites during warmer months (free), but there is no water. From Virgin, take the Kolob Terrace Road about 21 miles (34 km) north to the Lava Point turnoff; the viewpoint is 1.8 miles (2.9 km) farther on a well-marked but unpaved spur road. (Vehicles longer than 19 feet/6 meters are prohibited on the Lava Point road.) Expect the trip from Virgin to Lava Point to take about an hour.

Kolob Reservoir

This high-country lake north of Lava Point has good fishing for rainbow trout. An unpaved boat ramp is at the south end near the dam. People sometimes camp along the shore, although there are no facilities. Most of the surrounding land is private. To reach the reservoir, continue north 3.5 miles (5.6 km) on Kolob Terrace Road from the Lava Point turnoff. The fair-weather road can also be followed past the reservoir to the Cedar City area. Blue Springs Reservoir, near the turnoff for Lava Point, is closed to the public.

KOLOB CANYONS

North and west of Zion Canyon is the remote backcountry of the Kolob. This area became a second Zion National Monument in 1937, and then was added to Zion National Park in 1956.

The paved 5-mile (8-km) Kolob Canyons Road begins at the Kolob Canyons Visitor Center just off I-15 and ends at the Timber Creek Overlook Trail; it's open year-round.

Kolob Canyons Road

This 5-mile (8-km) scenic drive winds past the dramatic Finger Canyons of the Kolob to the Timber Creek Overlook Trail. The road is paved and has many pullouts where you can stop to admire the scenery. The first part of the drive follows the 200-mile-long (320-km) Hurricane Fault, which forms the west edge of the Markagunt Plateau. Look for the tilted rock layers deformed by friction as the plateau rose nearly 1 mile (1.6 km). The **Taylor Creek Trail,** which begins 2 miles (3.2 km) past the **Kolob Canyons Visitor Center** (3752 E. Kolob Canyon Rd., New Harmony, 435/772-3256, 8am-5pm daily mid-Mar.-mid-Oct., 8am-4:30pm daily mid-Oct.-mid-Mar.) provides a close look at the canyons.

Lee Pass, 4 miles (6.4 km) beyond the visitors center, was named after John D. Lee, who was the only person ever convicted of a crime in the infamous Mountain Meadows Massacre; he's believed to have lived nearby for a short time after the 1857 incident, in which a California-bound wagon train was attacked by an alliance of Mormons and local Native Americans. About 120 people in the wagon train were killed. Only small children too young to tell the story were spared. The close-knit Mormon community tried to cover up the incident and hindered federal attempts to apprehend the killers. Only Lee, who oversaw Indian affairs in Southern Utah at the time, was ever brought to justice; he was later executed.

La Verkin Creek Trail begins at the Lee Pass trailhead and offers trips to Kolob Arch and beyond. Signs at the end of the road identify the points, buttes, mesas, and mountains. The salmon-colored Navajo sandstone cliffs glow a deep red at sunset. The **Timber Creek Overlook Trail** begins from the **picnic area** at road's end and climbs 0.5 mile (0.8 km) to the overlook (elev. 6,369 ft/1,941 m); views encompass the Pine Valley Mountains, Zion Canyon, and distant Mount Trumbull.

Recreation

Zion's hiking trails are tailored to a range of abilities, making it easy to explore. Both the Pa'rus Trail and Riverside Walk are wheelchair-accessible; the latter passes lush hanging gardens. Casual hikers can spend several days riding the shuttle bus up Zion Canyon and hopping off for day hikes. But be forewarned that many of the best hikes in Zion Canyon require significant climbs up the canyon walls. These hikes up to vertiginous viewpoints or narrow canyons may whet your appetite for extended backpacking trips or an in-water hike up the Virgin River Narrows.

Experienced hikers can do countless off-trail routes in the canyons and plateaus surrounding Zion Canyon; rangers can suggest areas. Rappelling and other climbing skills may be needed to negotiate drops in some of the more remote canyons. Groups cannot exceed 12 hikers per trail or drainage. Overnight hikers must obtain **backcountry permits** from the Zion Canyon or Kolob Canyons Visitor Centers or from https://zionpermits. nps.gov ($5 nonrefundable fee for online reservations). The permit fees are based on group size: $15 for 1-2 people, $20 for 3-7, and $25 for 8-12. Some areas of the park—mainly those near roads and major trails—are closed to overnight use. Ask about shuttles to backcountry trailheads outside Zion Canyon at the visitors center's backcountry desk (435/772-0170). Shuttles are also available from **Zion Rock and Mountain Guides** (1458 Zion Park Blvd., Springdale, 435/772-3303, www.

zionrockguides.com) and **Zion Guru** (792 Zion Park Blvd., Springdale, 435/628-8329, www.zionguru.com) in Springdale.

Zion Canyon Hikes

HIKING IN ZION CANYON

The trails in Zion Canyon provide perspectives of the park that are not available from the roads. Many of the hiking trails require long ascents but aren't too difficult if taken at a leisurely pace. Carry water on all hikes, even the shortest walks. Descriptions of the following trails are given in order from the mouth of Zion Canyon to the Virgin River Narrows. **Trails are sometimes closed due to rockfall;** always check the park website (www.nps.gov/zion) or the visitor centers for the latest trail conditions.

Pa'rus Trail

Distance: 3.5 miles (5.6 km) round-trip
Duration: 2 hours
Elevation change: 50 feet (15 m)
Effort: easy
Trailheads: South Campground and Canyon Junction
Shuttle stops: Zion Canyon Visitor Center or Canyon Junction

This paved, mostly wheelchair-accessible trail runs from South Campground to the Canyon Junction shuttle-bus stop. For most of its distance, the trail skirts the Virgin River, and it makes for a nice early morning or evening stroll. Listen for the trilling song of the canyon wren (easy to hear), then try to spot the small bird in the bushes (not so easy to see). The Pa'rus Trail is the only trail in the park open to bicycles and pets. While most of the trail has a slope of 2-5 percent, there is one 30-foot section of the trail that has an 18 percent slope. Access to the Zion Human History Museum from the Pa'rus Trail is uneven and rocky with large log steps and tight turns; this part of the trail is not wheelchair accessible. The museum, however, is accessible as a regular shuttle stop.

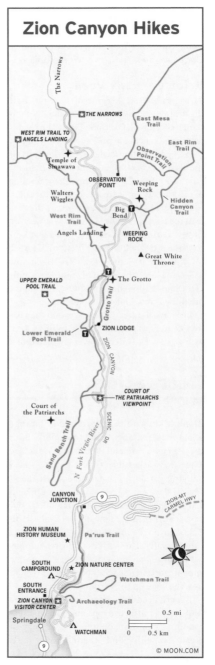

© MOON.COM

Zion Hikes

Trail	Effort	Distance	Duration
Weeping Rock Trail	easy	0.5 mi/0.8 km round-trip	30 minutes
Archeology Trail	easy-moderate	0.8 mi/1.3 km round-trip	30 minutes
Canyon Overlook Trail	easy	1 mi/1.6 km round-trip	1 hour
Sand Bench Trail	easy	4.5 mi/7.2 km round-trip	3 hours
Lower Emerald Pool Trail	easy	1.2 mi/1.9 km round-trip	1 hour
Riverside Walk	easy	2.2 mi/3.5 km round-trip	1.5-2 hours
Coalpits Wash	easy	3.5 mi/5.6 km round-trip	2 hours
Pa'rus Trail	easy	3.5 mi/5.6 km round-trip	2 hours
Northgate Peaks Trail	easy	4 mi/6.4 km round-trip	2 hours
Huber Wash	easy	5 mi/8 km round-trip	2.5 hours
Timber Creek Overlook Trail	easy-moderate	1 mi/1.6 km round-trip	30 minutes
★ Upper Emerald Pool Trail via Kayenta Trail	moderate	3 mi/4.8 km round-trip	1-3 hours
Watchman Trail	easy-moderate	3.3 mi/5.3 km round-trip	2 hours
Taylor Creek Trail	easy-moderate	5 mi/8 km round-trip	4 hours
Wildcat Canyon Trail	moderate	10 mi/16 km round-trip	5 hours
Hidden Canyon Trail	strenuous	3 mi/4.8 km round-trip	2.5-3 hours
★ West Rim Trail to Angels Landing	strenuous	5.4 mi/8.7 km round-trip	4 hours
Observation Point Trail	strenuous	8 mi/12.9 km round-trip	5 hours
The Subway	strenuous	9 mi/14.5 km round-trip	7 hours
East Rim Trail	strenuous	10.6 mi/17 km one-way	6-8 hours
West Rim Trail	strenuous	13.3 mi/21.4 km one-way	8 hours or overnight
Hop Valley Trail to Kolob Arch	strenuous	14 mi/22.5 km round-trip	8 hours
La Verkin Creek Trail to Kolob Arch	strenuous	14 mi/22.5 km round-trip	8 hours
★ The Narrows	strenuous	9.4 mi/15.1 km round-trip	8 hours
The Narrows (downstream)	strenuous	16mi/26km one-way	10-14 hours

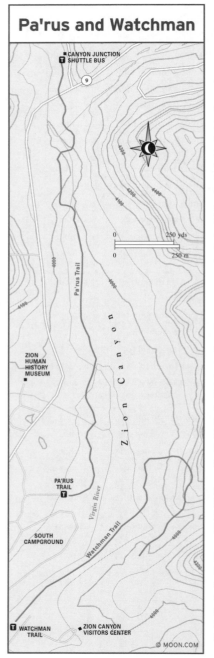

Archeology Trail

Distance: 0.8 mile (1.3 km) round-trip
Duration: 30 minutes
Elevation change: 80 feet (24 m)
Effort: easy-moderate
Trailhead: just north of Watchman Campground
Shuttle stop: Zion Canyon Visitor Center

This short uphill walk leads to an Ancestral Puebloan food storage site. The trail starts across the road from the visitors center parking lot, at the entrance to the Watchman Campground; look for the colorful interpretive sign and follow the trail. From the top of the hill, you'll get views of the lower canyon. Although it's not the park's most spectacular hike, it's worth exploring to get an idea of Ancestral Puebloan life. Artifacts from the site are exhibited at the Zion Human History Museum.

Watchman Trail

Distance: 3.3 miles (5.3 km) round-trip
Duration: 2 hours
Elevation change: 370 feet (113 m)
Effort: easy-moderate
Trailhead: just north of Watchman Campground
Shuttle stop: Zion Canyon Visitor Center

No, this hike doesn't go to the top of 6,555-foot (2,000-m) Watchman Peak, but it does lead to a mesa with a good view of this prominent mountain. The hike starts off unspectacularly, but it gets more interesting as it gains elevation. Be sure to look back over your shoulder for views of Zion Canyon's high walls.

At the top of the mesa, the Watchman pops into view. The short mesa-top loop trail is worth taking for its views of Springdale and its nice assortment of wildflowers, including barrel cacti.

During the middle of the day, this trail can bake in the sun. Try to hike it on a cool day or early or late in the day. It's a good shakedown hike to do on the evening you arrive at Zion. As soon as the sun drops behind the canyon walls, set out—on long summer evenings, you'll have plenty of time to complete it before dark.

Sand Bench Trail

Distance: 4.5 miles (7.2 km) round-trip
Duration: 3 hours
Elevation change: 500 feet (152 m)
Effort: easy
Trailhead: Zion Lodge
Shuttle stops: Court of the Patriarchs or Zion Lodge

This loop trail has good views of the Three Patriarchs, the Streaked Wall, and other monuments of lower Zion Canyon. During the main season, outfitters across the road from Zion Lodge organize three-hour horseback rides on the trail. The horses churn up dust and leave an uneven surface (among other things), so hikers usually prefer to go elsewhere during those times. The trail soon leaves the riparian forest along Birch Creek and climbs onto the dry benchland. Piñon pine, juniper, sand sage, yucca, prickly pear cactus, and other high-desert plants and animals live here. Hikers can get off the shuttle at the Court of the Patriarchs Viewpoint, walk across the scenic drive, and then follow a service road to the footbridge and trailhead. A 1.2-mile (1.9-km) trail extension runs north along the river and connects the trailhead with Zion Lodge. In warmer months, try to hike in the early morning or late afternoon.

Lower Emerald Pool Trail

Distance: 1.2 miles (1.9 km)
Duration: 1 hour
Elevation change: 69 feet (21 m)
Effort: easy
Trailhead: across the footbridge from Zion Lodge
Shuttle stop: Zion Lodge

This easy, relatively flat hike follows a paved trail to the lowest Emerald Pool. One of the highlights, at least when there's a lot of spring run-off, is the tall waterfall that feeds into the pool. At other times, especially during drought years, it may be just a trickle. Although this trail is good for families and can be navigated by people using wheelchairs, it can get crowded.

★ Upper Emerald Pool Trail via Kayenta Trail

Distance: 3 miles (4.8 km) round-trip
Duration: 1-3 hours
Elevation change: 350 feet (107 m)
Effort: moderate
Trailhead: across the footbridge from The Grotto
Shuttle stop: The Grotto

Pools, small waterfalls, and views of Zion Canyon make this hike a favorite. The trail begins at The Grotto picnic area, crosses a footbridge, and turns left onto the 1-mile (0.8-km)

The Watchman Trail leads to a good view but doesn't climb the peak itself.

Emerald Pools Trails

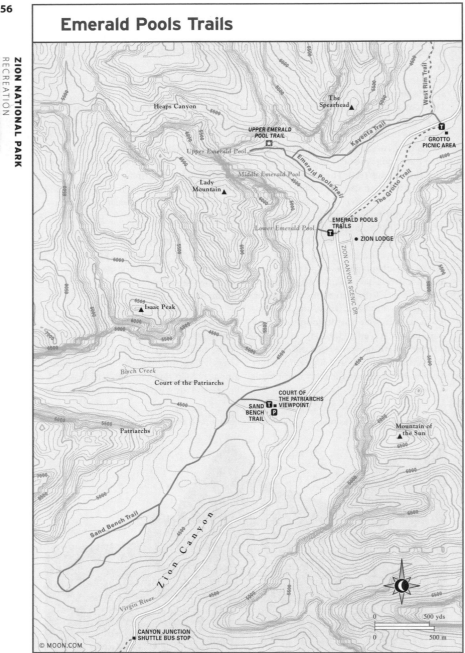

Heaps Canyon

The Spearhead ▲

West Rim Trail

UPPER EMERALD
POOL TRAIL ★

Upper Emerald Pool

Kayenta Trail

Emerald Pools Trail

🅣 GROTTO
PICNIC AREA

Middle Emerald Pool

Lady
Mountain ▲

The Grotto Trail

Lower Emerald Pool

EMERALD POOLS
TRAILS 🅣

● ZION LODGE

ZION CANYON SCENIC DR.

Isaac Peak ▲

Birch Creek

Court of the Patriarchs

Mountain of
▲ the Sun

COURT OF
THE PATRIARCHS
VIEWPOINT
SAND 🅣 ▪
BENCH 🅟
TRAIL

Patriarchs

Sand Bench Trail

Zion Canyon

Virgin River

CANYON JUNCTION
▪ SHUTTLE BUS STOP

0   500 yds
0   500 m

© MOON.COM

Kayenta Trail before continuing uphill to Upper Emerald Pool Trail. Follow this trail for 0.5 mile (0.8 km) and you'll reach the spring-fed pool. This magical spot has a white-sand beach and towering cliffs. Don't expect to find solitude; this trail is quite popular.

Although the Emerald Pool trails are relatively easy, they can get icy and slippery in winter. More people have died from falls on the Emerald Pool trails than on the hike to Angels Landing, so do hike with attention and care.

★ West Rim Trail to Angels Landing

Distance: 5.4 miles (8.7 km) round-trip
Duration: 4 hours
Elevation change: 1,488 feet (454 m)
Effort: strenuous
Trailhead: across the road from The Grotto picnic area
Shuttle stop: The Grotto

This strenuous trail leads to some of the best views of Zion Canyon. Start from The Grotto picnic area (elev. 4,300 ft/1,311 m) and cross the footbridge, then turn right along the river. The trail, which was blasted out of the cliff side by Civilian Conservation Corps workers during the 1930s, climbs the slopes and enters the cool and shady depths of Refrigerator Canyon. Walter's Wiggles, a series of 21

closely spaced switchbacks, wind up to Scout Lookout and a trail junction—it's 4 miles (6.4 km) round-trip and a 1,050-foot (320-m) elevation gain if you decide to turn around here. Scout Lookout has fine views of Zion Canyon. From the lookout, it's a daunting 0.5 mile (0.8 km) to the summit of Angels Landing.

Angels Landing rises as a sheer-walled monolith 1,500 feet (457 m) above the North Fork of the Virgin River. Although the trail to the summit is rough and very narrow, chains provide security in the more exposed places. Hike this final approach to Angels Landing with great caution and only in good weather; don't go if the trail is covered with snow or ice or if thunderstorms threaten. Children must be closely supervised, and people who are afraid of heights should skip this trail. Once on top, the panorama makes all the effort worthwhile. Not surprisingly, it's most pleasant to do this steep hike during the cooler morning hours. Start extra-early to avoid crowds, which can make the final stretch all the more frightening.

Energetic hikers can continue 4.8 miles (7.7 km) on the main trail from Scout Lookout to **West Rim Viewpoint,** which overlooks the Right Fork of North Creek. This strenuous 12.8-mile (20.6 km) round-trip hike from

Walter's Wiggles are a series of 21 tight switchbacks on the way to Angels Landing.

West Rim Trail to Angels Landing

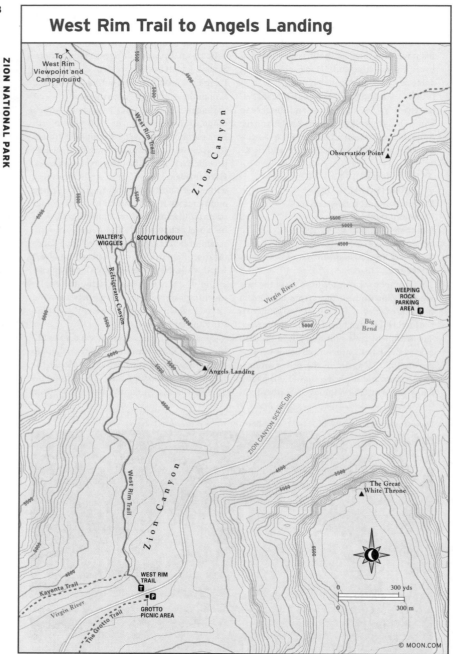

To West Rim Viewpoint and Campground

West Rim Trail

Zion Canyon

Observation Point

WALTER'S WIGGLES

SCOUT LOOKOUT

Refrigerator Canyon

Virgin River

WEEPING ROCK PARKING AREA

Big Bend

Angels Landing

ZION CANYON SCENIC DR

Zion Canyon

West Rim Trail

The Great White Throne

WEST RIM TRAIL

Kayenta Trail

Virgin River

The Grotto Trail

GROTTO PICNIC AREA

0   300 yds
0   300 m

© MOON.COM

The Grotto picnic area includes 3,070 feet (936 m) of elevation gain. West Rim Trail continues through Zion's backcountry to Lava Point (elev. 7,890 ft/2,405 m), where there's a primitive campground. A car shuttle and one or more days are needed to hike the 13.3 miles/21.4 kilometers (one-way) from The Grotto picnic area to Lava Point. You'll have an easier hike if you start at Lava Point and hike down to the picnic area; even so, be prepared for a long day hike. The trail has little or no water in some seasons.

Weeping Rock Trail

Distance: 0.5 mile (0.8 km) round-trip
Duration: 30 minutes
Elevation change: 100 feet (30 m)
Effort: easy
Trailhead: Weeping Rock parking area
Shuttle stop: Weeping Rock

This easy trail winds past lush vegetation and wildflowers to a series of cliff-side springs above an overhang. Thousands of water droplets glisten in the afternoon sun. The springs emerge where water seeping through more than 2,000 feet (610 m) of Navajo sandstone meets a layer of impervious shale. Signs along the way identify some of the trees and plants. **Note:** This trail may be closed, due to recent rockfall. Check its status at the visitors center or on the park's website.

Observation Point Trail

Distance: 8 miles (12.9 km) round-trip
Duration: 5 hours
Elevation change: 2,148 feet (655 m)
Effort: strenuous
Trailhead: Weeping Rock parking area
Shuttle stop: Weeping Rock

This strenuous trail climbs to Observation Point (elev. 6,507 ft/1,983 m) on the edge of Zion Canyon. Trails branch off along the way to Hidden Canyon, upper Echo Canyon, the east entrance, East Mesa, and other destinations. The trail starts off at the Weeping Rock parking area as the East Rim Trail and quickly makes the first of many switchbacks. You'll reach the junction for Hidden Canyon

Trail after 0.8 mile (1.3 km). Several switchbacks later, the trail enters sinuous Echo Canyon. This incredibly narrow chasm can be explored for short distances upstream and downstream to deep pools and pour-offs. **Echo Canyon Trail** branches to the right at about the halfway point; this rough trail continues up the canyon and connects with trails to Cable Mountain, Deertrap Mountain, and the east entrance station (on Zion-Mt. Carmel Highway). The East Rim Trail then climbs slickrock slopes above Echo Canyon with many fine views. Parts of the trail are cut right into the cliffs; this work was done in the 1930s by the Civilian Conservation Corps. You'll reach the rim at last after 3 miles (4.8 km) of steady climbing, and then it's an easy 0.6-mile (1-km) hike through a forest of piñon pine, juniper, Gambel oak, manzanita, sage, and some ponderosa pine to Observation Point. Impressive views take in Zion Canyon below and mountains and mesas all around. The **East Mesa Trail** turns right about 0.3 mile (0.5 km) before Observation Point and follows the plateau northeast to a dirt road outside the park. **Note:** These trails may be closed, due to recent rockfall. Check their status at the visitors center or on the park's website.

Hidden Canyon Trail

Distance: 3 miles (4.8 km) round-trip
Duration: 2.5-3 hours
Elevation change: 850 feet (259 m)
Effort: strenuous
Trailhead: Weeping Rock parking area
Shuttle stop: Weeping Rock

See if you can spot the entrance to Hidden Canyon from below. Inside the narrow canyon are small sandstone caves, a little natural arch, and diverse plant life. The high walls, rarely more than 65 feet (20 m) apart, block sunlight except for a short time at midday. From the trailhead at the Weeping Rock parking area, follow the East Rim Trail 0.8 mile (1.3 km) up the cliff face, then turn right and go 0.7 mile (1.1 km) on the Hidden Canyon Trail to the canyon entrance. Footing can be a bit difficult in places, but chains provide handholds

Weeping Rock Trails

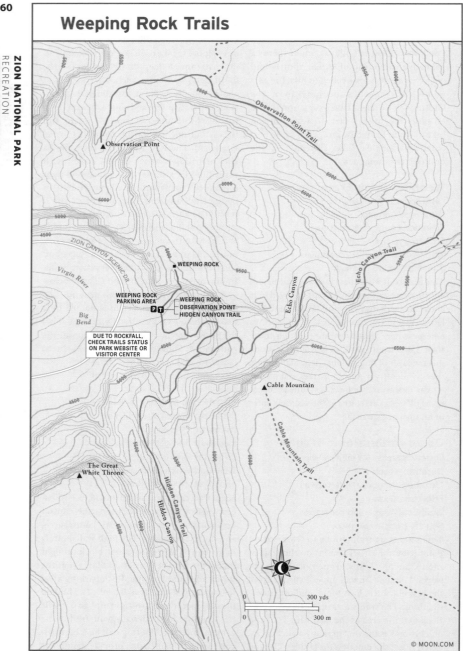

Observation Point

Observation Point Trail

Echo Canyon Trail

ZION CANYON SCENIC DR.

Virgin River

WEEPING ROCK

WEEPING ROCK PARKING AREA

WEEPING ROCK OBSERVATION POINT HIDDEN CANYON TRAIL

Echo Canyon

Big Bend

DUE TO ROCKFALL, CHECK TRAILS STATUS ON PARK WEBSITE OR VISITOR CENTER

Cable Mountain

Cable Mountain Trail

The Great White Throne

Hidden Canyon Trail

Hidden Canyon

0   300 yds
0   300 m

© MOON.COM

on the exposed sections. Steps chopped into the rock just inside Hidden Canyon help bypass some deep pools. After heavy rains and spring runoff, the creek forms a small waterfall at the canyon entrance. The canyon itself is about 1 mile (1.6 km) long and mostly easy walking, although the trail fades away. Look for the arch on the right about 0.5 mile (0.8 km) up the canyon. **Note:** This trail may be closed, due to recent rockfall. Check its status at the visitors center or on the park's website.

Riverside Walk

Distance: 2.2 miles (3.5 km) round-trip
Duration: 1.5-2 hours
Elevation change: 57 feet (17 m)
Effort: easy
Trailhead: Temple of Sinawava parking area
Shuttle stop: Temple of Sinawava

This is one of the most popular hikes in the park, and except for the Pa'rus Trail, it's the easiest. The nearly level paved trail begins at the end of Zion Canyon Scenic Drive and heads upstream along the Virgin River to the Narrows. Allow about two hours to fully take in the scenery—it's a good place to get a close-up view of Zion's lovely hanging gardens. Countless springs and seeps on the canyon walls support luxuriant plant growth and swamps. Most of the springs occur at the boundary between the porous Navajo sandstone and the less permeable Kayenta Formation below. The water and vegetation attract abundant wildlife; keep an eye out for birds and animals and their tracks. Late morning is the best time for photography. In autumn, cottonwoods and maples display bright splashes of color. At trail's end, the canyon is wide enough only for the river. Hikers continuing upstream on the Narrows hike must wade and sometimes even swim.

★ The Narrows

Distance: 9.4 miles (15.1 km) round-trip
Duration: 8 hours
Elevation change: 200 feet (61 m)
Effort: strenuous
Trailheads: end of Riverside Walk or Chamberlain's Ranch
Shuttle stop: Temple of Sinawava

Upper Zion Canyon is probably the most famous backcountry area in the park, yet it's also one of the most strenuous. There's no trail, and you'll be wading in the river much of the time, which can be knee- to chest-deep. In places, the high fluted walls of the upper North Fork of the Virgin River are only 20 feet (6 m) apart, and very little sunlight penetrates the depths. Mysterious side canyons beckon.

Hikers should be well prepared and in good condition—river hiking is more tiring than hiking over dry land. The major hazards are flash floods and hypothermia; even in the summer, expect water temperatures of about 68°F/20°C (winter temps run around 38°F/3°C). Finding the right time to go can be tricky: Spring runoff is usually too high, summer thunderstorms bring hazardous flash floods or toxic cyanobacteria, and winter is too cold, unless you hike in a dry suit. That leaves just early summer (mid-June-mid-July) and early autumn (mid-Sept.-mid-Oct.) as the best bets.

Don't be tempted to wear river sandals or sneakers up the Narrows; it's easy to twist an ankle on the slippery rocks. If you have a pair of hiking boots that you don't mind drenching, they'll work, but an even better solution is available from the **Zion Adventures** (36 Lion Blvd., Springdale, 435/772-1001, www.zionadventures.com) and other Springdale outfitters. They rent specially designed river-hiking boots, along with neoprene socks, walking sticks, and, in cool weather, dry suits. Boots, socks, and sticks rent for $27; with a dry suit, the package costs $57. They also provide valuable information about hiking the Narrows and lead tours of the section below Orderville Canyon (about $189 pp, depending on group size and the season). **Zion Outfitter** (7 Zion Park Blvd., Springdale, 435/772-5090, www.zionoutfitter.com), located just outside the park entrance, and **Zion Guru** (795 Zion Park Blvd., Springdale, 435/632-0432, www.

nguru.com) provide similar services at
ıparable prices.

'alk with rangers at the Zion Canyon
...or Center before starting a trip; they also
have a handout with useful information on
planning a Narrows hike. No permit is needed
if you're just going up as far as Big Springs,
although you must first check conditions and
the weather forecast with rangers.

A good half-day trip begins at the end of
the Riverside Walk and follows the Narrows
1.5 miles/2.4 kilometers (about 2 hours) upstream to Orderville Canyon, then back the
same way. Orderville Canyon makes a good
destination itself; it can be accessed via a
side road off Kolob Terrace Road. A permit
is required to explore this area beyond its
first quarter mile. In the main canyon of the
Narrows, non-permitted day hikers must turn
around at Big Springs, about 2.5 miles past
Orderville.

The Narrows (Downstream)

Distance: 16 miles (26 km) one-way
Duration: 10-14 hours
Elevation change: 334 feet (102 m)
Effort: strenuous
Trailheads: Chamberlain's Ranch
No shuttle access

Although it involves a considerable amount of
planning, a downstream hike of the Narrows
saves not only climbing but also the work of
fighting the river currents. If you're planning to hike the full length of the Narrows,
it is strongly recommended that you take the
downstream route. The main hitch is that
this requires a shuttle to the upper trailhead
near Chamberlain's Ranch, reached via an 18-
mile (29-km) dirt road that turns north from
Highway 9 east of the park.

During the summer, **Zion Adventures**
(36 Lion Blvd., Springdale, 435/772-1001,
www.zionadventures.com, 6:15am and
9:30am, $37 pp, reservations required) offers
a daily shuttle to Chamberlain's Ranch. There
is a small discount in the fare if you also rent
gear from them. **Zion Rock and Mountain
Guides** (1458 Zion Park Blvd., Springdale,

435/772-3303, www.zionrockguides.com) has
a similar service.

Permits are required for overnight
hikes, which must be "top down," starting at
Chamberlain's Ranch and hiking downstream
to the Riverside Walk; get permits from the
backcountry desk at the Zion Canyon Visitor
Center the day before you plan to hike or the
morning of your hike (7am-noon) or by applying at https://zionpermits.nps.gov. You will
also be issued a plastic bag specially designed
to collect human waste. Only one-night stays
are allowed. No camping is permitted below
Big Springs. Group size for hiking and camping is limited to 12 people along the entire
route.

You can get through the entire 16-mile/26-
kilometer (one-way) Narrows in about 12
hours, although two days is best to enjoy
the beauty of the place. Children under 12
shouldn't attempt to hike the entire canyon.

HIKING EAST OF ZION CANYON

You can't take the park shuttle bus to trailheads east of Zion Canyon, although the long-
distance East Rim Trail, which starts just
inside the park's eastern boundary, joins trails
that lead down to Zion Canyon's Weeping
Rock trailhead.

Canyon Overlook Trail

Distance: 1 mile (1.6 km) round-trip
Duration: 1 hour
Elevation change: 163 feet (50 m)
Effort: easy
Trailhead: parking area just east of the long
(westernmost) tunnel on the Zion-Mt. Carmel Highway

This fun hike starts on the road east of Zion
Canyon and features great views from the
heights without the stiff climbs found on
most other Zion trails. The trail winds in and
out along the ledges of Pine Creek Canyon,
which opens into a great valley. Panoramas at
trail's end take in lower Zion Canyon in the

1: The Narrows 2: the East Rim Trail 3: the Riverside
Walk

distance. A sign at the viewpoint identifies Bridge Mountain, Streaked Wall, East Temple, and other features. The Great Arch of Zion—termed a "blind arch" because it's open only on one side—is below; the arch is 580 feet (177 m) high, 720 feet (219 m) long, and 90 feet (27 m) deep. On a busy day, parking at and exiting from the parking area can be more challenging than the hike itself.

East Rim Trail

Distance: 10.6 miles (17 km) one-way
Duration: 6-8 hours
Elevation change: 2,300 feet (700 m)
Effort: strenuous
Trailheads: east entrance of Zion National Park; Weeping Rock trailhead

This trail is best done as a one-way trek. It's possible to do it as a long day hike but beautiful enough to encourage a slower-paced overnight trip. The great views start with a look at sandstone cliffs; the trail passes canyons, a ponderosa pine forest, and other trails (to Cable Mountain) and, eventually the big features of Zion Canyon come into view. The first half of the hike involves a steady climb, but then the trail tops out on a mesa and finishes by dropping into Zion Canyon. This downhill stretch is amazingly beautiful—even the slickrock that you walk on in places seems like a work of art. In the slickrock section, keep an eye out for the rock cairns that mark the way.

The Observation Point Trail joins this trail at 9 miles (14.5 km); it's a steep 2 miles (3.2 km) on this spur trail to Observation Point. The main trail continues down a paved path to Weeping Rock and the Zion Canyon shuttle bus.

A good turn-around point for a shorter round-trip day hike is Jolley Gulch, a deep canyon a couple of miles from the east entrance trailhead.

The East Rim Trail tops out at 6,725 feet (2,050 m), high enough that snow may linger into the spring. Check with the staff at the visitors center backcountry desk (435/772-0170) if you're hiking early in the season.

HIKING OFF HIGHWAY 9

During the summer, this area of the park can be extremely hot, and in the early spring, it's often too muddy to hike. These trails, which head north from Highway 9 west of the town of Springdale, are accessible without paying the park entrance fee.

Huber Wash

Distance: 5 miles (8 km) round-trip
Duration: 2.5 hours
Elevation change: 163 feet (50 m)
Effort: easy
Trailhead: Highway 9, about 6 miles (9.7 km) west of park entrance, near a power substation

From the parking area, this trail heads up Huber Wash through painted desert and canyons. One of the highlights of hiking in this area, besides the desert scenery, is the abundance of petrified wood. There's even a logjam of petrified wood at the 2.5-mile (4 km) mark, where the trail ends in a box canyon decked with a hanging garden. If you're up for a tricky climb over the petrified logjam, you can clamber up and catch the Chinle Trail, then hike 5 miles (8 km) back to the road. The Chinle Trail emerges onto Highway 9 about 2.5 miles (4 km) east of the Huber Wash trailhead.

This trail is too hot to hike during the summer, but it's a good cool-weather destination. Even then, remember to bring plenty of water.

Coalpits Wash

Distance: 3.5 miles (5.6 km) round-trip
Duration: 2 hours
Elevation change: 100 feet (30 m)
Effort: easy
Trailhead: Highway 9, about 7.3 miles (11.7 km) west of park entrance. The trailhead parking area may not be marked; it's between Rockville and Virgin, almost directly across Highway 9 from the turnoff to Grafton.

At 3,666 feet (1,117 m), the Coalpits Wash trailhead is the lowest spot in Zion. This low elevation makes it an ideal winter hike, and it's also the best place to look for early spring wildflowers, including mariposa lilies, purple sagebrush, and pale evening primrose. Birders also like this shrubby area.

The stream in this wash carries water for much of the year. After about 1.5 miles (2.4 km), Coalpits joins Scroggins Wash. Though most hikers turn around at this point, it's possible to keep going up the ever-narrowing wash (the Chinle Trail joins in at 3.75 mi/6 km) and turn this into a good cool-season backpacking trip.

HIKING FROM KOLOB TERRACE ROAD

From the town of Virgin, Kolob Terrace Road runs north and passes several trailheads, including the Subway, a popular canyoneering spot, and a couple of great trails at Lava Point. These trails are far less traveled than those in Zion Canyon, and at about 7,000 feet (2,134 m), they stay fairly cool in summer.

Snow blocks the access road to Lava Point for much of the year; the usual season is May or June to early November. Check road conditions with the Zion Canyon or Kolob Canyons Visitor Centers. From the south entrance station in Zion Canyon, drive west 15 miles (24 km) on Highway 9 to Virgin, travel north 21 miles (34 km) on Kolob Terrace Road (signed for "Kolob Reservoir"), then turn right and continue 1.8 miles (2.9 km) to Lava Point.

The Subway

Distance: 9 miles (14.5 km) round-trip
Duration: 7 hours
Elevation change: 2,000 feet (610 m)
Effort: strenuous
Trailheads: Left Fork or Wildcat Canyon

The Left Fork of North Creek, aka "The Subway," is a special semitechnical canyoneering hike for strong swimmers. This challenging day hike involves, at the very least, lots of route-finding, many stream crossings, and some rope work. Obviously, the Left Fork is not for everyone.

Like the Narrows, the Left Fork can be hiked either partway up and then back down, starting and ending at the Left Fork trailhead; or, with a shuttle, from an upper trailhead at Wildcat Canyon downstream to the Left Fork trailhead. The "top-to-bottom" route requires rappelling skills and at least 60 feet (18 m) of climbing rope or webbing. It also involves swimming through several deep sections of very cold water.

Even though the hike is in a day-use-only zone, the National Park Service requires a **special permit,** which, unlike other Zion backcountry permits, is available ahead of time through a somewhat convoluted **lottery process.** Prospective hikers should

Lose the crowds and get a new perspective on the park from Kolob Terrace trails.

visit the park's permitting website (https://zionpermits.nps.gov), where you will be introduced to the complicated lottery system of applying for a permit to hike the Subway. Lotteries are run monthly for hiking dates three months in the future. Each lottery entry costs $5, and each individual hiker can apply only once per month. There's also a last-minute lottery, held two days in advance of the hike. Finally, if there are any remaining permits available, they are dispensed the day before the hike at the visitors center.

The Left Fork trailhead is on Kolob Terrace Road, 8.1 miles (13 km) north of Virgin.

Hop Valley Trail to Kolob Arch

Distance: 14 miles (22.5 km) round-trip
Duration: 8 hours
Elevation change: 1,050 feet (320 m)
Effort: strenuous
Trailhead: Hop Valley trailhead, 13 miles (21 km) north of Virgin off the Kolob Terrace Road

Although most hikers reach Kolob Arch via La Verkin Creek Trail, you can also hike to the scenic arch on the Hop Valley Trail from Kolob Terrace Road. The Hop Valley Trail is 7 miles (11.3 km) one-way to Kolob Arch with an elevation drop of 1,050 feet (320 m); water is available in Hop Valley and La Verkin Creek. You may have to do some wading in the creek, and the trail crosses private land (no camping).

Northgate Peaks Trail

Distance: 4 miles (6.4 km) round-trip
Duration: 2 hours
Elevation change: 100 feet (30 m)
Effort: easy
Trailhead: Wildcat Canyon trailhead (southern end), 16 miles (26 km) north of Virgin off Kolob Terrace Road

Most of the trails in this remote area of the park are long and challenging. Northgate Peaks is the exception: an easy family hike along a sandy trail. Hike out from the southern Wildcat Canyon trailhead and pass the turnoff to the Hop Valley Trail; about 200 yards farther, turn right (south) onto the Northgate Peaks Trail. The trail passes through a pine-strewn meadow to a trail's-end overlook of the Great West Canyon, surrounded by highly textured sandstone domes. Wildflowers, including the strikingly pretty shooting stars, are abundant near the end of the trail. This is also a good place to look for raptors.

West Rim Trail

Distance: 13.3 miles (21.4 km) one-way
Duration: 8 hours or overnight
Elevation change: 3,600 feet (1,100 m)
Effort: strenuous
Trailhead: Lava Point trailhead

The West Rim Trail goes southeast to Zion Canyon, with an elevation drop of 3,600 feet/1,100 meters (3,000/915 of them in the last 6 mi/9.7 km). This is the western end of the same trail that takes hikers from Zion Canyon to Angels Landing. Water can normally be found along the way at Sawmill, Potato Hollow, and Cabin Springs.

From its start on the edge of the Kolob Plateau to its end in Zion Canyon, the West Rim Trail passes through a wide range of ecosystems, including sandstone domes and an unexpected pond at Potato Hollow, and many great views. The trail is most often done as a two-day backpacking trip, which gives hikers time to explore and enjoy the area.

You can also reach the Lava Point trailhead by hiking the 1-mile (1.6-km) Barney's Trail from Site 2 in Lava Point Campground.

Wildcat Canyon Trail

Distance: 10 miles (16 km) round-trip
Duration: 5 hours
Elevation change: 450 feet (137 m)
Effort: moderate
Trailhead: Lava Point trailhead

The Wildcat Canyon Trail heads southwest from Lava Point to a trailhead on Kolob Terrace Road (16 mi/26 km north of Virgin), so if it's possible to arrange a shuttle, you can do this as a one-way hike in about three hours. The trail, which travels across slick-rock, through forest, and past cliffs, has views of the Left Fork North Creek drainage, but it lacks a reliable water source. You can continue north and west toward Kolob Arch by taking the 4-mile (6.4-km) Connector Trail to the Hop Valley Trail.

You can also reach the Lava Point trailhead by hiking the 1-mile (1.6-km) **Barney's Trail** from Site 2 in Lava Point Campground.

HIKING IN KOLOB CANYONS

There are two good day hikes in Kolob Canyons: the short but steep Timber Creek Overlook Trail provides panoramic views, and the Taylor Creek Trail puts you right down into a canyon. Access these hikes from Kolob Canyons Road, which begins at I-15 south of Cedar City.

Taylor Creek Trail

Distance: 5 miles (8 km) round-trip
Duration: 4 hours
Elevation change: 450 feet (137 m)
Effort: easy-moderate
Trailhead: 2 miles (3.2 km) east of Kolob Canyons Visitor Center, left side of the road

This excellent day hike from Kolob Canyons Road heads upstream into the canyon of the Middle Fork of Taylor Creek. Double Arch Alcove is 2.7 miles (4.3 km) from the trailhead; a dry fall 350 yards farther blocks the way (water flows over it during spring runoff and after rains). A giant rockfall occurred here in 1990. From this trail you can also explore the North Fork of Taylor Creek. A separate trail along the South Fork of Taylor Creek leaves the road at a bend 3.1 miles from the visitors center, then goes 1.2 miles (1.9 km) upstream beneath steep canyon walls.

La Verkin Creek Trail to Kolob Arch

Distance: 14 miles (22.5 km) round-trip
Duration: 8 hours
Elevation change: 700 feet (213 m)
Effort: strenuous
Trailhead: Lee Pass

Kolob Arch's 287-foot (87-m) span makes it one of the world's largest arches. (Landscape Arch in Arches National Park is 3 feet longer, and a 400-foot-long (122-m) arch in China tops them both.) Kolob's height is over 300 feet (91 km), and its vertical thickness is 75 feet (23 m). The arch makes a fine destination for a backpacking trip. Spring and autumn are the best seasons to go; summer temperatures rise above 90°F (32°C), and winter snows make the trails hard to follow.

La Verkin Creek Trail begins at Lee Pass (elev. 6,080 ft/1,853 m) on Kolob Canyons Road, 4 miles (6.4 km) beyond the visitors center. The trail drops into Timber Creek (intermittent flow), crosses over hills to La Verkin Creek (flows year-round), then turns up side canyons to the arch. The 14-mile (22.5-km) round-trip hike can be done as a long day trip, but you'll enjoy the best lighting for photos at the arch if you camp in the area and see it the following morning. Carry plenty of water for the return trip; the climb to the trailhead can be hot and tiring.

Timber Creek Overlook Trail

Distance: 1 mile (1.6 km) round-trip
Duration: 30 minutes
Elevation change: 100 feet (30 m)
Effort: easy-moderate
Trailhead: at the end of Kolob Canyons Road, 5 miles (8 km) from the visitors center

It's a short but relatively steep jaunt from the parking lot at the road's end to the Timber Creek Overlook. Along the way, you'll have good views of the Kolob's Finger Canyons, and on a clear day, the North Rim of the Grand Canyon is visible from the overlook.

BIKING

One of the fringe benefits of the Zion Canyon shuttle bus is the great bicycling that's resulted from the lack of automobile traffic. It used to be way too scary to bike along the narrow, traffic-choked Zion Canyon Scenic Drive, but now it's a joy. When the shuttle buses get crowded (and they do), biking is a great way to get to the sights up the canyon.

On the stretch of road where cars are permitted—between the Zion Canyon Visitor

Center and Canyon Junction (where the Zion-Mt. Carmel Highway meets Zion Canyon Scenic Drive)—the 2-mile (3.2-km) paved Pa'rus Trail is open to cyclists as well as pedestrians and makes for easy, stress-free pedaling. Bicycles are allowed on the park road, but they must pull over to allow shuttle buses to pass.

If you decide you've had enough cycling, every shuttle bus has a rack that can hold two bicycles. Bike parking is plentiful at the visitors center, Zion Lodge, and most trailheads.

Outside the Zion Canyon area, Kolob Terrace Road is a good place to stretch your legs; it's 22 miles (35 km) to Kolob Reservoir.

There's no place to mountain bike off-road within the park, but there are good mountain-biking spots, including places to practice slickrock riding, just outside the park boundaries. It's best to stop by one of the local bike shops for advice and a map of your chosen destination.

Three-speed cruiser bikes are available in Springdale at Zion Outfitter (7 Zion Park Blvd., 435/772-5090, http://zionoutfitter.com, 7am-9pm daily). Zion Adventures (36 Lion Blvd., Springdale, 435/772-1001, www.zionadventures.com, 8am-8pm daily Mar.-Oct., 8am-7pm daily Nov., 9am-7pm daily Dec.-Feb.) rents road bikes ($35 per day) and e-bikes ($60 per day), both of which are good for park roads. Zion Cycles (868 Zion Park Blvd., Springdale, 435/772-0400, www.zioncycles.com, 9am-6pm daily), tucked behind Zion Pizza Noodle, has similar rentals.

HORSEBACK RIDING

Trail rides on horses and mules leave from the corral near Zion Lodge (435/679-8665, www.canyonrides.com, Mar.-Oct.) and head down the Virgin River. A one-hour trip ($45) goes to the Court of the Patriarchs, and a half-day ride ($90) follows the Sand Bench Trail. Riders must be at least age 7 for the short ride and age 10 for the half-day ride, and riders can weigh no more than 220 pounds.

CLIMBING

Rock climbers come to scale the high Navajo sandstone cliffs; after Yosemite, Zion is the nation's most popular big-wall climbing area. However, Zion's sandstone is far more fragile than Yosemite's granite, and it tends to crumble and flake, especially when wet. Beginners should avoid these walls—experience with crack climbing is a must.

For route descriptions, pick up a copy of *Desert Rock* by Eric Bjørnstad or *Rock Climbing Utah* by Stewart M. Green. Both books are sold at the Zion Canyon Visitor Center bookstore. The backcountry desk in the visitors center also has a notebook full of route descriptions supplied by past climbers. Check here to make sure your climbing area is open—some are closed to protect nesting peregrine falcons—and remember to bring a pair of binoculars to scout climbing routes from the canyon floor.

If you aren't prepared to tackle the 2,000-foot-high (610-m) canyon walls, you may want to check out a couple of bouldering sites, both quite close to the south entrance of the park. One huge boulder is 40 yards west of the park entrance; the other is a large slab with a crack, located 0.5 mile (0.8 km) north of the entrance.

During the summer, it can be intensely hot on unshaded walls. The best months for climbing are March-May and September-early November.

If watching the climbers at Zion gives you a hankering to scale a wall, the Zion Adventures (36 Lion Blvd., Springdale, 435/772-1001, www.zionadventures.com) runs half-day and day-long climbing clinics for beginning and experienced climbers. Similar offerings are provided by Zion Rock and Mountain Guides (1458 Zion Park Blvd., Springdale, 435/772-3303, www.zionrockguides.com), Red Desert Adventure (435/668-2888,

---

1: canyoneering in a slot canyon 2: biking in Zion National Park 3: horseback riding tour in Zion National Park

www.reddesertadventure.com), and **Zion Mountaineering School** (868 Zion Park Blvd., Springdale, 435/319-0313, www.guidesinzion.com), which specializes in private tours. All of these outfitters also guide clients on canyoneering expeditions. Outfitters are not permitted to lead climbs inside the park, so these activities are held outside the park's boundaries.

OUTFITTERS

Several good outfitters have shops in Springdale, just outside the park. Here you can buy all manner of gear and outdoor clothing. You can also pick up canyoneering skills, take a guided mountain-bike ride (outside the park), or learn to climb big sandstone walls.

Campers who left that crucial piece of equipment at home should visit **Zion Outdoor** (868 Zion Park Blvd., Springdale, 435/772-0630, www.zionoutdoor.com, 9am-9pm daily), as should anybody who needs to spruce up their wardrobe with some stylish outdoor clothing.

Rent a bike or equipment to hike the Narrows at **Zion Outfitter** (7 Zion Park Blvd., Springdale, 435/772-5090, http://zionoutfitter.com, 7am-9pm daily).

Canyoneering supplies, including gear to hike the Narrows or the Subway, are available from **Zion Adventures** (36 Lion Blvd., Springdale, 435/772-1001, www.zionadventures.com, 8am-8pm daily Mar.-Oct., 8am-7pm daily Nov., 9am-7pm daily Dec.-Feb.), **Zion Guru** (795 Zion Park Blvd., Springdale, 435/632-0432, www.zionguru.com), and **Zion Rock and Mountain Guides** (1458 Zion Park Blvd., Springdale, 435/772-3303, www.zionrockguides.com).

Food and Accommodations

Within the park, lodging is limited to Zion Lodge and three park campgrounds. Look to Springdale or the east entrance of the park for more options.

ZION LODGE

The rustic **Zion Lodge** (435/772-7700 or 888/297-2757, www.zionlodge.com, $229-284) is in the heart of Zion Canyon, 3 miles (4.8 km) up Zion Canyon Scenic Drive. Zion Lodge provides the only accommodations and food options within the park. It's open year-round; reservations for guest rooms can be made up to 13 months in advance. During high season, all rooms are booked months in advance. There are four accessible hotel rooms (two with grab bars, two with roll-in showers) and a wheelchair is available for loan. Accommodations in motel rooms near the main lodge or cute cabins (gas fireplaces but no TVs) run around $200.

The **Red Rock Grill** (435/772-7760, dinner reservations required, 6:30am-10:30am, 11:30am-3pm, and 5pm-10pm daily, dinner entrées $12-30), the lodge restaurant, offers a Southwestern and Mexican-influenced menu for breakfast, lunch, and dinner daily. A snack bar, the **Castle Dome Café** (breakfast, lunch, and dinner daily spring-fall) serves fast food; a cart on the patio sells beer.

The lodge also has evening programs, a gift shop, Wi-Fi in the lobby, and accessible public restrooms.

CAMPGROUNDS
Zion Canyon Campgrounds

Campgrounds in the park often fill up during Easter and other major holidays. During summer, they're often full by early afternoon. It's a good idea to make reservations in advance at the South and Watchman Campgrounds, both just inside the south entrance. Each has sites with water but no showers. **Watchman Campground** (reservations 877/444-6777, information 435/772-3256, www.recreation.gov, $20) has 197 sites, some of which have electrical hookups ($30). There are seven accessible sites with paved pads. There are also other flat sites and six accessible restrooms. Prime riverside spots are available. It stays open in winter. **South Campground** (reservations 877/444-6777, information 435/772-3256, www.recreation.gov, closed in winter $20) has 128 sites, including a few choice walk-in sites and easy access to the Pa'rus Trail. During April and May of some years, the park campgrounds may have an influx of western tent caterpillars, which defoliate trees; populations vary greatly from year to year.

Tenters shouldn't eschew Watchman, where loops C and D are for tents; these sites are more spacious than those at South. Some of the fruit trees planted in the campgrounds by early pioneers are still producing; you can pick your own.

It should be noted that camping in Zion's two big campgrounds is pretty easy; indeed, except for the lack of showers, it can be luxurious. Campers have easy access, via the park's shuttles, to good restaurants in Springdale. It's simple enough to find showers in Springdale; just outside the park, Zion Outfitter charges $4; it also has a laundry.

Private campgrounds are just outside the park in Springdale and just east of the park's east entrance. Camping supplies, sack lunches, and groceries are available just outside the park entrance at **Happy Camper Market** (Springdale shuttle stop, 95 Zion Park Blvd., 435/772-7805, 7am-10pm daily).

Kolob Campgrounds

Up the Kolob Terrace Road are six first-come, first-served sites at **Lava Point Campground** (no water, free), a small primitive campground open during warmer months. The **Red Ledge RV Park** (Kanarraville, 435/586-9150, https://www.redledgervandcampground.com, Apr.-Nov., $22 tents, $30-34 RVs) is the closest commercial campground to the Kolob Canyons area, and there's no other campground in this part of the park; go 2 miles (3.2 km) north on I-15, take exit 42, and continue 4.5 miles (7.2 km) into the center of Kanarraville. The campground is primarily geared toward RVs, but has some tent sites, a store, showers, and a laundry room.

The tiny agricultural community of Kanarraville was named after a local Paiute chief. A low ridge south of town marks the southern limit of prehistoric Lake Bonneville. Hikers can explore trails in Spring and Kanarra Canyons within the Spring Canyon Wilderness Study Area just east of town.

Transportation

GETTING THERE
Car

Zion National Park is 43 miles (69 km) northeast of St. George, 60 miles (97 km) south of Cedar City, 41 miles (66 km) northwest of Kanab, and 86 miles (138 km) southwest of Bryce Canyon National Park. There are two entrances to the main section of the park: From Springdale, you enter the south end of Zion Canyon, near the visitors center and the Zion Canyon shuttle buses; from the east, you come in on the Zion-Mt. Carmel Highway (Hwy. 9) and pass through a long tunnel before popping into Zion Canyon a few miles north of the visitors center.

If your vehicle is 7 feet, 10 inches wide, 11 feet, 4 inches tall, or larger, you will need a traffic-control escort through the narrow mile-long Zion-Mt. Carmel Tunnel. Vehicles of this size are too large to stay in one lane while traveling through the tunnel, which was built in the 1920s, when autos were not only small but few and far between. Most **RVs, buses, trailers,** and **fifth-wheels,** and some **camper shells,** will require an escort. Expect to pay a $15 fee per vehicle in addition to the park entrance fee (payable at the park entrance station before entering the tunnel). The fee is good for two trips through the tunnel for the same vehicle over a seven-day period.

Although the National Park Service persists in using the term *escort,* you're really on your own through the tunnel. Park staff will stop oncoming traffic, allowing you enough time to drive down the middle of the tunnel, but you do not follow an escort vehicle. Traffic-control staff are present at the tunnel 8am-8pm daily May-early September. During the winter season, oversize vehicle passage must be arranged at the **entrance station** (8am-6pm daily early to mid-March and late Sept.-Nov., 8am-7pm daily mid-Mar.-late April and early Sept.-late Sept., 8am-8pm daily late April-early Sept. and mid-Sept.-late Sept., 8am-4:30pm daily Nov.-early Mar.) at Zion Canyon Visitor Center, at Zion Lodge, or by phoning 435/772-3256. Bicycles and pedestrians are not allowed in the tunnel.

There's a separate entrance for the Kolob Canyons area, in the park's northwest corner. Reach this area via Kolob Canyons Road, which begins just off I-15 exit 40 at the Kolob Canyons Visitor Center and climbs to an overlook for great views of the Finger Canyons of the Kolob; the drive is 10 miles (16 km) round-trip.

A third entrance leads to the less traveled part of the park and is accessed by the Kolob Terrace Road, which heads north from Highway 9 at the tiny town of Virgin and goes to backcountry sites. (There's no entrance station or visitors center on Kolob Terrace Road.)

If you get to Zion before 10am or after 3pm, there may be **parking** spaces available in the visitors center lot. Midday visitors should just park in Springdale (at your motel or in a public lot) and catch a shuttle bus to the park entrance.

Zion-Springdale Shuttle

For majority of the year, one line of the Zion Canyon **shuttle bus** (www.nps.gov/zion,

mid-Feb.-Thanksgiving, runs every 6-10 minutes, starting at 7am daily, free) travels between Springdale and the park entrance, stopping within a short walk of every Springdale motel and near several large visitor parking lots at the edge of town. The last shuttle of the day leaves the Temple of Sinawava at 7:15pm. The shuttle bus is wheelchair accessible. Pets are not allowed on the shuttle; however, service animals are permitted.

GETTING AROUND
Car

Zion Lodge guests may obtain a pass authorizing them to drive to the lodge, but in general, private vehicles are not allowed to drive up Zion Canyon Road. It's fine to drive to the campgrounds; the road between the park entrance and the Zion-Mt. Carmel Highway junction is open to all vehicles. In the off-season, November-March, private vehicles are allowed on all roads.

Zion Canyon Shuttle

The road through Zion Canyon is narrow with few pullouts, so to keep the road from becoming a parking lot, a wheelchair-accessible **shuttle bus** (www.nps.gov/zion, runs every 6-10 minutes, starting at 7am during peak season) provides regular service through the canyon. The route starts just inside the park entrance, at the Zion Canyon Visitor Center, and runs the length of Zion Canyon Road, stopping at scenic overlooks, trailheads, and Zion Lodge. The last shuttle of the day leaves the Temple of Sinawava at 7:15pm. The shuttle service is unavailable during the off-season (Nov.-Mar.), and private vehicles are allowed on all roads during this time.

Advance reservations (www.recreation. gov, $1 per day) are required to ride the Zion Canyon shuttle, with a limited number of tickets sold for each day. Pets are not allowed; only service animals are permitted. Buses run as often as every seven minutes 7am-7:15pm daily, less frequently early in the morning and in the evening.

Springdale and Vicinity

Mormons settled tiny Springdale (population 650) in 1862; however, with its location just outside the park's south entrance, the town is not a typical Mormon settlement but rather is geared toward serving park visitors. Its many high-quality motels and B&Bs, as well as frequent shuttle bus service to the park's entrance, make Springdale an appealing base for a visit to Zion. Farther down the road toward Hurricane are the little towns of Rockville and Virgin, both quickly becoming B&B suburbs of Springdale.

SIGHTS

O. C. Tanner Amphitheater

The highlight at the open-air **O. C. Tanner Amphitheater** (435/652-7800, www. octannershows.com, admission varies) is a series of musical concerts held on Friday or Saturday evenings throughout the summer. The amphitheater is just outside the park entrance.

FOOD

A short walk from the park entrance, **Cafe Soleil** (205 Zion Park Blvd., Springdale, 435/772-0505, www.cafesoleilzionpark.com, 6am-9pm daily spring-fall, 7am-8pm winter, $8-12) is a bright, friendly place for breakfast or a lunchtime sandwich.

★ **Deep Creek Coffee** (932 Zion Park Blvd., Springdale, 435/669-8849, http:// deepcreekcoffee.com, 6am-2pm daily) is the hip place to hang out in the morning. Besides excellent coffee drinks and made-from-scratch chai, they serve tasty smoothies, quinoa bowls, and sandwiches ($5-12). For a truly substantial meal, head across the way to **Oscar's Café** (948 Zion Park Blvd., Springdale, 435/772-3232, www.cafeoscars. com, 7am-9pm daily, $12-19), where you can get a good burger or a Mexican-influenced breakfast or lunch. The patio is set back off the main road and is especially pleasant.

An old gas station has become the ★ **Whiptail Grill** (445 Zion Park Blvd., Springdale, 435/772-0283, www. whiptailgrillzion.com, noon-10pm daily mid-Feb.-Nov., $12-18), a casual spot serving innovative homemade Mexican-style food, such as incredibly good spaghetti squash enchiladas or fish tacos jazzed up with grape salsa. There's very little seating inside, so plan to eat at the outdoor tables (warmed and lit by gas torches during the evening) or take your meal to go.

A good, reasonably priced place to bring a family with picky eaters is **Zion Pizza and Noodle** (868 Zion Park Blvd., Springdale, 435/772-3815, www.zionpizzanoodle.com, 4pm-10pm daily, $11-16), housed in an old church and serving a good selection of microbrews. The menu at this busy restaurant is wide-ranging, with lots of pasta dishes, calzones, and salads in addition to the pizza.

The **Spotted Dog Café** (Flanigan's Inn, 428 Zion Park Blvd., Springdale, 435/772-3244, www.flanigans.com, breakfast buffet 7am-11am daily spring-fall, dinner 5pm-9:30pm daily spring-fall, 5pm-9:30pm Tues.-Sun. winter, dinner $14-21) is one of Springdale's top restaurants; it has a good wine list and a full bar and uses high-quality ingredients for its American bistro cuisine, including pepita-crusted grilled trout and game meatloaf (made with bacon, elk, buffalo, and beef). Be sure to order a salad with your dinner—the house salad is superb. If you want to eat outside, try to get a table on the back patio, which is quieter and more intimate than the dining area out front.

A long-time Springdale favorite is the **Bit & Spur Restaurant** (1212 Zion Park Blvd., Springdale, 435/772-3498, www.bitandspur. com, reservations recommended during busy season, 5pm-9:30pm daily spring-fall, weekends only winter, $16-38), a lively Mexican-influenced place with a menu that goes far

beyond the usual south-of-the-border con-coctions. The sweet-potato tamales keep us coming back year after year. The restaurant also offers full liquor service.

★ **King's Landing Bistro** (1515 Zion Park Blvd., Springdale, 435/772-7422, www.klbzion.com, 5pm-9:30pm Mon.-Sat., $18-30), located at the Driftwood Lodge, serves some of Springdale's most innovative dinners. Start off with bison carpaccio, and then move on to a pork steak topped with bacon lardons and an array of veggies or king salmon served with gnocchi. Sit outside and enjoy the views.

Springdale's sole brewpub is the **Zion Canyon Brew Pub** (95 Zion Park Blvd., 435/772-0036, www.zionbrewery.com, 11:30am-10pm daily, $13-29), right at the pedestrian gate to the park. The pub offers six flagship brews and many seasonal options, and its upscale pub grub is made from scratch and tasty. Pair a buffalo meatloaf burger with a chocolaty Conviction Stout.

The town's only full-fledged supermarket, **Sol Foods** (995 Zion Park Blvd., Springdale, 435/772-3100, www.solfoods.com, 7am-11pm daily), stocks groceries, deli items, hardware, and camping supplies.

ACCOMMODATIONS

The quality of lodgings in the area just outside Zion National Park is quite high. Springdale offers a wide range of accommodations. Rockville has several B&Bs, and Hurricane, the next town west of the park, has all the standard chain motels and the least expensive rooms in the area. During the off-season (late fall-early spring), rates drop substantially.

$100-150

The least expensive lodgings in Springdale are the motel rooms at **Zion Park Motel** (865 Zion Park Blvd., Springdale, 435/772-3251, www.zionparkmotel.com, $109-194), an older, well-kept motel with a small pool, located about 1 mile (1.6 km) from the park entrance.

1: Café Soleil 2: Cliffrose Lodge 3: Oscar's Café

The hosts at the **Bunkhouse at Zion B&B** (149 E. Main St., Rockville, 435/772-3393, www.bunkhouseatzion.com, $125) are dedicated to living sustainably, and they bring this ethic into their simple two-room B&B. The views are remarkable from this quiet spot in Rockville. There's a two-night minimum stay.

Also in quiet Rockville, just a short drive from the park, is **2 Cranes Inn** (125 E. Main St., Rockville, 435/216-7700, www.2craneszion.com, $95-115). Here you'll find a Zen-meets-Southwest atmosphere, with four rooms with private baths, great outdoor spaces (including a labyrinth), and a communal kitchen stocked with coffee, tea, and a few breakfast basics.

Under the Eaves B&B (980 Zion Park Blvd., Springdale, 435/772-3457, www.undertheeaves.com, $99-199) features six homey guest rooms, plus a spacious suite, all in a vintage home and a garden cottage. Children over age eight are welcome, and all guests get free breakfast at a nearby restaurant.

Over $150

★ **Flanigan's Inn** (428 Zion Park Blvd., Springdale, 435/772-3244, www.flanigans.com, $179-269 guest rooms) is a quiet and convenient place to stay. Guest rooms (and a handful of specialty suites) are set back off the main drag and face a pretty courtyard. Up on the hill behind the inn, a labyrinth provides an opportunity to take a meditative walk in a stunning setting. An excellent restaurant (the Spotted Dog Café), a pool, and spa services make this an inviting place to spend several days. Two villas, essentially full-size houses, are also available.

Probably the most elegant place to stay is the ★ **Desert Pearl Inn** (707 Zion Park Blvd., Springdale, 435/772-8888 or 888/828-0898, www.desertpearl.com, $289-319), a very handsome lodge-like hotel perched above the Virgin River. Some guest rooms have views of the river; others face the pool. Much of the wood used for the beams and the finish moldings was salvaged from a railroad trestle made of century-old Oregon fir and redwood that once spanned the north end of the Great Salt Lake. The guest rooms are all large and beautifully furnished, with a modern look.

The closest lodging to the park is at **Cable Mountain Lodge** (147 Zion Park Blvd., Springdale, 435/772-3366 or 877/712-3366, www.cablemountainlodge.com, $189-369 studios). Along with being extremely convenient, it's very nicely fitted out, with a pool, guest rooms with microwaves and fridges or small kitchens, and appealing architecture and decor to go along with the spectacular views. Regular hotel rooms are referred to as studios; a number of suite options are also available.

Just outside the south gates to Zion, the ★ **Cliffrose Lodge** (281 Zion Park Blvd., Springdale, 435/772-3234 or 800/243-8824, www.cliffroselodge.com, $322-381 regular rooms) sits on five acres of lovely, well-landscaped gardens with riverfront access. The guest rooms, suites, and villas (essentially three-bedroom condos) are equally nice, especially the riverside rooms, and there's a pool and a laundry room. The Cliffrose is favored by many longtime Zion fans. The entire lodge underwent a property "evolvement" in 2018, with upgrades to all guest rooms.

The **Driftwood Lodge** (1515 Zion Park Blvd., Springdale, 435/772-3262, www.driftwoodlodge.net, $159-249) is a six-building complex with a good restaurant, pool, and spa on its spacious grounds, and pet-friendly guest rooms with refrigerators and microwaves.

For a place with a bit of personality, or perhaps more accurately, with multiple personalities, try the **Novel House Inn at Zion** (73 Paradise Rd., Springdale, 435/772-3650 or 800/711-8400, www.novelhouse.com, $199-219), a small family-run inn with 10 guest rooms, each decorated with a literary theme and named after an author, including Mark Twain, Rudyard Kipling, and Louis L'Amour. All guest rooms have private baths, TVs, and great views, and the B&B is tucked off the main drag. All rooms come with a voucher for complimentary breakfast at Oscar's Café.

Expect a very friendly welcome at the **Harvest House B&B** (29 Canyon View Dr., 435/772-3880, www.harvesthouse.net, $150-180), which has four guest rooms at the center of Springdale within easy walking distance of the park entrance. All rooms have private bathrooms and you'll enjoy the garden setting and its year-round outdoor hot tub.

Red Rock Inn (998 Zion Park Blvd., Springdale, 435/772-3139, www.redrockinn.com, $279) offers accommodations in individual cabins and a cottage suite amid gardens and patios, all with canyon views. Full-breakfast baskets are delivered to your door.

Even though it's a chain motel, the **Holiday Inn Express** (1215 Zion Park Blvd., Springdale, 435/772-3200, www.hiexpress.com, $205-231) is an attractive option; it's part of a complex with a restaurant, a swimming pool, a gift shop, and some of the newest guest rooms in Springdale. In addition to regular hotel rooms, there are also various suites and kitchen units available.

Campgrounds

If you aren't able to camp in the park, the **Zion Canyon Campground** (479 Zion Park Blvd., Springdale, 435/772-3237, www.zioncamp.com) is a short walk from the park entrance. Along with tent sites (no dogs allowed, $49) and RV sites ($59-89), there are motel rooms ($140-170). The sites are crammed pretty close together, but a few are situated right on the bank of the Virgin River. Facilities at this busy place include a store, a pizza parlor, a game room, a laundry room, and showers.

The "glamping" phenomenon has come to the Zion area. **Under Canvas Zion** (3955 Kolob Terrace Rd., 435/359-2911, www.undercanvas.com/camps/zion, open early March-mid-Nov.) offers luxury safari tent experiences on 196 acres bordering the west side of the park. Lodging is in a variety of large wall tents or tepees, some with private en suite bathrooms, and all fitted with fine bedding and furniture. In other words, this isn't exactly roughing it. Tent accommodations that sleep four start at $219 per night, with modern plumbing and bathroom facilities in group shower houses. Top-of-the-line tents with private bathrooms are $450. Adventure packages are also available that customize outdoor activities to your preferences, and also include three camp-cooked meals a day. Under Canvas Zion is 6 miles (9.7 km) north of Virgin on the Kolob Terrace Road.

At the other end of the luxe spectrum, go off the grid at the **Zion Wright Family Ranch** (12120 W. Hwy 9, 435/231-2008, www. zionwrightfamilyranch.com, $29). The no-frills campground has dispersed sites in a beautiful and quiet spot several miles up the Kolob Terrace Road from Virgin. The hosts also offer horseback rides.

INFORMATION AND SERVICES

People traveling with their dogs have a bit of a dilemma when it comes to visiting Zion. No pets are allowed on the trails (except the Pa'rus Trail) or in the shuttle buses,

and it's unconscionable to leave a dog inside a car here in the warmer months. Fortunately, the **Doggy Dude Ranch** (800 E. Main St., Rockville, 435/772-3105, www. doggyduderanch.com) provides conscientious daytime and overnight pet care.

The **Zion Canyon Medical Clinic** (120 Lion Blvd., Springdale, 435/772-3226, http:// zioncanyonclinic.com) provides urgent-care services.

You may want to check out the art galleries along Zion Park Boulevard; some of them have high-quality merchandise.

GETTING THERE

Springdale is located at the mouth of Zion Canyon, just outside the park's main (south) entrance. From I-15 just north of St. George, take exit 16 and head east on Highway 9; it's about 40 miles (64 km) to Springdale. If you're coming from the north, take I-15 exit 22, head southeast through Toquerville, and meet Highway 9 at the town of La Verkin.

St. George

Southern Utah's largest city, St. George (pop. 93,000) sits between lazy bends of the Virgin River and rocky hills of red sandstone. Although it's one of the nation's fastest-growing cities and has gained a reputation as a retirement haven, thanks in part to its warm winter climate and its plethora of golf courses, the city itself will have limited appeal to most park travelers; if your focus is Zion, you'll most likely just use St. George as a jumping-off point. However, St. George's abundance of hotels, a clutch of good restaurants, public art and galleries in the old downtown core, and slickrock-laden state park a few miles away make it a handy place to begin or end your Utah parks adventure.

In 1861, more than 300 Mormon families in the Salt Lake City area answered the call to go south to start the Cotton Mission, of which St. George became the center (hence the frequent

use of the term "Dixie" to describe the area). The settlers overcame great difficulties to start farms and to build an attractive city in this remote desert. Brigham Young chose the city's name to honor George A. Smith, who had served as head of the Southern (Iron) Mission during the 1850s. The title *Saint* means simply that he was a Mormon—a Latter-Day Saint.

SIGHTS

Visits to some of the city's historic sites will add to your appreciation of St. George's past; ask for the "St. George Historic Walking Tour" brochure at the **Greater Zion Tourism Office** (20 N. Main St., Suite 105, 435/634-5747, www.greaterzion.com, 9am-5pm Mon.-Sat.).

Visitors can see the **St. George Temple** (250 E. 400 S., 435/673-5181) from the outside and stop in its visitors center, and you can tour

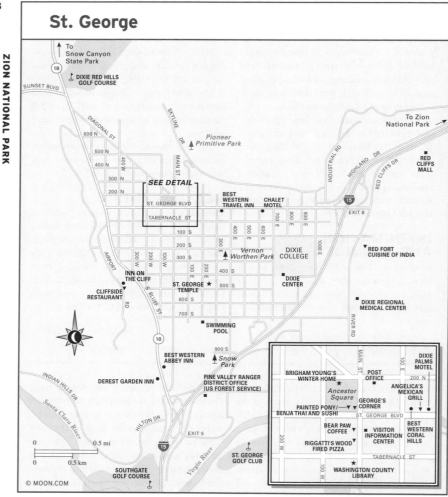

St. George

Brigham Young's Winter Home (67 W. 200 N., 435/673-2517, 9am-7pm Mon.-Sat., 1pm-7pm Sun. Apr.-Sept., 9am-5pm Mon.-Sat., 1pm-5pm Sun. Oct.-Mar., free).

Dinosaur Trackways

Back in the early Jurassic, when the supercontinent of Pangaea was just beginning to break up, lakes covered this part of present-day Utah, and dinosaurs were becoming the earth's dominant vertebrates. Two sites southeast of St. George preserve dinosaur tracks from this era. Of the two, the more recently discovered site at Johnson Farm is more impressive and much easier to get to; indeed, it has been called one of the world's 10 best dinosaur-track sites. The Fort Pearce site is good if you're hankering for some back-road travel and like scouting dino tracks and petroglyphs in remote washes.

ST. GEORGE DINOSAUR DISCOVERY SITE AT JOHNSON FARM

Tracks at the **St. George Dinosaur Discovery Site at Johnson Farm** (2180 E. Riverside Dr., 435/574-3466, www. utahdinosaurs.com, 10am-6pm daily, $8 adults, $7 seniors, $4 ages 4-11) were discovered in 2000 by a retired optometrist. Since then, a vast number of tracks, including those of three species of theropods (meat-eating dinosaurs), and important "trace fossils" of pond scum, plants, invertebrates, and fish have also been uncovered.

Excavation work is ongoing, and a visitors center provides a good look at some of the most exciting finds, including a wall-size slab of rock with footprints going to and fro. Also quite remarkable are the "swim tracks," which settled a long-standing argument over whether dinosaurs actually swam.

The track site is on the outskirts of St. George, about 2 miles (3.2 km) south of I-15 exit 10.

FORT PEARCE DINOSAUR TRACKS

A scenic back-road drive through the desert between St. George and Hurricane passes the ruins of Fort Pearce and more dinosaur tracks. Much of the road is unpaved, and it has rough and sandy spots, but it's usually suitable for cautious drivers in dry weather.

This group of tracks documents the passage of at least two different dinosaur species more than 200 million years ago. The well-preserved tracks, in the Moenave Formation, were made by a 20-foot-long (6-m) herbivore weighing an estimated 8-10 tons and by a carnivore half as long. No remains of the dinosaurs themselves have been found here.

In 1861 ranchers arrived in Warner Valley to run cattle on the desert grasslands. The Black Hawk War (1865-1872) and periodic raids by Navajo made life precarious for the settlers. Springs in Fort Pearce Wash— the only reliable water for many miles— proved the key to domination of the region. In December 1866 work began on a fort overlooking the springs. The stone walls stood about 8 feet (2.4 m) high and were more than 30 feet (9.1 m) long. No roof was ever added. Much of the fort and the adjacent corral (built in 1869) have survived to the present. Local cattle ranchers still use the springs for their herds. Petroglyphs can be seen in various places along the wash, including 0.25 mile (0.4 km) downstream from the fort along ledges on the north side of the wash.

To reach this somewhat remote site from St. George, head south on River Road, cross the Virgin River Bridge, and turn left onto 1450 South. Continue on this main road and keep bearing east through several 90-degree left and right turns. Turn left (east) onto the dirt Warner Valley Road at the Fort Pearce sign and continue 5.6 miles (9 km) to a road that branches right along a small wash to the Fort Pearce parking lot. The dinosaur tracks are in a wash about 2 miles (3.2 km) farther down the road from Fort Pearce; the parking area is signed.

Snow Canyon State Park

If St. George's outlet stores and chain restaurants threaten to close in on you, head a few miles north of town to the red-rock canyons, sand dunes, volcanoes, and lava flows of **Snow Canyon State Park** (1002 N. Snow Canyon Rd., 435/628-2255, http://stateparks. utah.gov, 6am-10pm daily year-round, $10 per vehicle day use). Walls of sandstone 50-750 feet (15-230 m) high enclose the 5-mile-long (8-km) canyon. **Hiking trails** trace the canyon bottom and lead into the backcountry for a closer look at the geology, flora, and fauna; take the 1.5-mile (2.4 km) **Hidden Pinyon Trail** for a good introduction. Common plants are barrel, cholla, and prickly pear cacti; yucca; Mormon tea; shrub live oak; cliffrose; and cottonwood. Delicate wildflowers bloom mostly in the spring and autumn, following the wet seasons, but cacti and the sacred datura can flower in the heat of summer.

Wildlife includes sidewinder and Great Basin rattlesnakes, Gila monsters, desert tortoises, kangaroo rats, squirrels, cottontails, kit

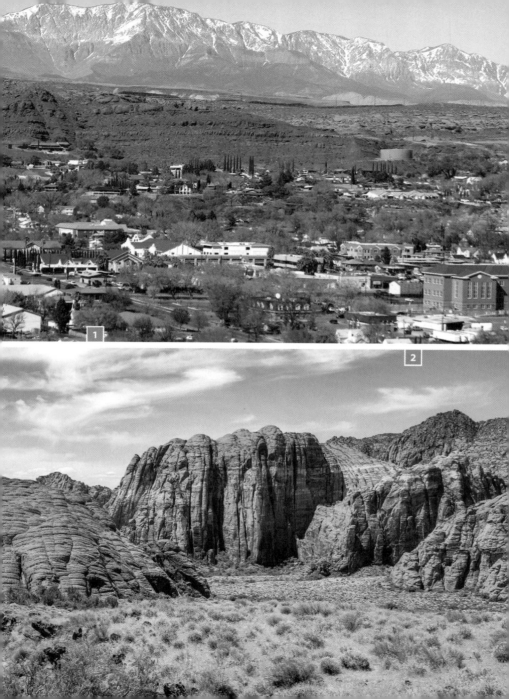

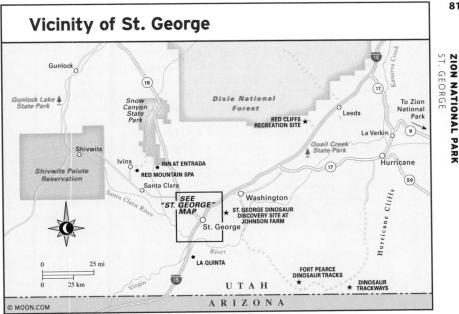

Vicinity of St. George

© MOON.COM

foxes, coyotes, and mule deer. During summer and fall thundershowers, the endangered desert tortoises may take to the park's roadways to drink from puddles; take extra care when driving at these times. You may find some Native American rock art, arrowheads, bits of pottery, and ruins. Many of the place names in the park honor Mormon pioneers. Snow Canyon was named for Lorenzo and Erastus Snow, not for the rare snowfalls.

Summer is too hot for comfortable hiking, except in the early morning. Highway 18 leads past an overlook on the rim of Snow Canyon and to the paved park road (Hwy. 300) that drops into the canyon and follows it to its mouth and the small town of Ivins. Snow Canyon is about 12 miles (19.3 km) northwest of St. George. It is reached either by Highway 18—the faster way—or through the towns of Santa Clara and Ivins by heading north on Bluff Street, turning left onto Snow

Canyon Parkway, and following the plentiful signs to the park. The campground here has a few lovely sites.

RECREATION
Golf

With over a dozen golf courses in the area, St. George enjoys a reputation as Utah's winter golf capital. Greens fees are highest in the winter (the rates listed here, without cart rental) and drop by nearly 50 percent during the hot summer months.

Red sandstone cliffs serve as the backdrop for **Dixie Red Hills** (1250 N. 645 W., 435/627-4444, www.sgcity.org/sportsandrecreation/golf, $22), the city's first golf course, built in the 1960s on the northwest edge of town; it's a nine-hole par-34 municipal course. The 18-hole par-71 **Green Spring Golf Course** (588 N. Green Spring Dr., 435/656-6300, https://washingtoncity.org/recreation/golf, $67), just west of I-15 exit 10 in the town of Washington, has a reputation as one of the finest courses in Utah.

1: a bird's-eye view of St. George **2:** Snow Canyon State Park

Professionals favor the cleverly designed 27-hole par-72 **Sunbrook Golf Course** (2366 Sunbrook Dr., 435/634-5866, www. sgcity.org/sportsandrecreation/golf, $56) off Dixie Downs Road, between Green Valley and Santa Clara. The **St. George Golf Club** (2190 S. 1400 E., 435/634-5854, www.sgcity. org/sportsandrecreation/golf, $35) has a popular 18-hole par-73 course south of town in Bloomington Hills. The **Southgate Golf Course** (1975 S. Tonaquint Dr., 435/627-4440, www.sgcity.org/sportsandrecreation/golf, $35), on the southwest edge of town, has 18 holes. The adjacent Southgate Game Improvement Center (435/674-7728) can provide golfers with computerized golf-swing analysis plus plenty of indoor practice space and lots of balls.

Entrada (2511 W. Entrada Trail, 435/986-2200, www.golfentrada.com) is a newer 18-hole private course that's fast on its way to becoming St. George's most respected. The Johnny Miller-designed course is northwest of St. George at beautiful Snow Canyon and incorporates natural lava flows, rolling dunes, and arroyos (dry riverbeds) into its design. Guests at the Inn at Entrada can get a package deal to golf; in peak winter season room rates start at around $160. The 18-hole par-72 **Sky Mountain** (1030 N. 2600 W., 435/635-7888, www.skymountaingolf.com, $57), northeast of St. George in nearby Hurricane, has a spectacular setting.

Mountain Biking

Mountain bikers in the know come to St. George fall-early spring to ride single-track trails and slickrock that is just as good as what you'll find in Moab. One of Utah's most spectacular trails is **Gooseberry Mesa,** southeast of Hurricane, a challenging but fun ride with both slickrock and single track. The **Green Valley Loop** starts at the Green Valley Spa and is mostly advanced single-track.

Less intense cycling can be found at **Snow Canyon State Park,** where the paved 6-mile (9.7-km) Whiptail Trail and the 8-mile (12.9-km) gravel and sand West Canyon Road are open to bicycles.

Climbing

Snow Canyon State Park (435/628-2255, http://stateparks.utah.gov, 6am-10pm daily year-round, $10 per vehicle) offers many technical rock-climbing routes in the park.

FOOD

Although its dining scene has improved in recent years, chain restaurants still rule in St. George.

The best place to head for lunch or dinner is the old downtown area, known as Ancestor Square, at the intersection of St. George Boulevard and Main Street. There you'll find several blocks of locally owned restaurants and art galleries. ★ **Painted Pony** (2 W. St. George Blvd., 435/634-1700, www.painted-pony.com, 11:30am-10pm Mon.-Sat., 4pm-9pm Sun., $28-36, reservations recommended for weekend dinner) is a stylish restaurant where the kitchen puts Southwestern and, in some cases, Asian touches on American standards; try ratatouille ravioli with sweet corn sauce and smoked pepper coulis. On a weekend evening, St. Georgians dress up and flock here. Downstairs from the Painted Pony is another pretty good restaurant, **Benja Thai and Sushi** (2 W. St. George Blvd., 435/628-9538, www.benjathai.com, 11:30am-10pm Mon.-Sat., $13-23), one of the very few Thai restaurants in Southern Utah.

Also in the Ancestor Square complex, at the corner of St. George Boulevard and Main Street, is an actual pub: **George's Corner** (2 W. St. George Blvd., 435/216-7311, http://georgescornerrestaurant.com, 8am-midnight daily, $10-24). It's a little shocking to look in a window in the heart of downtown and see people gathered at a bar, but for many visitors, it's also a small joy. In addition to the bar area, George's Corner also has a family-friendly restaurant section featuring typical pub fare; breakfast is also served.

Just down the street, **Bear Paw Cafe** (75 N.

Main St., 435/879-3410, http://bearpawcafe. com, 7am-3pm daily, $8-15) is a bright spot for coffee drinkers and anyone who wants a good breakfast; Belgian waffles are the house specialty. Next door, the deservedly popular **Riggatti's Wood Fired Pizza** (73 N. Main St., 435/674-9922, http://riggattis.com, 11am-9pm Mon.-Sat., medium pizza $8-18) serves pizza; a favorite is the CBR (chicken, bacon, ranch dressing). Although the staff is friendly, the dining atmosphere is pretty basic; take your pizza to go.

Find excellent tacos at **Angelica's Mexican Grill** (101 E. St. George Blvd., 435/628-4399, www.irmitas.com, 11am-8pm Mon.-Thurs., 11am-9pm Fri.-Sat., $8-14), an authentic Mexican restaurant near downtown.

A little farther from the downtown hub, near a freeway interchange and chain hotels and restaurants, is **Red Fort Cuisine of India** (148 S. 1470 E., 435/574-4050, redfortcuisine.com, 11:30am-9pm Mon.-Thurs., 11:30am-10pm Fri.-Sat., $13-20), which probably has the best Indian food you'll find in this part of the state, including many vegetarian options. It's a local favorite, and often crowded.

Also worth the 2-mile drive southwest of downtown is the **Cliffside Restaurant** (511 S. Tech Ridge Dr., 435/319-6005, www. cliffsiderestaurant.com, 11am-3pm and 5pm-9pm Mon.-Thurs., 11am-3pm and 5pm-10pm Fri.-Sat., $16-36), where the astounding views are nearly matched by the very good food (steaks, ribs, pizza, and fresh fish).

ACCOMMODATIONS

St. George offers many places to stay and eat, though the town fills up when events such as the early-October marathon or early-May triathlon are held. Motel prices vary wildly: They are highest during the cooler months and drop if business is slow in summer. (We've listed the higher prices here.) Golfers should ask about golf-and-lodging packages. You'll find most lodgings along the busy I-15 business route of St. George Boulevard (exit 8) and Bluff Street (exit 6).

Under $50

★ **Dixie Palms Motel** (185 E. St. George Blvd., 435/673-3531, www.dixiepalmsmotel. com, $40-55) is a classic old-fashioned courtyard motel on the main strip right downtown, with fridges and microwaves in the guest rooms. It's a top pick for budget travelers who won't be bothered by older furnishings (beds are fine) and small baths.

$50-100

Many of St. George's less expensive lodging choices are chains operating at exit 8 off I-15. Near downtown, there are some decent locally owned choices. The **Chalet Motel** (664 E. St. George Blvd., 435/628-6272, www. chaletmotelstgeorge.com, $74-99) offers fridges and microwaves or some efficiency kitchens in larger guest rooms. There's also a pool.

The Spanish-style **Best Western Travel Inn** (316 E. St. George Blvd., 435/673-3541 or 888/590-2835, www.stgeorgebestwestern.com, $66-80) is a relatively small motel with an outdoor pool, an indoor hot tub, and a pretty good free breakfast.

$100-150

A particularly nice standard motel, the **Desert Garden Inn** (1450 S. Hilton Inn Dr., 435/688-7477 or 800/662-2525, www. wyndhamhotels.com/trademark, $99-139) is located on a golf course and has beautiful public areas and nicely appointed guest rooms. Facilities include a pool, a sauna, and private tennis courts.

Close to downtown is one of St. George's best: the **Best Western Coral Hills** (125 E. St. George Blvd., 435/673-4844, www.coralhills. com, $98-150), a very attractive property with indoor and outdoor pools and two spas, an exercise room, and a complimentary continental breakfast.

Look for more motels at I-15 exit 6. Here you'll find the **Best Western Plus Abbey Inn** (1129 S. Bluff St., 435/652-1234 or 888/222-3946, www.bwabbeyinn.com, $130-199); all guest rooms have microwaves and fridges. There's a small outdoor pool, an indoor spa, recreation and fitness facilities, and hot breakfast included.

Over $150

Golfers and those who are willing to pay extra for bit of plushness should seriously consider the Inn at Entrada (2588 W. Sinagua Trail, 435/634-7100, www.innatentrada.com, $219-439), located near Snow Canyon State Park. A stay at the inn is the easiest way to gain access to the resort community's top-notch golf course. It's a lovely setting, the lodging comprises casitas, and there's a spa and a restaurant on-site.

The classy and friendly Inn on the Cliff (511 S. Tech Ridge Dr., 435/216-5864, www.innonthecliff.com, $159-189) indeed perches over the city, with a good restaurant, great views, and boutique-style amenities, including a pool, a fitness center, and free breakfast box delivered to the room. Note that weekend prices can be as much as $200 higher.

Spa Resort

St. George is home to a deservedly popular spa resort in a gorgeous natural setting.

It's not the swankiest spa ever but, with its outdoorsy atmosphere and focus on outdoor adventure and fitness, the ★ Red Mountain Resort (1275 E. Red Mountain Circle, 877/246-4453, http://redmountainresort.com, $225-350 room only) appeals to guests who want to explore. It's located near Snow Canyon, and morning hikes in the beautiful state park are a great part of the routine. Facilities include numerous swimming and soaking pools, a fitness center and gym, a salon, a spa, and conference rooms, plus access to lots of hiking and biking trails. Packages, which include all meals, lodging, and use of most spa facilities and recreation, start at about $365 per person, with special deals often available online. Spa services, including massage, facials, body polishing, and aromatherapy, cost extra. In addition to hotel-style rooms, the resort offers a variety of suites, including some with two bedrooms and full kitchens.

Campgrounds

The best camping in the area is at Snow Canyon State Park (435/628-2255, http://stateparks.utah.gov, reservations 800/322-3770, www.reserveamerica.com, $8 reservation fee, reservations required in spring, $20 without hookups, $25 with hookups). Sites are in a pretty canyon, and the campground has showers. From downtown St. George, head north on Bluff Street (Hwy. 18) and follow signs about 12 miles (19.3 km) to the park.

Other public campgrounds in the area include Quail Creek State Park (435/879-2378, http://stateparks.utah.gov, reservations www.reserveamerica.com, $25-35), north of town off I-15. Take exit 16 when coming from the south or exit 23 when approaching from the north. Quail Creek is on a reservoir with little shade, but it's a good option if you have a boat.

The Bureau of Land Management (BLM) Red Cliffs Recreation Area (435/688-3200, $15) is also north of St. George. Take I-15 exit 22 when coming from the south or exit 23 from the north. Red Cliffs is a more scenic than Quail Creek and has hiking trails, including Silver Reef, which leads to dinosaur tracks.

If you need a place to park an RV for the night right in town, McArthur's Temple View RV Resort (975 S. Main St., 435/673-6400 or 800/776-6410, www.templeviewrv.com, $42 tents and RVs) is near St. George Temple but has little shade.

INFORMATION AND SERVICES

Staff at downtown's Visitor Information Center (20 N. Main St., 435/634-5747, https://greaterzion.com, 9am-5pm Mon.-Fri.), can tell you about the sights, events, and services of southwestern Utah.

For information on fishing, hiking, and camping in national forestland, visit the Dixie

National Forest office (196 E. Tabernacle St., 435/652-3100, www.fs.usda.gov/main/dixie, 8am-5pm Mon.-Fri.).

There is a post office (180 N. Main St., 435/673-3312). The Dixie Regional Medical Center (1380 E. Medical Center Dr., 435/251-1000) provides hospital care.

GETTING THERE

St. George's airport (SGU) is 5 miles (8 km) southeast of downtown off I-15 exit 2. SkyWest Airlines, a local subsidiary of Delta (800/221-1212, www.delta.com), plus American (800/433-7330), and United (800/864-8331, www.ual.com) offer several daily direct flights to and from Salt Lake City, Denver, Phoenix, and Los Angeles.

Several of the usual rental-car companies operate at the St. George airport: Budget (435/673-6825), Avis (435/627-2002), and Hertz (435/652-9941).

It's an easy two-hour drive from Las Vegas to St. George, so travelers may want to consider flying into Vegas and renting a car there.

Greyhound (800/231-2222) buses depart from a Texaco station (1572 S. Convention Center Dr.) for Salt Lake City, Denver, Las Vegas, and other destinations. The St. George Shuttle (790 S. Bluff St., 435/628-8320 or 800/933-8320, www.stgshuttle.com) will take you to Las Vegas ($41), the Salt Lake City airport ($60), or Springdale ($70) in a passenger van.

Cedar City

Cedar City (population about 33,000), known for its scenic setting and its summertime Utah Shakespeare Festival, is a handy base for exploring a good chunk of Southern Utah. Just east of town are the high cliffs of the Markagunt Plateau—a land of panoramic views, colorful rock formations, desolate lava flows, extensive forests, and flower-filled meadows. Also on the Markagunt Plateau is the Cedar Breaks National Monument, an immense amphitheater eroded into the vividly hued underlying rock.

Zion National Park's Kolob Canyons area is less than 20 miles (32 km) from Cedar City. Within an easy day's drive are the Zion Canyon section of the park to the south, and Bryce Canyon National Park and Escalante Canyons unit to the east.

SIGHTS

Utah Shakespeare Festival

Cedar City's lively Utah Shakespeare Festival (435/586-7880, box office 435/586-7878 or 800/752-9849, www.bard.org) presents Shakespearean plays, contemporary

theatre, and musicals each summer season in the Beverley Taylor Sorenson Center for the Arts on the campus of Southern Utah University. This theater complex opened in 2016 and boasts three performance areas, including the Engelstad Shakespeare Theatre, an open-air space reminiscent of Elizabethan theaters but with modern amenities and technology. The indoor Randall Jones Theatre presents the "Best of the Rest"—often recent Broadway hits—while the "black box" Eileen and Allen Anes Studio Theatre offers more experimental performances and seats just 200. A total of eight or nine plays are staged each season (late June-mid-Oct.).

Costumed actors stage the popular free Greenshow (7pm Mon.-Sat. late June-Aug.) before the performances, with a variety of Elizabethan comedy skits, Punch-and-Judy shows, period dances, music, juggling, and other good-natured 16th-century fun. Backstage tours ($8) of the costume shop, makeup room, and performance space show you how the festival works. At literary seminars each morning, actors and Shakespearean

Cedar City

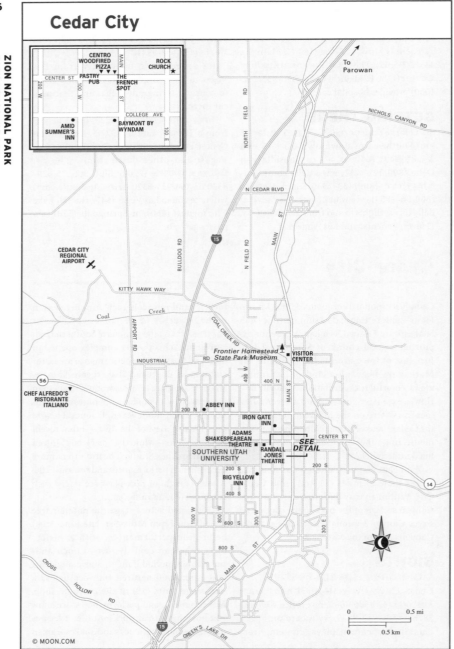

CENTRO WOODFIRED PIZZA
ROCK CHURCH
CENTER ST
PASTRY PUB
THE FRENCH SPOT
MAIN
200 W
100 W
ST
COLLEGE AVE
AMID SUMMER'S INN
BAYMONT BY WYNDAM
100 E

To Parowan

NICHOLS CANYON RD

N CEDAR BLVD

NORTH FIELD RD

MAIN ST

15

CEDAR CITY REGIONAL AIRPORT

BULLDOG RD

N FIELD RD

KITTY HAWK WAY

Coal   Creek

AIRPORT RD

COAL CREEK RD

INDUSTRIAL   RD

Frontier Homestead State Park Museum
VISITOR CENTER

400 W

400 N

MAIN ST

56

CHEF ALFREDO'S RISTORANTE ITALIANO

200 N   ABBEY INN

IRON GATE INN

ADAMS SHAKESPEAREAN THEATRE
SOUTHERN UTAH UNIVERSITY
RANDALL JONES THEATRE
CENTER ST
SEE DETAIL

200 S

BIG YELLOW INN

200 S

14

400 S

1100 W
800 W
600 S
300 W

300 E

800 S

MAIN ST

CROSS

HOLLOW

RD

0   0.5 mi

0   0.5 km

15

GREEN'S LAKE DR

© MOON.COM

scholars discuss the previous night's play. Production seminars, held daily except Sunday, take a close look at acting, costumes, stage props, special effects, and other details of play production.

The Greenshow and seminars are free, but most plays are $24-82, depending on seats, and it's wise to purchase tickets well in advance; last-minute theatergoers, however, can usually find tickets to something.

The theaters are near the corner of Center Street and 300 West. Rain occasionally dampens the performances (the Engelstad Theatre is open to the sky), and plays may move to a conventional indoor theater next door.

Frontier Homestead State Park Museum

The **Frontier Homestead State Park Museum** (635 N. Main St., 435/586-9290, https://frontierhomestead.org, 9am-6pm daily June-Aug., 9am-5pm Mon.-Sat. Sept.-May, $4), an in-town state park, focuses on history rather than recreation. Cedar City was a center for iron mining and processing starting in 1850, when Brigham Young, hoping to increase Utah's self-sufficiency, sent workers to develop an "Iron Mission." The ironworks eventually became a private company, although it never really prospered financially. Indoor and outdoor exhibits focus on the iron foundry and other aspects of local history.

SCENIC DRIVES
Parowan Gap

Ten miles (16 km) west of the small I-15 town of Parowan is a pass where Native Americans created many petroglyphs, designs pecked into the rocks. Wildlife—and the people pursuing it—commonly passed through this gap in the Red Hills, and it may have served as an important site for hunting rituals. The meaning of the rock art hasn't been deciphered, but it probably represents the thoughts of many different Native American groups over the past 1,000 or more years. Geometric designs, snakes, lizards, mountain sheep, bear claws, and human figures are all still recognizable.

You can get here on a good gravel road from Parowan by going north on Main Street, turning left, and continuing 10.5 miles (16.9 km) on the last street (400 North). Or, from Cedar City, go north on Main Street, which becomes Highway 130 at I-15 exit 62, and follow signs north for 13.5 miles (21.7 km), then turn right and go 2.5 miles (4 km) on a good gravel road (near milepost 19). In Cedar City, you can get an interpretive brochure and map at the **BLM Cedar City District Office** (176 E. D. L. Sargent Dr., 435/865-3000).

Markagunt High Plateau Scenic Byway

Starting at Cedar City's eastern boundary, Highway 14 plunges into a narrow canyon flanked by steep rock walls before climbing to the top of the Markagunt Plateau. This scenic route passes dramatic rock cliffs and pink-rock hoodoos that echo the formations at Zion and Bryce Canyon National Parks. Although it's not a quick drive—especially if you get caught behind a lumbering RV—the scenic qualities of the canyon and the incredible vistas, which extend across Zion and down into Arizona, will amply repay your patience. The route also passes several wooded campgrounds and small mountain resorts. Because of their elevations—mostly 8,000-9,000 feet (2,438-2,743 m)—these high-mountain getaways are popular when the temperatures in the desert basin towns begin to soar. The route ends at Long Valley Junction, at U.S. 89, which is 41 miles (66 km) east of Cedar City.

FOOD

Cedar City has a few good casual restaurants. The brightest spot is ★ **Centro Woodfired Pizzeria** (50 W. Center St., 435/867-8123, www.centropizzeria.com, 11am-10pm Mon.-Sat., 11am-9pm Sun., $10-15), a stylish place with very good pizza (cooked to a char unless you specify otherwise), large salads, and a decent selection of beer and wine. It's a busy spot in the evening, especially when the Shakespeare Festival is in session, so plan accordingly.

1

2

Grind Coffeehouse (19 N. Main St., 435/867-3333, 7am-5pm Mon.-Sat., 9am-3pm Sun., $5-8) has the best coffee in town and a good selection of sandwiches. The cavernous space isn't especially inviting, but it does have the feeling of a community gathering place. Nearby, **The French Spot** (5 N. Main St., 435/866-8587, www.thefrenchspotcafe.com, 10am-9pm Mon.-Sat., 10am-8pm Sun., $5-15) is a sweet café run by a French pastry chef and his family. Stop in for an omelet, crepes, or a croissant.

At the **Pastry Pub** (86 W. Center St., 435/867-1400, www.cedarcitypastrypub.com, 8am-10pm Mon.-Sat., $6-9), you'll find pastries, good sandwiches, and coffee; although the atmosphere here is a bit fusty, it's a good place for lunch or a quick bite to eat before a play.

Chef Alfredo Ristorante Italiano (2313 W. 400 N., 435/586-2693, www.chefalfredos.com, 11am-2pm and 4pm-9pm Mon.-Fri., 4pm-9pm Sat., 4pm-8pm Sun., $16-30) has a wide-ranging and well-executed Italian menu and an elegance that belies its location in a strip mall some distance from downtown. Come prepared for generous servings.

ACCOMMODATIONS

During the Shakespeare Festival, Cedar City is a popular destination, so it's best to reserve a room at least a day or two in advance during the summer. There are two major concentrations of motels. A half-dozen large chain hotels cluster around the I-15 exits, together with lots of fast-food restaurants and strip malls. Downtown along Main Street are even more motels. You can easily walk from most of the downtown motels to the Shakespeare Festival. Many of Cedar City's B&Bs are also within a stroll of the festival grounds.

Note that the following prices are for the summer festival high season. Outside high season, expect rates to drop by about one-third.

$100-150

Located conveniently downtown, **Baymont by Wyndam Cedar City** (80 S. Main St., 435/586-6518, www.elreyinncedarcity.com, $115) is an old-style motel with a remodel in the works.

One of the best places to stay in Cedar City is the **Abbey Inn** (940 W. 200 N., 435/586-9966 or 800/325-5411, www.abbeyinncedar.com, $97-155), which has remodeled guest rooms, an indoor pool, and a good breakfast included.

Bed-and-breakfast inns and Shakespeare seem to go hand in hand. Near the festival, at the edge of the Southern Utah University campus, the **Big Yellow Inn** (234 S. 300 W., 435/586-0960, www.bigyellowinn.com, $119-199) is easy to spot: It's yellow and full of antiques. Several of the guest rooms are in a house directly across the street from the main inn. The antiques-filled **Amid Summer's Inn** (140 S. 100 W., 435/589-2600, www.amidsummersinn.com, $119-179) has eight sumptuously decorated guest rooms in a restored 1930s cottage.

The **Iron Gate Inn** (100 N. 200 W., 435/867-0603, www.theirongateinn.com, $129-149), built in 1897, nicely remodeled in the early 2000s, is a rare pet-friendly B&B.

Campgrounds

East of Cedar City on Highway 14 are a handful of campgrounds in the Dixie National Forest. The closest, **Cedar Canyon** (635/865-3200, www.fs.usda.gov/main/Dixie, Memorial Day-Labor Day, $19), is 12 miles (19.3 km) from town in a pretty canyon along Cow Creek. It's at 8,100 feet (2,469 m) elevation and has water.

Cedar City KOA (1121 N. Main St., 435/586-9872 or 800/562-9873, https://koa.com/campgrounds/cedar-city, year-round, $34 tents, $56 RVs) has cabins ($63-74 no linens, $78-145 linens provided), showers, a playground, and a pool.

1: Frontier Homestead State Park **2:** Centro Woodfired Pizzeria

INFORMATION AND SERVICES

The **Cedar City Brian Head Tourism Bureau** (581 N. Main St., 435/586-5124, www.visitcedarcity.com, 8:30am-5pm Mon.-Fri., 9am-5pm Sat.) is just south of Frontier Homestead State Park. The Dixie National Forest's **Cedar City Ranger District Office** (1789 N. Wedgewood Lane, 435/865-3200) has information on recreation and travel on the Markagunt Plateau. The **BLM's Cedar City District Office** (176 E. D. L. Sargent Dr., 435/865-3000) is just off Main Street on the north edge of town.

GETTING THERE

Just east of I-15, Cedar City is 52 miles (84 km) northeast of St. George and 253 miles (407 km) southwest of Salt Lake City; take I-15 exit 57, exit 59, or exit 62. **Delta** (800/221-1212, www.delta.com) has flights operated by SkyWest between the small **Cedar City Regional Airport** (CDC, 2560 Aviation Way, 435/867-9408) and Salt Lake City. Rent a car from **Avis** (435/867-9898) at the airport.

Bryce Canyon National Park

In Bryce Canyon, a geologic fairyland of rock spires rises beneath the high cliffs of the Paunsaugunt Plateau. This intricate maze, eroded from soft limestone, now glows with warm shades of red, orange, pink, yellow, and cream. The sun's rays and cloud shadows moving across the landscape provide a continuous show of changing color.

Looking at these rock formations is like looking at puffy clouds in the sky; it's easy to find images in the shapes of the rocks. Some see the natural rock sculptures as Gothic castles, others as Egyptian temples, subterranean worlds inhabited by dragons, or vast armies of a lost empire. The Paiute tale of the Legend People relates how various animals and birds once lived in a beautiful city built for them by

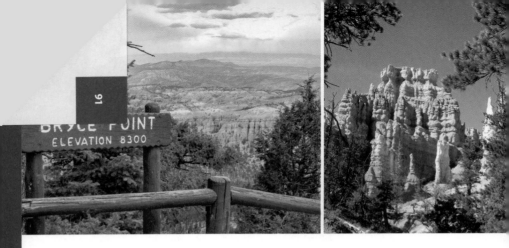

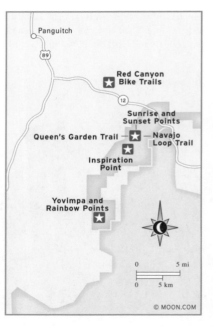

Highlights

Look for ★ to find recommended sights, activities, dining, and lodging.

★ **Watch the Sun Rise and Set:** At their namesake hours, **Sunrise and Sunset Points** are irresistible. Don't forget your camera (page 96)!

★ **See the "Silent City" from Inspiration Point:** From Sunset Point, walk south along the Rim Trail to see this fantastic maze of hoodoos. Many rows of narrow gullies here are more than 200 feet (61 m) deep (page 96).

★ **Drive to Yovimpa and Rainbow Points:** The views the scenic road are spectacular—with a climax at the highest are of the park at 9,115 feet (2,778-m) (page 99).

★ **Trek the Queen's Garden Trail:** This trail drops from Sunrise Point through the middle of Bryce Amphitheater to a hoodoo resembling a portly Queen Victoria. While it's the easiest hike below the rim, it can still leave flatlanders huffing and puffing (page 102).

★ **Hike Navajo Loop Trail:** From Sunset Point, hike down through a narrow canyon and into deep, dark Wall Street—an even narrower canyon—before returning to the rim (page 103).

★ **Bike Red Canyon:** Put rubber to the road on the paved trail that parallels Highway 12. Adventurous mountain bikers should seek thrills on the **Castro Canyon Trail** (page 113).

Bryce Canyon National Park

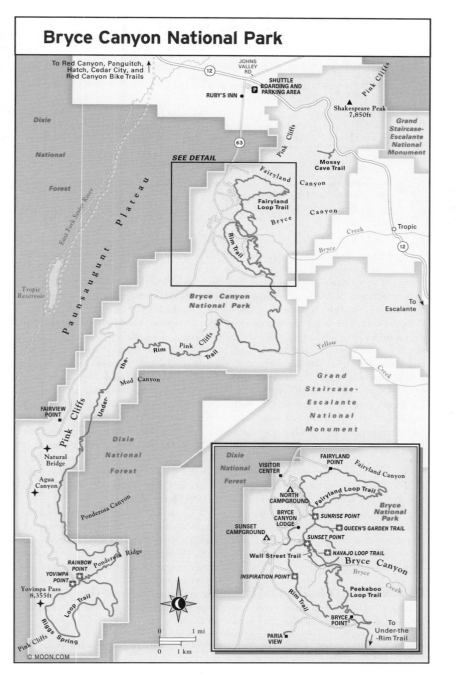

To Red Canyon, Panguitch, Hatch, Cedar City, and Red Canyon Bike Trails

JOHNS VALLEY RD.

12

SHUTTLE BOARDING AND PARKING AREA

RUBY'S INN

Pink Cliffs

Shakespeare Peak 7,850ft

Grand Staircase-Escalante National Monument

Dixie

National

63

Pink Cliffs

Forest

SEE DETAIL

Fairyland Canyon

Mossy Cave Trail

East Fork Sevier River

Fairyland Loop Trail

Canyon

Plateau

Bryce

Creek

Tropic

Rim Trail

Bryce

12

Paunsaugunt

Tropic Reservoir

Bryce Canyon National Park

To Escalante

Rim

Pink Cliffs

Trail

Yellow

Creek

the-

Mud Canyon

Grand Staircase-Escalante National Monument

Under-

FAIRVIEW POINT

Pink Cliffs

Dixie

National

Natural Bridge

Forest

Dixie

FAIRYLAND POINT

National

VISITOR CENTER

Fairyland Canyon

Agua Canyon

Forest

NORTH CAMPGROUND

Fairyland Loop Trail

Bryce National Park

Ponderosa Canyon

BRYCE CANYON LODGE

SUNRISE POINT

QUEEN'S GARDEN TRAIL

SUNSET CAMPGROUND

SUNSET POINT

RAINBOW POINT

Ponderosa Ridge

Wall Street Trail

NAVAJO LOOP TRAIL

YOVIMPA POINT

INSPIRATION POINT

Bryce Canyon

Yovimpa Pass 8,355ft

Loop Trail

Rim Trail

Bryce

Creek

Peekaboo Loop Trail

Pink Cliffs

Riggs Spring

0   1 mi

0   1 km

BRYCE POINT

PARIA VIEW

To Under-the-Rim Trail

© MOON.COM

Bryce in One Day

- If you wake up early enough, catch the scene at **Sunrise Point** (it's worth it).

- If you choose to sleep in, drive to **Rainbow Point,** at the end of the parkway, with views over much of Southern Utah.

- From there, drive back toward the amphitheater area, where you can descend from the rim on the **Navajo Loop Trail.** At the bottom of the loop, turn onto the **Queen's Garden Trail** and follow that back up to the rim. This hike is about three miles and will take a little over an hour. The Rim Trail connects the two trailheads.

- From here it's easy to get lunch and snacks at the **General Store.**

- Spend the afternoon walking along the **Rim Trail.** Head to **Lodge at Bryce Canyon** for dinner; it's the best food in the area.

Coyote; when the Legend People began behaving badly toward Coyote, he transformed them all into stone.

Bryce Canyon isn't a canyon at all, but rather the largest of a series of massive amphitheaters cut into the Pink Cliffs. In Bryce Canyon National Park, you can gaze into the depths from viewpoints and trails on the plateau rim or hike down moderately steep trails and wind your way among the spires. A 17-mile (27-km) scenic drive traces the length of the park and passes many overlooks and trailheads. Away from the road, the nearly 36,000 acres of Bryce Canyon National Park offer many opportunities to explore spectacular rock features, dense forests, and expansive meadows.

The park's elevation ranges 6,600-9,100 feet (2,012-2,743 m), so it's usually much cooler here than at Utah's other national parks. Expect pleasantly warm days in summer, frosty nights in spring and fall, and snow at almost any time of year. The visitors center, the scenic drive, and one campground stay open throughout the year.

PLANNING YOUR TIME

Allow a full day to see the visitors center exhibits, enjoy the viewpoints along the scenic drive, and take a few short walks. Because of the layout of the park, with viewpoints all on the east side of the scenic drive, rangers recommend driving all the way south to Rainbow Point, and then stopping at viewpoints on your way back toward the park entrance; this means you won't constantly need to turn left across oncoming traffic.

The hike into Queen's Garden is a good, relatively short hike, and it's easy to fit into a one-day tour of the park. If you have more time to hike, try the Navajo Loop Trail; it can be combined with the Queen's Garden for a pretty substantial trek. Another good bet for strong hikers is the outstanding Peekaboo Loop. These trails are often crowded near the rim, less so the farther out you get. If the crowds begin to get to you, it's time to visit the Fairyland Loop Trail, which is off the main drag and less traveled.

If you're interested in photographing the hoodoos—and it's hard to resist the urge—it makes sense to spend the night in or near the park. Photographers usually obtain the best results early and late in the day, when shadows set off the brightly colored rocks. Memorable sunsets and sunrises reward visitors who stay overnight. Moonlit nights reveal yet another spectacle.

Previous: clear skies and red sandstone hoodoos; Bryce Point offers one of the park's grandest vistas; hoodoos in Bryce Canyon National Park.

If you want to travel into the backcountry, be sure to consult with a ranger about your plans. Remember that winter can last a long time at this elevation, and many trails can be blocked by snow and ice into the spring. The weather can also take a toll on the trails, and it's not uncommon to learn that your selected trail has been closed by rockfall.

Exploring the Park

Bryce Canyon National Park (435/834-5322, www.nps.gov/brca, $35 per vehicle, $30 motorcycles, $20 pp cyclists or pedestrians, admission good for 7 days and unlimited shuttle use) is just south of the incredibly scenic Highway 12, between Bryce Junction and Tropic.

Special hazards you should be aware of include crumbly ledges and lightning strikes. People who have wandered off trails or got too close to the drop-offs have had to be pulled out by rope. Avoid cliffs and other exposed areas during electrical storms, which are most common in late summer.

Rangers note that most serious injuries in the park could be prevented by wearing proper supportive footwear with lug soles; don't head down the trail in flip-flops!

VISITORS CENTER

From the turnoff on Highway 12, follow signs past Ruby's Inn for 4.5 miles (7.2 km) south to the park entrance; the Bryce Canyon Visitor Center (435/834-4747, 8am-8pm daily May-Sept., 8am-6pm daily mid-Mar.-Apr. and Oct., 8am-4:30pm daily Nov.-mid-Mar.) is a short distance farther on the right. A 20-minute video, shown every half hour, introduces the park. Geologic exhibits illustrate how the land was formed and how it has changed. Historical displays cover the Paiute people, early nonnative explorers, and the first settlers; trees, flowers, and wildlife are identified. Rangers present a variety of naturalist programs, including short hikes, mid-May-early September; see the posted schedule.

TOURS

The most basic tour of the park, which comes with the price of admission, is a ride on the park shuttle bus. Shuttle buses run every 15 minutes or so during the peak part of the day, and the trip from Ruby's Inn to Yovimpa Point takes 50 minutes. Of course, the beauty of the shuttle is that you can get off at any stop, hike for a while, and then catch another bus. However, if you're not really planning to hike, consider joining one of the free, twice-daily **shuttle bus tours** (435/834-5290, 9am and 1:30pm daily May-Sept., reservations required and available at Ruby's Inn, Ruby's Campground, or the shuttle parking area) of the park. These 3.5-hour tours go all the way to Rainbow Point. Shuttle season is early May-mid-October; shuttle use is voluntary but note that rigs longer than 20 feet (6 m) aren't allowed on the main park road during times that the shuttle is running.

Ruby's Inn (26 S. Main St., 866/866-6616, www.rubysinn.com), a hotel, restaurant, and recreation complex at the park entrance, is a good place to take measure of the opportunities for organized recreation and sightseeing excursions around Bryce Canyon. The lobby is filled with outfitters who are eager to take you out on the trail; you'll find lots of recreational outfitters, along with vendors who organize horseback rides ($68-135), hay rides, barn dances, chuckwagon dinners, and even virtual reality tours of southern Utah. During the summer, Ruby's also sponsors a **rodeo** (866/782-0002, 7pm Wed.-Sat., $13 adults, $9 ages 5-11) across from the inn.

Parkgoers have long explored Bryce

Canyon's hoodoos on horseback, and it's still an option offered at Ruby's and at the park lodge. You can also explore the area around Bryce Canyon on a noisier steed: Guided all-terrain vehicle (ATV) tours of Red Canyon are offered by **Ruby's ATV Tours** (435/834-5231, 1-hour trip $70-140 depending on vehicle choice).

If you'd like to get a look at Bryce and the surrounding area from the air, take a scenic flightseeing tour with **Bryce Canyon Airlines** (Ruby's Inn, 435/834-8060), which offers both plane and helicopter tours. There's quite a range of options, but a 35-minute airplane tour ($175 pp, 2-person minimum) provides a good look at the surroundings.

Sights

SCENIC DRIVE

From elevations of about 8,000 feet (2,438 m) near the visitors center, the park's scenic drive gradually winds 1,100 feet (335 m) higher to Rainbow Point. About midway you'll notice a change in the trees from largely ponderosa pine to spruce, fir, and aspen. On a clear day, you can enjoy vistas of more than 100 miles (161 km) from many of the viewpoints. Because of parking shortages on the drive, trailers or RVs longer than 20 feet (6 m) must be left at the visitors center or your campsite. Visitors wishing to see all of the viewpoints from Fairyland Point to Bryce Point should take a walk on the 5.5-mile (8.9-km) Rim Trail.

Note that even though the viewpoints are described here in north-to-south order, when the park is bustling, it's better to drive all the way to the southern end of the road and visit the viewpoints from south to north, thus avoiding left turns across traffic. Of course, if you're just heading to one viewpoint or trailhead, it's fine to drive directly to it.

Fairyland Point

The turnoff for Fairyland Point is just inside the park boundary, but before you get to the booth where payment is required; go north 0.8 mile (1.3 km) from the visitors center, then east 1 mile (1.6 km). Whimsical rock formations line Fairyland Canyon a short distance below. You can descend into the fairyland on the **Fairyland Loop Trail** or follow the **Rim Trail** for other panoramas.

TOP EXPERIENCE

★ Sunrise and Sunset Points

These overlooks are off to the left about 1 mile (1.6 km) south of the visitors center, and they're connected by a 0.5-mile (0.8-km) paved section of the **Rim Trail.** Panoramas from each point take in large swathes of Bryce Amphitheater and beyond. The lofty Aquarius and Table Cliff Plateaus rise along the skyline to the northeast; you can see the same colorful Claron Formation in cliffs that faulting has raised about 2,000 feet (610 m) higher. A short walk down either the **Queen's Garden Trail** or the **Navajo Loop Trail** from Sunset Point will bring you close to Bryce's **hoodoos** and provide a totally different experience from what you get atop the rim.

★ Inspiration Point

It's well worth the 0.75-mile (1.2-km) walk south along the **Rim Trail** from Sunset Point to see a fantastic maze of hoodoos in the "Silent City." It's also accessible by car, from a spur road near the Bryce Point turn-off. Weathering along vertical joints has cut many rows of narrow gullies, some more than 200 feet (61 m) deep. It's a short but steep 0.2-mile (0.3-km) walk up to Upper Inspiration Point.

1: Fairyland Loop Trail **2:** Navajo Loop Trail **3:** Sunset Point

Where to See Hoodoos

Bryce Canyon's spectacular hoodoos were carved by cycles of freezing and melting.

Many visitors assume that the tall rock spires called hoodoos have been shaped by wind. In fact, they were created in the interaction of water, ice, and gravity. When the Colorado Plateau uplifted, vertical breaks—called joints—formed in the plateau. Joints allowed water to flow into the rock, and over time, erosion widened them into rivulets, gullies, and eventually deep slot canyons. Bryce Canyon is composed of layers of limestone, siltstone, dolomite, and mudstone, and each rock type erodes at a different rate, carving these strange shapes. Ice is arguably an even more powerful force than erosion in their formation. About 200 days a year, water will freeze, melt, and freeze again, causing ice wedges to form within the rock joints, eventually breaking the rock.

The word *hoodoo* derives from the same source as *voodoo;* both words describe religious beliefs and practices. Early Spanish explorers transferred the mystical sense of the word to the towering, vaguely humanoid rock formations that rise above the Southwestern landscape. The Spaniards believed that Native Americans worshipped these "enchanted rocks." In fact, while early Indigenous people considered many hoodoo areas sacred, there is no evidence that they worshipped the stones themselves.

Bryce Point is a good spot for a huge panoramic view filled with hoodoos. To pack the most hoodoos into a short visit, hike the 1-mile (1.6-km) section of the **Rim Trail** between Sunrise and Sunset Points. This area of the **Bryce Amphitheatre** has the highest concentration of hoodoos and offers the most up-close and personal views. To further immerse yourself in their geology, hike the **Queen's Garden** or **Navajo Trails** (or connect the two to form a loop).

Bryce Point

This overlook at the south end of Bryce Amphitheater has expansive views to the north and east. It's also the start for the **Rim, Peekaboo Loop,** and **Under-the-Rim Trails.** From the turnoff 2 miles (3.2 km) south of the visitors center, follow signs 2.1 miles (3.4 km) in.

Paria View

Cliffs drop precipitously into the headwaters of Yellow Creek, a tributary of the Paria River. You can see a section of the Under-the-Rim Trail winding up a hillside near the mouth of the amphitheater below. Distant views take in the Paria River Canyon, White Cliffs (of Navajo sandstone), and Navajo Mountain. The plateau rim in the park forms a drainage divide. Precipitation falling west of the rim flows gently into the East Fork of the Sevier River and the Great Basin; precipitation landing east of the rim rushes through deep canyons in the Pink Cliffs to the Paria River and on to the Colorado River and the Grand Canyon. Take the turnoff for Bryce Point, and then keep right at the fork.

Farview Point

This sweeping panorama takes in a lot of geology. You'll see levels of the Grand Staircase that include the Aquarius and Table Cliff Plateaus to the northeast, Kaiparowits Plateau to the east, and White Cliffs to the southeast. Look beyond the White Cliffs to see a section of the Kaibab Plateau that forms the North Rim of the Grand Canyon. The overlook is on the left, 9 miles (14.5 km) south of the visitors center.

Natural Bridge

This large feature lies just off the road to the east, 1.7 miles (2.7 km) past Farview Point. The span is 54 feet (16.5 m) wide and 95 feet (29 m) high. Despite its name, this is an arch formed by weathering from rain and freezing, not by stream erosion, as with a true natural bridge. Once the opening reached ground level, runoff began to enlarge the hole and to dig a gully through it.

Agua and Ponderosa Canyons

You can admire sheer cliffs and hoodoos from the Agua Canyon overlook to the east, 1.4 miles (2.3 km) past Natural Bridge. With a little imagination, you may be able to pick out the Hunter and the Rabbit below. The Ponderosa Canyon overlook, 1.8 miles (2.9 km) farther east, offers a panorama similar to that at Farview Point.

★ Yovimpa and Rainbow Points

The land drops away in rugged canyons and fine views at the end of the scenic drive, 17 miles (27 km) south of the visitors center. At an elevation of 9,115 feet (2,778 m), this is the highest area of the park. Yovimpa and Rainbow Points are only a short walk apart yet offer different vistas. The **Bristlecone Loop Trail** is an easy 1-mile (1.6-km) loop from Rainbow Point to ancient bristlecone pines along the rim. The **Riggs Spring Loop Trail** makes a good day hike; you can begin from either Yovimpa Point or Rainbow Point and descend into canyons in the southern area of the park. The **Under-the-Rim Trail** starts from Rainbow Point and winds 23 miles (37 km) to Bryce Point; day hikers can make a 7.5-mile (12 km) trip by using the Agua Canyon Connecting Trail and a car shuttle.

Recreation

Although it's possible to have an entirely pleasant visit to Bryce by just riding the shuttle and hopping off to snap pictures at various viewpoints, a short hike or horseback ride down off the rim will give you an entirely different perspective on the hoodoos, native plants, and, perhaps, wildlife of the park.

HIKING

Hikers enjoy close-up views of the wonderfully eroded features and gain a direct appreciation of Bryce's geology. Because almost all of the trails head down off the canyon's rim, they're moderately difficult, with many ups and downs, but the paths are well graded and signed. Hikers not accustomed to the 7,000-9,000-foot (2,134-2,743-m) elevation will find the going relatively strenuous and should allow extra time. Be sure to carry water and drink frequently—staying well hydrated will give you more energy.

Wear sturdy shoes with ankle support and lugged soles as well as a hat and sunscreen to protect against sunburn, which can be a

Bryce Canyon Hikes

Trail	Effort	Distance	Duration
Bristlecone Loop Trail	easy	1 mi/1.6 km round-trip	30 minutes-1 hour
Mossy Cave Trail	easy	1 mi/1.6 km round-trip	30 minutes-1 hour
Rim Trail	easy	11 mi/17.7 km round-trip	5-7 hours
★ Queen's Garden Trail	easy-moderate	1.8 mi/2.9 round-trip	1.5 hours
★ Navajo Loop Trail	moderate	1.3 mi/2.1 km round-trip	1.5 hours
Swamp Canyon Loop	moderate	4.3 mi/7 km round-trip	2-3 hours
Peekaboo Loop Trail	moderate-strenuous	5.5 mi/8.9 km round-trip	3-4 hours
Hat Shop Trail	moderate-strenuous	4 mi/6.4 km round-trip	3-4 hours
Fairyland Loop Trail	strenuous	8 mi/12.9 km round-trip	4-5 hours
Riggs Spring Loop	strenuous	8.5 mi/13.7 round-trip	5-6 hours
Under-the-Rim Trail	strenuous	23 mi/37 km one-way	2 days or longer

problem at these elevations. Don't forget rain gear, because storms can come up suddenly. Always carry water for day trips; only a few natural sources exist. Ask at the visitors center for current trail conditions and water sources; you can also pick up a free hiking map. Snow may block some trail sections in winter and early spring. Horses are permitted only on Peekaboo Loop. Pets must stay above the rim; they're allowed on a half-mile stretch of the Rim Trail only between Sunset and Sunrise Points.

Overnight hikers can obtain the required **backcountry permit** ($5 pp) at the visitors center. Camping is allowed only on the Under-the-Rim and Riggs Spring Loop Trails. Backpack stoves must be used for cooking; wood fires are prohibited. Although there are several isolated springs in Bryce's backcountry, it's prudent to carry at least one gallon of water per person per day. Ask about the location and flow of springs when you register for the backcountry permit.

Don't expect much solitude during the summer on the popular Rim, Queen's Garden, Navajo, and Peekaboo Loop Trails. Fairyland Loop Trail is less used, and the backcountry trails are almost never crowded. September-October are the choice hiking months—the weather is best and the crowds are smallest, although nighttime temperatures in late October can dip well below freezing.

Rim Trail

Distance: 11 miles (17.7 km) round-trip
Duration: 5-7 hours
Elevation change: 540 feet (165 m)
Effort: moderate
Trailheads: Fairyland Point, Bryce Point
Shuttle Stops: Fairyland Point, Bryce Point

This easy trail follows the edge of Bryce Amphitheater. Most people walk short sections of the rim in leisurely strolls or use the trail to connect with one of the five other trails that head down beneath the rim. Near the lodge, there's a 0.5-mile (0.8-km) stretch of trail between Sunrise and Sunset Points that is paved, nearly level, and wheelchair accessible; other parts are gently rolling.

Rim Trail

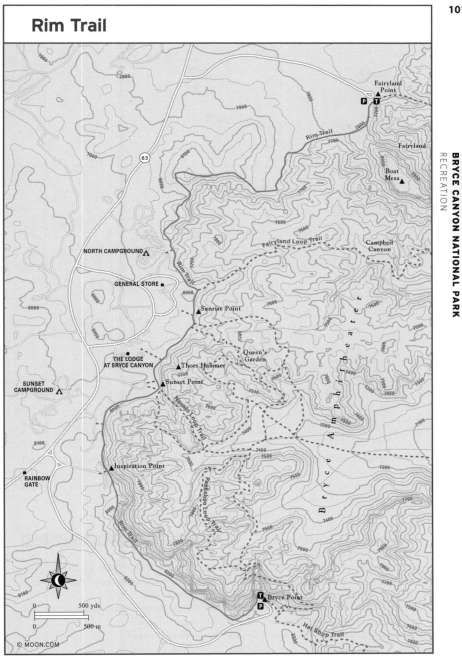

© MOON.COM

Fairyland Loop Trail

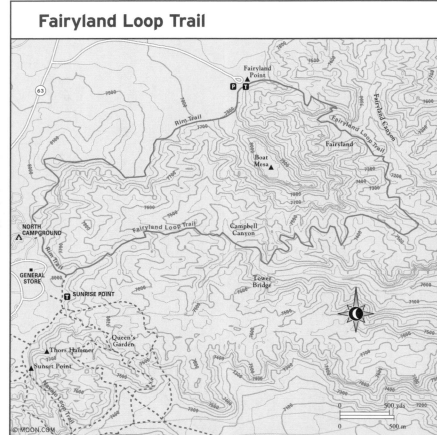

Fairyland Loop Trail

Distance: 8 miles (12.9 km) round-trip
Duration: 4-5 hours
Elevation change: 2,300 feet (701 m)
Effort: strenuous
Trailheads: Fairyland Point, Sunrise Point
Shuttle Stops: Fairyland Point, Sunrise Point

This trail winds in and out of colorful rock spires in the northern part of Bryce Amphitheater, a somewhat less-visited area 1 mile (1.6 km) off the main park road. Although the trail is well graded, remember the steep, unrelenting climb you'll make when you exit. You can take a loop hike of 8 miles (12.9 km) from either Fairyland Point or Sunrise Point by using a section of the **Rim Trail;** a car shuttle saves 3 hiking miles (4.8 km). The whole loop is too long for many visitors, who enjoy short trips down and back to see this "fairyland."

★ Queen's Garden Trail

Distance: 1.8 miles (2.9 km) round-trip
Duration: 1.5 hours
Elevation change: 320 feet (98 m)
Effort: easy-moderate
Trailhead: Sunrise Point
Shuttle Stop: Sunrise Point

A favorite of many people, this trail drops from Sunrise Point through impressive features in the middle of Bryce Amphitheater to a **hoodoo** resembling a portly Queen Victoria. This is the easiest excursion below the rim. Queen's Garden Trail also makes a good loop hike with the **Navajo Loop** and **Rim Trails;** most people who do the loop prefer to descend the steeper Navajo and climb out on Queen's Garden Trail for a 3.5-mile (5.6-km) hike. Trails also connect with the **Peekaboo Loop Trail** and go to the town of Tropic.

★ Navajo Loop Trail

Distance: 1.3 miles (2.1 km) round-trip
Duration: 1.5 hours
Elevation change: 520 feet (158 m)
Effort: moderate
Trailhead: Sunset Point
Shuttle Stop: Sunset Point

From Sunset Point, the trail drops 520 vertical feet (158 m) in 0.75 mile (1.2 km) through a narrow canyon. At the bottom, the loop leads into deep, dark **Wall Street**—an even narrower canyon 0.5 mile (0.8 km) long—and then returns to the rim. Of all the trails in the park, this is the most prone to rockfall, so hikers should be alert to slides or sounds of falling rocks; it's not uncommon for at least part

of the trail to be closed because of the danger of falling rocks. Other destinations from the bottom of Navajo Trail are **Twin Bridges, Queen's Garden Trail, Peekaboo Loop Trail,** and the town of Tropic. The 1.5-mile (2.4 km) spur trail to Tropic isn't as scenic as the other trails, but it does provide another way to enter or leave the park; ask at the visitors center or in Tropic for directions to the trailhead.

Peekaboo Loop Trail

Distance: 5.5 miles (8.9 km) round-trip
Duration: 3-4 hours
Elevation change: 1,500 feet (457 m)
Effort: moderate-strenuous
Trailhead: Bryce Point
Shuttle Stop: Bryce Point

This enchanting walk is full of surprises at every turn—and there are lots of turns. The trail is in the southern part of Bryce Amphitheater, which has some of the most striking rock features. The loop segment itself is 3.5 miles (5.6 km) long, with many ups and downs and a few tunnels. The elevation change is 500-800 feet (152-244 m), depending on the trailhead you choose. The loop hooks up with the Navajo and the Queen's Garden Trails and can be extended by combining

descending the Peekaboo Loop Trail

Bristlecone Pine

The Bristlecone Pine Loop Trail is named for these ancient trees.

Somewhere on earth, a bristlecone pine tree may be among the planet's oldest living organisms. The trees here, while not the world's oldest, are up to 1,700 years old (there's a bristlecone in California that's nearly 4,800 years old). These twisted, gnarly trees are easy to spot in the area around **Rainbow Point** because they look their age.

What makes a bristlecone live so long? For one, its dense, resinous wood protects it from insects, bacteria, and fungi that kill many other trees. It grows in a harsh dry climate where there's not a lot of competition from other plants. During droughts that would kill most other plants, the bristlecone can slow its metabolism until it's practically dormant, then spring back to life when conditions are less severe. Although the dry desert air poses its own set of challenges, it also keeps the tree from rotting.

Besides its ancient look, a bristlecone pine can be recognized by its distinctive needles—they're packed tightly, five to a bunch, with the bunches running along the length of a branch, making it look like a bottle brush.

these loops. Peekaboo is the only trail in the park shared by horses and hikers; remember to give horseback travelers the right of way and, if possible, to step to higher ground when you allow them to pass.

Hat Shop Trail

Distance: 4 miles (6.4 km) round-trip
Duration: 3-4 hours
Elevation change: 1,075 feet (328 m)
Effort: moderate-strenuous
Trailhead: Bryce Point
Shuttle Stops: Bryce Point
The **Hat Shop,** an area of delicate spires

capped by erosion-resistant rock, is one of the landmarks along the 23-mile (37-km) Under-the-Rim Trail. If you don't want to take that full two-day trek, this section makes a good day hike. Begin at Bryce Point and follow the Under-the-Rim Trail for about 2 miles (3.2 km). The trail heads downhill to the Hat Shop; it's a steep uphill climb on the way back.

Under-the-Rim Trail

Distance: 23 miles (37 km) one-way
Duration: 2 days or longer
Elevation change: 1,500 feet (457 m)
Effort: strenuous

Bryce Canyon Festivals

Several festivals offer a chance to dig a little deeper into the park's astronomy, geology, and natural history. Although these are regular events, dates vary from year to year; check the park's website (www.nps.gov/brca) for details.

If you want to delve into Bryce's geology, plan a trip in mid-July, when the free two-day **GeoFest** offers geologist-guided hikes and bus tours as well as evening programs, exhibits, and activities for kids. Check under Things To Do on the park's website for more information. Reserve seats on the bus tour in advance by calling 435/834-5290 and pick up tickets for guided hikes at the visitors center.

Bryce has been designated a Night Sky Sanctuary, and it's a great place to stargaze. Check the park's website for the date of the June **Astronomy Festival,** when you can explore stars, the planets, and the Milky Way in one of the darkest spots in the Lower 48. During the day, there's safe solar viewing through special telescopes at the visitors center, a workshop on telescope basics, and a star lab in the lodge auditorium. Evening talks get visitors ready for stargazing through huge telescopes. Special shuttles run to the stargazing site; check at the visitors center or visit the park website for full schedules and shuttle details.

Trailheads: Bryce Point, Rainbow Point
Shuttle Stops: Bryce Point, Rainbow Point
The longest trail in the park winds 23 miles (37 km) below the Pink Cliffs, between Bryce Point to the north and Rainbow Point to the south. Allow at least two days to hike the entire trail; the elevation change is about 1,500 feet (457 m), with many ups and downs. Four connecting trails from the scenic drive also make it possible to travel the Under-the-Rim Trail as a series of day hikes. Another option is to combine the Under-the-Rim and **Riggs Spring Loop Trails** for a total of 31.5 miles (51 km).

Swamp Canyon Loop

Distance: 4.3 miles (7 km) round-trip
Duration: 2-3 hours
Elevation change: 800 feet (244 m)
Effort: moderate
Trailhead: Swamp Canyon
Shuttle Stop: Swamp Canyon
This loop comprises three trails: the Swamp Canyon Connecting Trail, a short stretch of the Under-the-Rim Trail, and the Sheep Creek Connecting Trail. Drop below the rim on the Swamp Canyon trail to a smaller sheltered canyon that is, by local standards, a wetland. Swamp Canyon's two tiny creeks and a spring provide enough moisture for a lush growth of grass and willows. Salamanders live here, as do a variety of birds; this is usually a good trail for bird-watching.

Bristlecone Loop Trail

Distance: 1 mile (1.6 km) round-trip
Duration: 30 minutes-1 hour
Elevation change: 195 feet (59 m)
Effort: easy
Trailheads: Rainbow Point, Yovimpa Point
Shuttle Stop: Rainbow Point
This easy 1-mile (1.6-km) loop begins from either Rainbow or Yovimpa Point and goes to viewpoints and ancient bristlecone pines along the rim. These hardy trees survive fierce storms and extremes of hot and cold that no other tree can. Some of the bristlecone pines here are 1,700 years old.

Riggs Spring Loop

Distance: 8.5 miles (13.7 km) round-trip
Duration: 5-6 hours
Elevation change: 1,625 feet (495 m)
Effort: strenuous
Trailhead: Rainbow Point
Shuttle Stop: Rainbow Point
One of the park's more challenging day hikes or a leisurely overnighter, this trail begins

Bryce Canyon in Winter

Although Bryce is most popular during the summer months, it is especially beautiful and otherworldly during the winter, when the rock formations are topped with snow. Because of the high elevation (8,000-9,000 ft/2,438-2,743 m), winter lasts a long time, often into April.

The main park roads and most viewpoints are plowed. The **Rim Trail** makes an excellent, easy snowshoe or cross-country ski route. The unplowed **Paria Ski Trail** (a 5-mile/8-kilometer loop) and **Fairyland Ski Trail** (a 2.5-mile/4-kilometer loop) are also good routes. Rent cross-country ski equipment just outside the park at Ruby's Inn.

At the visitors center, the **Bryce Canyon Snowshoe Program** (435/834-4747, www.nps.gov/brca,1pm daily when possible, free) offers free snowshoes and poles when you join a guided hike with a snowshoe ranger. These 1-mile (1.6-km) outings are designed for beginners and depend on snow depth and ranger availability. On full-moon nights November to March, rangers add a moonlit snowshoe hike.

Bryce Canyon in winter

Although trail closures are relatively common due to rockfall or slick conditions, winter can be a fabulous time to explore the hoodoos. Crampons or simpler traction devices (such as Yaktrax) are often far safer than snowshoes for hiking steep trails with packed snow or ice.

During the winter, most of the businesses around the park entrance shut down. The notable exception is **Ruby's Inn** (26 S. Main St., 435/834-5341 or 866/866-6616, www.rubysinn.com), which is a wintertime hub of activity. Rates are considerably lower this time of year: January to March, most guest rooms go for about $70. The inn hosts the **Bryce Canyon Winter Festival** during Presidents Day weekend in February. The three-day festival includes cross-country skiing and snowshoeing clinics, demos, and tours. This is also the time and place to pick up tips on ski archery and winter photography.

from Rainbow Point and descends into canyons in the southern area of the park. Of the three backcountry campgrounds along the trail, the Riggs Spring site is most conveniently located; it's about halfway around the loop. Great views of the hoodoos, lots of aspen trees, a couple of pretty meadows, and good views off to the east are some of the highlights of this hike. A fire in 2018 burned the area of the trail near Rainbow Point; the burned area is now particularly rich with flowers. Day hikers often take a shortcut that bypasses Riggs Spring and saves 0.75 mile (1.2 km).

Mossy Cave Trail

Distance: 1 mile (1.6 km) round-trip
Duration: 30 minutes-1 hour
Elevation change: 209 feet (64 m)
Effort: easy
Trailhead: Highway 12, between mileposts 17 and 18

This easy trail is just off Highway 12, northwest of Tropic, near the east edge of the park (which means that park entrance fees aren't required). Hike up Water Canyon to a cool alcove of dripping water and moss. Sheets of ice and icicles add beauty to the scene in winter. The hike is only 1 mile (1.6 km) round-trip with a small elevation change. A side trail just before the cave branches right a short distance to a little waterfall; look for several small arches in the colorful canyon walls above. Although the park lacks perennial natural streams, the stream in Water Canyon flows even during dry spells. Mormon pioneers labored for three years to channel water from the East Fork of the Sevier River through a canal and down this wash to the town of Tropic. Without this irrigation, the town might not even exist. To reach the trailhead from the visitors center, return to Highway 12 and turn east, then travel 3.7 miles (6 km) toward Escalante; the parking area is on the right just after a bridge, between mileposts 17 and 18.

HORSEBACK RIDING

If you'd like to get down among the hoodoos but aren't sure you'll have the energy to hike back up to the rim, consider letting a horse help you along. **Canyon Trail Rides** (Lodge at Bryce Canyon, 435/679-8665, www.canyonrides.com, Apr.-Oct.), a park concessionaire, offers two-hour ($65) and half-day ($90) guided rides near Sunrise Point. Both rides descend to the floor of the canyon; the longer ride follows the Peekaboo Loop Trail. Riders must be at least seven years old and weigh no more than 220 pounds; the horses and wranglers are accustomed to novices.

Ruby's Horseback Adventures (435/834-5341 or 866/782-0002, www.horserides.net, Apr.-Oct.) offers horseback riding in and near Bryce Canyon. There's a choice of half-day ($90) and full-day ($135, including lunch) trips, as well as a 1.5-hour trip ($68). During the summer, Ruby's also sponsors a rodeo (7pm Wed.-Sat., $14 adults, $9 ages 5-11) across from the inn.

OUTFITTERS

You guessed it: If there's a piece of gear or clothing that you need, the **General Store at Ruby's Inn** (26 S. Main St., 435/834-5484, www.rubysinn.com, 7am-10:30pm daily) is the best place to look for it. Here you'll find a large stock of groceries, camping and fishing supplies, Native American crafts, books, souvenirs, and a post office. Horseback rides, helicopter tours, and airplane rides are arranged in the lobby just outside the store. In winter, cross-country skiers can rent gear and use trails located near the inn as well as in the park. Snowmobile trails are also available, but snowmobiles may not be used within the park. Western-fronted shops across from Ruby's Inn offer trail rides, chuckwagon dinners, mountain bike rentals, souvenirs, and a petting farm.

Inside the park, there's another **General Store** (8am-9pm daily, Apr.-mid-Nov.) with groceries, camping supplies, coin-operated showers, and a laundry room. It is located between North Campground and Sunrise Point.

If you need specialized outdoor gear, you're more likely to find it 50 miles (81 km) east in the town of Escalante than in the Bryce Canyon neighborhood.

Food and Accommodations

FOOD

The dining room at the ★ **Lodge at Bryce Canyon** (435/834-8700, www.brycecanyonforever.com, 7am-10am, noon-3pm, and 5pm-9pm daily Apr.-Oct., $17-34) is classy and atmospheric, with a large stone fireplace and white tablecloths, and offers food that's better than anything else you're going to find in the area. For lunch ($10-15), the snack bar is a good bet in nice weather; the only seating is outside on the patio or in the hotel lobby.

A short walk from the Lodge is **Valhalla Pizzeria and Coffee Shop** (435/834-8700, www.brycecanyonforever.com, 6am-10pm daily mid-May-mid-Oct., $11-23). Although the pizza is described as "artisanal," don't set your hopes too high. Close by, the **General Store** (by the Lodge near Sunrise Point) also serves perfectly acceptable slices of pizza (11:30am to 3pm, less than $5).

If you're up for a high-volume dining experience, Ruby's Inn **Cowboy Buffet and Steak Room** (26 S. Main St., 435/834-5341, www.rubysinn.com, 6:30am-9:30pm daily summer, 6:30am-9pm winter, $16-32) is an incredibly busy place. It's also one of the better Ruby's-associated restaurants, with sandwiches, steaks, and pasta. Casual lunch and dinner fare, including pizza, is served in the inn's snack bar, the **Canyon Diner** (6:30am-9:30pm daily May-mid-Oct., noon-7pm mid-Oct.-Apr., $4-12). Note that the vegetarian sandwich here consisted of a slice of American cheese, some lettuce, and a few cucumber slices on a hot dog bun. A third Ruby's restaurant, **Ebenezer's Barn & Grill** (7pm dinner, 8pm show daily late Apr.-mid-Oct., $32-38) features cowboy-style food and entertainment that's very expensive for its quality.

Bryce Canyon Resort (13500 E. Hwy. 12, 435/834-5351 or 800/834-0043, www.brycecanyonresort.com, 7am-10pm daily, $14-30), located near the turnoff for the park, has an on-site restaurant, the **Cowboy Ranch House,** which features grilled steaks and burgers; they also serve Utah beers.

Two long-established restaurants west of the park entrance have a low-key, noncorporate atmosphere and pretty good food compared to what's available closer to the park. The small family-run restaurant attached to **Bryce Canyon Pines** (Hwy. 12, milepost 10, 435/834-5441 or 800/892-7923, https://brycecanyonrestaurant.com, 7am-8pm daily, $11-27) is a homey place to stop for burgers, soup, or sandwiches (lunches run $8-10). The restaurant, which touts its fruit pies, sells boxed lunches to go. Two miles (3.2 km) west of the park turnoff is **Bryce Uptop Lodge** (1152 Hwy. 12, 435/834-5227, https://bryceuptoplodge.com, 7am-11am, 5pm-9pm daily, $13-35), a steak house with an Old West atmosphere and nice views; there's also an on-site market and bakery here.

ACCOMMODATIONS

Travelers may have a hard time finding accommodations and campsites April-October in both the park and nearby areas. Advance reservations at lodges, motels, and the park campground are a good idea; otherwise, plan to arrive by late morning if you expect to find a room without reservations. You'll also find that there's a huge variation in room prices from day to day and from season to season. Use the prices cited below, for summer high season, only as a general guide; what you may find on the Internet or by phone on a particular evening may differ markedly.

The Lodge at Bryce Canyon is the only lodge inside the park, and you'll generally need to make reservations months in advance to get a room at this historic landmark (although it doesn't hurt to ask about last-minute vacancies). Other motels are clustered near the park entrance road, but many do not offer much for the money. The quality of lodgings is generally quite low in areas around the park; they're somewhat better in Tropic, 11 miles (17.7 km) east on Highway 12, and in Panguitch, 25 miles (40 km) to the northwest.

$100-150

During the winter, it's easy to find inexpensive accommodations in this area; even guest rooms at Ruby's Inn start at about $80. The rest of the year, expect to pay handsomely for the convenience of staying close to the park. Several motels are clustered on Highway 12, right outside the park boundary. Many of these have seen a lot of use over the years, usually without a lot of attendant upkeep. If you want something more sumptuous and relaxing, consider staying at a B&B in nearby Tropic.

A reasonably good value for the area can be found at the **Bryce View Lodge** (105 E. Center St., 435/834-5180, www.bryceviewlodge.com, $130), which has starkly basic guest rooms set back from the road near the park entrance, across the road from Ruby's Inn (it's owned by Ruby's). The lodge offers an indoor pool and hot tub. Check for deals here; rates can be as low as $60.

Although "resort" may be stretching it, **Bryce Canyon Resort** (13500 E. Hwy. 12, 435/834-5351, from $128-165) is an older hotel complex with a small pool, a restaurant, a store, and lodging options that include standard motel rooms, suites, and rustic cabins that sleep up to six.

Bryce Uptop Lodge (1152 Hwy. 12, 435/834-5227, https://bryceuptoplodge.com, $100) has pine-paneled motel rooms in what appear to be older prefab modular structures; these are best suited for budget travelers who don't want to camp and don't plan to spend a lot of time in their rooms. It's 4 miles (6.4 km) west of the park entrance in a small complex with a restaurant and a supermarket.

The sprawling **Best Western Ruby's Inn** (26 S. Main St., 435/834-5341 or 866/866-6616, www.rubysinn.com, $150-160) offers many year-round services on Highway 63 just north of the park boundary; winter rates are considerably lower. The hotel features many separate buildings with guest rooms, as well as an indoor pool and a hot tub and all the bustling activity you could ever want. Kitchenettes and family rooms are also available; pets are allowed. Ruby's Inn is more than just a place to stay, however: This is one of the area's major centers for all manner of recreational outfitters, dining, entertainment, and shopping. Many tour bus groups bed down here.

Lodge at Bryce Canyon

Six miles (9.7 km) west of the park turnoff, **Bryce Canyon Pines Motel** (Hwy. 12, milepost 10, 435/834-5441 or 800/892-7923, www.brycecanyonmotel.com, $145-150 standard rooms) is an older motel with motel rooms, cottages, two-bedroom family suites with full kitchens, a seasonal covered pool, horseback rides, an RV park, and a restaurant (breakfast, lunch, and dinner daily early Apr.-late Oct.).

OVER $150

The newest and best-appointed hotel in the area is the **Best Western Bryce Canyon Grand Hotel** (30 N. 100 E., 435/834-5700 or 866/866-6634, www.brycecanyongrand.com, $219-289). It's across the road from Ruby's, but it's actually a bit of a walk. Rooms have microwaves and refrigerators (unlike many in the area) and the sort of higher-end comforts that are expected in hotels in this price range, including a good breakfast buffet. An outdoor pool is open in the summer; during the winter guests can go across the highway to use the indoor pool at Ruby's.

Set among ponderosa pines a short walk from the rim, the ★ **Lodge at Bryce Canyon** (435/834-8700 or 877/386-4383, www.brycecanyonforever.com, Apr.-Oct., rooms $223-271, cabins $231) was built in 1923 by a division of the Union Pacific Railroad; a spur line once terminated at the front entrance. The lodge is the only lodging in the park itself and has lots of charm; it's listed in the National Register of Historic Places. It also has by far the best location of any Bryce-area accommodations. Options include suites in the lodge, motel-style guest rooms, and lodgepole pine cabins; all are clean and pleasant but fairly basic in terms of amenities. Reserving up to a year in advance is a good idea for the busy spring, summer and early fall season; these are popular lodgings.

Activities at the lodge include horseback rides, park tours, evening entertainment, and ranger talks. A gift shop sells souvenirs, while food can be found at both a restaurant and a snack bar.

CAMPGROUNDS
Bryce Canyon Campgrounds

The park's two campgrounds, **North Campground** and **Sunset Campground** ($20 tents, $30 RVs, no hookups), both have water and some pull-through spaces; each campground has about 100 sites. Both campgrounds accept reservations, which are a good idea. During the busy summer season, they usually fill by 1pm or 2pm. If you don't have a reservation, try to arrive early.

North Campground (877/444-6777, www.recreation.gov, year-round, first come, first served; $20 tents, $30 RVs, no hookups) is on the left just past the visitors center. The best sites here are just a few yards downhill from the Rim Trail, with easy hiking access to many park trails. North Campground Loop A is open year-round.

Sunset Campground (877/444-6777, www.recreation.gov, late spring-early fall, $20 tents, $30 RVs, no hookups), about 2.5 miles (4 km) farther on the right, across the road from Sunset Point, has good access to hiking trails. Sunset has two campsites on Loop A are accessible to people with disabilities. **Reservations** are accepted May-Oct.; make reservations at least two days in advance.

Basic groceries, camping supplies, coin-operated showers, and a laundry room are available at the General Store (mid-Apr.-late Sept.), between North Campground and Sunrise Point. During the rest of the year, you can go outside the park to Ruby's Inn for these services.

Public Campgrounds

Dixie National Forest has three Forest Service campgrounds located in scenic settings among ponderosa pines. They often have room when campgrounds in the park are full. Sites can be reserved (877/444-6777, www.recreation.gov, $8 reservation fee) at Pine Lake, King Creek, and Red Canyon Campgrounds. **Pine Lake Campground** (late May-mid-Sept., $17) is at 8,300 feet (2,530 m) elevation, just east of its namesake lake, in a forest of ponderosa pine, spruce, and juniper. From the highway junction north of the park, head northeast 11 miles (17.7 km) on gravel-surfaced Highway 63, then turn southeast and go 6 miles (9.7 km). Contact the Escalante Ranger District Office in Escalante (435/826-5499) for information on Pine Lake.

King Creek Campground (usually May-late Sept., $17) is on the west shore of Tropic Reservoir, which has a boat ramp and fair trout fishing. Trails for hikers and OHVs begin at the campground. Sites are at 8,000 feet (2,438 m) elevation. Go 2.8 miles (4.5 km) west of the park turnoff on Highway 12, and then head 7 miles (11.3 km) south on the gravel East Fork Sevier River Road. **Red Canyon Campground** (late May-late Sept., $20) is just off Highway 12, 4 miles (6.4 km) east of U.S. 89. It's at 7,400 feet (2,456 m) elevation, below brilliantly colored cliffs. Contact the Red Canyon Visitor Center (435/676-2676, www.fs.usda.gov/recarea/dixie) for more information on King Creek and Red Canyon Campgrounds.

Camping is available a little farther away at beautiful **Kodachrome Basin State Park** (801/322-3770 or 800/322-3770, www.reserveamerica.com, $25 tents, $35 RVs)

with hookups, $85 bunkhouse, $8 reservation fee). From Bryce, take Highway 12 east to Cannonville, then head 9 miles (14.5 km) south to the park.

Private Campgrounds

Private campgrounds in the area tend to cost $35 or more; the base price for camping at Ruby's increases when there are more than two campers. The convenient **Ruby's Inn Campground** (26 S. Main St., 435/834-5301 or 866/878-9373, Apr.-Oct.) has spaces for tents ($32) and RVs ($42-51); full hookups are available, and showers and a laundry room are open year-round. They've also got a few tepees (from $41) and bunkhouse-style cabins (bedding not provided, $60). All of the considerable facilities at Ruby's are available to campers, and the park shuttle stops here. **Bryce Canyon Pines Campground** (Hwy. 12, milepost 10, 435/834-5441 or 800/892-7923, www.brycecanyonmotel.com, Apr.-Oct., $35 tents, $50 RVs), 4 miles (6.4 km) west of the park entrance, has an indoor pool, a game room, groceries, and shaded sites.

Transportation

GETTING THERE
Car
Bryce Canyon National Park is just south of the incredibly scenic Highway 12, between Bryce Junction and Tropic. To reach the park from Bryce Junction (7 mi/11.3 km south of Panguitch at the intersection of U.S. 89 and Hwy. 12), head 14 miles (22.5 km) east on Highway 12, then south 3 miles (4.8 km) on Highway 63. From Escalante, it's about 50 miles west on Highway 12 to the turnoff for Bryce; turn south onto Highway 63 for the final 3 miles (4.8 km) into the park (winter snows occasionally close this section). Both approaches have spectacular scenery. **Free parking** is available at the visitors center or near Ruby's Inn, outside the park entrance but near shuttle bus stops.

GETTING AROUND
Car
You can drive your own vehicle into Bryce Canyon National Park. However, if you do drive into the park, don't plan to pull a trailer all the way to Rainbow Point: Trailers aren't allowed past Sunset Campground. Trailer parking is available at the visitors center.

Bryce Canyon Shuttle
During the summer, Bryce hosts an enormous number of visitors. In order to keep the one main road along the rim from turning into a parking lot, the National Park Service runs the **Bryce Canyon Shuttle** (every 15-20 minutes 8am-8pm daily mid-April-mid-Oct., shorter hours early and late in season, free). Wheelchair-accessible

run during the peak summer season he shuttle parking and boarding area tersection of Highways 12 and 63 to ιsitors center, with stops at Ruby's Inn and Ruby's Campground. From the visitors center, the shuttle travels to the park's developed areas, including all the main amphitheater viewpoints, Sunset Campground, and the Bryce Canyon Lodge. Passengers can take as long as they like at any viewpoint, then catch a later bus. The shuttle bus service also makes it easier for hikers, who don't need to worry about car shuttles between trailheads.

Use of the shuttle bus system is included in the cost of admission to the park, but it is not mandatory; you can still bring in your own vehicle. However, park officials note that there is generally one parking space for every four cars entering the park.

Vicinity of Bryce Canyon

Sometimes the tour-bus bustle at Bryce's rim and at the large commercial developments right at the entrance to the park can be a little off-putting. It's easy to escape the crowds by heading just a few miles west on scenic Highway 12.

RED CANYON

The drive on Highway 12 between U.S. 89 and the turnoff for Bryce Canyon National Park passes through this well-named canyon. Because Red Canyon is not part of Bryce—it's part of Dixie National Forest—many of the trails are open to mountain biking and ATV riding. In fact, this canyon has become very popular as other Utah mountain biking destinations have become crowded. Red Canyon's bike trails are spectacularly scenic and exhilarating to ride. Ruby's Inn provides a shuttle service for Red Canyon mountain bikers.

Staff members at the **Red Canyon Visitor Center** (Hwy. 12, between mileposts 3 and 4, 435/676-2676, www.fs.usda.gov/recarea/dixie, 10am-4pm Fri.-Sun. Apr.-Oct.) can tell you about the trails and scenic backcountry roads that wind through the area. Books and maps are available.

The U.S. Forest Service maintains many scenic hiking trails that wind back from the highway for a closer look at the geology. The following trails are open to hikers only. Because this is not part of the national park, dogs are permitted on these trails.

Pink Ledges Trail

Distance: 1 mile (1.6 km) round-trip
Duration: 30 minutes
Elevation change: 100 feet (30 m)
Effort: easy
Trailhead: Red Canyon Visitor Center

The Pink Ledges Trail, the easiest and most popular trail in the area, loops past intriguing geological features. Signs identify some of the trees and plants.

Birdseye Trail

Distance: 1.6 miles (2.6 km) round-trip
Duration: 1 hour
Elevation change: 150 feet (46 m)
Effort: easy-moderate
Trailhead: Red Canyon Visitor Center

The Birdseye Trail winds by red-rock formations, offers a bird's-eye view, and connects the visitors center with the short Photo Trail and its parking area on Highway 12, just inside the forest boundary.

Buckhorn Trail

Distance: 1.8 miles (2.9 km) round-trip
Duration: 1.5 hours
Elevation change: 250 feet (76 m)
Effort: moderate-strenuous
Trailhead: Red Canyon Campground, site 23

This trail climbs to views of the interesting geology of Red Canyon. It's a good choice if you'd like to burn off a little energy and get a sense of the surrounding country. The

Vicinity of Bryce Canyon

Beaver

Circleville

62

89

130

20

15

Parowan

Enoch

Panguitch

RED CANYON
BIKE TRAILS

Brian Head

Red Canyon

BRYCE WILDLIFE ADVENTURE ★

Cedar
City

14

Cedar Breaks
Nat'l Monument

Bryce
Canyon
National
Park

Tropic

12

Alton

Grand Staircase-
Escalante National
Monument

Zion
National
Park

89

Glendale

0   10 mi

0   10 km

9

© MOON.COM

campground is on the south side of Highway 12 between mileposts 3 and 4.

For a longer hike (4 mi/6.4 km one-way), turn left off the Buckhorn Trail after about 0.6 mile (1 km) onto the Golden Wall Trail. Follow the Golden Wall Trail south past yellow limestone walls, and then north again back to Highway 12, where it comes out across from the visitors center. A short spur, the Castle Bridge Trail, climbs to a ridge overlooking the Golden Wall before rejoining the Golden Wall Trail.

Tunnel Trail

Distance: 1 mile (1.6 km) round-trip
Duration: 1 hour
Elevation change: 300 feet (91 m)
Effort: moderate
Trailhead: Highway 12 pullout, just west of the tunnels

The Tunnel Trail ascends to fine views of the canyon and the two highway tunnels. The trail crosses a streambed and then climbs a ridge to access the views.

★ Red Canyon Bike Trails

A rather wonderful paved bike trail parallels Highway 12 for 8.6 miles (13.8 km) through Red Canyon. Parking lots are located at either end of town, at the Thunder Mountain trailhead and Coyote Hollow Road.

True mountain bikers will eschew the pavement and head to **Casto Canyon Trail,** a 5.5-mile (8.9 km) one-way trail that winds through a variety of red-rock formations and forest. This ride starts west of the visitors center, about 2 miles (3.2 km) east of U.S. 89. Turn north from Highway 12 onto Forest Road 118 and continue about 3 miles (4.8 km) to the Casto Canyon parking lot. For part of the way, the trail is shared with ATVs, but then the bike trail splits off to the right. The usual turnaround point is at Sanford Road.

This ride can be linked with other trails to form a 17-mile (27-km) one-way test of biking skills and endurance, with the route starting and ending along Highway 12. If you don't have a shuttle vehicle at each of the trailheads, you'll need to pedal back another 8 miles (12.9 km) along the paved roadside trail to retrieve your vehicle. Start at Tom Best Road, just east of Red Canyon. You'll climb through forest, turning onto Berry Spring Creek Road and then Cabin Hollow Road. Once the trail heads into Casto Canyon, you'll have 5 downhill miles (8 km) of wonderful red-rock scenery. When you reach the Casto Canyon trailhead, you can choose to return to Highway 12 or pedal out to U.S. 89 and Panguitch. Much of the trail is strenuous, and you must take water along because there's no source along the way. There are several side trails you could use to make this into a shorter ride; stop by the **Red Canyon Visitor Center** (Hwy. 12, between mileposts 3 and 4, 435/676-2676, www.fs.usda. gov/recarea/dixie/recarea/?recid=24942, 10am-4pm Fri.-Sun.) for more information; you can also download a map from the website.

Campground

Red Canyon Campground (Hwy. 12, 435/676-2676, www.fs.usda.gov/recarea/dixie, late May-late Sept., $20) is located at 7,400 feet (2,256 m) and has 37 first-come, first-served sites and easy access to trails. Drinking water and showers ($2) are available.

BRYCE MUSEUM AND WILDLIFE ADVENTURE

A museum and natural history complex, **Bryce Museum and Wildlife Adventure** (1945 W. Hwy. 12, 435/834-5555, www. brycewildlifeadventure.com, 9am-7pm daily Apr. 1-Nov. 15, $8, $2 under age 11) is a wildlife showcase housed in a large building just west of the turnoff to Bryce Canyon. This taxidermy collection depicts more than 800 animals from around the world displayed in dioramas resembling their natural habitats. It's actually quite well done, and kids seem to love it. There's also a good collection of Native American artifacts and a beautiful butterfly display. You can also rent ATVs here.

TOP EXPERIENCE

CEDAR BREAKS NATIONAL MONUMENT

If you're driving between Zion and Bryce National Parks, consider stopping at Cedar Breaks. But take note: This is high country, and the road is closed mid-October-late May. **Cedar Breaks National Monument** (435/586-0787 summer, 435/586-9451 winter, www.nps.gov/cebr, $10 pp, free under age 16) is much like Bryce Canyon, but it's on a different high plateau and lacks the crowds that flock to Bryce. Here on the west edge of the Markagunt Plateau, a giant amphitheater 2,500 feet (762 m) deep and more than 3 miles (4.8 km) across has been eroded into the stone. A fairyland of forms and colors appears below the rim. Ridges and pinnacles extend like buttresses from the steep cliffs. Traces of iron, manganese, and other minerals have tinted the normally white limestone a rainbow of warm hues. The intense colors blaze during **sunsets** and glow

even on cloudy days. Rock layers look much like those at Bryce Canyon National Park, but here they're 2,000 feet (610 m) higher. Elevations range from 10,662 feet (3,250 m) at the rim's highest point to 8,100 feet (2,469 m) at Ashdown Creek. Cottony patches of clouds often drift above the craggy landscape. In the distance, beyond the amphitheater, are Cedar City and the desert's valleys and ranges. Dense forests broken by large alpine meadows cover the rolling plateau country away from the rim. More than 150 species of wildflowers brighten the meadows during summer; the colorful display peaks during early July, when the **Annual Wildflower Festival** (435/586-0787, www.nps.gov/cebr) takes place. Designated an **International Dark Sky Park,** Cedar Breaks is popular for stargazing. **Star parties** are held in the summer (8:30pm most Saturday nights) and winter seasons (check www.nps.gov/cebr/star-parties.htm).

Three easy trails near the rim provide added appreciation of the geology and forests. Allow extra time on foot—walking can be tiring at high elevations. Regulations prohibit pets on the trails.

A 7.5-mile (12-km) scenic drive leads past four spectacular overlooks, each with a different perspective. Avoid overlooks and other exposed areas during thunderstorms, which are common on summer afternoons. Heavy snows close the road for much of the year. You can drive in only from about late May, sometimes later, until the first big snowstorm of autumn, usually in October. Winter visitors can ski, snowshoe, or travel by snowmobile (only on unplowed roads) from Brian Head (2 mi/3.2 km north of the monument) or Highway 14 (2.5 mi/4 km south).

Cedar Breaks National Monument is 24 miles (39 km) east of Cedar City, 17 miles (27 km) south of Parowan, 30 miles (48 km) southwest of Panguitch, and 27 miles (43 km) northwest of Long Valley Junction (Hwy. 14 and U.S. 89).

1: Red Canyon **2:** Cedar Breaks National Monument

Visitors Center

A log cabin **visitors center** (435/586-0787 summer, 435/586-9451 winter, www.nps.gov/cebr, 9am-6pm daily late May-mid-Oct.) includes exhibits, an information desk, and a bookstore. The exhibits provide a good introduction to the Markagunt Plateau and identify local rocks, wildflowers, trees, animals, and birds. Staff members offer nature walks, geology talks, and campfire programs; see the schedules posted in the visitors center and at the campground. The Point Supreme Overlook is located west of the visitors center. The entrance fee ($10 pp) is collected near the visitors center; there's no charge if you're just driving through the monument without stopping.

Campground Trail

Distance: 1 mile (1.6 km) round-trip
Duration: 45 minutes
Elevation change: 20 feet (6 m)
Effort: easy
Trailheads: visitors center and campground

Travel between the visitors center and the campground on this paved, ADA-compliant trail that follows the rim of the amphitheater, crosses the road, and passes meadows and forested stands. Because it passes through three different habitat types, it's a good place to see wildflowers. It's also the only trail in the park that permits pets.

Spectra Point/Ramparts Trail

Distance: 4 miles (6.4 km) round-trip
Duration: 2 hours
Elevation change: 400 feet (122 m)
Effort: moderate-strenuous
Trailhead: visitors center

The Spectra Point/Ramparts Trail begins at the visitors center, then follows the rim along the south edge of the amphitheater to an overlook. Hikers who are short on time or feeling the effects of the 10,000-foot (3,048-m) elevation can cut the distance in half by stopping after 1 mile (1.6 km) at Spectra Point, where weather-beaten bristlecone pines grow. The trail's end is marked by an overlook.

Alpine Pond Trail

Distance: 2 miles (3.2 km) round-trip
Duration: 1 hour
Elevation change: 20 feet (6 m)
Effort: easy
Trailhead: Chessmen Ridge Overlook

The Alpine Pond Trail drops below the rim into one of the few densely wooded areas of the amphitheater. The trail winds through enchanting forests of aspen, subalpine fir, and Engelmann spruce. You can cut the hiking distance in half with a car shuttle between the two trailheads or by taking a connector trail that joins the upper and lower parts of the loop near Alpine Pond. Begin from either Chessmen Ridge Overlook or the trailhead pullout 1.1 miles (1.8 km) farther north. A trail guide ($1) is available at the start or at the visitors center. Even though this is not a strenuous trail, don't be surprised if you huff and puff your way around it...you're at over 10,000 feet (3,048 m) elevation!

Food and Accommodations

Point Supreme Campground (www.recreation.gov, mid-June-late Sept., $24), east of the visitors center, offers 25 sites (10 reservable) with water. If you plan to visit in June or September, it's best to call ahead to check that it's open; in some years the season is short. There's a picnic area near the campground.

The nearest accommodations and restaurants are 2 miles (3.2 km) north in Brian Head, where **Cedar Breaks Lodge** (223 Hunter Ridge Rd., Brian Head, 435/677-3000 or 800/438-2929, www.cedarbreakslodge.com, $85-125 summer, $100-250 winter, plus $17 resort fee) has fairly plush guest rooms with basic kitchenettes, a day spa, and lower rates during the summer (Brian Head is busiest during the ski season).

Tropic

Mormon pioneer Ebenezer Bryce homesteaded near the town site of Tropic in 1875, but the work of scratching a living from the rugged land became too difficult. He is remembered as saying of the area, "Well, it's a hell of a place to lose a cow." He left five years later for more promising land in Arizona. The name of Bryce Canyon National Park commemorates his efforts. Other pioneers settled six villages near the upper Paria River between 1876 and 1891. The towns of Tropic, Cannonville, and Henrieville still survive.

FOOD

There are a few dining options in town. The best place to start your search for a meal is **Rustler's Restaurant** (141 N. Main St., 435/679-8383, 7am-9pm daily, $10-27), which is part of Clark's Grocery, an all-around institution that, in addition to selling groceries, serves Mexican food, pasta, pizza, ice cream, and steaks from a variety of venues within a complex that's essentially the town center.

Hungry for brisket or pulled pork? Order at the counter at **IDK Barbecue** (161 N. Main St., 435/679-8353, www.idkbarbecue.com, 11am-9pm Mon.-Sat., $8-17) and sample what some have called the state's best barbecue.

At the Stone Canyon Inn, the **Stone Hearth Grille** (1380 W. Stone Canyon Lane, 435/679-8923, www.stonehearthgrille.com, 5pm-9pm daily Mar.-Oct., $26-38, reservations recommended) has an upscale atmosphere and menu. The food is the best for miles around. In good weather, have your meal on the terrace and enjoy the lovely off-the-beaten-path setting.

ACCOMMODATIONS

Travelers think of Tropic primarily for its cache of motels lining Main Street (Hwy. 12), but several pleasant B&Bs also grace the town.

$50-100

At the **Bryce Canyon Inn** (21 N. Main St., 435/679-8502 or 800/592-1468, www.brycecanyoninn.com, Mar.-Oct., $77 motel rooms, $99-199 cabins), the tidy cabins are nicely furnished and are one of the more appealing options in the Bryce neighborhood. The economy motel rooms are small but clean and a good deal, and there's a good coffee shop on the premises.

$100-150

At the east end of town, on a family farm, the **Bullberry Inn B&B** (412 S. Hwy 12, 435/668-9911, http://bullberryinn.com, late Mar.-Oct., $135-145) has wraparound porches and simple but pleasant guest rooms with private baths and rustic-style pine furniture.

Over $150

The ★ **Stone Canyon Inn** (1380 W. Stone Canyon Lane, 435/679-8611 or 866/489-4680, www.stonecanyoninn.com, $195-375), a couple of miles west of downtown Tropic with views of Bryce, is a strikingly handsome, modern structure with several comfortable two-bedroom guest cabins with kitchens and newly built bungalows configured as suites that can sleep up to four; there are even "treehouses" that allow you to sleep above the trees. A sauna is shared by guests; it's tucked in between the inn and the cottages. Along with these accommodations, which are the region's most luxurious, the Stone Canyon has a notably good restaurant.

Red Ledges Inn (181 N. Main St., 435/679-8811, www.redledgesinn.com, $159-184) has conventional motel rooms in an attractive wood-fronted, Western-style motel. Pets are permitted for an additional fee.

Bryce Trails B&B (1001 W. Bryce Way, 435/231-4436, www.brycetrail.com, $189-229) is comfortably off the main drag. Every guest room has a good view as well as a stunning photograph taken by one of the owners, who also sometimes teaches one-on-one photo classes.

Campgrounds

Head east to Cannonville for **Cannonville/ Bryce Valley KOA** (215 N. Red Rock Dr., Cannonville, 435/679-8988, www.koa.com, $33-37 tents, $43-72 RVs, $70-79 camping cabins), or continue south from Cannonville to **Kodachrome Basin State Park** (801/322-3770 or 800/322-3770, www.reserveamerica. com, $20 tents, $30 RVs).

GETTING THERE

Tropic is 11 miles (17.7 km) east of Bryce Canyon National Park on Highway 12, and is visible from many of the park's viewpoints.

Panguitch

Pioneers arrived here in 1864, but the Ute people forced them to evacuate just two years later. A second attempt by settlers in 1871 succeeded, and Panguitch (the name is from the Paiute word for "big fish") is now the largest town in the area.

Panguitch is one of the more pleasant towns in this part of Utah, and it has an abundance of reasonably priced motels, plus a couple of good places to eat. It's a convenient stopover on the road between Zion and Bryce National Parks.

SIGHTS

The **city park** on the north edge of town has picnic tables, a playground, tennis courts, and a visitor information cabin. A **swimming pool** (250 E. Center St., 435/676-2259) is by the high school.

Travelers in the area during the second weekend in June should try to swing by for the annual **Quilt Walk** (www.quiltwalk.org), an all-out festival with historic home tours, quilting classes, and lots of food. The Quilt Walk commemorates a group of seven pioneers who trudged through snow to bring food back to starving townspeople—they spread quilts on the deep, soft snow and walked on them in order not to sink.

FOOD

A longtime favorite in Panguitch is the mesquite-grilled meat at **Cowboy's**

Smokehouse Bar-B-Q (95 N. Main St., 435/676-8030, www.thecowboysmokehouse. com, 11am-10pm Mon.-Sat. mid-Mar.-mid-Oct., $15-29). The **Big Fish Family Restaurant** (608 S. Main St., 435/676-8999, 11am-9pm daily, $9-16) serves standard American food dinners, including decent burgers. Depart from the standard American fare at **Tandoori Taqueria** (5 N. Main St., 435/962-9395, www.thetandooritaqueria.com, 4pm-9pm Mon.-Thurs., noon-9pm Fri.-Sun. $10-15), where a fusion of Indian and Mexican flavors includes a three-taco plate with posole, chorizo-and-beef, and tandoori chicken tacos. This is the best place in miles around for veggie food.

ACCOMMODATIONS
$50-100

Panguitch is the best place in greater Bryce Canyon to find an affordable motel room—there are more than a dozen older motor court lodgings, most quite basic but nicely maintained. Of these, the **Blue Pine Motel** (130 N. Main St., 435/676-8197 or 800/299-6115, www.bluepinemotel.com, $74-94) is one of the most attractive, with a friendly welcome and clean, well-furnished guest rooms that include microwaves and refrigerators.

Nothing to do with either Zane Grey or Jerry Garcia, the older but well-kept **Purple Sage Motel** (132 E. Center St., 435/676-8536, www.purplesagemotel.biz, $55-110) is nothing fancy, but a good value (the most expensive room is a family suite).

Another good budget pick is the **Canyon Lodge Motel** (210 N. Main St., 435/676-8292, www.canyonlodgemotel.com, $69-119), an older property with clean, unpretentious guest rooms plus a three-bed suite.

Over $150

Cottonwood Meadow Lodge (milepost 123, U.S. 89, 435/676-8950, www.brycecanyoncabins.com, Apr.-Oct., $185-325, one-time cleaning fee in addition, 2-night minimum) is the exception to the modest-accommodations rule in the Panguitch area. This upscale lodge features four units, all with kitchen facilities: a bunkhouse, a log cabin dating from the 1860s, a three-bedroom farmhouse, and an attractively rehabbed barn that sleeps six. It's about 15 minutes from town and about 20 minutes from Bryce Canyon National Park. Ranch animals are available for visits, and the Sevier River runs through the property, located 2 miles (3.2 km) south of Highway 12 on U.S. 89.

Campgrounds

Hitch-N-Post Campground (420 N. Main St., 435/676-2436, www.hitchnpostrv.com, year-round) offers spaces for tents ($20) and RVs ($33-37) and has showers and a laundry room. The **Panguitch KOA Campground** (555 S. Main St., 435/676-2225, Apr.-Oct., $29-34 tents, $42-57 RVs, $53 camping cabins, $110-140 deluxe cabins), on the road to Panguitch Lake, includes a pool, a recreation room, laundry, and showers. The closest public campground is in **Red Canyon** (Hwy. 12, 435/676-2676, $18).

INFORMATION AND SERVICES

Contact **Bryce Canyon Country** (435/676-1160 or 800/444-6689, www.brycecanyoncountry.com) for information on Panguitch and the nearby area. The **Powell Ranger District Office** (225 E. Center St., 435/676-9300, 8am-4:30pm Mon.-Fri.) of the Dixie National Forest has information on campgrounds, hiking trails, fishing, and scenic drives in the forest and canyons surrounding Bryce Canyon National Park.

There is a **post office** (65 N. 100 W.). **Garfield Memorial Hospital** (200 N. 400 E., hospital 435/676-8811, clinic 435/676-8811) is the main hospital in this part of the state.

GETTING THERE

Panguitch is on U.S. 89, 7 miles (11.3 km) north of Bryce Junction (Hwy. 12 and U.S. 89). From Bryce Junction, it is 11 miles (17.7 km) east on Highway 12 to Bryce Canyon National Park.

Grand Staircase-Escalante

Grand Staircase-Escalante contains a vast and

scenic collection of slickrock canyon lands, desert, prehistoric village sites, Old West ranch land, and arid plateaus. Miles of back roads link stone arches, mesas, and abstract rock formations.

There's little dispute that the Escalante canyons are the primary reason people visit the monument area. The river and its tributaries cut deep and winding slot canyons through massive slickrock formations; hiking these canyon bottoms is an extremely popular adventure. A multiday trek is a rite of passage for many devoted hikers, but you don't have to be a hardened backcountry trekker to enjoy this landscape: Two backcountry roads wind through the area, and many day hikes are possible.

Highlights

Look for ★ to find recommended sights, activities, dining, and lodging.

★ **Explore Kodachrome Basin State Park:** Strange-looking rock pillars, or "sand pipes," are the attraction at this state park. Its campground and hiking trails make it a good base for exploring south into the monument (page 127).

★ **Photograph Grosvenor Arch:** Actually two sandstone arches, Grosvenor has been drawing photographers for decades, including a famed *National Geographic* expedition in the 1940s (page 128).

★ **Investigate the Past at Anasazi State Park Museum:** An excavated village displays a wide range of Ancestral Puebloan building styles, while indoor exhibits at the park's museum offer information and insight (page 132).

★ **Cruise along Burr Trail Road:** Views of the astounding Long Canyon, the Waterpocket Fold, the Circle Cliffs, and distant mountains make this road a treat via car or mountain bike (page 132).

★ **Hike to Lower Calf Creek Falls:** Expect to see desert varnish, beaver ponds, Native American ruins, and pictographs along the trail—with the misty 126-foot-high (38-m) waterfall as a climax (page 142)

★ **Go Canyoneering:** Hike the enchanting slot canyons in the **Dry Fork of Coyote Gulch,** accessible via the bumpy dirt Hole-in-the-Rock Road (page 143).

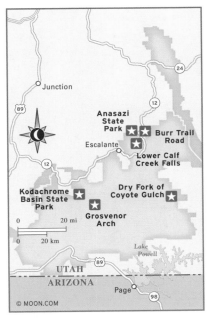

Grand Staircase-Escalante National Monument

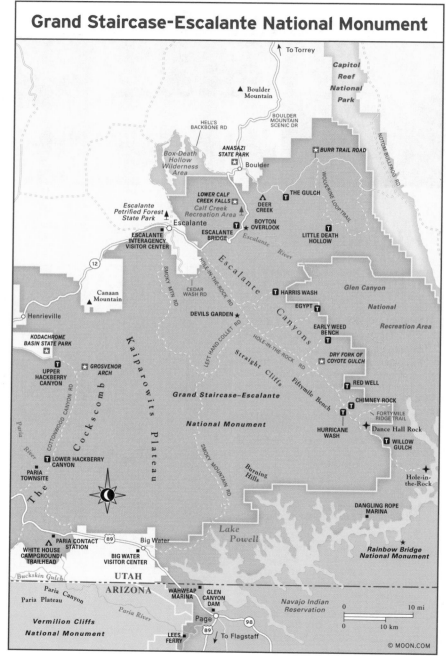

To Torrey

Capitol Reef National Park

Boulder Mountain

HELL'S BACKBONE RD

BOULDER MOUNTAIN SCENIC DR

NOTOM-BULLFROG RD

ANASAZI STATE PARK

BURR TRAIL ROAD

Box-Death Hollow Wilderness Area

Boulder

WOLVERINE LOOP TRAIL

LOWER CALF CREEK FALLS

THE GULCH

Escalante Petrified Forest State Park

Calf Creek Recreation Area

DEER CREEK

Escalante

BOYTON OVERLOOK

LITTLE DEATH HOLLOW

ESCALANTE BRIDGE

Escalante River

ESCALANTE INTERAGENCY VISITOR CENTER

12

HOLE-IN-THE-ROCK RD

Escalante Canyons

Glen Canyon

Canaan Mountain

CEDAR WASH RD

HARRIS WASH

EGYPT

National

Henrieville

SMOKY MTN RD

DEVILS GARDEN

LEFT HAND COLLET RD

EARLY WEED BENCH

Recreation Area

KODACHROME BASIN STATE PARK

HOLE-IN-THE-ROCK RD

DRY FORK OF COYOTE GULCH

UPPER HACKBERRY CANYON

GROSVENOR ARCH

Kaiparowits Plateau

Straight Cliffs

Fiftymile Bench

RED WELL

COTTONWOOD CANYON RD

Grand Staircase-Escalante

CHIMNEY ROCK

FORTYMILE RIDGE TRAIL

The Cockscomb

National Monument

HURRICANE WASH

Dance Hall Rock

Paria River

LOWER HACKBERRY CANYON

SMOKY MOUNTAIN RD

WILLOW GULCH

PARIA TOWNSITE

Burning Hills

Hole-in-the-Rock

DANGLING ROPE MARINA

Lake Powell

PARIA CONTACT STATION

Big Water

Rainbow Bridge National Monument

89

WHITE HOUSE CAMPGROUND/ TRAILHEAD

BIG WATER VISITOR CENTER

Buckskin Gulch

UTAH

ARIZONA

WAHWEAP MARINA

GLEN CANYON DAM

Navajo Indian Reservation

Paria Canyon

Paria Plateau

Paria River

Page

98

Vermilion Cliffs National Monument

LEES FERRY

89

To Flagstaff

0   10 mi

0   10 km

© MOON.COM

Grand Staircase-Escalante in One Day

- Begin your day at the **visitors center** in Escalante, which has excellent natural history exhibits.

- Then drive 15 miles (24 km) east to the mostly level trail to **Lower Calf Creek Falls** for a snapshot of what makes the Escalante canyons so alluring (with a 126-foot-high waterfall as a reward).

- Stop at **Kiva Koffeehouse,** 13 miles (21 km) east of Escalante on Highway 12, for Southwestern specialties and excellent coffee.

- After lunch, drive 26 miles (42 km) on the Hole-in-the-Rock Road to the **Dry Fork of Coyote Gulch,** which provides the thrills and wonderment of Escalante slot canyons as a day hike.

- Refuel your weary bones at **Circle D Eatery** in Escalante, with excellent locally raised beef ribs and steaks, smoked in-house.

The other destinations in this rugged landscape offer striking but less-well-defined opportunities for adventure. Backcountry drivers and long-distance mountain bikers will find mile after mile of desert and canyon to explore. Grosvenor Arch, with double windows, is a popular back-road destination. At the southern edge of the park, along the Arizona border, is another rugged canyon system popular with long-distance hikers. The Paria River Canyon is even more remote than the Escalante, and hiking these slot canyons requires experience and preparation.

This vast protectorate of remote slot canyons, geologic curiosities, and rugged backcountry wilderness has undergone some change since President Bill Clinton established the Grand Staircase-Escalante National Monument (GSENM) in 1996. This designation caused an uproar among local ranchers, mining interests, and Utah's congressional delegation. That coalition won concessions in 2018, when President Donald Trump modified the boundaries of the GSENM, reducing its size. Critics say the goal was to remove the area's protection from coal and mineral exploitation. When President Joseph Biden took office in 2021, he moved to reinstate the monument to its original size. The original 1996 GSENM infrastructure remains in place with no changes to public access or recreation.

The GSENM is now divided into three separate units. To the east, the narrow wilderness canyons of the Escalante River and its tributaries comprise the **Escalante Canyons unit** (242,836 acres). In the center of the former GSENM is a vast swath of arid rangeland and canyons that's now the **Kaiparowits Plateau unit** (551,034 acres). The western third, which edges the Gray, White, and Pink Cliffs of the Grand Staircase, has become the **Grand Staircase unit** (209,993 acres). President Joseph Biden will likely restore the original boundaries.

PLANNING YOUR TIME

If you only have one day, plan to drive stunning Highway 12. The Lower Calf Creek Falls hike begins right off the highway between Escalante and Boulder, and hiking it is a great way to spend half a day.

If you have an additional day or two, it makes sense to base yourself either in Escalante (convenient camping and moderately priced accommodations) or in Boulder (where it's possible to sleep and eat in luxury). Spend your second day here exploring

Previous: Willis Creek narrows; the Dry Fork of Coyote Gulch; abandoned *Gunsmoke* set off Johnson Canyon-Skutumpah Road.

Hole-in-the-Rock Road, where you can hike slot canyons in the Dry Fork of Coyote Gulch and explore Devils Garden. It's possible to stay in this area of the monument for several days, either backpacking along the Escalante River or exploring its various canyons as day hikes. If you're at all up to backpacking, it's only a one-nighter to hike from the town of Escalante along the river to the Highway 12 bridge.

If you have more time, drive between the Kanab area and Cannonville on Cottonwood Canyon Road (be sure to check road conditions before heading out). Stop and walk up through the Cottonwood Narrows, and at the north end of the road, visit Grosvenor Arch and Kodachrome Basin State Park. If you want to make a loop drive, return on the Johnson Canyon and Skutumpah Roads, with a hike along Lick Wash.

Exploring the Park

There is no entrance fee to visit **Grand Staircase-Escalante National Monument** (435/826-5499 visitor center, 435/644-1200 headquarters, www.blm.gov/programs/national-conservation-lands/utah/grand-staircase-escalante-national-monument). Free permits are required for all overnight backcountry camping or backpacking. There are fees to camp in the monument's three developed campgrounds.

Hikers in the Paria Wilderness area, which includes Paria Canyon and Coyote Buttes, are required to buy a permit, as are hikers at the Calf Creek Recreation Area (Park Wilderness fees: $6 per day for day hikers, $5 per day for overnight trips; Calf Creek Recreation area day use fee: $5 per vehicle).

It's best to have a travel strategy when visiting this huge national monument. Just as important, especially for a visit of more than a couple of days, is a vehicle that can take on some rugged roads. (A Subaru wagon proved perfectly adequate in dry weather, but when the clay was wet and muddy, the back roads were virtually impassable to all but 4WD vehicles with significantly higher clearance than a station wagon.)

Only two paved roads pass through the monument areas, both on a west-east trajectory. To the north, Highway 12 links Bryce Canyon and Capitol Reef National Parks with access to the Escalante River canyons. This is one of the most scenic roads in Utah—in fact,

Car and Driver magazine has rated this route as one of the 10 most scenic in the United States. Its innumerable vistas and geologic curiosities will keep you on the edge of your seat. U.S. 89, which runs along the southern edge of the monument between Kanab and Lake Powell, is no scenery slouch either. It is also the access road for the North Rim of the Grand Canyon in Arizona.

Three fair-weather dirt roads, each with a network of side roads and trails, cut through the rugged heart of the monument, linking the two paved roads. Before heading out on these back roads, check with the visitors center for conditions; high-clearance vehicles are recommended.

VISITORS CENTERS

The monument's **field office** (669 S. U.S. 89A, Kanab, 435/644-1200, 8am-4:30pm Mon.-Fri.) is in Kanab, but the regional visitors centers, listed below, are the best places for practical travel information.

Escalante Interagency Visitor Center (755 W. Main St., Escalante, 435/826-5499, 8am-4:30pm daily) is housed in a sprawling building at the west end of the town of Escalante. Staff are very knowledgeable and helpful, and exhibits focus on the monument's ecology and biological diversity.

Kanab Visitor Center (745 E. U.S. 89, Kanab, 435/644-1300, 8am-4:30pm daily mid-Mar.-mid-Nov., 8am-4:30pm Mon.-Fri.

mid-Nov.-mid-Mar.) is the place to stop if you're planning to drive Cottonwood or Johnson Canyon and Skutumpah Roads from the south. Staff can give you updates on the road conditions and suggest driving and hiking strategies. A walk-in lottery for permits to hike Coyote Buttes is held at 8:30am daily. Exhibits at this visitors center concentrate on geology and archaeology.

Cannonville Visitor Center (10 Center St., Cannonville, 435/826-5640, 8am-4:30pm daily mid-Mar.-mid-Nov.) is an attractive building at the north end of Cottonwood and Johnson Canyon-Skutumpah Roads. Even if the office is closed, stop by to look at the outdoor exhibits, which depict the different cultures that have lived in the area.

Big Water Visitor Center (100 Upper Revolution Way, Big Water, 435/675-3200, 8am-4:30pm Thurs.-Mon.), a spiral-shaped building designed to resemble an ammonite, is home to a small but distinctive collection of dinosaur bones and a wild mural depicting late-Cretaceous life in the area. Stop here to learn about local paleontology.

Anasazi State Park Museum (460 N. Hwy. 12, Boulder, 435/335-7382, www. stateparks.utah.gov, 9am-5pm daily mid-Mar.-mid-Nov., $5) has a ranger on duty at an information desk inside the museum. The museum is worth a visit, so don't be stingy with your five bucks!

Paria Contact Station (U.S. 89, 44 mi/71 km east of Kanab, 435/644-4628, 8am-4:30pm daily mid-Mar.-mid-Nov.) is a small visitors center, but it's an important stop for anyone planning to hike Paria Canyon.

TOURS

For guided tours of the Escalante canyons, contact **Utah Canyon Outdoors** (325 W. Main St., Escalante, 435/826-4967, www. utahcanyonoutdoors.com). Trips focus on day hikes (full-day $140-150 pp), with popular trips going to less crowded slot canyons and riparian areas. It also offers hiker shuttles and runs a good gear shop in the salmon-colored building in downtown Escalante.

The guides at **Excursions of Escalante** (125 E. Main St., Escalante, 435/826-4714 or 800/839-7567, www.excursionsofescalante. com) lead trips into more remote canyons, including some that require some technical canyoneering to explore, and some multiday backpacking trips. Straightforward hiking trips ($155 pp) are also offered, either cross-country (easiest) or in slot canyons (more

The land around Escalante is barren and harsh; consider hiring a guide to explore the outback.

GRAND STAIRCASE-ESCALANTE
EXPLORING THE PARK

challenging). A day of basic canyoneering ($195 pp) includes instruction.

Many local outfitters use pack animals. With **Escape Goats** (435/826-4652, www.escalantecanyonguides.com), you can hike with goats (and a friendly, goat-loving human guide) into canyons. This is a good bet for families with kids. A variety of hikes are available; full-day hikes run around $150 pp.

Saddle up for day rides or horsepacking trips with **Hell's Backbone Ranch and Trail** (435/335-7581, www.bouldermountaintrails.com, 1.5-2-hour ride $60-75), located next to the Boulder Mountain Guest Ranch up the Hells Backbone/Salt Gulch Road.

Boulder-based **Earth Tours** (307/733-4261 or 435/335-7475, www.earth-tours.com) offers guided hikes ($120 pp and up) as well as backroads driving tours ($125) of the area. Most trips are led by a geologist with a wide-ranging interest in natural history.

Sights

ALONG HIGHWAY 12

Highway 12 runs west-east from Bryce Canyon National Park and Tropic along the north edge of the Grand Staircase and Kaiparowits Plateau units to the town of Escalante, where the route cuts through Escalante Canyons to Boulder. Stop at the **Cannonville Visitor Center** (10 Center St., Cannonville, 435/826-5640, 8am-4:30pm daily mid-Mar.-mid-Nov.) for information about back-road conditions and hikes in the western parts of the monument. Two backcountry roads depart from Cannonville and lead to remote corners of the monument.

Johnson Canyon-Skutumpah Road

The northern end of the Johnson Canyon-Skutumpah Road (46 mi/74 km one-way) is in Cannonville, and its southern terminus is at U.S. 89, just east of Kanab. From the northernmost stretch of this road, Bryce Canyon rises to the west; about 6 miles (9.7 km) from the southern end and off to the east on private land (look from the road but don't trespass) is a weathered set from the TV show *Gunsmoke*.

The unpaved portions of the road are rough and rutted in places, and after rains, the bentonite soils that make up the roadbed turn to goo. In good weather, cars with good clearance can usually make the journey. The road follows the Pink and White Cliff terraces of the Grand Staircase, with access to some excellent and comparatively undersubscribed hiking trails. Several steep slot canyons make for excellent canyoneering. The best views (and the worst roads) are in the northernmost 20 miles (32 km) or so, above Lick Wash. Much of the rest of the way is rangeland, so watch for cattle grazing by the roadway. The lower 16 miles (26 km) of Johnson Canyon Road are paved.

Scenic Back Way: Cottonwood Canyon Road

The 46-mile (74-km) Cottonwood Canyon Road also connects Cannonville with U.S. 89, but it passes through quite different terrain and landscapes. One of the most scenic backcountry routes in the monument, Cottonwood Canyon Road not only offers access to dramatic Grosvenor Arch, but it also passes along the Cockscomb, a soaring buckle of rock that divides the Grand Staircase and the Kaiparowits Plateau. Cottonwood Creek, which this road parallels, is a normally dry streambed that cuts through the angular rock beds of the Cockscomb. Several excellent hikes lead into the canyons and narrows, where the Paria River, Hackberry Canyon, and Cottonwood Creek all meet, about 20 miles (32 km) south of Cannonville.

Check at the Cannonville or Big Water Visitor Centers for information about road

Down the Grand Staircase

The broad tilted terraces of the Grand Staircase step down through time. Some 200 million years of sedimentation are visible here, starting with pink in the north, then traveling through gray, white, and vermilion cliffs.

A freshwater lake deposited the limey siltstones that became the Pink Cliffs (see these same rocks in Bryce Canyon National Park). This layer formed on top of the shale of the Gray Cliffs, deposited when an ocean covered the area; the Gray Cliffs step is rich with marine fossils and coal, formed from ancient wetland plants. The next older step, the White Cliffs, is composed of Navajo sandstone, one of the main rocks seen in Zion National Park. The bottom step, the bright Vermilion Cliffs, visible around Kanab, is also sandstone, laden with fossils of fish and dinosaurs. At the base of the whole staircase, the striped brick-colored Chinle badlands form the bed for the Paria River.

These sandstone steps are stacked like pancakes. As in much of the Colorado Plateau region, erosion by water and wind produces amazing geological displays, including the intricate network of deep canyons, uplifted plateaus, sheer cliffs, beautiful sandstone arches and natural bridges, water pockets, sandstone monoliths, pedestals and balanced rocks, domes, and buttes.

conditions. Although the road is sometimes passable for cars, several road crossings are susceptible to washouts after rainstorms, and the northern portion is impassable even to 4WD vehicles when wet because of the extremely unctuous nature of the roadbed. Check conditions before setting out if you plan to go beyond Grosvenor Arch.

★ Kodachrome Basin State Park

Located in a basin southeast of Bryce, **Kodachrome Basin State Park** (435/679-8562, http://stateparks.utah.gov, 6am-10pm daily, $10 day use) is well worth a visit. Here you'll see not only colorful cliffs but also strange-looking rock pillars that occur nowhere else in the world. Sixty-seven pillars (called "sand pipes") found in and near the park range in height from 6 feet (4.9 m) to nearly 170 feet (52 m). One theory of their origin is that earthquakes caused sediments deep underground to be churned up by water under high pressure. The particles of calcite, quartz, feldspar, and clay in the sand pipes came from underlying rock formations, and the pipes appeared when the surrounding rock eroded away. Most of the other rocks visible in the park are Entrada sandstone: The lower orange layer is the Gunsight Butte Member,

and the white layer with orange bands is the Cannonville Member. Signs name some of the rock features. "Big Stoney," the phallus-shaped sand pipe overlooking the campground, is so explicit that it doesn't need a sign.

The article "Motoring into Escalante Land" by Jack Breed in the September 1949 *National Geographic* magazine brought attention to the scenery and earned the area the name "Kodachrome Flat," for the then-experimental Kodak film used by the expedition. The state park is a worthwhile stop, both as a day trip to see the geology and as a pleasant spot to camp. The park also offers several good half-day hiking trails, including the 3-mile (4.8-km) Panorama Trail that links many of the park's top sights, and a host of shorter hikes. You'll also find horseback trail rides offered by **Red Canyon Trail Rides** (near the park entry gate, 800/892-7923, www.redcanyontrailrides.com, 1-hour ride $40), which explores red-rock canyons and sand pipes along the Panorama Trail.

The state park has two **campgrounds** (435/679-8562, reservations 800/322-3770 or www.reserveamerica.com, year-round). The **Basin Campground** ($25 tents, $35 RVs with hookups) is in a natural amphitheater at an elevation of 5,800 feet (1,770 m). It has restrooms, showers, and a dump station. During the winter, restrooms and showers may close, but pit toilets are available. The campground usually has space except on summer holidays. The smaller **Bryce View Campground** ($25) is more primitive, and, not surprisingly, has good views of Bryce Canyon. In addition, at the park's Oasis group camping site are two bunkhouse camping cabins that sleep up to six (bring your own bedding; no running water, bathrooms and showers adjacent, $85 a night).

GETTING THERE

To reach the park, take Highway 12 south to Cannonville and follow the signs for 7 miles (11.3 km) along paved Cottonwood Canyon Road. Adventurous drivers can also approach the park from U.S. 89 to the south via Cottonwood Canyon Road (35 mi/56 mi) or Skutumpah Road through Bull Valley Gorge and Johnson Canyon (48 mi/77 mi). These routes may be impassable in wet weather but are generally OK in dry weather for cars with good clearance.

★ Grosvenor Arch

Just 1 mile (1.6 km) off Cottonwood Canyon Road, a side road leads to the magnificent Grosvenor Arch. It takes a bit of effort to get here (the 10-mile/16-kilometer dirt road between the turnoff to Kodachrome Basin State Park and the arch can be bumpy and should be avoided in wet weather), so a visit to the arch can take on the qualities of a pilgrimage. There are actually two arches here, which is a rare occurrence for the erosion-formed structures. Their position, jutting like flying buttresses out of a soaring cliff, is also quite stunning. The larger of the two openings is 99 feet (30 m) across. A 1949 National Geographic Society expedition named the double arch in honor of the society's president. From Highway 12, take the Cottonwood Canyon Road turnoff to Kodachrome Basin State Park. Continue for 10 miles (16 km) to the Grosvenor Arch parking area. Alternatively, the turnoff is 29 miles (47 km) north from U.S. 89.

Escalante Petrified Forest State Park

The pleasant **Escalante Petrified Forest State Park** (435/826-4466, http://stateparks. utah.gov, 7am-10pm daily summer, 8am-10pm daily winter, $8 day use), just northwest of the town of Escalante, offers camping, boating, fishing, picnicking, hiking, a visitors center with displays of petrified wood and dinosaur bones, and a chance to see petrified wood along hiking trails. Rivers of 140 million years ago carried trees to the site of present-day Escalante and buried them in sand and gravel. Burial prevented decay as crystals of silicon dioxide gradually replaced the wood cells. Mineral impurities added a rainbow of colors to the trees as they turned to stone. Weathering has exposed this petrified wood and the water-worn pebbles and sand of the Morrison Formation.

For a look at some colorful petrified wood, follow the **Petrified Forest Trail** from the campground up a hillside wooded with piñon pine and juniper. At the top of the 240-foot-high (73-m) ridge, continue on a loop trail to the petrified wood; allow 45-60 minutes for the 1-mile (1.6-km) round-trip hike. The steep **Rainbow Loop Trail** (0.75 mi/1.2 km) branches off the Petrified Forest Trail to more areas of petrified wood.

The **campground** (reservations 800/322-3770, www.reserveamerica.com, year-round, $20 tents, $28 RVs with water and electric hookups) offers drinking water, flush toilets, showers (mid-Mar.-mid-Nov.), and RV hookups. The adjacent 139-acre Wide Hollow Reservoir offers fishing, boating, and birdwatching. The park is 1.5 miles (2.4 km) west of Escalante on Highway 12, then 0.7 mile (1.1 km) north on a gravel road.

Town of Escalante

The town of Escalante, 38 miles (61 km) east of Bryce Canyon and 23 miles (37 km) south of Boulder, has a full range of services and

1: Grosvenor Arch **2:** Kodachrome Basin State Park
3: Devils Garden

is the headquarters for explorations of the Escalante River canyons. The **Escalante Interagency Visitor Center** (755 W. Main St., Escalante, 435/826-5499, 8am-4:30pm daily) provides information on local hikes and road conditions.

Smokey Mountain Road

From Escalante, it's 78 miles (126 km) south to U.S. 89 at Big Water, just shy of Lake Powell, along Smokey Mountain Road. This road is rougher than other cross-monument roads. Be sure to check conditions before setting out; a 4WD vehicle is required. As this route passes across the Kaiparowits Plateau, the landscape is bleak and arid. After that, the road drops precipitously onto a bench where side roads lead through badlands to Lake Powell beaches. Big Water is 19 miles (31 km) from Page, Arizona, and 57 miles (92 km) from Kanab.

Hole-in-the-Rock Road

The building of this road by determined Mormons is an epic story of the colonization of the West. Church leaders organized the Hole-in-the-Rock Expedition to settle the wildlands around the San Juan River of southeastern Utah, believing that a Mormon presence would aid in ministering to the Native Americans there and prevent non-Mormons from moving in. In 1878 the Parowan Stake issued the first call for a colonizing mission to the San Juan, even before a site had been selected.

Preparations and surveys took place the following year as the 236 men, women, and children received their calls. Food, seed, farming and building tools, 200 horses, and more than 1,000 head of cattle were brought along. Planners ruled out lengthy routes through northern Arizona or eastern Utah in favor of a straight shot via Escalante that would cut the distance in half. The expedition set off in the fall of 1879, convinced that they were part of a divine mission.

Hints of the trouble to come filtered back from the group as they discovered the Colorado River crossing to be far more difficult than first believed. Lack of water sources along the way added to their worries. From their start at Escalante, road building progressed rapidly for the first 50 miles (80 km), then slowly over rugged slickrock for the final 6 miles (9.7 km) to Hole-in-the-Rock. A sheer 45-foot (14-m) drop below this narrow notch was followed by almost 1 mile (1.6 km) of extremely steep slickrock to the Colorado River. The route looked impossible, but three crews of workers armed with picks and blasting powder worked simultaneously to widen the notch and construct a precarious wagon road down to the river and up the cliffs on the other side.

The job took six weeks. Miraculously, all of the people, animals, and wagons made it down and were ferried across the Colorado River without serious incident. Canyons and other obstacles continued to block the way as the weary group pressed on. Only after six months of exhausting travel did they stop at the present-day site of Bluff on the San Juan River.

Today, on a journey from Escalante, you can experience a bit of the same adventure the pioneers knew. Except for scattered signs of ranching, the land remains unchanged. If the road is dry, vehicles with good clearance can drive to within a short distance of Hole-in-the-Rock. The rough conditions encountered past Dance Hall Rock require more clearance than most cars allow. Bring sufficient gas, food, and water for the entire 124-mile (200-km) round-trip from Escalante; there are no services along this route.

SIGHTS

Metate Arch and other rock sculptures decorate **Devils Garden,** 12.5 miles (20.1 km) down Hole-in-the-Rock Road. Turn west and continue 0.3 mile (0.5 km) at the sign to the parking area, because you can't really see the "garden" from the road. Red and cream-colored sandstone formations sit atop pedestals or tilt at crazy angles. Delicate bedding lines run through the rocks. There are no trails or markers—just wander around as you like. The Bureau of Land Management (BLM) has provided picnic tables, grills, and outhouses for day use. No overnight camping is permitted at Devils Garden.

Dance Hall Rock (38 mi/61 km down Hole-in-the-Rock Rd.) jumped to the fiddle music and lively steps of the expedition members in 1879. Its natural amphitheater has a relatively smooth floor and made a perfect gathering spot when the Hole-in-the-Rock group had to wait three weeks at nearby Fortymile Spring for road work to be completed ahead. Dance Hall Rock is an enjoyable place to explore and only a short walk from the parking area. Solution holes, left by water dissolving in the rock, pockmark the sandstone structure.

At road's end, 57 miles (92 km) from Highway 12, continue on foot across slickrock to the notch and views of the blue waters of **Lake Powell** below. Rockslides have made the descent impossible for vehicles, but hikers can scramble down to the lake and back in about one hour. The elevation change is 600 feet (183 m). The 0.5-mile (0.8-km) round-trip hike is strenuous. After a steep descent over boulders, look for steps of Uncle Ben's Dugway at the base of the notch. Below this point, the grade is gentler. Drill holes in the rock once held oak stakes against which logs, brush, and earth supported the outer wagon wheels. The inner wheels followed a narrow rut 4 to 6 inches deep. About two-thirds of the route down is now under water, although the most impressive roadwork can still be seen.

GETTING THERE

The turnoff from Highway 12 is 5 miles (8 km) east of Escalante. In addition to rewarding you with scenic views, Hole-in-the-Rock Road passes many side drainages of the Escalante River to the east and some remote country of the Kaiparowits Plateau high above the west. Staff at the **Escalante Interagency Visitor Center** (755 W. Main St., Escalante, 435/826-5499, 8am-4:30pm daily), just west of Escalante, can give current road conditions and suggest hikes.

Boynton Overlook and Hundred Hands Pictograph

Be sure to pull off Highway 12 at the **Boynton Overlook** (Hwy. 12, 14 mi/22.5 km east of Escalante, at the Escalante River Bridge) and scan the walls on the far side of the Escalante River for the Hundred Hands pictograph (binoculars help immensely). For a closer look, take a 30-minute hike up from the trailhead parking area at the bottom of the hill at the Escalante River crossing. Rather than hike along the river, go up above the house (don't stray onto fenced-in private property), scramble up the face of the first cliff, and follow faint trails and rock cairns across the bench. It is easiest if you've located the pictographs first from the overlook. The Hundred Hands are high up on a cliff face that's larger than the one you scrambled up. Follow the cliff to the right, where pictographs of goats are lower on the wall.

Back down at river level, head downstream a few hundred yards and look up to the left to see Ancestral Puebloan ruins, known as the Moki House.

Calf Creek Recreation Area

This stunning canyon and park at **Calf Creek Recreation Area** (Hwy. 12, 15 mi/24 km east of Escalante, day use $5 per vehicle) offers the most accessible glimpse of what Escalante canyon country is all about. The trailhead to 126-foot (38-m) **Lower Calf Creek Falls** is here, and you should definitely make plans for the half-day hike (6 mi/9.7 km round-trip, 3-4 hours), especially if you have no time for further exploration of this magical landscape. Otherwise, stop here to picnic in the shade of willows and cottonwoods. This is also the most convenient **campground** ($15) for dozens of miles. The 13 campsites have water, fire pits, and picnic tables.

The Million-Dollar Road

Highway 12 between Escalante and Boulder was completed in 1935 by workers from the Civilian Conservation Corps. The cost was a budget-busting $1 million. Before then, mules carried supplies and mail across this wilderness of slickrock and narrow canyons. The section of Highway 12 between Calf Creek and Boulder is extraordinarily scenic—even jaded travelers used to the wonders of Utah will have to pull over and ogle the views from the **Hog's Back,** where the road crests a fin of rock above the canyons of the Escalante. Be here for sunset on a clear evening and you'll have a memory to carry for the rest of your life.

Boulder

Boulder is a tiny community in a lovely location at the base of Boulder Mountain, where the alpine air mixes with the desert breezes. The single best lodging choice in the Escalante region—the Boulder Mountain Lodge—is here, so plan accordingly.

★ Anasazi State Park Museum

At the excellent **Anasazi State Park Museum** (Hwy. 12, 1 mi/1.6 km north of Boulder, 435/335-7308, http://stateparks. utah.gov, 8am-6pm daily Mar.-Oct., 8am-4pm daily Nov.-Feb., $5 pp, $10 family), indoor museum exhibits, an excavated village site, and a pueblo replica provide a look into the life of these ancient people. The Ancestral Puebloans stayed here for 50-75 years sometime between 1050 and 1200. They grew corn, beans, and squash in fields nearby. The village population peaked at about 200, with an estimated 40 to 50 dwellings. Why the Ancestral Puebloans left or where they went isn't known for certain, but a fire swept through much of the village before they abandoned it. Perhaps they burned the village on purpose, knowing they would move on. University of Utah students and faculty excavated the village, known as the Coombs Site, in 1958 and 1959. You can view pottery, ax heads, arrow points, and other tools found at the site in the museum, along with delicate items like sandals and basketry that came from more protected sites

elsewhere. A diorama shows how the village might have appeared in its heyday. You can see video programs on the Ancestral Puebloans and modern Native Americans on request.

The self-guided tour of the ruins begins behind the museum. You'll see a whole range of Ancestral Puebloan building styles—a pit house, masonry walls, jacal walls (mud reinforced by sticks), and combinations of masonry and jacal. Replicas of habitation and storage rooms behind the museum show complete construction details.

Fuel up for your museum tour at the food truck parked out front.

TOP EXPERIENCE

★ Burr Trail Road

Burr Trail Road, originally a cattle trail blazed by stockman John Atlantic Burr, extends from the town of Boulder on Highway 12 to the Notom-Bullfrog Road, which runs between Highway 24 near the eastern entrance to Capitol Reef National Park and Bullfrog Marina on Lake Powell, off Highway 276. Starting at Boulder, this beautiful road is paved as far as the boundary between the Escalante Canyons unit of the monument and Capitol Reef National Park (31 mi/50 km), where the route traverses the Circle Cliffs, as well as spectacular canyon areas such as Long Canyon and the Gulch. As the route meets the Waterpocket Fold in Capitol Reef National Park, breathtaking switchbacks drop some 800 feet (244 m) in just 0.5 mile (0.8 km). These switchbacks are not considered suitable for RVs or vehicles towing trailers. The unpaved sections of the road may be impassable in poor weather. Visitors should inquire about road and weather conditions before setting out. Also inquire about hiking trails that depart from side roads.

Burr Trail Road joins Notom-Bullfrog Road just before it exits Capitol Reef National Park.

1: Boynton Overlook **2:** Anasazi State Park **3:** the Hundred Hands pictograph **4:** Burr Trail Road

The Gore King of the Southwest

In 2009, a Bureau of Land Management employee discovered some unusual dinosaur bones in a remote area of the Grand Staircase-Escalante National Monument. After a year of excavation, the skull and other bones were proclaimed to belong to an ancestor of *Tyrannosaurus rex*, named *Lythronax argestes*, or "gore king of the Southwest." Paleontologists dated the *Lythronax* to the late Cretaceous Period, about 80 million years ago, making it by far the earliest tyrannosaur species to be found in North America.

At that time, western North America was an island continent called Laramidia. Utah was on the east coast of this island, fronting onto a shallow sea covering what is now the U.S. Midwest. Because the dinosaurs evolved on this island, they're quite different from those found in eastern North America or in Europe or Asia.

At 24 feet (7.3 m) long and 2.5 tons, *Lythronax* was smaller than *T. rex*, but still large enough to be the largest carnivore in its ecosystem. Along with its size, its smallish snout and wide back of the skull allowed it to have the structural strength to attack prey; forward-oriented eyes gave it depth perception.

The discovery was announced in late 2013, and the dinosaur is now on exhibit at the Natural History Museum of Utah in Salt Lake City.

ALONG U.S. 89

In this region, U.S. 89 runs between Kanab in the west to the Utah-Arizona border in the Glen Canyon National Recreation Area. From Kanab to Page, Arizona, at the Colorado River's Glen Canyon Dam, is 80 miles (129 km).

Johnson Canyon Road

Eight miles (12.9 km) east of Kanab, Johnson Canyon Road heads north in the Grand Staircase unit before joining Skutumpah Road and Glendale Bench Road. This road system links up with several more remote backcountry roads in the Grand Staircase and Kaiparowits units, and it eventually leads to Cannonville along Highway 12. From U.S. 89, Johnson Canyon Road is paved for the first 16 miles (26 km). The road passes an abandoned movie set where the TV series *Gunsmoke* was sometimes filmed. The road then climbs up through the scenic Vermilion and then White Cliffs of the Grand Staircase. The road eventually passes over Skutumpah Terrace, a rather featureless plateau covered with scrub.

Paria Canyon and Vermilion Cliffs National Monument

Paria Canyon—a set of magnificent slot canyons that drain from Utah down through northern Arizona to the Grand Canyon—is the focus of popular multiday canyoneering expeditions. Paria Canyon and 293,000 acres of surrounding desert grasslands are now protected as **Vermilion Cliffs National Monument** (www.blm.gov). Although the monument spreads south from the Utah-Arizona border, access to the monument's most famous sites is from back roads in Utah. In addition to the long Paria Canyon backpacking route, some shorter but strenuous day hikes explore this area. For more information, contact the **Kanab Visitor Center** (745 E. U.S. 89, Kanab, 435/644-4680, 8am-4:30pm daily mid-Mar.-mid-Nov., 8am-4:30pm Mon.-Fri. mid-Nov.-mid-Mar.) or stop at the **Paria Contact Station** (U.S. 89, 44 mi/71 km east of Kanab, 435/644-4628, 8am-4:30pm daily mid-Mar.-mid-Nov.) near milepost 21 on U.S. 89.

Cottonwood Canyon Road

A few miles east of the Paria Contact Station (milepost 21 on U.S. 89), Cottonwood Canyon Road leads north. The unpaved road's lower portions, usually passable with a car in dry weather, pass through scenic landscapes as the road pushes north. The route climbs up across a barren plateau before dropping down to the Paria River. Several good hikes lead from roadside trailheads into steep side canyons. The route continues north along the Cockscomb, a long wrinkle of rock ridges that runs north and south across the desert. At the northern end of this 46-mile (72-km) route are Grosvenor Arch, Kodachrome Basin State Park, and Highway 12 at Canyonville.

Big Water and Smokey Mountain Road

At the little crossroads of Big Water, a BLM **visitors center** (100 Upper Revolution Way, Big Water, 435/675-3200, 8:30am-4:30pm daily Apr.-Oct., 8am-4:30pm Thurs.-Mon. Nov.-Mar.) serves the needs of travelers to the monument and to Glen Canyon National Recreation Area (NRA), which is immediately adjacent to this area. The visitors center is worth a stop—it houses bones from a 75-million-year-old, 30-foot-long (9-m) duck-billed dinosaur. The backbone, bearing tooth marks from a tyrannosaur, and the 13-foot-long (4-m) tail are especially impressive.

Joining U.S. 89 at Big Water is Smokey Mountain Road. This long and rugged road links Big Water to Highway 12 at Escalante, 78 miles (126 km) north. The southern portions of the route pass through Glen Canyon NRA, and side roads lead to remote beaches and flooded canyons. The original *Planet of the Apes* movie was shot here, before the area was inundated by Lake Powell.

From Big Water it is 19 miles (31 km) to Page, Arizona, on U.S. 89.

Recreation

The three monument units of the Grand Staircase-Escalante region preserve some of the best long-distance hiking trails in the American Southwest, but they also have shorter trails for travelers who want to sample the wonderful slot canyons and backcountry without venturing too far afield.

Be sure to check at local visitors centers for road and trail conditions, up-to-date maps, and, if you're backpacking, a free backcountry permit, which is required for overnight stays. Many of the following hikes require extensive travel on backcountry roads, which can be impassable after rains and rough the rest of the time. In summer, these trails are hot and exposed; always carry plenty of water, use sunscreen, and wear a hat.

Hiking the **Escalante River Canyon** is one of the world's greatest wilderness treks. Most people devote 4-6 days to exploring its slickrock canyons, which involves frequent scrambling (if not rock climbing), stream fording (if not swimming), and exhausting detours around rockfalls and logjams. Most of the day hikes are along side canyons of the Escalante River and can be reached by trailheads off Hole-in-the-Rock Road or Burr Trail. A couple of shorter hikes—Lower Calf Creek Falls and Escalante Natural Bridge—start quite conveniently from Highway 12. Another good jumping-off point for day hikers is the Dry Fork Coyote Gulch trailhead, 26 miles (42 km) south of Highway 12 on Hole-in-the-Rock Road; trails here lead to two fascinating and beautifully constricted slot canyons.

The **Paria Canyon** is another famed long-distance slickrock canyon hike that covers 37 miles (60 km) between the border of Utah and the edge of the Colorado River's Marble Canyon. Several long day hikes leave from trailheads on the Paria Plateau, along the border with Arizona.

Other areas with developed hiking trails include the Skutumpah Road area and Cottonwood Canyon, in the Kaiparowits Plateau unit. Otherwise, hiking in the monument is mostly on unmarked routes. Call one of the visitors centers and ask for help from the rangers to plan a hiking adventure where there are no trails.

Walk Softly

Only great care and awareness can preserve these pristine canyons. You can help by minimizing the trace of your passage in the area.

- Travel in groups of **12 or fewer.**
- To protect soil crust and vegetation, **park** only in already disturbed areas.
- Don't touch or disturb **Native American artifacts.**
- **Protect wildlife** by leaving your dogs at home.
- Build **campfires** in developed or designated campgrounds with fire grates, fire pits, or fire pans. Wood collection in these areas is not permitted. The National Park Service and the Bureau of Land Management recommend the use of backpacking stoves.
- Most important, **pack out all waste** and use portable human waste disposal bags.

Leave No Trace (www.lnt.org) is a national organization dedicated to awareness, appreciation, and respect for our wildlands. The organization also promotes education about outdoor recreation that is environmentally responsible.

HIKING JOHNSON CANYON-SKUTUMPAH ROAD

The northern portions of this road pass through the White Cliffs area of the Grand Staircase, and several steep and narrow canyons are trenched into these terraces. Rough hiking trails explore these slot canyons. As when hiking any slot canyon, be sure to check the weather report before venturing up-canyon and beware of changes in weather; flash floods can strike fast, and they are especially common in mid-late summer.

Willis Creek Narrows

Distance: 4.4 miles (7.1 km) round-trip
Duration: 3-4 hours
Elevation change: 40 feet
Effort: easy
Trailhead: 9 miles (14.5 km) south of Cannonville along Skutumpah Road

This relatively easy trail follows a small stream as it etches a deep and narrow gorge through the sandstone. It's a perfect introduction to slot-canyon hiking. From the parking area, where Skutumpah Road crosses Willis Wash, walk downstream along the wash. Follow the streambed, which quickly descends between slickrock walls. The canyon is at times no more than 6-10 feet (1.8-3 m) across, while the walls rise 200-300 feet (61-91 m). The trail follows the streambed through the canyon for nearly 2.5 miles (4 km). To return, backtrack up the canyon. Use caution when hiking during flash flood season.

Bull Valley Gorge

Distance: 2 miles (3.2 km) round-trip
Duration: 1-2 hours
Elevation change: 850 feet (259 m)
Effort: moderate-strenuous
Trailhead: 10.5 miles (16.9 km) south of Cannonville along Skutumpah Road

Approximately 1.5 miles (2.4 km) south of Willis Creek on Skutumpah Road, a narrow bridge vaults over the Bull Valley Gorge. Like the Willis Creek Narrows, this is a steep and narrow cleft in the slickrock; however, scrambling along the canyon bottom is a greater challenge. From the bridge, walk upstream along a faint trail on the north side of the crevice until the walls are low enough to scramble down. From here, the canyon deepens quickly, and you'll have to negotiate several dry falls along the way (a rope will come in handy). When you reach the area below the bridge, look up to see a 1950s-era pickup truck trapped between the canyon walls. Three men died in this 1954 mishap; their bodies were recovered, but the pickup was left in place. The canyon continues another mile (1.6 km) from this point; after that the valley widens out a bit. There is no loop trail out of the canyon, so turn back when you've seen enough.

Lick Wash

Distance: 4 miles (6.4 km) one-way to Park Wash
Duration: 4-5 hours
Elevation change: 200 feet (61 m)
Effort: easy
Trailhead: 20 miles (32 km) south of Cannonville along Skutumpah Road

From Lick Wash, trails lead downstream into slot canyons to a remote arroyo (dry riverbed) surrounded by rock-topped mesas. One of these lofty perches contains a preserve of now-rare native grasses. Although this area can be reached in a day's hike, this is also a good base for a multiday camping trip. The trail starts just below the road crossing on Lick Wash and follows the usually dry streambed as it plunges into a narrow slot canyon. The canyon bottom is mostly level and easy to hike. After 1 mile (1.6 km), the canyon begins to widen; after 4 miles (6.4 km), Lick Wash joins Park Wash, a larger desert canyon.

Looming above this canyon junction are mesas topped with deep sandstone terraces. Rising to the east is **No Mans Mesa,** skirted on all sides by steep cliffs. The 1,788 acres atop the mesa were grazed by goats for six months in the 1920s, but since then the pristine grassland has been protected by the Bureau of Land Management (BLM) as an Area of Critical Environmental Concern. Hardy hikers can scramble up a steep trail—used by the goats—to visit this wilderness preserve. The ascent of No Mans Mesa is best considered an overnight trip from the Lick Wash trailhead.

HIKING COTTONWOOD CANYON ROAD

The northern portion of this route passes Kodachrome Basin State Park, which has a fine selection of hiking trails through colorful rock formations. The first five hikes in this section are in the state park. For a brief introduction to the park's ecology, follow the short **Nature Trail.** Be sure to pick up a map of hiking trails when you enter the park.

Panorama Trail

Distance: 3 miles (4.8 km) round-trip
Duration: 2 hours
Elevation change: 350 feet (107 m)
Effort: easy
Trailhead: west side of park road, south of Trailhead Station

The Panorama Trail loops through a highly scenic valley with sand pipes and colorful rocks. The trail then leaves the valley and climbs up the rocks, offering good views of the park's formations. The most spectacular views are found at Panorama Point, which requires a short, steep climb up a few switchbacks. If the 3-mile (4.8-km) loop leaves you thirsty for more hiking (and you're carrying an adequate supply of water), several spur trails offer the opportunity for a longer loop.

Angel's Palace Trail

Distance: 1.5 miles (2.4 km) round-trip
Duration: 30-45 minutes
Elevation change: 300 feet (91 m)
Effort: easy-moderate
Trailhead: Kodachrome Basin State Park, just east of group campground

From the trailhead, hike up the butte to its top, where you're rewarded with fine views of the park and the surrounding area, including Bryce Canyon. Once on top of the butte, the trail is level, and the hike becomes a pleasant amble. It's easy to spend quite a bit of time exploring the plateau. Note that horseback riders share this trail.

Grand Parade Trail

Distance: 1.5 miles (2.4 km) round-trip
Duration: 1.5 hours
Elevation change: 100 feet (30 m)
Effort: easy
Trailhead: Kodachrome Basin State Park, Trailhead Station

The Grand Parade Trail makes a loop with good views of rock pinnacles. It stays on the floor of the canyon, so it's much gentler than some of the park's other hikes. But it's not dull—the trail visits a couple of box canyons and rock formations that resemble marchers in a parade. Horses and bicycles are permitted on this trail.

Eagle's View Trail

Distance: 1 mile (1.6 km) round-trip
Duration: 30 minutes
Elevation change: 1,000 feet (305 m)
Effort: moderate-strenuous
Trailhead: north of Kodachrome Basin State Park campground

Eagle's View Trail, a segment of a historic cattle trail, climbs steep cliffs above the campground. The highest overlook is a steep 0.25-mile (0.4 km) ascent from the campground, but if you just want a good view, only hike to the top of the second set of stairs—after this point, the trail gets very narrow and exposed. Because this trail is so steep and has significant exposure, it's not good for young children. It's also best to avoid it in gusty winds.

Shakespeare Arch Trail

Distance: 1 mile (1.6 km) round-trip
Duration: 30 minutes
Elevation change: 50 feet (15 m)
Effort: easy
Trailhead: From the main park road, head east past the Arch group campground, turn right (south), and follow signs to Shakespeare Arch.

Although the trail's namesake arch collapsed in 2019 (thus fulfilling its natural life cycle), the trailside plants and excellent views still make this easy hike worthwhile. Pick up a brochure at the trailhead to help with plant identification.

Hackberry Canyon

Distance: 22 miles (35 km) one-way
Duration: 3 days
Elevation change: 1,300 feet (396 m)
Effort: strenuous
Trailhead: southern end of BLM Road 422

Directions: Head south on Cottonwood Canyon Road for 7.5 miles (12 km), from where the pavement ends at Kodachrome Basin State Park to the crossing of Round Valley Draw. From here, turn south onto BLM Road 422.

Hikers can travel the 22-mile (35-km) length of this scenic canyon in three days, or take day hikes from either end of the trail. The lower canyon meets Cottonwood Canyon at an elevation of 4,700 feet (1,435 m), just above the mouth of the Paria River. Cottonwood Canyon Road provides access to both ends. A small spring-fed stream flows down the lower half of Hackberry Canyon; hikers should expect to get their feet wet. Many side canyons invite exploration. One of them, Sam Pollock Canyon, is on the west side, about 4.5 miles (7.2 km) upstream from the junction of Hackberry and Cottonwood Canyons; follow it 1.75 miles (2.8 km) up to **Sam Pollock Arch** (60 ft/18 m high and 70 ft/21 m wide). Available topographic maps include Slickrock Bench and Calico Peak. Michael Kelsey's *Hiking and Exploring the Paria River* contains trail and trailhead information and a history of the Watson homestead, located a short way below Sam Pollock Canyon.

Cottonwood Narrows

Distance: 3 miles (4.8 km) round-trip
Duration: 2 hours
Elevation change: minimal
Effort: easy
Trailhead: From the pavement's end at Kodachrome Basin State Park, head south on Cottonwood Canyon Road. The northern end of the Cottonwood Narrows is 15 miles (24-km) down the dirt road; the southern end is 1 mile (1.6 km) farther south. Access is easier from the southern end.

This hike, through a narrow, high-walled Navajo sandstone canyon, is good for casual hikers. The sandy-bottomed wash offers an easy path through the Cockscomb and a good look at the layers of warped rocks. Several side canyons join the wash; if you're up for some scrambling, they can make for good exploring. Even on this short hike, remember to bring water. Use caution during flash flood season.

Box of the Paria River

Distance: 7 miles (11.3 km) round-trip
Duration: 4-5 hours
Elevation change: 500 feet (152 m)
Effort: strenuous
Trailheads: at the confluence of Cottonwood Creek and the Paria River, 2.5 miles (4 km) south of the lower Hackberry Canyon trailhead (29 mi/47 km south of the pavement's end at Kodachrome Basin State Park, or from the south, 11.5 miles (18.5 km) north of U.S. 89)

The confluence of Paria, Hackberry, and Cottonwood Canyons provides the backdrop to an excellent if strenuous day hike. The Box of the Paria River involves some steep climbs up rocky slopes as it traverses a tongue of slickrock between the mouth of the Hackberry and Paria Canyons. The route then follows the Paria River through its "box," or cliff-sided canyon, in the Cockscomb Formation. The trail returns to the trailhead by following Cottonwood Canyon upstream to the trailhead. For an easier hike up the box, start at the Old Paria townsite, at the northern end of Movie Set Road. Hike 1 mile (1.6 km) down the Paria River, and then turn east into the box. Inquire at visitors centers for maps and about trail conditions.

HIKING THE ESCALANTE RIVER

The maze of canyons that drain the Escalante River presents exceptional hiking opportunities. You'll find everything from easy day hikes to challenging backpacking treks. The Escalante's canyon begins just downstream from the town of Escalante and ends at Lake Powell, about 85 miles (137 km) beyond. In all this distance, only one road, Highway 12, bridges the river. Many side canyons provide additional access to the Escalante, and most are as beautiful as the main gorge. The river system covers such a large area that you can find solitude even in spring, the busiest hiking season. The many eastern canyons remain virtually untouched.

The Escalante canyons preserve some of the quiet beauty once found in Glen Canyon, which is now lost under the waters of Lake

Powell. Prehistoric Ancestral Puebloan and Fremont people have left ruins, petroglyphs, pictographs, and artifacts in many locations. These archaeological resources are protected by federal law: Don't collect or disturb them.

Before setting out, visit the rangers at the **Escalante Interagency Visitor Center** (755 W. Main St., 435/826-5499, 8am-4:30pm daily), on the west edge of Escalante, for the required free permit to backpack overnight, and to check on the latest trail and road conditions. Restrictions on group size may be in force on some of the more popular trails. You can also obtain topographic maps and literature that show trailheads, mileages, and other information that may be useful in planning trips. Some of the more popular trailheads have self-registration stations for permits.

The best times for a visit are early March to early June and mid-September to early November. Summertime trips are possible, but be prepared for higher temperatures and greater flash flood danger in narrow canyons. Travel along the Escalante River involves frequent crossings, and there's always water in the main canyon, usually ankle- or knee-deep. Pools in the Narrows between Scorpion Gulch and Stevens Canyon can be up to chest-deep in spots (which you can bypass), but that's the exception. Occasional springs, some tributaries, and the river itself provide drinking water. Always purify the water first; the BLM warns of the unpleasant disease giardiasis, which is caused by the invisible giardia protozoan. Don't forget insect repellent—mosquitoes and deer flies seek out hikers in late spring and summer. Long-sleeved shirts and long pants also discourage biting insects and protect against the brush.

For guided day hikes and hiking shuttles into the Escalante canyons, contact **Utah Canyon Outdoors** (325 W. Main St., Escalante, 435/826-4967, www.utahcanyonoutdoors.com).

Escalante Canyon Trailheads

The many approaches to the area allow all sorts of trips. Besides the Highway 12 access at

GRAND STAIRCASE-ESCALANTE
RECREATION

Escalante and the Highway 12 bridge, hikers can reach the Escalante River through western side canyons from Hole-in-the-Rock Road or eastern side canyons from Burr Trail Road. The western-canyon trailheads on Hole-in-the-Rock Road can be more easily reached by car, thus facilitating vehicle shuttles. To reach eastern-canyon trailheads, with the exceptions of Deer Creek and the Gulch on Burr Trail Road, you'll need lots of time and, if the road is wet, a sturdy 4WD vehicle. You must carry water for trips in these more remote canyons. Except for Deer Creek, they're usually dry.

Escalante to Highway 12 Bridge

Distance: 15 miles (24 km) one-way
Duration: 1-2 days
Elevation change: 500 feet (152 m)
Effort: moderate-strenuous
Trailhead: near the town of Escalante
Directions: Follow signs from Highway 12 on the east side of town (by the high school) to the trailhead.

This section of the Escalante River offers easy walking and stunning canyon scenery. Tributaries and sandstone caves invite exploration. You'll find good camping areas the entire way (be sure to get a permit for overnight camping). Usually the river here is only ankle-deep. Almost immediately, the river knifes its way through the massive cliffs of the Escalante Monocline, leaving the broad valley of the upper river behind. Although there is no maintained trail along this stretch of the east-flowing river, it is relatively easy to pick your way along the riverbank.

Death Hollow, which is far prettier than the name suggests, meets the Escalante from the north after 7.5 miles (12 km). Several good swimming holes carved in rock are a short hike upstream from the Escalante; watch for poison ivy among the greenery. Continue farther up Death Hollow to see more pools, little waterfalls, and outstanding canyon scenery. You can bypass some pools, but others you'll have to swim—bring a small inflatable

boat, air mattress, or waterproof bag to ferry backpacks.

Sand Creek, on the Escalante's north side, 4.5 miles (7.2 km) downstream from Death Hollow, is also worth exploring; deep pools begin a short way up from the mouth. Another 0.5 mile (0.8 km) down the Escalante, a natural arch appears high on the canyon wall. Then Escalante Natural Bridge comes into view, just 2 miles (3.2 km) from the Highway 12 bridge.

Escalante Natural Arch and Bridge

Distance: 2 miles (3.2 km) one-way
Duration: 2 hours
Elevation change: 100 feet (30 m)
Effort: easy
Trailhead: Highway 12 bridge over the Escalante River, between Escalante and Boulder

This hike upstream from the highway gives day hikers a taste of the Escalante River. After about 1.5 miles (2.4 km) of hiking, you'll see the arch (look up) and then the 130-foot-high (40-m) natural bridge. Hike upstream from the bridge for better views of the arch. Continue hiking for another 0.5 mile (0.8 km) beyond the arch to the point where Sand Creek enters the Escalante. Hot-weather hikers may want to head a short distance up Sand Creek to find deep pools.

Phipps Wash

Distance: 2 miles (3.2 km) one-way to Maverick Bridge
Duration: 3 hours
Elevation change: 300 feet (91 m)
Effort: easy
Trailhead: Highway 12 bridge over the Escalante River, between Escalante and Boulder

Start this hike from the highway crossing and follow the Escalante River downstream 1.5 miles (2.4 km) to Phipps Wash, a lovely side canyon. A sign directs you to cross the Escalante River—heed it. In several other places, you'll have to wade in the river, which is usually shallow and warm enough to make it a fairly simple task. Highlights of the hike are Maverick Bridge, about 0.5 mile (0.8 km) up the wash in a side canyon, and Phipps Arch, about 0.75 mile (1.2 km) up Phipps Wash, visible high on the canyon wall above the wash. If you want to continue up the wash, the streambed trail gives way to a sandy wash, then slickrock. The head of Phipps Wash is about 4 miles (6.4 km) from the Escalante River.

The head of the wash is also accessible from above; rather than hiking up the Escalante River, descend a steep slickrock slope from Sheffield Road (Road 103, about 0.5 mile (0.8 km) east of the Head of the Rocks overlook). The main parking area for this route is about 0.75 mile (1.2 km) from the Highway 12 turn-off. Because this route isn't marked, be sure to take topographic maps or go with a guide.

Highway 12 Bridge to Harris Wash

Distance: 26.5 miles (43 km) one-way
Duration: 4-6 days
Elevation change: 700 feet (213 m)
Effort: moderate
Trailhead: Highway 12 bridge over the Escalante River, between Escalante and Boulder

This is where many long-distance trekkers begin their exploration of the Escalante canyons. In this section, the Escalante Canyon offers a varied show: In places the walls close in to make constricted narrows; at others they step back to form great valleys. Side canyons filled with lush greenery and sparkling streams contrast with dry washes of desert, yet all can be fun to explore. A good hike of 4-6 days begins at the Highway 12 bridge, goes down the Escalante to Harris Wash, then travels up Harris to a trailhead off Hole-in-the-Rock Road (37 mi/60 km total).

From the Highway 12 bridge parking area, a trail leads to the river. Canyon access goes through private property; cross the river at the posted signs. **Phipps Wash** comes in from the south (the right side) after 1.5 miles (2.4 km) and several more river crossings. Turn up its wide mouth for 0.5 mile (0.8 km) to see Maverick Bridge in a drainage to the right. To reach Phipps Arch, continue another 0.75 mile (1.2 km) up the main wash, turn left into a box canyon, and scramble up the left side (see the 7.5-minute Calf Creek topographic map).

Bowington (Boynton) Arch is an attraction in a north side canyon known locally as Deer Creek. Look for this small canyon on the left, 1 mile (1.6 km) beyond Phipps Wash; hike up it for about 1 mile (1.6 km), past three deep pools, and then turn left into a tributary canyon. In 1878 gunfire resolved a quarrel between local ranchers John Boynton and Washington Phipps. Phipps was killed, but both their names live on.

Waters of **Boulder Creek** come rushing into the Escalante from the north in the next major side canyon, 5.75 miles (9.3 km) below the Highway 12 bridge. The creek, along with its Dry Hollow and Deer Creek tributaries, provides good canyon walking; deep areas may require swimming or climbing up on the plateau. (You could also start down Deer Creek from Burr Trail Road, where they meet, 6.5 miles (10.5 km) southeast of Boulder at a primitive BLM campground. Starting at the campground, follow Deer Creek 7.5 miles (12 km) to Boulder Creek, then 3.5 miles (5.6 km) down Boulder Creek to the Escalante.) Deer and Boulder Creeks have water year-round.

High sheer sandstone walls constrict the Escalante River in a narrow channel below Boulder Creek, but the canyon widens again above the **Gulch** tributary, 14 miles (22.5 km) below the highway bridge. Hikers can head up the Gulch on a day hike.

Most springs along the Escalante are difficult to spot. One that's easy to find is in the first south bend after the Gulch; water comes straight out of the rock a few feet above the river. Escalante Canyon becomes wider as the river lazily meanders along. Hikers can cut off some of the bends by walking in the open desert between canyon walls and riverside willow thickets. A bend cut off by the river itself loops to the north just before Horse Canyon, 3 miles (4.8 km) below the Gulch. Along with its tributaries **Death Hollow** and **Wolverine Creek**, **Horse Canyon** drains the Circle

Cliffs to the northeast. Floods in these mostly dry streambeds wash down pieces of black petrified wood. Vehicles with good clearance can reach the upper sections of all three canyons from a loop road off Burr Trail Road. Horse and Wolverine Creek Canyons offer good easy-to-moderate hiking, but if you really want a challenge, try Death Hollow, sometimes called Little Death Hollow to distinguish it from the larger one near Hell's Backbone Road. Starting from the Escalante River, go about 2 miles (3.2 km) up Horse Canyon and turn right into Death Hollow; rugged scrambling over boulders takes you back into a long section of twisting narrows. Carry water for Upper Horse Canyon and its tributaries. Lower Horse Canyon usually has water.

About 3.5 miles (5.6 km) down the Escalante from Horse Canyon, you'll enter Glen Canyon NRA and come to Sheffield Bend, a large grassy field on the right. Only a chimney remains from Sam Sheffield's old homestead. Two grand amphitheaters are beyond the clearing and up a stiff climb in loose sand. Over the next 5.5 river miles (8.9 km) to Silver Falls Creek, you'll pass long bends, dry side canyons, and a huge slope of sand on the right canyon wall. Don't look for any silver waterfalls in **Silver Falls Creek**—the name comes from streaks of shiny desert varnish on the cliffs.

Harris Wash is to the right (west) side of the Escalante River, almost opposite Silver Falls Creek. When the Hole-in-the-Rock route proved so difficult, pioneers figured there had to be a better way to the San Juan Mission. Their new wagon road descended Harris Wash to the Escalante River, climbed part of Silver Falls Creek, crossed the Circle Cliffs, descended Muley Twist Canyon in the Waterpocket Fold, and then followed Hall's Creek to Hall's Crossing on the Colorado River. Charles Hall operated a ferry there from 1881 to 1884. Old maps show a jeep road through Harris Wash and Silver Falls Creek Canyons, used before the National Park Service closed off the Glen Canyon NRA

section. Harris Wash is just 0.5 mile (0.8 km) downstream and across the Escalante from Silver Falls Creek.

★ Lower Calf Creek Falls

Distance: 3.1 miles (5 km) one-way
Duration: 4 hours
Elevation change: 250 feet (76 m)
Effort: easy-moderate
Trailhead: Calf Creek Campground ($5 day use), 16 miles (26 km) east of Escalante on Highway 12

Calf Creek is a tributary of the Escalante River, entering it near Highway 12. The hike to Lower Calf Creek Falls is quite accessible for ordinary folks and is, for many people, the highlight of their first trip to the Escalante area. It's the dazzling enticement that brings people back for longer and more remote hiking trips. From the trailhead and parking area just off Highway 12, the trail winds between high cliffs of Navajo sandstone streaked with desert varnish, where you'll see beaver ponds, Native American ruins and pictographs, and the misty 126-foot-high (38-m) Lower Calf Creek Falls. A brochure available at the trailhead next to the campground identifies many of the desert and riparian plant species along the way. Bring water and perhaps lunch. Summer temperatures can soar, but the falls and the crystal-clear pool beneath stay cool. Sheer cliffs block travel farther upstream.

Calf Creek Campground (early Apr.-late Oct., $15), near the road, has 13 sites with drinking water.

Upper Calf Creek Falls

Distance: 1 mile (1.6 km) one-way
Duration: 1.5 hours
Elevation change: 500 feet (152 m)
Effort: moderate
Trailhead: just east of milepost 81 on Highway 12
Directions: From Escalante, drive about 20.5 miles (33 km) east on Highway 12. Turn left onto a dirt road between mileposts 80 and 81; the road may be marked by a black boulder with a white stripe. Drive 0.25 mile (0.4 km) up the bumpy dirt road to the trailhead (park low-clearance vehicles at the turnoff and walk to the trailhead).

The hike to Upper Calf Creek Falls is more strenuous and less used than the trail to the lower falls. It's also entirely different in nature, so don't feel that if you've hiked to the lower falls, the upper falls trip will be a mere repeat. This hike starts with a fairly steep descent across slickrock and then continues along a sandy trail. At a fork, you can choose to hike down to the base of the 87-foot-high (27-m) falls or stay high and continue across more slickrock to the top of the falls and some deep pools in the stream. Near the bottom of the falls are hanging gardens and thick vegetation. At the top, paintbrush grows out of cracks in the slickrock.

Harris Wash

Distance: 10.25 miles (16.5 km) one-way from trailhead to Escalante River
Duration: 2-3 days round-trip
Elevation change: 700 feet (213 m)
Effort: moderate
Trailhead: Harris Wash trailhead off Hole-in-the-Rock Road
Directions: From Highway 12, turn south and travel on Hole-in-the-Rock Road for 10.8 miles (17.4 km), then turn left and go 6.3 miles (10.1 km) on a dirt road (keep left at the fork near the end).

Clear shallow water glides down this gem of a canyon. High cliffs streaked with desert varnish are deeply undercut and support lush hanging gardens. Harris Wash provides a beautiful route to the Escalante River, but it can also be a destination in itself; tributaries and caves invite exploration along the way. The sand and gravel streambed makes for easy walking. Don't be dismayed by the drab appearance of upper Harris Wash: The canyon and creek appear a few miles downstream. The Harris Wash trailhead is restricted to a maximum of 12 people per group.

TOP EXPERIENCE

★ Dry Fork of Coyote Gulch

Distance: 3.5 miles (5.6 km) round-trip
Duration: 5 hours
Elevation change: 300 feet (91 m)

Effort: moderate
Trailhead: Dry Fork of Coyote Gulch
Directions: From Highway 12, turn south onto Hole-in-the-Rock Road and follow it for 26 miles (42 km). Turn left at the sign for Dry Fork and continue 1.7 miles (2.7 km) along a rutted dirt road to the trailhead.

Twenty-six miles (42 km) south of Highway 12 is a series of narrow, scenic, and exciting **slot canyons** reached by a moderate day hike. The canyons feed into the Dry Fork of Coyote Gulch, reached from the Dry Fork trailhead. These three enchanting canyons are named **Peek-a-boo, Spooky,** and **Dry Creek.** Exploring these slots requires basic canyoneering skills and the ability to pass through some fairly narrow (12-inch) spaces. From the trailhead parking lot, follow cairns down into the sandy bottom of the Dry Fork of Coyote Gulch. The slot canyons all enter the gulch from the north; watch for cairns and trails because the openings can be easy to miss. You'll have to scramble up some rocks to get into Peek-a-boo. The slots sometimes contain deep pools of water; choke stones and pour-offs can make access difficult. No loop trail links the three slot canyons; follow each until the canyon becomes too narrow to continue, then come back out. Making a full circuit of these canyons requires about 3.5 miles (5.6 km) of hiking. A side trail from Coyote Gulch also leads to stunning Stevens Arch, which spans 225 feet (69 m). Because they are relatively accessible, these canyons draw a crowd and the parking area has a tendency to get strewn with garbage. Get an early start and remember to pack your garbage out!

HIKING IN PARIA CANYON AND VERMILION CLIFFS

The wild and twisting canyons of the Paria River and its tributaries offer a memorable experience for seasoned hikers. Silt-laden waters have sculpted the colorful canyon walls, revealing 200 million years of geologic history. *Paria* means "muddy water" in the Paiute language. You enter the 2,000-foot-deep (610-m) gorge of the Paria in Southern Utah, then hike

37 miles (60 km) downstream to Lee's Ferry in Arizona, where the Paria empties into the Colorado River. A handful of shorter but rugged day hikes lead to superb scenery and geologic curiosities.

Ancient petroglyphs and campsites show that Pueblo people traveled the Paria more than 700 years ago. They hunted mule deer and bighorn sheep while using the broad lower end of the canyon to grow corn, beans, and squash. The Dominguez-Escalante Expedition stopped at the mouth of the Paria in 1776, and these were the first nonnatives to see the river. John D. Lee and three companions traveled through the canyon in 1871 to bring a herd of cattle from the Pahreah settlement to Lee's Ferry. After Lee began a Colorado River ferry service in 1872, he and others farmed the lower Paria Canyon. Prospectors came here to search for gold, uranium, and other minerals, but much of the canyon remained unexplored. In the late 1960s, the BLM organized a small expedition whose research led to protection of the canyon as a primitive area. The Arizona Wilderness Act of 1984 designated Paria Canyon a wilderness, along with parts of the Paria Plateau and Vermilion Cliffs. Vermilion Cliffs National Monument was created in 2000.

The **BLM Paria Contact Station** (435/644-4628, 8am-4:30pm daily mid-Mar.-mid-Nov.) is in Utah, 44 miles (71 km) east of Kanab on U.S. 89 near milepost 21. It's on the south side of the highway, just east of the Paria River. Self-serve day-use permits ($5 pp, $6 per dog) are required for day hiking in Paria Canyon and to visit other sites in Vermilion Cliffs National Monument.

Paria Canyon

Distance: 38.5 miles (62 km) one-way
Duration: 4-6 days
Elevation change: 1,300 feet (396 m)
Effort: moderate
Trailhead: Whitehouse Campground
Directions: The trailhead is 2 miles (3.2 km) south of the Paria Contact Station, on a dirt road near a campground and old homestead site called White

House Ruins. The exit trailhead is in Arizona at Lonely Dell Ranch of Lee's Ferry, 44 miles (71 km) southwest of Page via U.S. 89 and U.S. 89A (or 98 mi/158 km southeast of Kanab on U.S. 89A).

Allow plenty of time to hike Paria Canyon—there are many river crossings, and you'll want to make side trips up at least some of the tributary canyons. Hikers should have enough backpacking experience to be self-sufficient, as help may be days away. Flash floods can race through the canyon, especially during summer. Rangers close the Paria if they think a danger exists. Because the upper end is narrowest (between miles 4.2 and 9.0), rangers require that all hikers start here so they have up-to-date weather information for their passage.

You must register at a trailhead or the **Kanab BLM Office** (318 N. 100 E., Kanab, 435/644-2672, 8am-4:30pm Mon.-Fri. year-round). **Permits** to hike the canyon are $5 per person per day. Backpackers should get a permit online (www.recreation.gov, reserve up to four months in advance) or at the ranger station; note that only a limited number are issued and competition for them can be fierce, so it's best to go online at the first of the month for reservations four months out. Day hikers can just register and pay the fee at the trailhead. The visitors center and the office both provide weather forecasts and brochures with a map and hiking information. The visitors center always has the weather forecast posted at an outdoor information kiosk.

The full hike requires a 150-mile (242-km) round-trip car shuttle. For a list of shuttle services, ask at the **Paria Contact Station** (U.S. 89, 44 mi/71 km east of Kanab, 435/644-4628, 8am-4:30pm daily mid-Mar.-mid-Nov.) or the Kanab BLM Office. Expect to pay about $200 for this service.

All visitors should take special care to minimize their impact on this beautiful canyon. Check the BLM's "Visitor Use Regulations" for the Paria before you go. Regulations include no campfires in the Paria and its

---

1: Calf Creek Falls 2: Coyote Gulch

tributaries, a pack-in, pack-out policy, and a requirement that latrines be made at least 100 feet (30 m) away from river and campsite locations. Human waste and toilet paper must be transported out in plastic bags (available at the ranger station).

The Paria rangers recommend a maximum group size of six, though regulations specify a 10-person limit. No more than 20 people per day can enter the canyon for overnight trips. The best times to travel along the Paria are usually mid-March to June and October to November. May, especially Memorial Day weekend, tends to be crowded. Winter hikers often complain of painfully cold feet. Wear shoes suitable for frequent wading; canvas shoes are better than heavy leather hiking boots. You can get good drinking water from springs along the way (see the BLM hiking brochure for locations); it's best not to use the river water because of possible chemical pollution from farms and ranches upstream. Normally the river is only ankle-deep, but in spring or after rainy spells, it can become much deeper. During thunderstorms, levels can rise to more than 20 feet (6 m) in the Paria Narrows, so heed weather warnings. Quicksand, which is most prevalent after flooding, is more a nuisance than a danger—usually it's just knee-deep. Many hikers carry a walking stick to probe the opaque waters for good crossing places.

Wrather Canyon Arch, one of Arizona's largest natural arches, is about 1 mile (1.6 km) up a side canyon of the Paria. The massive structure has a 200-foot (61 m) span. Turn right (southwest) at mile 20.6 on the Paria hike. (The mouth of Wrather Canyon and other points along the Paria are unsigned; you have to follow your map.)

Buckskin Gulch and Wire Pass

Distance: 1.7 miles (2.7 km) one-way
Duration: 3 hours
Elevation change: 300 feet (91 m)
Effort: moderate
Trailhead: Wire Pass trailhead
Directions: From Kanab, head 37 miles (60 km) east

on U.S. 89 to BLM Road 700 (also called House Rock Valley Road), between mileposts 25 and 26. Turn south for 8.5 bumpy miles (13.7 km) to the trailhead.

Buckskin Gulch is an amazing slot-canyon tributary of the Paria, with convoluted walls reaching hundreds of feet high and narrowing to as little as 4 feet (1.2 m) in width. In places the walls block out so much light that it's like walking in a cave. Be very careful to avoid flash floods.

Day hikers can get a taste of this incredible canyon country by driving to the Wire Pass trailhead. From the trailhead, a relatively easy trail leads into Wire Pass, a narrow side canyon that joins Buckskin Gulch. The trail runs the length of Wire Pass to its confluence with Buckskin Gulch. From here, you can explore this exceptionally narrow canyon or follow Buckskin Gulch to its appointment with Paria Canyon (12.5 mi/20 km).

For the full experience of Buckskin Gulch, long-distance hikers can begin at the Buckskin Gulch trailhead, 4.5 miles (7.2 km) south of U.S. 89 on BLM Road 700. From here, it's 16.3 miles/26.2 kilometers (one-way) to Paria Canyon. Hikers can continue down the Paria or turn upstream and hike 6 miles (9.7 km) to exit at the White House trailhead near the ranger station. Hiking this gulch can be strenuous, with rough terrain, deep pools of water, and log and rock jams that may require the use of ropes. Conditions vary considerably from one year to the next. Regulations mandate packing your waste out of this area.

Hiking permits ($6 pp per day) are required; backpackers should get an overnight permit (www.recreation.gov, $5 pp per day) online, up to four months in advance, or at the ranger station, but day hikers can simply register and pay the fee at the trailhead.

Coyote Buttes

You've probably seen photos of these dramatic rock formations: towering sand dunes frozen into rock. These much-photographed buttes are located on the Paria Plateau, just south of Wire Pass. Access is strictly controlled, and you can only enter the area with reservations and by permit. The number of people allowed into the area is also strictly limited; however, the permit process, fees, and restrictions are the same as for Paria Canyon.

Advance permits ($5-7) are required for day use and are available online and at the **Paria Contact Station** (U.S. 89, 44 mi/71 km east of Kanab, 435/644-4628, 8am-4:30pm daily mid-Mar.-mid-Nov.); no overnight camping is allowed. Group size is limited to no more than six people. Dogs are allowed but require their own $5 permits. All trash must be packed out, and campfires are not allowed. See the Vermilion Cliffs Monument website (www.blm.gov/programs/recreation/permits-and-passes/lotteries-and-permit-systems/arizona/coyote-buttes) for complete information and go to www.recreation.gov to obtain permits.

The BLM has divided the area into Coyote North and Coyote South. The Wave—the most photographed of the buttes—is in Coyote North, so this region is more popular (and easier to reach from the Wire Pass trailhead); BLM staff will give you a map and directions when you get your permit. After the trailhead, you're on your own, because the wilderness lacks signs. Permits are more difficult to obtain in spring and fall—the best times to visit—and on weekends. The fragile sandstone can break if climbed on, so it's important to stay on existing hiking routes and wear soft-soled footwear.

MOUNTAIN BIKING

Mountain bikes are allowed on all roads in the monument but not on hiking trails. Mountain bikers are not allowed to travel cross-country off roads or to make their own routes across slickrock; however, there are hundreds of miles of primitive roads in the monument, with dozens of loop routes available for cyclists on multiday trips. In addition to following the scenic **Burr Trail** from Boulder to the Waterpocket Fold in Capitol Reef National Park, cyclists can loop off this route and follow the Circle Cliffs-Wolverine Trail. This 45-mile (72-km) loop traverses the headwaters

of several massive canyons as they plunge to meet the Escalante River.

Hole-in-the-Rock Road is mostly a one-way-in, one-way-out affair, but cyclists can follow side roads to hiking trailheads and big vistas over the Escalante canyons. Popular side roads include a 10-mile (16-km) round-trip road to the area known as Egypt and the Fifty Mile Bench Road, a 27-mile (43-km) loop from Hole-in-the-Rock Road that explores the terrain above Glen Canyon. Left Hand Collet Road, a rough jeep trail that a mountain bike can bounce along easily enough, links Hole-in-the-Rock Road with the Smokey Mountain Road system, with links to both Escalante in the north and Big Water in the south.

Other popular routes in the **Big Water area** include the Nipple Butte loop and the steep loop around Smoky Butte and Smoky Hollow, with views over Lake Powell. **Cottonwood Canyon Road,** which runs between U.S. 89 and Cannonville, is another long back road with access to a network of less traveled trails.

Request more information on mountain biking from the visitors centers. They have handouts and maps and can help cyclists plan backcountry bike adventures. This country is remote and primitive, so cyclists must carry everything they are likely to need. Also, there are few sources of potable water in the monument, so cyclists must transport all drinking water or be prepared to purify it

4WD EXPLORATION

Without a mountain bike or a pair of hiking boots, the best way to explore the backcountry Grand Staircase-Escalante is with a high-clearance 4WD vehicle; however, the scale of the landscape, the primitive quality of many of the roads, and the extreme weather conditions common in the desert mean that you shouldn't head into the backcountry unless you are confident in your skills as a mechanic and driver. Choose roads that match your vehicle's capacity and your driving ability, and you should be OK. Some of the roads that appear on maps are slowly going back to nature:

Rather than close some roads, park officials are letting the desert reclaim them. Other roads are being closed, so it's best to check access and road conditions before setting out. Remember that many of the roads in the monument are very slow going. If you've got somewhere to be in a hurry, these corrugated, boulder-dodging roads may not get you there in time. Be sure to take plenty of water—not only for drinking but also for overheated radiators. It's also wise to carry wooden planks or old carpet scraps for help in gaining traction should your wheels get mired in the sand.

RAFTING

Most of the year, shallow water and rocks make boat travel impossible on the Escalante River, but for two or three weeks during spring runoff, which peaks in mid-May and early June, river levels may rise high enough to be passable. (In some years there may not be enough water in any season.) Contact the **Escalante Interagency Visitor Center** (755 W. Main St., Escalante, 435/826-5499, 8am-4:30pm daily) for ideas on when to hit the river at its highest. A shallow draft and maneuverability are essential, so inflatable canoes or kayaks work best (also because they are easier to carry out at trip's end or if water levels drop too low for floating). Not recommended are rafts (too wide and bulky) and hard-shelled kayaks and canoes (they get banged up on the many rocks). The usual launch is the Highway 12 bridge. Coyote Gulch—a 13-mile (21-km) hike—is a good

spot to get out, as is Crack in the Wall, which is a 2.75-mile (4.4-km) hike on steep sand from the junction of Coyote and Escalante Canyons to the Forty-Mile Ridge trailhead; a 4WD vehicle is needed, and a rope is required to negotiate the vessel over the canyon rim. Hole-in-the-Rock is another pullout (a 600-foot/183-meter ascent over boulders; rope suggested). You could also arrange for a friend to pick you up by boat from Halls Crossing or Bullfrog Marina. River boaters must obtain a free backcountry permit from either the BLM or the National Park Service.

OUTFITTERS

There aren't many places to shop for gear in this remote area. The most centrally located shops are in the town of Escalante, where you'll find **Utah Canyon Outdoors** (325 W. Main St., Escalante, 435/826-4967, www.utahcanyonoutdoors.com), which stocks books, maps, and some outdoor gear. Right across the street, **Escalante Outfitters** (310 W. Main St., Escalante, 435/826-4266, www.escalanteoutfitters.com) has a little bit of everything, including a small liquor store, and is a good place to pick up a warm jacket or a stylish tank top; they can also set you up with a guide for fishing, biking, or hiking trips.

Another shop with a good selection of clothing and gear is in Kanab: **Willow Canyon Outdoor** (263 S. 100 E., Kanab, 435/644-8884 www.willowcanyon.com), which also serves good coffee and has an excellent book shop.

Escalante

Escalante (elev. 5,813 ft/1,772 m) is a natural hub for exploration of the Kaiparowits Plateau and Escalante Canyons units of the monument. Even if you don't have the time or the inclination to explore the rugged canyon country, you'll discover incredible scenery just by traveling Highway 12 through the Escalante area.

At first glance, Escalante looks like a town that time has passed by. Just under 1,000 people live here, in addition to the resident cows, horses, and chickens that you'll meet just one block off Main Street. Yet this little community is the biggest place for scores of miles around and a center for ranchers and travelers. Escalante has the neatly laid-out streets and trim little houses typical of Mormon settlements.

FOOD

Escalante Outfitters (310 W. Main St., 435/826-4266, www.escalanteoutfitters.com, 8am-9pm daily), runs a little café that's a reliable place to eat in this little town. It serves espresso, sandwiches, handmade pizza ($12-25), and microbrew beer. The breakfast pastries are also delicious.

Stock up on food for the trail or the road at the **Escalante Mercantile and Natural Grocery** (210 W. Main St., 435/826-4114, 7am-6pm Mon.-Sat., 9am-5pm Sun. Mar.-Oct.). You know you need some fresh fruit by now, and you can also pick up bottled iced tea, juice, or kombucha. For the region's best breakfast pastries, quiche, and brown-bag sandwiches, stop by **Mimi's Bakery & Deli** (190 W. Main St., 435/690-0576, 8am-3pm Wed.-Sat., $9-11).

Nemo's Drive Thru (40 E. Main St., 435/826-4500, 11am-7pm Mon.-Sat., $8-13) is the perfect place to refuel after a long hike. The tiny restaurant doesn't look too impressive from the street, but the food is far better than what you'll find at most small-town

burger joints. In addition to regular burgers, they serve veggie burgers, fish-and-chips, sweet potato fries, and good milk shakes.

As close as you'll get to fine dining in Escalante is the ★ **Circle D Eatery** (485 W. Main St., 435/826-4125, www.escalantecircledeatery.com, 11am-9pm Wed.-Mon., 4:30pm-9pm Tues., $13-25), which offers local open-range beef and a variety of house-smoked meats. The steaks are dependably good, as is the smoked brisket. If you're around for breakfast, chow down on some good Mexican-style eggs.

The only true bar (at least according to Utah's arcane liquor laws) on the entire length of Highway 12 is **4th West Pub** (425 W. Main St., 435/826-4525, 5pm-10pm Sun.-Thurs., 5pm-midnight Fri.-Sat., $8-12). The food is simple—sandwiches, tacos, salads—but good, and if you're simply thirsty, you don't need to order food just to enjoy a cocktail.

East of town, **Kiva Koffeehouse** (Hwy. 12, milepost 73.86, 435/826-4550, www.kivakoffeehouse.com, 8am-4pm Wed.-Sun. Apr.-Oct., $6-12) has just about the best setting in the state, with windows looking out at the landscape. It's worth a stop for a latte or for a simple lunch of delicious Southwestern-style food, much of it organic, and for a look at the view.

ACCOMMODATIONS

Accommodations in Escalante range from simple to luxurious. Add a hefty 13.3 percent room tax to the listed rates.

$50-100

The seven small but comfy log cabins at ★ **Escalante Outfitters** (310 W. Main St., 435/826-4266, www.escalanteoutfitters.com, $55) share men's and women's bathhouses and a common grassy area. A larger ADA-accessible cabin with a bath ($150) sleeps four. Tucked behind the store, which also houses

The Petrified Forest

Trees fall into water, are washed downstream, and are buried by mud, silt, and ash. Minerals and elements like silica—from the volcanic ash—enter the wood either from water or the ground, filling in its pores. When the pores of the wood have been filled, its color changes depending on the minerals present. This mineral-loaded wood is resistant to rotting and is often quite beautiful, displaying the original cellular structure and grain.

Two especially good places to see petrified wood are along Huber Wash, in the western section of Zion National Park just west of Springdale, and at Escalante Petrified Forest State Park, just west of the town of Escalante.

Although it should go without saying that the petrified wood in these places should stay here—and not travel home in a hiker's pack or pocket—this general ethical guideline is backed up by a potent mythology of misfortune befalling people who steal petrified wood. Posted on a bulletin board at the base of the Petrified Forest Trail in the state park are many letters from people who decided to return bits of petrified wood they'd secreted away from the park, and the tales of how their lives went down the tubes after they stole it.

a casual pizza and espresso restaurant and a tiny liquor store, these cabins are convenient to all the action the town has to offer and include wireless Internet access. Dogs are permitted for $10 in some cabins.

On the west edge of town, the **Circle D Motel** (475 W. Main St., 435/826-4297, www.escalantecircledmotel.com, $80-115) reaches out to bicyclists and hikers with clean, basic guest rooms. Pets are welcome in some guest rooms; a restaurant is part of the complex.

The **Prospector Inn** (380 W. Main St., 435/826-4653, $79) is a large motor lodge near the center of town; there's a restaurant and lounge on the premises. A pleasant and modern establishment is **Rainbow Country B&B** (586 E. 300 S., 435/826-4567, www.bnbescalante.com, $89-125), with four guest rooms; guests have the use of a hot tub, a pool table, and a TV lounge.

$100-150

In downtown Escalante, ★ **Canyons B&B** (120 E. Main St., 435/826-4747, www.canyonsbnb.com, late Mar.-Nov., $130-150) is a modern three-bedroom bunkhouse that's been built behind an old farmhouse, which offers its own lodge room. There's nothing rustic about the guest rooms: All are attractively decorated and equipped with TV,

telephones, and Wi-Fi. Minimum-stay requirements may apply.

Right on the edge of town, find cozy log cabins, vacation houses, and RV sites at **Escalante Cabins and RV Park** (680 W. Main St., 435/826-4433, www.escalantepark.com, $119-129 cabins, $150-189 houses, $38-49 RVs, Mar.-Nov.). The cabins have bathrooms and microwaves, mini-fridges, and coffeemakers.

A remodeled motel with a fanciful Old West theme, the **Cowboy Country Inn** (75 S. 100 W., 435/616-4066, www.cowboycountryinn.com, $80-150) is half a block off the highway and offers 22 rooms, ranging from a small "bunkhouse" with bunk beds to a two-bedroom suite.

Over $150

Head east from Escalante on Highway 12 to the landmark Kiva Koffeehouse, a quirky hilltop restaurant just east of the Boynton Overlook high above the Escalante River, and its beautiful ★ **Kiva Kottage** (Hwy. 12, milepost 73.86, 435/826-4550, www.kivakoffeehouse.com, $220, breakfast included). The two spacious and beautifully decorated guest rooms each include a remarkable

1: cabins at Escalante Outfitters 2: Escalante Yurts
3: Escalante Mercantile 4: Hell's Backbone Bridge

view of the surrounding country. With their grand views, fireplaces, and big, deep, jetted bathtubs, these rooms are wonderful places to relax after a day of exploring, and the absence of TVs makes it all the better. The Kiva is just above the spot where the Escalante River crosses Highway 12 and is a good base for hikers. You'll have to drive to Escalante or Boulder for dinner, though the rooms do have microwaves and refrigerators.

The ★ **Slot Canyons Inn B&B** (3680 W. Hwy. 12, 435/826-4901 or 866/889-8375, www.slotcanyonsinn.com, $177-227) is a newer, purpose-built lodging about 5 miles (8 km) west of Escalante on a dramatically scenic 160-acre ranch. Although the structure has adobe-like features and blends into the rustic environment, the eight guest rooms are very comfortable and modern, some with patios and balconies. A spacious pioneer cabin has also been moved to the property and restored; it sleeps six ($300). There's even the North Creek Grill (6pm-9pm Tues.-Sat. May-Oct., $18-32, reservations recommended) so you don't have to drive into Escalante for your dinner. This is a very lovely place to stay—think of it not so much as a B&B (although breakfast is included in the rates) but as an exclusive small country inn.

The newest and most upscale of Escalante's hotels is the **Canyon Country Lodge** (760 E. Hwy. 12, 435/826-4545 or 844/367-3080, https://canyoncountrylodge.com, $209), just east of town. Rooms are large and nicely appointed, and an indoor pool and outdoor hot tub await, as does a charging station for your Tesla.

If you're traveling with a family or group of friends, consider renting the architecturally striking, solar-heated **La Luz Desert Retreat** (680 W. 600 S., 888/305-4708, www.laluz. net, high season $210 for 4 people, plus $75 cleaning fee, seasonal minimum stay requirements), in a private setting just south of town. The house, designed in the Usonian tradition of Frank Lloyd Wright, can sleep up to six.

Campgrounds

Escalante Petrified Forest State Park (435/826-4466, www.stateparks.utah.gov, reservations 800/322-3770, www.reserveamerica. com, year-round, $20 tents, $28 RVs), just northwest of the town of Escalante, is conveniently located and full of attractions of its own, most notably trails passing big chunks of petrified wood and boating and swimming in the reservoir (canoe, kayak, and paddleboard rentals available). Drinking water and showers are available, as are RV hookups.

In town, you can stay at **Canyons of the Escalante RV Park** (495 W. Main St., 435/826-4959, www.canyonsofescalantervpark.com, Mar.-Nov. 15), which has simple and deluxe cabins ($54-83; the more expensive ones have half baths) and sites for tents ($18) and RVs ($34-44), plus showers and a coin laundry. **Escalante Cabins and RV Park** (680 W. Main St., 435/826-4433, www.escalantepark. com, $38-49 RVs, Mar.-Nov.) is also a good bet for RV travelers.

A couple of miles north of town in a lovely grove of cottonwoods and junipers, ★ **Escalante Yurts** (1605 N. Pine Creek Rd., 435/826-4222 or 844/200-9878, https:// escalanteyurts.lodgify.com, $285-408) offers glamping comforts in 450-900-square-foot yurts (smaller yurts sleep up to four, the larger sleep seven). Each yurt has a private bathroom, high-quality furnishings, and a private patio platform. Continental breakfast is included.

Calf Creek Campground (early Apr.-late Oct., $15) is in a pretty canyon 15.5 miles (25 km) east of Escalante on Highway 12. Lower Calf Creek Falls Trail (5.5 mi/8.9 km round-trip) begins at the campground and follows the creek upstream to the falls.

INFORMATION AND SERVICES

The **Escalante Interagency Visitor Center** (755 W. Main St., 435/826-5499, 8am-4:30pm daily), on the western edge of town, has an information center for visitors to U.S. Forest Service, BLM, and National Park Service areas around Escalante; this is also one of the best spots for information on the national monument. Hikers or bikers headed for overnight trips in the monument system can obtain permits at the information center.

Kazan Memorial Clinic (65 N. Center St., 435/826-4374) offers medical care, but isn't open on weekends. The nearest hospital is 70 miles (113 km) west in Panguitch.

GETTING THERE

Located on Highway 12, Escalante is 38 miles (61 km) east of Bryce Canyon and 23 miles (37 km) south of Boulder. A word of warning: Drive slowly through town. The local police seem to have a refined eye for out-of-towners exceeding the speed limit.

AROUND ESCALANTE

Hell's Backbone Scenic Drive

This scenic 38-mile (61-km) drive climbs high into the pine forests north of Escalante with excellent views of the distant Navajo, Fifty-Mile, and Henry Mountains. The highlight, though, is the one-lane **Hell's Backbone Bridge,** which vaults a chasm between precipitous Death Hollow and Sand Creek Canyons. You'll want to stop here for photographs of the outstanding vistas—and to quell your vertigo.

Hell's Backbone Road reaches an elevation of 9,200 feet (2,805 m) on the slopes of Roger Peak before descending to a bridge. Mule teams used this narrow ridge, with sheer canyons on either side, as a route to Boulder until the 1930s. At that time, a bridge built by the Civilian Conservation Corps allowed the first vehicles to make the trip.

To reach Hell's Backbone Road from

Escalante, turn north on 300 East and follow the initially paved road out of town. The bridge is about 25 miles (40 km) from town. Alternatively, you can turn onto Hell's Backbone Road 3 miles (4.8 km) south of Boulder on Highway 12. From this corner, the bridge is 13 miles (21 km).

Cars can usually manage the gravel and dirt road when it's dry. Snows and snowmelt, however, block the way in winter until about late May. Check with the **Escalante Interagency Visitor Center** (755 W. Main St., Escalante, 435/826-5499, 8am-4:30pm daily) for current conditions. Trails and rough dirt roads lead deeper into the backcountry to more vistas and fishing lakes.

Campgrounds

Amid aspen and ponderosa pines, Posey Lake (elev. 8,700 ft/2,650 m) is stocked with rainbow and brook trout. The adjacent **Posey Lake Campground** (www.fs.usda.gov/recarea/dixie, Memorial Day-Labor Day, $13) has drinking water. A hiking trail (2 mi/3.2 km round-trip) begins near space number 14 and climbs 400 feet (122 m) to an old fire-lookout tower, with good views of the lake and surrounding country. Posey Lake is 14 miles (22.5 km) north of Escalante, and then 2 miles (3.2 km) west on a side road.

Blue Spruce Campground (www.fs.usda.gov/recarea/dixie, $9) is another pretty spot at an elevation of 7,860 feet (2,395 m), but it has only six sites. Anglers can try for pan-size trout in a nearby stream. The campground, surrounded by blue spruce, aspen, and ponderosa pine, has drinking water Memorial Day-Labor Day; go north 19 miles (31 km) from town, then turn left and drive 0.5 mile (0.8 km).

Boulder

About 200 people live in this farming community at the base of Boulder Mountain. Ranchers began drifting in during the late 1870s, although not with the intent to form a town. By the mid-1890s, Boulder had established itself as a ranching and dairy center. Remote and hemmed in by canyons and mountains, Boulder remained one of the last communities in the country to rely on pack trains for transportation; motor vehicles couldn't drive in until the 1930s. Today, Boulder is worth a visit to see an excavated Ancestral Puebloan village and the spectacular scenery along the way, and to eat in its excellent restaurants.

FOOD

The Boulder Mountain Lodge restaurant, ★ **Hell's Backbone Grill** (Hwy. 12, 435/335-7464, http://hellsbackbonegrill. com, 4pm-9pm daily mid-Mar.-Nov., $16-33, dinner reservations strongly recommended) has gained something of a cult following across the West. Run by two American Buddhist women, supplied with vegetables from their own farm, and typically filled with well-heeled guests from Boulder Mountain Lodge, the restaurant has a menu that changes with the seasons, but you can count on finding chipotle-rubbed meat, outstanding meatloaf, tasty posole, and excellent desserts.

For simpler but still very good fare, the **Burr Trail Grill** (10 N. Hwy. 12, 435/335-7511, 11:30am-9pm daily, late Mar.-Oct., $12-25) is at the intersection of Highway 12 and Burr Trail Road. The atmospheric dining room, sided with weathered wood planking and filled with whimsical art, monument visitors, and local families, offers sophisticated soup and sandwiches for lunch, and dinner main courses such as grilled pork loin, steaks, chicken, and trout, all with subtle Southwestern spicing.

Stop by **Magnolia's Street Food** (460 N. Hwy. 12, 801/643-3510, https:// magnoliasstreetfood.com, 9am-4pm daily Mar.-Nov., $5-11) for a breakfast burrito or some lunchtime tacos. It's a food truck parked outside the Anasazi State Park Museum.

ACCOMMODATIONS

You wouldn't expect to find one of Utah's nicest places to stay in tiny Boulder, but the ★ **Boulder Mountain Lodge** (Hwy. 12, 435/355-7460 or 800/556-3446, www.boulder-utah.com, $145-340), along the highway right in town, offers the kinds of facilities and setting that make this one of the few destination lodgings in the state. The lodge's buildings are grouped around the edge of a private 15-acre pond that serves as an ad hoc wildlife refuge. You can sit on the deck or wander paths along the pond, watching and listening to the amazing variety of birds that make this spot their home. The guest rooms and suites are in handsome and modern Western-style lodges facing the pond; rooms are nicely decorated with quality furniture and bedding, and there's a central great room with a fireplace and library and a large outdoor hot tub. One of Utah's best restaurants, **Hell's Backbone Grill** (435/355-7460, http://hellsbackbonegrill. com), is on the premises.

More modest but perfectly acceptable accommodations, with no Wi-Fi, are available at **Pole's Place** (435/335-7422, www. boulderutah.com/polesplace, spring-fall, $90), across the road from Anasazi State Park. While you're there, drop into the motel's gift shop and chat with the owner about local history.

Cowboy up at the **Boulder Mountain Guest Ranch** (3621 Hells Backbone Rd., 435/355-7480, http:// bouldermountainguestranch.com), 7 miles (11.3 km) from Boulder on Hell's Backbone Road. Guests have a choice of tepees with stone flooring and a queen bed, yurts, or canvas-walled tents ($65-95), simple bunk rooms with shared baths ($87), and queen-bed guest rooms with private baths ($100-125) in the main lodge, or in freestanding cabins that can sleep up to 6-8 guests each ($235-265) with full kitchen facilities and private baths. Also in the lodge is the excellent **Sweetwater Kitchen** (open April-Oct., 5:30pm-9:30 Thurs.-Tues., $16-30, reservations recommended), open to guests and nonguests alike (continental breakfast comes with room, box lunch to go $10). This is a good base for horseback trail rides; right next door is **Hell's Backbone Ranch and Trail** (435/335-7581, www.bouldermountaintrails.com, 1.5-2-hour ride $60-75).

Campgrounds

The best bet for tent campers is **Deer Creek Campground** (www.blm.gov/visit/deer-creek-campground, year-round, $10), 6.5 miles (10.5 km) from Boulder on Burr Trail Road; bring your own drinking water. During the summer, an alternative is to head north on Highway 12 up Boulder Mountain to a cluster of Fishlake National Forest campgrounds—**Singletree** (www.recreation.gov, $12), **Pleasant Creek** ($12), and **Oak Creek** ($12).

INFORMATION AND SERVICES

A good stop for visitor information is the **Anasazi State Park Museum** (460 N. Hwy. 12, 435/335-7308, http://stateparks.utah.gov, 8am-6pm daily Apr.-Oct., 8am-4pm daily Nov.-Mar., museum admission fee $5 pp), where there's an info desk for the national monument. The two gas stations in Boulder sell groceries and snack food; at **Hills and Hollows Mini-Mart** (on the hill above Hwy. 12, 435/335-7349, www.hillshollows.com, hours vary, generally 8:30am-7pm daily), you'll find provisions as diverse as soy milk and organic cashews. Every other Friday night during the summer, Hills and Hollows fires up a wood oven to make pizzas and holds an acoustic music jam.

GETTING THERE

Take paved Highway 12 either through the canyon and slickrock country from Escalante or over Boulder Mountain from Torrey, near Capitol Reef National Park. Burr Trail Road connects Boulder with Capitol Reef National Park's southern district via the Waterpocket Fold and Circle Cliffs. A fourth way in is from Escalante on the dirt Hell's Backbone Road, which comes out 3 miles (4.8 km) west of Boulder at Highway 12.

AROUND BOULDER

Boulder Mountain Scenic Drive

Utah Highway 12 climbs high into forests of ponderosa pine, aspen, and fir on Boulder Mountain between the towns of Boulder and Torrey. Travel in winter is usually possible, although heavy snows can close the road. Viewpoints along the drive offer sweeping panoramas of Escalante canyon country, the Circle Cliffs, the Waterpocket Fold, and the Henry Mountains. Hikers and anglers can explore the alpine country of Boulder Mountain and seek out the 90 or so trout-filled lakes. The Great Western Trail, which was built with ATVs in mind, runs over Boulder Mountain to the west of the highway. The Fishlake National Forest map (Teasdale District) shows the back roads, trails, and lakes.

Campgrounds

The U.S. Forest Service has three developed campgrounds about midway along Boulder Mountain Scenic Drive: **Oak Creek** (18 mi/29 km from Boulder, elev. 8,800 ft/2,680 m, $12), **Pleasant Creek** (19 mi/31 km from Boulder, elev. 8,600 ft/2,620 m, $12), and **Singletree** (24 mi/39 km from Boulder, elev. 8,200 ft/2,500 m, www.recreation.gov, $12); the last of these is the largest of the three and the best pick for larger RVs. The season runs from about late May to mid-September with water available; the campgrounds may also be open in spring and fall without water. **Lower Bowns Reservoir** (elev. 7,000 ft/2,135 m) has primitive camping (no water, free) and fishing for rainbow and cutthroat trout; turn east and go 5 miles (8 km) on a rough dirt road (not recommended for cars) just south of Pleasant Creek Campground.

Contact the **Fremont River District Office** (138 S. Main St., Loa, 435/836-2800) for information about camping or recreation on Boulder Mountain.

Kanab

Striking scenery surrounds this small town in Utah's far south. The Vermilion Cliffs to the west and east glow with a fiery intensity at sunrise and sunset. Streams have cut splendid canyons into surrounding plateaus. The Paiutes knew the spot as *kanab*, meaning "place of the willows," and the trees still grow along Kanab Creek. Mormon pioneers arrived in the mid-1860s and tried to farm along the unpredictable creek. Irrigation difficulties culminated in the massive floods of 1883, which gouged a section of creek bed 40 feet (12 m) below its previous level in just two days. Ranching proved better suited to this rugged and arid land.

Hollywood discovered this dramatic scenery in the 1920s and has filmed more than 150 movies and TV series here since. Famous films shot hereabouts include movies as varied as *My Friend Flicka*, *The Lone Ranger*, and *The Greatest Story Ever Told*. The TV series *Gunsmoke* and *F Troop* were shot locally. Film crews have constructed several Western sets near Kanab, but most are on private land and are difficult to visit.

While most park visitors see Kanab (population 4,300) as a handy stopover on trips to Bryce, Zion, and Grand Canyon National Parks and the southern reaches of the Grand Staircase unit of the monument, a few interesting sites around town warrant more than a sleep-eat-dash visit. In fact, the presence of several nicely refurbished motels, excellent choices for dining, and a pleasantly alternative vibe in town make this one of the nicest and most affordable places to stay in southwest Utah.

SIGHTS
Moqui Cave
The natural **Moqui Cave** (U.S. 89, 5 mi/8 km north of Kanab, 435/644-8525, www.moqui-cave.com, 9am-7pm Mon.-Sat. Memorial Day-Labor Day, 10am-4pm Mon.-Sat. Labor Day-Memorial Day, $6) has been turned into a roadside tourist attraction with a large collection of Native American artifacts. Most of the arrowheads, pottery, sandals, and burial items on display have been excavated locally. A diorama recreates an Ancestral Puebloan ruin located 5 miles (8 km) away in Cottonwood Wash. Fossils, rocks, and minerals are exhibited as well, including what's claimed to be one of the largest fluorescent mineral displays in the country. There's even a Prohibition-era speakeasy (not open for drinks). The collections and a gift shop are within a spacious cave that stays pleasantly cool even in the hottest weather.

Best Friends Animal Sanctuary
Best Friends Animal Sanctuary (5001 Angel Canyon Rd., 435/644-2001, www.bestfriends.org, 8am-5pm daily, check website for tour times, donations accepted, reservations required), the largest no-kill animal shelter in the country, takes in unwanted or abused animals and provides whatever rehabilitation is possible. Giant octagonal doghouses are filled with animals no one else wants: former research animals, aggressive dogs, old dogs, sick dogs, and dogs who have been abused or neglected. There are also plenty of cats, rabbits, birds, pot-bellied

Kanab

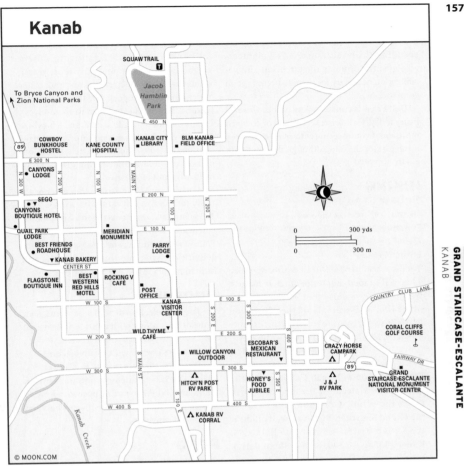

To Bryce Canyon and
Zion National Parks

SQUAW TRAIL

Jacob Hamblin Park

E 450 N

89

COWBOY BUNKHOUSE HOSTEL

KANE COUNTY HOSPITAL

KANAB CITY LIBRARY

BLM KANAB FIELD OFFICE

E 300 N

CANYONS LODGE

N 300 W
N 200 W
N 100 W
N MAIN ST
N 100 E
N 200 E

E 200 N

SEGO

CANYONS BOUTIQUE HOTEL

E 100 N

QUAIL PARK LODGE

MERIDIAN MONUMENT

BEST FRIENDS ROADHOUSE

PARRY LODGE

KANAB BAKERY

CENTER ST

FLAGSTONE BOUTIQUE INN

BEST WESTERN RED HILLS MOTEL

ROCKING V CAFÉ

POST OFFICE

W 100 S

KANAB VISITOR CENTER

E 100 E

S 200 E
S 300 E

WILD THYME CAFÉ

W 200 S

E 200 S

S MAIN ST

ESCOBAR'S MEXICAN RESTAURANT

S 400 E

CRAZY HORSE CAMPARK

WILLOW CANYON OUTDOOR

W 300 S

E 300 S

COUNTRY CLUB LANE

CORAL CLIFFS GOLF COURSE

FAIRWAY DR

89

HITCH'N POST RV PARK

HONEY'S FOOD JUBILEE

S 350 E

J & J RV PARK

GRAND STAIRCASE-ESCALANTE NATIONAL MONUMENT VISITOR CENTER

W 400 S

S 100 E
E 400 S

KANAB RV CORRAL

Kanab Creek

0   300 yds
0   300 m

© MOON.COM

pigs, and horses. Many animals are adopted out, but even the unadoptable ones are given homes for life, with plenty of care and attention from the sanctuary's roster of employees and volunteers.

The shelter's origins date back to the 1970s, when a group of animal lovers began trying to prevent unadoptable animals from being euthanized by rescuing animals that were about to be put to sleep by shelters, rehabilitating them as necessary, and finding them homes.

In the early 1980s this group of dedicated rescuers bought land in Angel Canyon just north of Kanab and, with their motley crew of unadoptable animals, established this sanctuary. Now over 1,600 animals live here at any given time, and the shelter is the county's largest employer, with more than 200 staff members caring for the animals and the grounds.

But even the large staff can't take care of all of the animals' needs. The shelter's volunteers spend anywhere from a couple of days to a couple of months feeding, walking, petting, and cleaning up after the animals. Kanab is usually full of shelter volunteers, who are spending their vacations here. Volunteers also give the animals the attention and socialization necessary for them to become good companions.

Best Friends runs a variety of tours several times a day. Call for reservations or to learn more about volunteering at the shelter. There's no charge for the tour, although donations are gladly accepted.

HIKING
Squaw Trail

Distance: 1.5 miles (2.4 km) one-way
Duration: 2 hours
Elevation change: 800 feet (245 m)
Effort: moderate
Trailhead: north end of 100 East, near the city park

This well-graded, but unfortunately named, trail provides a close look at the geology, plant life, and animals of the Vermilion Cliffs just north of town. To cut the hike down by 1 mile (1.6 km) and cut the elevation gain in half, turn around at the first overlook, where views to the south take in Kanab, Fredonia, Kanab Canyon, and the vast Kaibab Plateau. At the top, look north to see the White, Gray, and Pink Cliffs of the Grand Staircase. Pick up a trail guide at the **Kanab Visitor Center** (745 E. U.S. 89, Kanab, 435/644-1300, 8am-4:30pm daily). Brochures may also be available at the trailhead. Bring water with you, and in summer, try to get a very early start.

TOURS

Kanab is central to an amazing number of sights, and if you'd like the pros to handle the logistics of your visit, turn to **Dreamland Safari Tours** (435/412-1615, www.dreamlandtours.net, tours start around $90 adult, $45 child). Dreamland offers half-day and full-day tours of sights that include slots canyon hikes, petroglyphs, and dinosaur tracks.

ENTERTAINMENT AND EVENTS

A unique Kanab event is the **Sighthound Shivoo/Greyhound Gathering** (www.greyhoundgang.com, mid-May most years), when hundreds of greyhounds and other sighthounds converge on the town accompanied by their people (a breed to themselves). Events include a parade, a race, and a howl-in. The Greyhound Gang, a nonprofit organization dedicated to the rescue, rehabilitation, and adoption of former racing greyhounds, hosts this unlikely festival.

Also during May, Kanab is the center of activity for the **Amazing Earthfest** (435/644-3735, http://amazingearthfest.com), which celebrates land and life on the Colorado Plateau with lectures, workshops, and outdoor activities delving into the area's natural and human history. Most events are free.

SHOPPING

Find a good selection of books, camping gear, and clothing, along with a little coffee bar, at **Willow Canyon Outdoor** (263 S. 100 E., 435/644-8884, www.willowcanyon.com).

Denny's Wigwam (78 E. Center St., 435/644-2452, www.dennyswigwam.com) is a landmark Old West trading post with a broad selection of Western jewelry, cowboy hats and boots, and souvenirs.

FOOD

Start the day at ★ **Kanab Creek Bakery** (238 West Center St., 435/644-5689, https://kanabcreekbakery.com, 6:30am-5pm Tues.-Sun., breakfast $7-11), a European-style bakery-café operated by a Belgian-born woman. The breads and pastries are thoroughly authentic, and you'll have the option of omelets or quiche for breakfast, or fresh sandwiches and crepes for lunch.

★ **Sego** (190 N. 300 W., 435/644-5680, www.segokanab.com, 6pm-10pm Mon.-Sat., $11-25) is a surprisingly good find in this little town. Located in the Canyon Boutique Hotel, it has a cutting-edge menu, with starters of artisanal toast or a pork belly and watermelon salad and seafood dishes such as shrimp with mango puree and mandarin orange salsa. Most of the dishes are small plates, designed for sharing (expect the bill to run up as you order more and more!).

Another good bet is the ★ **Rocking V Café** (97 W. Center St., 435/644-8001, www.rockingvcafe.com, 11:30am-10pm Thurs.-Mon., dinner $18-48). The setting is casual, and the food has a modern Southwestern flair. Rocking V, which caters to vegans as well as steak lovers, pays homage to the "slow food" movement and makes everything from scratch. Be sure to check out the art gallery upstairs.

It's small and often crowded, but friendly, family-run **Escobar's Mexican Restaurant** (373 E. 300 S., 435/644-3739, 11am-9pm Sun.-Fri., $11-25) is the place for a Mexican lunch or dinner.

Wild Thyme Café (198 S. 100 E., 435/644-2848, https://wildthymekanab.com, noon-9pm daily, $12-31) focuses on Southwest and Cajun flavors, supported by the restaurant's home-grown greens and vegetables. Pistachio chicken with poblano cream is a standout. No liquor is served. Call to confirm winter hours.

Travelers setting out into the national monument from Kanab should note that this is the best place for many miles around to stock up on groceries. **Honey's Marketplace** (260 E. 300 S., 435/644-5877, 7am-10pm Mon.-Sat.) is a good grocery store on the way out of town to the east; note that it's closed on Sunday.

ACCOMMODATIONS

While a number of new hotels from the major chains line the edge of town, Kanab is blessed with a number of carefully refurbished vintage motor court hotels to fit diverse tastes and budgets. They're fun and within easy walking distance of downtown's notable dining options. Reservations are a good idea during the busy summer months, and during mid-May, when most rooms are occupied by greyhounds and their people. Almost all the lodgings are on U.S. 89, which follows 300 West, Center, 100 East, and 300 South through town.

Under $100

Framed by red cliffs, the low-slung **Cowboy Bunkhouse Hostel** (210 W. 300 N., 435/644-8244, www.thecowboybunkhouse.com, $30-75) pays homage to the cowboy life. The spartan but clean accommodations range from dorm beds ($30 pp) to en-suite private rooms for two ($60-75) to family bunkrooms ($60-125). Pets can stay for a $10, though they're not allowed in dorm rooms.

$100-150

Relive Kanab's Hollywood heyday at the **Parry Lodge** (89 E. Center St., 435/627-5308 or 877/386-4383, www.parrylodge.com, $142-193). Built during Kanab's glory days as a movie-making center, the Parry Lodge was where the stars and movie crews stayed; more than 80 years later, this is still a pleasantly old-fashioned place to spend the night, and it has lots of character. At the very least you'll want to stroll through the lobby, where lots of photos of the celebrities who once stayed here are displayed.

★ **Canyons Lodge** (236 U.S. 89 N., 844/322-8824, www.canyonslodge.com, $89-139) is an extensively renovated motel with pleasant log cabin-style guest rooms, all with fridges and microwaves, plus an outdoor pool and breakfast included. What was once a typical mom-and-pop motel is now a stylish place to stay, though most rooms are still relatively small, as you'd expect in an older property. Several rooms here are pet-friendly, and because it's a popular place for visitors to Best Friends Animal Sanctuary to stay, it's best to reserve in advance. Canyons Lodge is one of several properties in town that have been renovated by local hotel group Canyons Collection (www.thecanyonscollection.com).

Another offering from Canyons Collection, the **Quail Park Lodge** (125 U.S. 89 N., 435/215-1447, www.quailparklodge.com,

$99-119), is a tricked out and updated early 1960s motel, with a well-thought-out combination of vintage kitsch, mid-century modern, and quality linens and toiletries. The motel has a pool and accepts pets. The lodge also has cruiser bicycles to rent (free to guests).

Over $150

Most of Kanab's accommodations accept dogs, but only the ★ **Best Friends Roadhouse** (30 N. 300 W., 435/644-3400, https://www.bestfriendsroadhouse.org, $159-289) offers dog-washing stations, a fenced dog park, snuggle zones, pet walkers (for a fee), and a shuttle to the Best Friends Animal Sanctuary. The sparse (and easy to clean) décor is attractive, with comfy pet beds; the most expensive room is a two-story kitchenette suite. A vegan continental breakfast is included at the adjoining mercantile, which also sells snacks for pets and their people.

A Canyons Collection property, the ★ **Canyons Boutique Hotel** (190 N. 300 W., 435/644-8660, www.canyonshotel.com, $149-169) seems to have taken its color scheme from the nearby Coral Pink Sand Dunes, but the decor is actually pretty classy and the beds are comfy. The entire top floor is taken up by a three-bedroom penthouse ($259), and most rooms have large spa bathtubs; breakfast is included for all guests.

Another stylish entry from Canyons Collections is **Flagstone Boutique Inn and Suites** (233 W. Center St., 435/644-2020 or 844/322-8824, www.theflagstoneinn.com, $159-189), a former 1940s motor lodge that's been updated with contemporary pizzazz. A number of rooms have full or partial kitchens and are set up for extended stays, so daily maid service is not provided. The on-site Peekaboo Canyon Wood-fired Kitchen (open for three meals daily) makes vegetarian and vegan pizza and other specialties. This is a perfect spot if you are hubbing out of Kanab during your parks exploration.

Especially nice if you're traveling with a group that plans to spend several nights in Kanab are the **Kanab Garden Cottages** (various locations, 435/644-2020, www.kanabcottages.com, $149-189). These beautifully furnished three- or four-bedroom houses can easily sleep up to eight and are pet friendly and within walking distance of town.

North of Kanab, at Mount Carmel Junction, is the **Best Western East Zion Thunderbird Resort** (4530 State St., Mount Carmel, 435/648-2203, www.bestwestern.com, $160-210), with a pool, a nine-hole golf course, and a restaurant. This pleasant crossroads motel is convenient if you're heading to Zion or Bryce Canyon National Parks. All guest rooms have balconies or patios.

Northwest of Kanab, just a few miles east of Zion National Park, are the very appealing log cabins and lodges of the **Zion Mountain Ranch** (E. Hwy. 9, 435/648-2555 or 866/648-2555, www.zmr.com, cabins starting at $200). The cabins all have king beds and private baths plus microwaves and fridges; family lodges offer two or three bedrooms; the larger lodges can sleep up to 12. The setting is great, with expansive views, a buffalo herd, and a decent on-site restaurant. Horseback riding and other outdoor recreation are offered. The lodging options are boggling; explore the selection online and then give the ranch a call to discuss all the alternatives.

Campgrounds

The campground at **Coral Pink Sand Dunes State Park** (435/648-2800, www.stateparks.utah.gov, $25-35) has restrooms with showers, paved pull-through sites, and a dump station. It's a pleasant, shady spot, but it can hum with ATV traffic. It's open year-round, but the water is shut off from late October until Easter; winter campers must bring their own. Reservations are recommended for the busy Memorial Day-Labor Day season. The campground is about 10 miles (16 km) due west of Kanab, but the two are not directly connected by a road. Reach the campground by turning west off U.S. 89 about 10 miles (16 km) north

1: Canyons Lodge **2:** Coral Pink Sand Dunes State Park

of Kanab onto Hancock Road and following it 12 miles (19.3 km) to the campground. The route is well marked by signs.

Just north of the state park, the BLM maintains **Ponderosa Grove Campground** ($5) on the north edge of the dunes. There's no water here. From Kanab, head 8 miles (12.9 km) north on U.S. 89, turn west onto Hancock Road (between mileposts 72 and 73), and continue 7.3 miles (11.7 km) to the campground.

The **Kanab RV Corral** (483 S. 100 E., 435/644-5330, www.kanabrvcorral.com, year-round, $35-46) has RV sites (no tents) with hot showers, a pool, and laundry service. The **Hitch'n Post RV Park** (196 E. 300 S., 435/644-2142, www.hitchnpostrvpark.com, $23 tents, $38 RVs, $50-55 cabins) has showers. The **J & J RV Park** (584 E. 300 S., 435/899-1956, https://jandjrvpark.com, mid-Apr.-late Oct., $38-43 RVs) is a newer campground without much shade; it's not so appealing for tent campers, but is a good bet for larger RVs.

INFORMATION AND SERVICES

Staff members at the **Kane County Visitor Center** (78 S. 100 E., 435/644-5033, www.visitsouthernutah.com, 8am-7pm Mon.-Fri., 8am-5pm Sat.) offer literature and advice for services in Kanab and travel in Kane County. For information about the Grand Staircase and Kaiparowits Plateau units of the monument, go to the **BLM Kanab Visitor Center** (745 E. U.S. 89, Kanab, 435/644-1300, 8am-4:30pm daily) on the east edge of town.

GETTING THERE

Situated on U.S. 89, Kanab is 15 miles (24 km) south of Mount Carmel Junction (Hwy. 9 and U.S. 89), a total of 40 miles (64 km) from Zion National Park, and just 7 miles (11.3 km) north of the Arizona-Utah border. From Kanab, U.S. 89 continues southeast, providing access to the southern reaches of

Grand Staircase and Kaiparowits Plateau and, 74 miles (119 km) later, Glen Canyon Dam at Page, Arizona.

CORAL PINK SAND DUNES STATE PARK

Churning air currents funneled by surrounding mountains have deposited huge sand dunes in this valley west of Kanab. The ever-changing dunes, formed from eroded Navajo sandstone, reach heights of several hundred feet and cover about 2,000 of the park's 3,700 acres. Different areas in **Coral Pink Sand Dunes State Park** (435/648-2800, www.stateparks.utah.gov, day use $10 per vehicle, camping $25-35) have been set aside for hiking, off-road vehicles, and camping.

From Kanab, the shortest route is to go north 8 miles (12.9 km) on U.S. 89 to Hancock Road (between mileposts 72 and 73), turn left, and travel 9.3 miles (15 km) on the paved road to its end, then turn left (south) and go 1 mile on a paved road into the park. From the north, you can follow U.S. 89 for 3.5 miles (5.6 km) south of Mount Carmel Junction (Hwy. 9 and U.S. 89), then turn right (south) and go 11 miles (17.7 km) on a paved road. The back road from Cane Beds in Arizona has about 16 miles (26 km) of gravel and dirt with some sandy spots; ask a park ranger for current conditions.

The canyon country surrounding the park has good opportunities for hiking and off-road vehicle travel; the Kanab Visitor Center can supply maps and information. Drivers with 4WD vehicles can turn south on Sand Springs Road (1.5 mi/2.4 km east of Ponderosa Grove Campground) and go 1 mile (1.6 km) to Sand Springs, and another 4 miles (6.4 km) to the South Fork Indian Canyon Pictograph Site, in a pretty canyon. Visitors may not enter the Kaibab-Paiute Indian Reservation, which is south across the Arizona state line, from this side.

Capitol Reef National Park

Capitol Reef gets far less attention than Utah's other national parks, and its comparative lack of crowds enhances its many charms, which include excellent hiking and splendid scenery. Sculpted rock layers in a rainbow of colors put on a fine show. You'll find these same rocks throughout much of the Four Corners region, but their artistic variety has no equal outside this park.

About 70 million years ago, gigantic forces within the earth began to uplift, squeeze, and fold more than a dozen rock formations into the central feature of the park today—the Waterpocket Fold, so named for the many small pools of water trapped by the tilted strata. Erosion has since carved spires, graceful curves, canyons, and arches. The Waterpocket Fold extends 100 miles (161 km) between Thousand Lake

Highlights

Look for ★ to find recommended sights, activities, dining, and lodging.

★ **Savor the Sunset:** Watch the sun sink into the west from **Sunset Point,** while enjoying panoramic views of the Fremont River gorge, the Capitol Reef cliffs, and the distant Henry Mountains (page 168).

★ **Take the Scenic Drive:** Capitol Reef's 21-mile (34-km) round-trip Scenic Drive encompasses not only beautiful scenery and fascinating geology, but also human history, pioneer sites, and even fresh fruit in season (page 168).

★ **Follow Notom-Bullfrog Road:** Driving this road exposes the Waterpocket Fold's geologic wonders. You're rewarded with distinctive panoramas and scenic hikes into side canyons (page 171).

★ **Hike through Wildflowers:** The **Grand Wash Trail** offers easy hiking, great scenery, and an abundance of wildflowers along the way into the Narrows, where canyon walls rise to 200 feet (61 m) (page 177).

★ **Hike Cohab Canyon Trail:** After a short steep section, this trail enters a beautiful canyon, with many narrow side canyons along the way (page 177).

★ **See Rock Art:** From **Capitol Gorge,** you can hike past petroglyphs left by the Fremont people and a Mormon "pioneer register" on your way to natural water pockets (page 178).

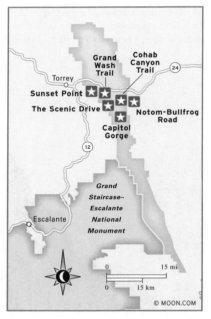

© MOON.COM

Capitol Reef National Park

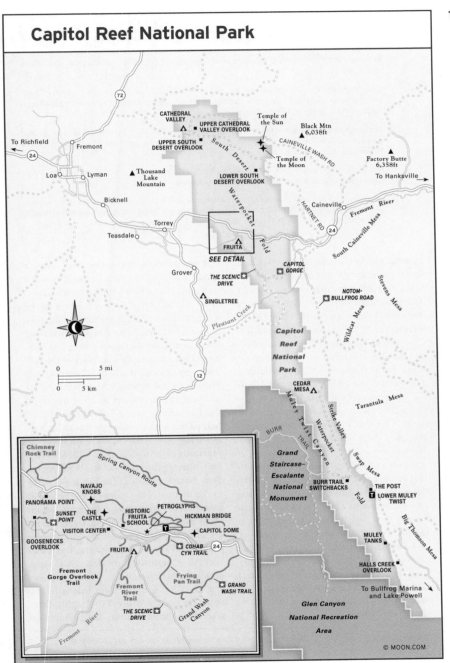

© MOON.COM

Capitol Reef in One Day

- Wake up with a walk among the pioneer-era orchards at the cliff-lined village of **Fruita** and take in the **visitors center.**

- Hike the 2.5-mile (4-km) round-trip **Fremont River Trail,** which starts at the Fruita Campground and climbs from the oasis-like valley up to a viewpoint that takes in the orchards, Boulder Mountain, and the reef's arched back.

- Unpack your picnic lunch at the shady picnic area of the **Gifford Farmhouse,** a renovated pioneer home in the verdant Fremont River valley. Stop in the farmhouse for a piece of pie or homemade baked goods for the road.

- For an after-lunch hike, the **Capitol Gorge** cuts a chasm through the Capitol Reef lined with petroglyphs, pioneer graffiti, and towering rock walls.

- Other than pie and snacks at the Gifford Farmhouse, there are no dining options in the park, so you'll need to drive 11 miles (17.7 km) west to nearby Torrey for dinner. Enjoy something healthy and locally grown at **Capitol Reef Inn and Cafe** or go upscale at **Hunt & Gather.**

Mountain to the north and Lake Powell to the south. (Look for it if you ever fly south from Salt Lake City—we never really grasped its magnitude until we flew over it on the way to Mexico.) The most spectacular cliffs and rock formations of the Waterpocket Fold form Capitol Reef, located north of Pleasant Creek and curving northwest across the Fremont River toward Thousand Lake Mountain. The reef was named by explorers who found the Waterpocket Fold a barrier to travel and likened it to a reef blocking passage on the ocean. One specific rounded sandstone hill reminded them of the U.S. Capitol dome in Washington DC.

Roads and hiking trails in the park provide access to the colorful rock layers and to the plants and wildlife that live here. You'll also see remnants of the area's long human history—petroglyphs and storage bins of the prehistoric Fremont people, a schoolhouse and other structures built by Mormon pioneers, and several small uranium mines from the 20th century. Legends tell of Butch Cassidy and other outlaw members of the Wild Bunch who hid out in these remote canyons in the 1890s.

Even travelers short on time will enjoy a quick look at visitors center exhibits and a drive on Highway 24 through an impressive cross section of Capitol Reef cut by the Fremont River. You can see more of the park on the Scenic Drive, a narrow paved road that heads south from the visitors center. The drive passes beneath spectacular cliffs of the reef and enters Grand Wash and Capitol Gorge Canyons; allow at least 1.5 hours for the 21-mile (34-km) round-trip and any side trips. The fair-weather Notom-Bullfrog Road (about half paved, with paved segments at both its north and south ends) heads south along the other side of the reef for almost 70 miles (113 km), offering fine views of the Waterpocket Fold. Burr Trail Road (dirt inside the park) in the south actually climbs over the fold in a steep set of switchbacks, connecting Notom Road with the town of Boulder. Only drivers with high-clearance vehicles can explore Cathedral Valley in the park's northern district. All of these roads provide access to viewpoints and hiking trails.

Expect hot summer days (highs in the upper 80s and low 90s) and cool nights. Late-afternoon thunderstorms are common in

Previous: dusk at Capitol Reef; "Welcome to Capitol Reef National Park"; the Cohab Canyon Trail.

July-August; be alert for impending storms, which can bring flash flooding. Winter brings cool days (highs in the 40s) and night temperatures in the low 20s and teens. Snow accents the colored rocks while rarely hindering traffic on the main highway. Winter travel on the back roads and trails may be halted by snow, but it soon melts when the sun comes out. Annual precipitation averages only seven inches, peaking in the late-summer thunderstorm season.

PLANNING YOUR TIME

Many Southern Utah travelers treat Capitol Reef as a pass-through, and indeed, it's easy to get a feel for the park by taking a short hike off Highway 24, perhaps just the walk out to Goosenecks and Sunset Point. But a short visit here may leave you longing for more. On a one-day visit, be sure to stop at the visitors center for the short film, hike either Grand Wash or Capitol Gorge, and spend some time exploring the park's human history, from petroglyphs left by the Fremont people to the Fruita blacksmith shop. It's easy to spend two or three days camping at the Fruita campground or staying in nearby Torrey and taking day hikes in the park's core district. But if you've got the proper vehicle, after a couple of days you'll want to explore the Notom-Bullfrog Road. If you're just driving, this is easy to do in a day; if you get out of the car to explore every canyon, it can take all the time you have.

Exploring the Park

The most accessible part of **Capitol Reef National Park** (435/425-3791, www.nps.gov/care, $20 per vehicle for travel on scenic drive, $10 cyclists and pedestrians, $15 motorcyclists) is along Highway 24, about 11 miles (17.7 km) east of Torrey. Several trails start right off the highway, which means that it's not necessary to pay the admission fee to get a taste of this park.

VISITORS CENTER

At the **visitors center** (Hwy. 24, 8am-6pm daily mid-May-Sept., 8am-4:30pm daily Oct.-May), start with the 15-minute film that introduces Capitol Reef's natural wonders and history. Rock samples and diagrams illustrate the park's geologic formations, and photos identify local plants and birds. Prehistoric Fremont artifacts on display include petroglyph replicas, sheepskin moccasins, pottery, basketry, stone knives, spear and arrow points, and bone jewelry. Other historical exhibits outline exploration and early Mormon settlement.

Hikers can pick up a map of trails that are near the visitors center and of longer routes in the northern and southern areas of the park; naturalists will want the checklists of plants, birds, mammals, and other wildlife, while history buffs can learn more about the area's settlement and the founding of the park. Rangers offer talks, campfire programs, and other special events from Easter through October; the bulletin board outside the visitors center lists what's going on. The visitors center is on Highway 24 at the turnoff for Fruita Campground and the Scenic Drive.

ALONG HIGHWAY 24

From the west, Highway 24 drops from the broad mountain valley near Torrey onto Sulphur Creek, with dramatic rock formations soaring to the horizon. A huge amphitheater of stone rings the basin, with formations such as Twin Rocks, Chimney Rock, and the Castle glowing in deep red and yellow tones. Ahead, the canyon narrows as the Fremont River slips between the cliffs to carve its chasm through the Waterpocket Fold.

Panorama Point

Take in the incredible view from Panorama

Point, 2.5 miles (4 km) west of the visitors center on the south side of Highway 24. Follow signs south for 250 yards to Panorama Point and views of Capitol Reef, the distant Henry Mountains to the east, and looming Boulder Mountain to the west. The large black basalt boulders were swept down from Boulder Mountain to the reef as part of giant debris flows between 8,000 and 200,000 years ago.

Goosenecks Overlook
On a gravel road 1 mile (1.6 km) south of Panorama Point are the Goosenecks of Sulphur Creek. A short trail leads to Goosenecks Overlook (elev. 6,400 ft/1,950 m) on the rim for dizzying views of the creek below. Canyon walls display shades of yellow, green, brown, and red.

TOP EXPERIENCE

★ Sunset Point
Enjoy panoramic views of the Fremont River gorge, the Capitol Reef cliffs, and the distant Henry Mountains at **Sunset Point.** Plan your evening around viewing the sunset; it's worth hanging out for the whole show. From the Goosenecks Overlook parking area, it's an easy 0.3-mile (0.5-km) hike across the slickrock to Sunset Point. There's a sign at the trailhead. Bring a flashlight and use caution when hiking back in the dark.

Historic Fruita School
Remnants of the pioneer community of Fruita stretch along the narrow Fremont River Canyon. The Fruita Schoolhouse is just east of the visitors center on the north side of Highway 24. Early settlers completed this one-room log structure, housing grades one through eight, in 1896. Mormon church meetings, dances, town meetings, elections, and other community gatherings took place here. A lack of students caused the school to close in 1941. Although the schoolhouse is locked, you can peer inside the windows and take photos. You can also listen to stories about the Fruita Schoolhouse on audioposts.

Fremont Petroglyphs
Farther down the canyon, 1.2 miles (1.9 km) east of the visitors center on the north side of Highway 24, are several panels of Fremont petroglyphs; watch for the road signs and parking area. Several mountain sheep and human figures with headdresses decorate the cliff. You can see more petroglyphs by walking to the left and right along the cliff face. Stay on the trail, and do not climb the talus slope. During the summer, rangers give talks about Fremont culture at 3pm daily.

Behunin Cabin
Behunin Cabin is 6.2 miles (10 km) east of the visitors center on the south side of Highway 24. Elijah Cutlar Behunin used blocks of sandstone to build this cabin around 1882. For several years, Behunin, his wife, and 11 of their 13 children shared this sturdy but quite small cabin (the kids slept outside). They moved on when flooding made life too difficult. Small openings allow a look inside the dirt-floored structure, but no furnishings remain.

TOP EXPERIENCE

★ THE SCENIC DRIVE
Turn south from Highway 24 at the visitors center to experience some of the reef's best scenery and to learn more about its geology. A quick tour of this 21-mile (34-km) out-and-back trip requires about 1.5 hours, but several hiking trails may tempt you to extend your stay. It's worth picking up a brochure at the visitors center for descriptions of geology along the road. The Scenic Drive is paved, although side roads have gravel surfaces. Note that drivers must pay the $20 park entrance fee to travel this road.

Fruita
In the Fruita Historic District, you'll first pass orchards and several of Fruita's buildings. A

1: Panorama Point **2:** Fremont petroglyphs **3:** the Notom-Bullfrog Road **4:** Fruita orchards

The Scenic Drive

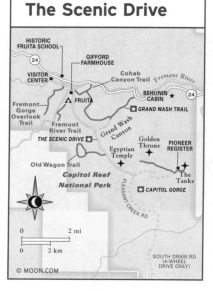

HISTORIC
FRUITA SCHOOL
24
GIFFORD
FARMHOUSE
VISITOR
CENTER
Cohab
Canyon Trail
Fremont River
BEHUNIN
CABIN
24
Fremont
Gorge
Overlook
Trail
FRUITA
GRAND WASH TRAIL
Fremont
River Trail
*Grand Wash
Canyon*
THE SCENIC DRIVE
Golden
Throne
PIONEER
REGISTER
Egyptian
Temple
Old Wagon Trail
*Capitol Reef
National Park*
The
Tanks
PLEASANT CREEK RD
CAPITOL GORGE

0   2 mi

0   2 km

SOUTH DRAW RD
(4-WHEEL
DRIVE ONLY)

© MOON.COM

blacksmith shop (0.7 mi/1.1 km from the visitors center, on the right) displays tools, harnesses, farm machinery, and Fruita's first tractor. The tractor didn't arrive until 1940, long after the rest of the country had modernized. In a recording, a rancher tells about living and working in Fruita. The nearby orchards and fields are still maintained using old-time farming techniques.

Ripple Rock Nature Center, just under 1 mile (1.6 km) south of the visitors center, has activities and exhibits for kids, many centering on pioneer life. Kids can also earn certification as Junior Rangers and Junior Geologists.

The **Gifford Farmhouse** (8am-5pm mid-Mar.-Oct., free), 1 mile (1.6 km) south on the Scenic Drive, is typical of rural Utah farmhouses of the early 1900s. Cultural demonstrations and handmade baked goods (pie!) and gifts are available. A picnic area is just beyond; with fruit trees and grass, this is a pretty spot for lunch. A short trail crosses orchards and the Fremont River to the **Historic Fruita School.**

Grand Wash

The Scenic Drive leaves the Fremont River valley and climbs a desert slope, with the rock walls of the Waterpocket Fold rising to the east. Turn east to explore Grand Wash, a dry channel etched through the sandstone. A dirt road follows the twisting gulch 1 mile (1.6 km), with sheer rock walls rising along the sandy streambed. At the road's end, an easy hiking trail follows the wash 2.5 miles (4 km) to its mouth along Highway 24.

Back on the paved Scenic Drive, continue south past Slickrock Divide to where the rock lining the reef deepens into a ruby red and forms odd columns and spires that resemble statuary. Called the **Egyptian Temple,** this is one of the most striking and colorful areas along the road.

Capitol Gorge

Capitol Gorge is at the end of the Scenic Drive, 10.7 miles (17.2 km) from the visitors center. Capitol Gorge is a dry canyon through Capitol Reef, much like Grand Wash. Believe it or not, narrow, twisting Capitol Gorge was the route of the main state highway through south-central Utah for 80 years. Mormon pioneers laboriously cleared a path so wagons could get through, a task they repeated every time flash floods rolled in a new set of boulders. Cars bounced their way down the canyon until 1962, when Highway 24 opened, but few traces of the old road remain today. Walking is easy along the gravel riverbed, but don't enter if storms threaten. An easy 1-mile (1.6-km) saunter down the gorge will take day hikers past petroglyphs and a "register" rock where pioneers carved their names. If you're lucky, you may get a glimpse of desert bighorn sheep in this area. Native to the area and often depicted in rock art, the sheep had disappeared from the park but were successfully reintroduced in the 1990s.

Pleasant Creek Road

The Scenic Drive curves east toward Capitol Gorge and onto Pleasant Creek Road (turn right 8.3 miles from the visitors center), which continues south below the face of the reef. After 3 miles (4.8 km), the sometimes rough dirt road passes Sleeping Rainbow-Floral Ranch (closed to the public) and ends at Pleasant Creek. A rugged road for 4WD vehicles—South Draw Road—continues on the other side, but it is much too rough for cars. Floral Ranch dates back to the early years of settlement at Capitol Reef. In 1939 it became the Sleeping Rainbow Guest Ranch, from the translation of the Native American name for Waterpocket Fold. Now the ranch belongs to the park and is used as a field research station by students and faculty of Utah Valley University. Pleasant Creek's perennial waters begin high on Boulder Mountain to the west and cut a scenic canyon completely through Capitol Reef. Hikers can head downstream through the 3-mile-long canyon and then return the way they went in, or continue another 3 miles (4.8 km) cross-country to Notom Road.

NORTH DISTRICT

Only the most adventurous travelers enter the remote canyons and desert country of the park's northern district. The few roads cannot be negotiated by 4WD vehicles, let alone ordinary cars, in wet weather. In good weather, high-clearance vehicles (good clearance is more important than four-wheel drive) can enter the region from the east, north, and west. The roads lead through stately sandstone monoliths of Cathedral Valley, volcanic remnants, badlands country, many low mesas, and vast sand flats. Foot travel allows closer inspection of these features or lengthy excursions into the canyons of Polk, Deep, and Spring Creeks, which cut deeply into the flanks of Thousand Lake Mountain.

Mountain bikers enjoy these challenging roads as well, but they must stay on established roads. Much of the north district is good for horseback riding too.

The district's two main roads—Hartnett Road and Cathedral Road (aka Caineville Wash Rd.)—combine with a short stretch of Highway 24 to form a loop, with a campground at their junction. **Cathedral Valley Campground**'s six sites (no fee, no water) provide a place to stop for the night; rangers won't permit car camping elsewhere in the district. The campground is on the 4WD Cathedral Valley loop road about 36 miles (58 km) from the visitors center (from the park entrance, head 12 miles (19.3 km) east on Highway 24 to mile marker 91, turn north and ford the Fremont River, and then follow Hartnett Road about 24 mi/39 km to the campground); check on road conditions at the visitors center before heading out. The **Upper Cathedral Valley Trail**, just below the campground, is a 1-mile (1.6-km) walk offering excellent views of the Cathedrals. Backcountry hikers must have a **permit** and camp at least 0.5 mile (0.8 km) from the nearest road. Be prepared to take care of yourself in this remote district; **cell phone service** is **limited** or non-existent. (The nearest **pay phones** are at the Visitor Center or Fruita Campground.) Guides to the area can be purchased at the visitors center.

SOUTH DISTRICT
★ Notom-Bullfrog Road

Capitol Reef is only a small part of the Waterpocket Fold. By taking the Notom-Bullfrog Road, you'll see over 70 miles (113 km) of the fold's eastern side. This route crosses some of the younger geologic layers, such as those of the Morrison Formation, which form colorful hills. In other places, eroded layers of the Waterpocket Fold jut up at 70-degree angles. The Henry Mountains to the east and the many canyons on both sides of the road add to the memorable panoramas. The northernmost 10 miles (16 km) of the road have been paved, and about 25 miles (40 km) are paved on the southern end near Bullfrog, a settlement on the shores of Lake Powell. The rest of the road is dirt and gravel, and it can get pretty washboarded and bumpy. Most cars should have no trouble negotiating this road in good weather. Keep an eye on the weather and contact the visitors center for current road conditions before setting out,

The Waterpocket Fold

The Waterpocket Fold is a vast wrinkle nearly 100 miles (161 km) long.

About 65 million years ago, well before the Colorado Plateau uplifted, sedimentary rock layers in south-central Utah buckled, forming a steep-sided monocline, a rock fold with one very steep side in an area of otherwise nearly horizontal layers. A monocline is a "step-up" in the rock layers along an underlying fault. The rock layers on the west side of the Waterpocket Fold have been lifted more than 7,000 feet (2,134 m) higher than the layers to the east. The 100-mile-long fold was then subjected to millions of years of erosion, which slowly removed the upper layers to reveal the warped sedimentary layers at its base. Continued erosion of the sandstone has left many basins, or "water pockets," along the fold. These seasonal water sources, often called "water tanks," are used by desert animals, and they were a water source for prehistoric people. Erosion of the tilted rock layers continues today, forming colorful cliffs, massive domes, soaring spires, stark monoliths, twisting canyons, and graceful arches. Getting a sense of the Waterpocket Fold requires some off-pavement driving. The best viewpoint is along **Burr Trail Road,** which climbs up the fold between Boulder and Notom-Bullfrog Road.

though: The dirt-and-gravel surface is usually OK for cars when dry but can be dangerous for any vehicle when wet, and sandy spots and washouts may present a problem for low-clearance vehicles. Have a full tank of gas and carry extra water and food; no services are available between Highway 24 and Bullfrog Marina. Stop at the visitors center for information sheets if you're planning to hike or canyoneer in the slot canyons; a permit is required for overnight backcountry camping. Features and mileage along the drive from north to south include the following:

- **Mile 0.0:** The turnoff from Highway 24 is 9.2 miles (14.8 km) east of the visitors center and 30.2 miles (48.6 km) west of Hanksville (another turnoff from Highway 24 is 3 mi/4.8 km east).

- **Mile 4.1:** Notom Ranch is to the west; once a small town, Notom is now a private ranch.

- **Mile 8.1:** Burrow Wash; experienced hikers can explore the slot canyon upstream. A 2.5-mile (4-km) hike up the sandy wash leads to narrow slots.

- **Mile 9.3:** Cottonwood Wash; a 2.5-mile

(4-km) trek along the wash leads to a slot canyon hike.

- **Mile 10.4:** Five Mile Wash; yet another sandy wash. Pavement ends.
- **Mile 13.3:** Sheets Gulch; a slot canyon is upstream of here; the trail goes for 6.7 miles (10.8 km) and is sometimes done as an overnight (permit required).
- **Mile 14.4:** Oak Creek crossing.
- **Mile 20.0:** Entering Capitol Reef National Park; a small box has information sheets.
- **Mile 22.3:** Cedar Mesa Campground is to the west; the small five-site campground is surrounded by junipers and has fine views of the Waterpocket Fold and the Henry Mountains. Free sites have tables and grills; there's a pit toilet but no drinking water. The Red Canyon Trail (5.6 mi/9 km round-trip) begins here and heads west into a box canyon in the Waterpocket Fold.
- **Mile 26.0:** Bitter Creek Divide. Streams to the north flow to the Fremont River; Halls Creek on the south side runs through Strike Valley to Lake Powell, 40 miles (64 km) away.
- **Mile 34.1:** Burr Trail Road Junction; turn west up the steep switchbacks to ascend the Waterpocket Fold and continue to Boulder and Highway 12 (36 mi/58 km). Burr Trail is the only road that actually crosses the top of the fold, and it's one of the most scenic in the park. Driving conditions are similar to the Notom-Bullfrog Road—OK for cars when dry. Pavement begins at the park boundary and continues to Boulder. Although paved, the Burr Trail still must be driven slowly because of its curves and potholes. The section of road through Long Canyon has especially pretty scenery.
- **Mile 36.0:** Surprise Canyon trailhead; the 2-mile (3.2-km) round-trip hike into this narrow, usually shaded canyon takes 1-2 hours. This is your best bet for a shorter hike in this area of the park.
- **Mile 36.6:** Post Corral; a small trading post here once served sheepherders and some cattle ranchers, but today this spot is just a reference point. Park here to hike to Headquarters Canyon (3.2 mi/5.1 km round-trip). A trailhead for Lower Muley Twist Canyon via Halls Creek is at the end of a 0.5-mile-long (0.8 km) road to the south.
- **Mile 37.5:** Leaving Capitol Reef National Park. Much of the road between here and Glen Canyon National Recreation Area has been paved.
- **Mile 45.5:** Road junction; turn right (south) to continue to Bullfrog Marina (25 mi/40 km) or go straight (east) for Starr Springs Campground (23 mi/37 km) in the Henry Mountains.
- **Mile 46.4:** The road to the right (west) goes to Halls Creek Overlook. This turn-off is poorly signed and easy to miss; look for it 0.9 mile (1.4 km) south of the previous junction.
- **Mile 49.0:** Colorful clay hills of deep red, cream, and gray rise beside the road. This clay turns to goo when wet, providing all the traction of axle grease.
- **Mile 54.0:** Beautiful panorama of countless mesas, mountains, and canyons; Lake Powell and Navajo Mountain can be seen to the south.
- **Mile 65.3:** Junction with paved Highway 276; turn left (north) for Hanksville (59 mi/95 km) or right (south) to Bullfrog Marina (5.2 mi/8.4 km).
- **Mile 70.5:** End at Bullfrog Marina in Glen Canyon National Recreation Area.

Muley Twist Canyon
LOWER CANYON

"So winding that it would twist a mule pulling a wagon," said an early visitor. This canyon has some of the best hiking in the southern district of the park. In the 1880s Mormon pioneers used the canyon as part of a wagon route between Escalante and new settlements in southeastern Utah, replacing the even more difficult Hole-in-the-Rock route.

Unlike most canyons of the Waterpocket Fold, Muley Twist runs lengthwise along the crest for about 18 miles (29 km) before finally turning east and leaving the fold. Hikers starting from Burr Trail Road can easily follow the twisting bends down to Halls Creek, 12 miles (19.3 km) away. Two trailheads and the Halls Creek route allow a variety of trips.

Start from Burr Trail Road near the top of the switchbacks (2.2 mi/3.5 km west of Notom-Bullfrog Rd.) and hike down the dry gravel streambed. After 4 miles (6.4 km), you have the option of returning the same way, taking the Cut Off route east 2.5 miles (4 km) to the Post Corral trailhead (off Notom-Bullfrog Rd.), or continuing 8 miles (12.9 km) down Lower Muley Twist Canyon to its end at Halls Creek. On reaching Halls Creek, turn left (north) and travel 5 miles (8 km) up the creek bed or the old jeep road beside it to the Post. This section of creek is in an open dry valley. With a car shuttle, the Post would be the end of a good two-day, 17-mile (27-km) hike. Check the weather beforehand and avoid the canyon if storms threaten.

Cream-colored sandstone cliffs lie atop the red Kayenta and Wingate Formations. Impressively deep undercuts have been carved into the lower canyon. Spring and fall offer the best conditions; summer temperatures can exceed 100°F. Elevations range from 5,640 feet (1,664 m) at Burr Trail Road to 4,540 feet (1,384 m) at the confluence with Halls Creek to 4,894 feet (1,492 m) at the Post.

An information sheet is available online (www.nps.gov/care), at the visitors center, and at the trailheads. You'll also find this hike described in David Day's *Utah's Favorite Hiking Trails* and in the small spiral-bound *Explore Capitol Reef Trails* by the Capitol Reef Natural History Association, available at the visitors center. Carry all the water you'll need for the trip because natural sources are often dry or polluted.

UPPER CANYON

This part of the canyon has plenty of scenery. Large and small natural arches along the way add to its beauty. Upper Muley Twist Road turns north off Burr Trail Road about 1 mile (1.6 km) west from the top of a set of switchbacks. Cars can usually go in 0.5 mile (0.8 km) to a trailhead parking area; high-clearance 4WD vehicles can head another 3 miles (4.8 km) up a wash to the end of the primitive road. Look for natural arches on the left along this last section. The **Strike Valley Overlook Trail** (0.75 mi/1.2 km round-trip) begins at the end of the road and leads to a magnificent panorama of the Waterpocket Fold and beyond. Return to the canyon, where you can hike as far as 6.5 miles (10.4 km), to the head of Upper Muley Twist Canyon.

Two large arches are a short hike upstream; Saddle Arch, the second one, on the left, is 1.7 miles (2.7 km) away. The **Rim Route** begins across from Saddle Arch, climbs the canyon wall, follows the rim (offering good views of Strike Valley and the Henry Mountains), and descends back into the canyon at a point just above the narrows, 4.75 miles (7.6 km) from the end of the road. The Rim Route is most easily followed in this direction. Proceed up-canyon to see several more arches. A narrow section of canyon beginning about 4 miles (6.4 km) from the end of the road must be bypassed to continue; look for rock cairns showing the way around to the right. Continuing up the canyon past the Rim Route sign will take you to several small drainages marking the upper end of Muley Twist Canyon. Climb a high tree-covered point on the west rim for great views; experienced hikers with a map can follow the rim back to Upper Muley Twist Road. There is no trail and no markers on this route. Bring all the water you'll need; there are no reliable sources in Upper Muley Twist Canyon.

Recreation

Fifteen trails for day hikes begin within a short drive of the visitors center. Of these, only Grand Wash, Capitol Gorge, and the short paths to Sunset Point and Goosenecks are easy. The others involve moderately strenuous climbs over irregular slickrock. Signs and rock cairns mark the way, but it's all too easy to wander off if you don't pay attention to the route.

Although most hiking trails can easily be done in a day, backpackers and hikers might want to try longer trips in Chimney Rock-Spring Canyons to the north or Muley Twist Canyon and Halls Creek to the south. Obtain the required **backcountry permit** (free) from a ranger and camp at least 0.5 mile (0.8 km) from the nearest maintained road or trail. (Cairned routes like Chimney Rock Canyon, Muley Twist Canyon, and Halls Creek don't count as trails but are backcountry routes.) Bring a stove for cooking; backcountry users are not permitted to build fires. Avoid camping or parking in washes at any time—torrents of mud and boulders can carry away everything.

HIKING FROM HIGHWAY 24

Stop by the visitors center to pick up a map showing hiking trails and trail descriptions. These trailheads are located along the main highway through the park and along the Fremont River. Note that the Grand Wash Trail cuts west through the reef to the Scenic Drive.

Chimney Rock Loop

Distance: 3.5 miles (5.6 km) round-trip
Duration: 2.5 hours
Elevation change: 590 feet (180 m)
Effort: moderate-strenuous
Trailhead: 3 miles (4.8 km) west of the visitors center on the north side of Highway 24

Towering 660 feet (201 m) above the highway, Chimney Rock (elev. 6,100 ft/1,860 m)

is a fluted spire of dark red rock (Moenkopi Formation) capped by a block of hard sandstone (Shinarump Member of the Chinle Formation). The trail leads pretty much straight uphill from the parking lot to a ridge overlooking Chimney Rock, and then levels off a bit. Panoramic views take in the face of Capitol Reef. Petrified wood along the trail has been eroded from the Chinle Formation (the same rock layer found in Petrified Forest National Park in Arizona). It is illegal to take any petrified wood.

Spring Canyon Route

Distance: 10 miles (16 km) one-way
Duration: 6 hours
Elevation change: 540 feet (165 m)
Effort: moderate
Trailhead: Chimney Rock parking lot

Except for its length, this hike, through the deep and narrow Spring Canyon, is not particularly difficult. It begins at the top of the Chimney Rock Trail and runs to the Fremont River and Highway 24; because it begins and ends on the highway, a car shuttle can eliminate the need to hike out and back. The wonderfully eroded forms of Navajo sandstone present a continually changing exhibition. The riverbed is normally dry. (Some maps show all or part of this as "Chimney Rock Canyon.") Check with rangers for the weather forecast before setting off, because flash floods can be dangerous, and the Fremont River (which you must wade across) can rise quite high. Normally, the river runs less than knee-deep to Highway 24 (3.7 mi/6 km east of the visitors center). With luck, you'll have a car waiting for you. Summer hikers can beat the often intense heat with a crack-of-dawn departure. Carry water, as this section of canyon lacks a reliable source.

From the Chimney Rock parking area, hike Chimney Rock Trail to the top of the ridge and follow the signs for Chimney Rock

Canyon. Enter the unnamed lead-in canyon and follow it downstream. A sign marks Chimney Rock Canyon, which is 2.5 miles (4 km) from the start. From this point, it's an additional 6.5 miles downstream to reach the Fremont River. A section of narrows requires some rock-scrambling (bring a cord to lower backpacks), or the area can be bypassed on a narrow trail to the left above the narrows. Farther down, a natural arch high on the left marks the halfway point.

Upper Chimney Rock Canyon could be explored on an overnight trip (permit required). A spring (purify the water before drinking it) is in an alcove on the right side, about 1 mile (1.6 km) up Chimney Rock Canyon from the lead-in canyon. Wildlife uses this water source, so camp at least 0.25 mile (0.4 km) away. Chimney Rock Canyon, the longest in the park, begins high on the slopes of Thousand Lake Mountain and descends nearly 15 miles (24 km) southeast to join the Fremont River.

Sulphur Creek Route

Distance: 5.5 miles (8.9 km) one-way
Duration: 3-5 hours
Elevation change: 540 feet (165 m)
Effort: moderate-strenuous
Trailhead: across Highway 24 from Chimney Rock parking lot

This moderately difficult hike begins by following a wash across the highway from the Chimney Rock parking area, then descends to Sulphur Creek and heads down the narrow canyon to the visitors center; it's 5 miles (8 km) if you've arranged a car or bike shuttle, and double that if you have to hike back to your starting point. It's best to hike Sulphur Creek during warm weather, because you'll be wading in the normally shallow creek through a slot canyon. Wear sneakers or other shoes that you don't mind getting wet. Before starting out, check to make sure the water level isn't too high for hiking. You can do this by examining the route's endpoint behind the visitors center; it should be ankle-deep or less for a safe and fun hike. *Don't* hike here if

there's a chance of rain or if the visitors center posts flash flood warnings!

Three small waterfalls are along the route, but it's fairly easy to climb down rock ledges to the side of the water; two falls are just below the Goosenecks and the third is about 0.5 mile (0.8 km) before the visitors center. Carry water with you.

Hickman Natural Bridge

Distance: 2 miles (3.2 km) round-trip
Duration: 1.5 hours
Elevation change: 400 feet (122 m)
Effort: easy-moderate
Trailhead: 2 miles (3.2 km) east of the visitors center on the north side of Highway 24

The graceful Hickman Natural Bridge spans 133 feet (41 m) across a small streambed. Numbered stops along the self-guided trail correspond to descriptions in a pamphlet available at the trailhead or visitors center. Starting from the parking area (elev. 5,320 ft/1,622 m), the trail follows the Fremont River's green banks a short distance before climbing to the bridge. The last section of trail follows a dry wash shaded by cottonwoods, junipers, and piñon pines. You'll pass under the bridge (eroded from the Kayenta Formation) at trail's end. Capitol Dome and other sculptured sandstone features surround the site. Joseph Hickman, for whom the bridge was named, served as principal of Wayne County High School and later in the state legislature; he and another local, Ephraim Pectol, led efforts to promote Capitol Reef.

Rim Overlook Trail

Distance: 4.5 miles (7.2 km) round-trip
Duration: 3-5 hours
Elevation change: 1,110 feet (335 m)
Effort: moderate-strenuous
Trailhead: Hickman Natural Bridge trailhead

A splendid overlook 1,000 feet (305 m) above Fruita beckons hikers up the Rim Overlook Trail. Take the Hickman Natural Bridge Trail from the parking area, turn right at the signed fork, and hike for about 2 miles (3.2 km). Allow 3.5 hours from the fork for this hike.

Panoramic views take in the Fremont River valley below, the great cliffs of Capitol Reef above, the Henry Mountains to the southeast, and Boulder Mountain to the southwest.

Continue another 2.2 miles (3.5 km) from the Rim Overlook to reach **Navajo Knobs.** Rock cairns lead the way over slickrock along the rim of the Waterpocket Fold. A magnificent view at trail's end takes in much of southeastern Utah.

★ Grand Wash Trail

Distance: 4.5 miles (7.2 km) round-trip
Duration: 2-3 hours
Elevation change: 200 feet (61 m)
Effort: easy
Trailhead: 4.7 miles (7.6 km) east of the visitors center on the south side of Highway 24

One of only five canyons cutting completely through the reef, Grand Wash offers easy hiking, great scenery, and an abundance of wildflowers. There's no trail—just follow the dry riverbed. (Flash floods can occur during storms.) Only a short distance from Highway 24, canyon walls rise 800 feet (244 m) above the floor and narrow to as little as 20 feet (6 m) in width; this stretch of trail is known as the Narrows. After the Narrows, the wash widens, and wildflowers grow everywhere. The Cassidy Arch trailhead is 2 miles (3.2 km) from Highway 24.

The hike can also be started from a trailhead at the end of Grand Wash Road, off the Scenic Drive. A car or bike shuttle can make it a one-way hike of 2.2 miles (3.5 km).

HIKING THE SCENIC DRIVE

These hikes begin from trailheads along the Scenic Drive. Drivers must pay the $15 national park admission fee to travel this road.

Fremont Gorge Overlook Trail

Distance: 4.5 miles (7.2 km) round-trip
Duration: 2-3 hours
Elevation change: 1,000 feet (305 m)
Effort: moderate-strenuous
Trailhead: Fruita blacksmith shop

From the start at the Fruita blacksmith shop, the trail climbs a short distance, then crosses a lovely native prairie on Johnson Mesa and climbs steeply to the overlook about 1,000 feet (305 m) above the Fremont River. The overlook is not a place for the acrophobic—even people who aren't ordinarily afraid of heights might find it a little daunting.

★ Cohab Canyon Trail

Distance: 3.5 miles (5.6 km) round-trip
Duration: 2.5 hours
Elevation change: 440 feet (134 m)
Effort: moderate-strenuous
Trailheads: across the road from Fruita Campground (1 mi/1.6 km south of the visitors center) and across Highway 24 from the Hickman Natural Bridge trailhead

Cohab is a pretty little canyon overlooking the campground. Mormon polygamists ("cohabitationists") supposedly used the canyon to escape federal marshals during the 1880s. It's possible to hike this trail starting from either trailhead. Starting from the campground, the trail first follows steep switchbacks before continuing along more gentle grades to the top of the reef, 400 feet (122 m) higher and 1 mile (1.6 km) from the campground. You can take a short trail to viewpoints or continue 0.75 mile (1.2 km) down the other side of the ridge to Highway 24.

Another option is to turn right at the top on Frying Pan Trail and head to Cassidy Arch (3.5 mi/5.6 km one-way) and Grand Wash (4 mi/6.4 km one-way). The trail from Cassidy Arch to Grand Wash is steep. All of these interconnecting trails offer many hiking possibilities, especially if you can arrange a car shuttle. For example, you could start up Cohab Canyon Trail from Highway 24, cross over the reef on Frying Pan Trail, make a side trip to Cassidy Arch, descend Cassidy Arch Trail to Grand Wash, walk down Grand Wash to Highway 24, then walk (or car shuttle) 2.7 miles (4.3 km) along the highway back to the start, for 10.5 miles (16.9 km) total.

Hiking the Frying Pan Trail involves an additional 600 feet (183 m) of climbing from either Cohab Canyon or Cassidy Arch Trail. Once atop Capitol Reef, the trail follows the gently rolling slickrock terrain.

Fremont River Trail

Distance: 2 miles (3.2 km) round-trip
Duration: 2 hours
Elevation change: 480 feet (146 m)
Effort: moderate-strenuous
Trailhead: Fruita Campground amphitheater

The trail starts out quite easy, passing orchards along the Fremont River (elev. 5,350 ft/1,631 m). This part of the trail is wheelchair-accessible. After 0.5 mile (0.8 km), it climbs sloping rock to a Miners Mountain viewpoint overlooking Fruita, Boulder Mountain, and Capitol Reef. This is a good early-morning hike from the campground; bring a thermos of coffee and enjoy the panoramic views from the top.

Cassidy Arch

Distance: 3.5 miles (5.6 km) round-trip
Duration: 3 hours
Elevation change: 670 feet (204 m)
Effort: moderate-strenuous
Trailhead: end of the drivable section of Grand Wash Road
Directions: Turn left off the Scenic Drive, 3.6 miles (5.8 km) from the visitors center, and follow Grand Wash Road to the trailhead.

Cassidy Arch Trail begins near the end of Grand Wash Road, ascends the north wall of Grand Wash, and then winds across slickrock to a vantage point close to the arch. Energetic hikers will enjoy good views of Grand Wash, the great domes of Navajo sandstone, and the broad, sturdy arch itself, which is wide enough for non-agorophobes to walk on. The notorious outlaw Butch Cassidy may have traveled through Capitol Reef and seen this arch. Frying Pan Trail branches off Cassidy Arch Trail at the 1-mile (1.6-km) mark, and then wends its way across 3 miles (4.8 km) of slickrock to Cohab Canyon.

Old Wagon Trail Loop

Distance: 3.8 miles (6.1 km) round-trip
Duration: 3 hours
Elevation change: 1,080 feet (329 m)
Effort: moderate-strenuous
Trailhead: on the Scenic Drive, 6 miles (9.7 km) south of the visitors center, between Grand Wash and Capitol Gorge

Wagon drivers once used this route as a shortcut between Grover and Capitol Gorge. The old trail crosses a wash to the west, and then ascends steadily through piñon and juniper woodland on Miners Mountain. After 1.5 miles (2.4 km), the trail leaves the wagon road and continues north for 0.5 mile (0.8 km) to a high knoll and the best views of the Capitol Reef area.

★ Capitol Gorge

Distance: 2 miles (3.2 km) round-trip
Duration: 1-2 hours
Elevation change: 100 feet (30 m)
Effort: easy-moderate
Trailhead: Capitol Gorge parking area

Follow the well-maintained dirt road to the parking area in Capitol Gorge to begin this hike. The first mile (1.6 km) downstream is the most scenic: Fremont petroglyphs (in poor condition) appear on the left after 0.1 mile (0.2 km); narrows of Capitol Gorge close in at 0.3 mile (0.5 km); a "pioneer register" on the left soon after consists of names and dates of early travelers and ranchers scratched in the canyon wall. If you're able to, scramble up some rocks and follow a cairn-marked trail across the slickrock, then head up out of the wash at the trail marker to see natural water tanks, about 0.8 mile (1.3 km) from the trail. These depressions in the rock collect water and give the Waterpocket Fold its name. Back in the wash, listen for canyon wrens—their song starts on a high note and then trills down the scale. From the turnoff to the water tanks, hikers can continue another 3 miles (4.8 km) downstream to Notom Road.

1: Cassidy Arch Trail **2:** Capitol Gorge

Golden Throne Trail

Distance: 4 miles (6.4 km) round-trip
Duration: 3 hours
Elevation change: 730 feet (223 m)
Effort: strenuous
Trailhead: Capitol Gorge parking area

The Golden Throne Trail begins at the trailhead at the end of the drivable part of Capitol Gorge. Instead of heading down Capitol Gorge from the parking area, turn left up this trail for a steady climb to dramatic views of the reef and surrounding area. The Golden Throne is a massive monolith of yellow-hued sandstone capped by a thin layer of red rock. This is a good hike to take around sunset, when the rocks take on a burnished glow.

MOUNTAIN BIKING

Ditch the car and really get to know this country with a big loop tour. For a strenuous ride with steep grades, take the **Boulder Mountain Loop.** Start from Highway 24 near Capitol Reef, take the Notom-Bullfrog Road to Burr Trail Road, and then take Highway 12 over Boulder Mountain to Highway 24 and back to Capitol Reef. This is definitely the sort of trip that requires some touring experience and a decent level of training (Boulder Mountain is quite a haul). This route can run 80-125 miles (129-201 km) over several days. A car shuttle for the Highway 24 portion can shorten the ride.

In the remote northern section of the park, cyclists can ride the challenging **Cathedral Valley Loop.** The complete loop is more than 60 miles (97 km). Little water is available along the route, so it's best ridden in spring or fall, when temperatures are low. Access the loop on either Hartnett Road (11.7 mi/18.9 km east of the visitors center) or Caineville Wash Road (18.6 mi/30 km east of the visitors center). A small campground is located about 36 miles into the loop.

Although the Scenic Drive doesn't have much of a shoulder, it's not a bad bicycling road, especially early in the morning before car traffic has picked up. Dirt spur roads off the Scenic Drive lead up Grand Wash, into Capitol Gorge, and up South Draw to Pleasant Creek.

Contact the visitors center for more information on these and other routes.

CLIMBING

Rock climbing is allowed in the park. Check the park website (www.nps.gov/care) for information about recommended climbing zones; also check with rangers to learn

Golden Throne

The Orchards of Capitol Reef

Capitol Reef was one of the last places in the West to be found by settlers. The first reports came in 1866 from a detachment of Mormon militia pursuing insurgent Utes. In 1872, Professor Almon H. Thompson of the Powell Expedition led the first scientific exploration in the fold country and named several park features along the group's Pleasant Creek route. Mormons, expanding their network of settlements, arrived in the upper Fremont Valley in the late 1870s and spread downriver to Hanksville. Junction (renamed Fruita in 1902) and nearby Pleasant Creek (Sleeping Rainbow-Floral Ranch) were settled about 1880. Floods, isolation, and transportation difficulties forced many families to move on, especially downstream from Capitol Reef. Irrigation and hard work paid off with prosperous fruit orchards and the sobriquet "The Eden of Wayne County." The aptly named Fruita averaged about 10 families, who grew alfalfa, sorghum (for syrup), vegetables, and a wide variety of fruit. Getting the produce to market required long and difficult journeys by wagon. The region remained one of the most isolated in Utah until after World War II.

Fruita orchards

Although Fruita's citizens have departed, the National Park Service still maintains the old orchards. They are lovely in late April, when the trees are in bloom beneath the towering canyon walls. Visitors are welcome to pick and carry away the cherries, apricots, peaches, pears, and apples during harvest seasons. Harvest begins in late June-early July and ends in October. You'll be charged about the same as in commercial pick-your-own orchards. You can also wander through any orchard and eat all you want on the spot for free before and during the designated picking season.

about restricted areas and obtain the required **permit** (free at visitors center or by email: care_permits@nps.gov). Climbers must use "clean" techniques (no pitons or bolts) and keep at least 100 feet (30 m) from rock-art panels and prehistoric structures. Because of the abundance of prehistoric rock art found there, the rock wall north of Highway 24—between the Fruita School and the east end of Kreuger Orchard (mile 81.4)—is closed to climbing. Other areas closed to climbing include Hickman Natural Bridge and all other arches and bridges, Temple of the Moon and Temple of the Sun, and Chimney Rock.

The harder, fractured sandstone of the Wingate Formation is better suited to climbing than the more crumbly Entrada sandstone. The rock is given to flaking, however, so climbers should use caution. Be sure that your chalk matches the color of the rock; white chalk is prohibited.

CAMPGROUNDS

Fruita Campground (year-round, $20), 1 mile (1.6 km) south of the visitors center on the Scenic Drive, has 71 sites for tents and RVs, with drinking water and heated restrooms but no showers or hookups. Campers must get their water from the visitors center during winter. The surrounding orchards and lush grass make this an attractive, though somewhat suburban, spot. It has excellent access to hiking trails. Most sites can be reserved in advance (www.recreation.gov). Five sites are wheelchair accessible and can be reserved from March-October. One group campground (Mar.-Oct., reservations required, www.recreation.gov, $4 pp, $75 minimum) and a picnic area are also nearby.

Two campgrounds offer first-come, first-served primitive sites with no water. The five-site **Cedar Mesa Campground** (year-round, free) is in the park's southern district, just off Notom-Bullfrog Road (dirt); campers enjoy fine views of the Waterpocket Fold and the Henry Mountains. From the visitors center, go east 9.2 miles (14.8 km) on Highway 24, then turn right and go 22 miles (35.4 km) on Notom-Bullfrog Road (avoid this road if it's wet). **Cathedral Valley Campground** (year-round, free) serves the park's northern district; it has six sites near the Hartnett Junction, about 30 miles (48 km) north of

Highway 24. Take either Caineville Wash Road or Hartnett Road. Both roads are dirt and should be avoided when wet. Hartnett has a river ford.

If you're just looking for a place to park for the night, check out the public land east of the park boundary, off Highway 24. Areas on both sides of the highway (about 9 mi/14.5 km east of the visitors center) can be used for free primitive camping. Several Forest Service campgrounds are south of Torrey on Boulder Mountain, along Highway 12, and private campgrounds catering mostly to RVs are in Torrey.

Backcountry camping is allowed in the park; obtain a free **backcountry permit** at the visitors center.

Getting There

Capitol Reef National Park flanks Highway 24, which is a major (by Southern Utah standards) east-west road, roughly paralleling and south of I-70. Highway 24 intersects I-70 at the town of Green River, which is north and east of the park; follow the road down through Hanksville to reach Capitol Reef. This is the quickest way to get from the Moab area to Capitol Reef.

Travelers coming from the Escalante area should head north on Highway 12 toward the town of Boulder. (This is also the most scenic route from Zion and Bryce.) Twisty Highway 12 will take you over Boulder Mountain to Highway 24 at the town of Torrey; Capitol Reef is just 11 miles (17.7 km) east.

Torrey

Torrey (pop. 240) is an attractive little village with a real Western feel. Only 11 miles (17.7 km) west of the Capitol Reef National Park visitors center, at the junction of Highways 12 and 24, it's a friendly and convenient place to stay, with several excellent lodgings and a few good restaurants.

There are other little towns along the Fremont River, which drains this steep-sided valley. Teasdale is a small community just 4 miles (6.4 km) west, situated in a grove of

piñon pines. Bicknell, a small farm and ranch town, is 8 miles (12.9 km) west of Torrey.

OUTFITTERS

Hondoo Rivers and Trails (435/425-3519, www.hondoo.com), run by longtime locals, offers guided horseback riding adventures for multiday backcountry excursions; for a real treat, check out the inn-to-inn trail rides. They also provide guided hiking tours and backpacking trips, jeep tours, and shuttle services.

ENTERTAINMENT AND EVENTS

The **Entrada Institute** (www. entradainstitute.org), a nonprofit organization that seeks to further understanding and appreciation of the natural, historical, cultural, and scientific heritage of the Colorado Plateau, sponsors a cultural event as part of its **Saturday Sunset Series** (7:30pm Sat. late May-late Oct., usually free). Events range from talks by local ranchers on the cattle industry to musical performances. The institute is housed at the **Robber's Roost Bookstore** (185 W. Main St., 435/425-3265, www.robbersroostbooks.com, 8am-6pm daily spring-fall), which is a good place to visit any time of day.

FOOD

At **Hunt & Gather** (599 W. Main St., 435/425-3070, www.huntandgatherrestaurant.com, 8am-11am Wed.-Fri., 8am-noon Sat.-Sun. and 5pm-10pm Wed.-Sun., dinner entrées $20-42), you'll find meals that reflect the restaurant's name. On the "hunter" side of the menu, there's wild game, beef, and fish; vegetarians should look at the "gather" options. The chef has worked at some of Salt Lake City's finest restaurants, and this is the most upscale dining you'll find in this small town.

A good, reliable Torrey standard is the **Capitol Reef Inn and Cafe** (360 W. Main St., 435/425-3271, www.capitolreefinn.com, 7am-9pm daily, $10-21), where there's an emphasis on healthy and, when possible, locally grown food. It's easy to eat your veggies here—the 10-vegetable salad will make up for some of the less nutritious meals you've had on the road. An additional perk is the lobby gift shop, which has a good selection of books and crafts.

For something a little less elevated, try the burgers and milk shakes at **Slacker's Burger Joint** (165 E. Main St., 435/425-3710, 11am-8pm Mon.-Sat., $6-15), in the center of Torrey. The pastrami burger is rightfully famous, and an afternoon milk shake hits the spot after a day of hiking.

Stop by the **Wild Rabbit Cafe** (135 E. Main St., 435/425-3074, http://thewildrabbitcafe.com, 8am-3pm Thurs.-Sun., $8-19) for a good cup of coffee and a homemade pastry (including vegan and gluten-free options), a full breakfast, or lunch. They offer a hiker's box you can take with you for your day in the park. It's a simple counter-service place with seating both indoors and out.

About 24 miles (39 km) east of the Capitol Reef visitors center, stop by the tiny ★ **Mesa Market** (mile marker 102, Hwy. 24, Caineville, 435/456-9156, www.mesafarmmarket.com, 7am-7pm daily late Mar.-Oct.) for artisanal cheese and yogurt, sourdough bread baked in a wood-fired oven, and whatever produce is growing in the back 40. You won't find better picnic makings anywhere in southeastern Utah.

ACCOMMODATIONS
$50-100

A few small bunkhouse cabins are available at the center of town at the **Torrey Trading Post** (75 W. Main St., 435/425-3716, www.torreytradingpost.com, $50). These snug, recently built cabins aren't loaded with frills—the toilets and showers are in men's and women's bathhouses—but the price is right, pets are permitted, and there's a place to do laundry. In addition, a fully furnished studio cabin with a king bed, twin foldout bed, full bath, and full kitchen is $105, and a fully furnished larger cabin that sleeps six, with two full baths and kitchen, goes for $165.

The **Capitol Reef Inn and Cafe** (360 W. Main St., 435/425-3271, www.capitolreefinn.com, spring-fall, $84, pets allowed) has large but somewhat dated motel rooms and a good café serving breakfast, lunch, and dinner. In the front yard, the motel's owner and his brother have built a kiva resembling those used by Native Americans. It's obviously a labor of love, and a pretty cool place to explore.

In a grove of trees immediately behind downtown Torrey's old trading post and country store is **Austin's Chuck Wagon Lodge**

(12 W. Main St., 435/425-3335 or 800/863-3288, www.austinschuckwagonmotel.com, Mar.-Dec., rooms $77-119, cabins $183), with guest rooms in an older motel, a newer lodge-like building, or newer two-bedroom cabins. There's also a pool and a hot tub.

$100-150

At the east end of Torrey, the **Rim Rock Inn** (2523 E. Hwy. 24, 435/425-3388 or 888/447-4676, www.therimrock.net, Mar.-Dec., $109-119) does indeed perch on a rim of red rock; it's just about as close as you can get to the park. The motel and its two restaurants are part of a 120-acre ranch, so the views are ex-pansive, though the rooms themselves are fairly basic.

In a pretty setting 3 miles (4.8 km) south of town, **Cowboy Homestead Cabins** (Hwy. 12, 435/425-3414 or 888/854-5871, www.cowboyhomesteadcabins.com, $119-129) has attractive one- and two-bedroom cabins with private baths, kitchenettes, and outdoor gas barbecue grills.

In Teasdale, 4 miles (6.4 km) west of Torrey, **Pine Shadows** (195 W. 125 S., Teasdale, 435/425-3939, www.pineshadowcabins.net, $109-169, 2-night minimum) offers spacious modern cabins, equipped with two queen beds plus full baths and kitchens, in a piñon forest.

Muley Twist Inn (245 W. 125 S., outside Teasdale, 435/425-3640 or 800/530-1038, www.muleytwistinn.com, $125-165), an el-egantly decorated five-bedroom B&B, is on a 30-acre parcel with great views. One guest room is fully accessible to wheelchair users. It's another really wonderful place to come home to at the end of a day of driving or hiking.

Stay in a 1914 schoolhouse: The **Torrey Schoolhouse Bed and Breakfast** (150 N. Center St., 435/633-4643, www.torreyschoolhouse.com, Apr.-Oct., $130-165) has been renovated but retains many period touches and an old-fashioned atmosphere. Modern amenities include a shiatsu massage chair in every room, memory foam mattress toppers, flat-screen TVs, and a wheelchair-accessible suite.

Over $150

If you're looking for comfortable motel rooms with an outdoor pool and nice views, a good choice is the **Capitol Reef Resort** (2600 E. Hwy. 24, 435/425-3761, www.capitolreefresort.com, $169-209). If a standard motel room seems too tame, stay in one of the air-conditioned Conestoga wagon (sleeps six, $319), with private bath, a little walk away. Tepees ($289) and cabins ($269-379) are also available.

The ★ **Lodge at Red River Ranch** (2900 W. Hwy. 24, 435/425-3322, www.redriverranch.com, $184-274) is between Bicknell and Torrey beneath towering cliffs of red sandstone on the banks of the Fremont River. This wood-beamed lodge sits on a 2,200-acre working ranch, but there's noth-ing rustic or unsophisticated about the ac-commodations. The three-story structure is built in the same grand architectural style as old-fashioned mountain lodges. The great room has a massive stone fireplace, cozy chairs and couches, and a splendid Old West atmosphere. There are 15 guest rooms, most decorated according to a theme, and all have private baths. Guests are welcome to wander ranch paths, fish for trout, or meander in the gardens and orchards. Breakfast and dinner are served in the lodge restaurant but are not included in the price of lodgings; box lunches can be ordered.

The lovely **SkyRidge Inn Bed and Breakfast** (1012 E. Hwy. 24, 435/425-3222, www.skyridgeinn.com, $165-195) is 1 mile (1.6 km) east of downtown Torrey. The mod-ern inn has been decorated with high-quality Southwestern art and artifacts; all six guest rooms have private baths. SkyRidge sits on a bluff amid 75 acres, and guests are invited to explore the land on foot or bicycle.

Campgrounds

Although most campers will try for a site at Capitol Reef National Park, the campground there fills up quickly. Torrey has a couple of private campgrounds that cater to both RV and tent campers. Right in town, the **Sand Creek RV Park** (540 W. Hwy. 24, 435/425-3577, www.sandcreekrv.com, Mar.-Oct., $20 tents, $40-42 RVs, $48-65 camping cabins, $45 vintage trailer) has shaded tent spaces in a pleasant grassy field. Showers ($5 for nonguests) and laundry facilities ($5 to wash and dry) are available. Sand Creek is smaller than many RV parks, but it's particularly appealing. **Thousand Lakes RV Park** (1110 W. Hwy. 24, 1 mi/1.6 km west of Torrey, 435/425-3500 or 800/355-8995, www.thousandlakesrvpark.com, Apr.-late Oct., $20 tents, $41 RVs with full hookups) has showers, wireless Internet, a laundry room, and a store. Thousand Lakes also has cabins, ranging from Spartan (no linens, $39) to deluxe (sleeps up to 6, linens provided, $109).

The U.S. Forest Service's **Sunglow Campground** (Forest Rd. 143, east of Bicknell, 435/836-2811, www.recreation.gov, open with water May-Oct., $12) is just east of Bicknell at an elevation of 7,200 feet (2,195 m). The surrounding red cliffs really light up at sunset, hence the name. Several other Forest Service campgrounds are on the slopes of Boulder Mountain along Highway 12 between Torrey and Boulder. These places are all above 8,600 feet (2,621 m) and usually don't open until late May-early June.

INFORMATION AND SERVICES

The **Fremont River Ranger District** (138 S. Main St., Loa, 435/836-2800, www.fs.fed.us/r4/fishlake, 8am-4:30pm Mon.-Fri.) of the Fishlake National Forest has information about hiking, horseback riding, and road conditions in the northern and eastern parts of Boulder Mountain and the Aquarius Plateau.

Canyonlands National Park

The canyon country stages its supreme performance in this vast park, which spreads across 527 square miles (1,365 sq. km). The deeply entrenched Colorado and Green Rivers meet in its heart, after which the Colorado continues south through the tumultuous Cataract Canyon Rapids.

The park is divided into four districts and a separate noncontiguous unit. The Colorado and Green Rivers form the River District and divide Canyonlands National Park into three other regions. Island in the Sky is north, between the rivers; the Maze is to the west; and Needles is to the east. The small Horseshoe Canyon Unit, farther west, preserves a canyon on Barrier Creek, a tributary of the Green River, in which astounding petroglyphs and ancient rock paintings are protected.

DRUID ARCH   4.5 MI/7.2 KM
ELEPHANT HILL   2.7 MI/4.4 KM
SQUAW FLAT CG   4.7 MI/7.6 KM

DEVIL'S KITCHEN   2.3 MI/3.7 KM
CAMPGROUND LOOP
CHESLER PARK   2.2 MI/3.5 KM

Highlights

Look for ★ to find recommended sights, activities, dining, and lodging.

★ **Take a Ride on White Rim Road:** Only high-clearance 4WD rigs or sturdy mountain bikes can make this scenic drive along the Colorado and Green Rivers (page 196).

★ **Hit the Mesa Arch Trail:** This easy trail leads to a dramatic cliff-side arch. If you have time for just one hike, make it this one—the sun rising through the arch is a sight to behold (page 199).

★ **Hike Grand View Trail:** This short hike along slickrock cliffs captures the essence of the Island in the Sky. A sheer mile below the trail, the gorges of the Colorado and Green Rivers join to form Cataract Canyon, while needles punctuate the skyline (page 200).

★ **See 2000-year-old Art:** The distinctive petroglyphs at **BLM Newspaper Rock Historical Monument** span centuries (page 204).

★ **Go Slickrock Hiking:** The **Cave Spring Trail** is a good introduction to slickrock hiking, with rock cairns that mark the way and ladders to assist with the steeper sections (page 208).

★ **Check out Chesler Park:** A trail winds through sand and slickrock before ascending to a lovely desert meadow that contrasts with the Needles District's characteristic red and white spires (page 212).

★ **Find Adventure in the Land of Standing Rocks:** Rock spires stand guard over myriad canyons in this remote section of the Maze District, accessible via a high-clearance 4WD vehicle (page 218).

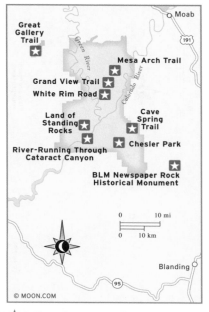

★ **Follow the Great Gallery Trail:** Ghostly life-size pictographs are located in remote Horseshoe Canyon. Hike through pleasant scenery and spring wildflowers to get there (page 221).

★ **Ride the Rapids:** The Colorado River picks up speed through **Cataract Canyon,** especially in spring, with 26 or more rapids guaranteeing a wild ride (page 224).

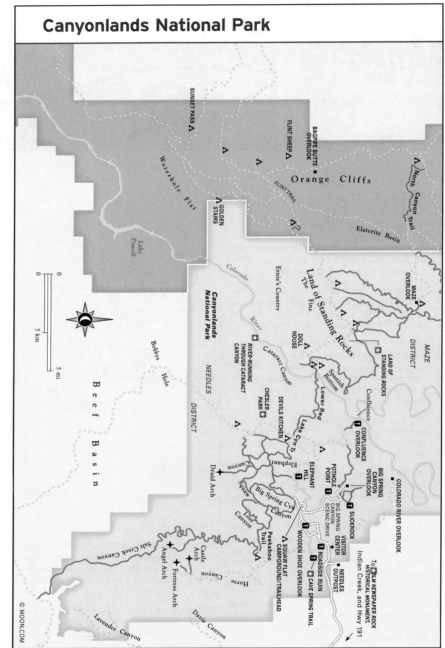

Canyonlands National Park

SUNSET PASS

FLINT SHEEP

BAGPIPE BUTTE
OVERLOOK

Waterhole Flat

FLINT TRAIL

Orange Cliffs

North Canyon Trail

GOLDEN STAIRS

Elaterite Basin

Lake Powell

Colorado

Ernie's Country

Land of Standing Rocks
The Fins

MAZE OVERLOOK

0
0

5 km
5 mi

Canyonlands National Park

River

RIVER-RUNNING THROUGH CATARACT CANYON

DOLL HOUSE

MAZE DISTRICT

LAND OF STANDING ROCKS

Bobbys Hole

Cataract Canyon

Spanish Bottom

Confluence

NEEDLES DISTRICT

CHESLER PARK

DEVILS KITCHEN

Lower Red

Lake Cyn Tr

CONFLUENCE OVERLOOK

BIG SPRING CANYON OVERLOOK

Beef Basin

Squaw Canyon

Druid Arch

Elephant Canyon

ELEPHANT HILL

POTHOLE POINT

COLORADO RIVER OVERLOOK

Big Spring Cyn

BIG SPRING CANYON SCENIC DRIVE

SLICKROCK

Lost Canyon

Peekaboo Trail

WOODEN SHOE OVERLOOK

SQUAW FLAT CAMPGROUND/TRAILHEAD

VISITOR CENTER

NEEDLES OUTPOST

Salt Creek Canyon

Angel Arch

Castle Arch

ROADSIDE RUIN

CAVE SPRING TRAIL

To NEWSPAPER ROCK HISTORICAL MONUMENT, Indian Creek, and Hwy 191

Fortress Arch

Horse Canyon

Davis Canyon

Lavender Canyon

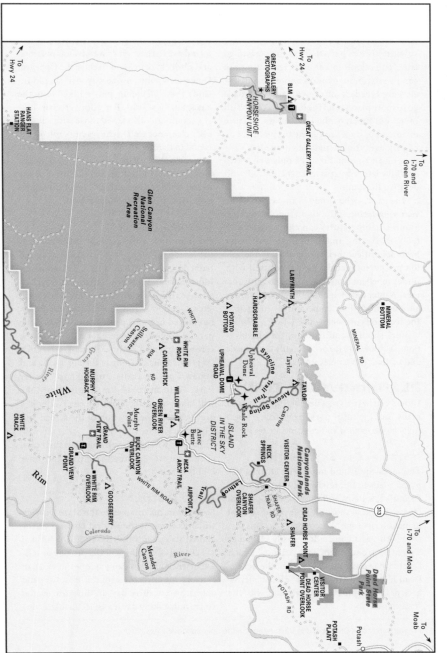

Each district has its own distinct character. No bridges or roads directly connect the three land districts and the Horseshoe Canyon Unit, so most visitors have to leave the park to go from one region to another. The huge park can be seen in many ways and on many levels. Paved roads reach a few areas, 4WD roads go to more places, and hiking trails reach still more, but much of the land shows no trace of human passage. To get the big picture, you can fly over this incredible complex of canyons on an air tour; however, only a river trip or a hike lets you experience the solitude and detail of the land.

The park can be visited in any season of the year, with spring and autumn the best choices. Summer temperatures can climb past 100°F (38°C); carrying and drinking lots of water becomes critical then (bring at least one gallon per person per day). Arm yourself with insect repellent from late spring to midsummer. Winter days tend to be bright and sunny, although nighttime temperatures can dip into the teens or even below 0°F (-18°C). Winter visitors should inquire about travel conditions, as snow and ice occasionally close roads and trails at higher elevations.

PLANNING YOUR TIME

Unless you have a great deal of time, you can't really "do" the entire park in one trip. It's best to pick one section and concentrate on it.

Island in the Sky District

The mesa-top Island in the Sky District has paved roads to impressive belvederes such as Grand View Point and the strange Upheaval Dome. If you're short on time or don't want to make a rigorous backcountry trip, this district is the best choice. It is easily visited as a day trip from Moab. The "Island," which is actually a large mesa, is much like nearby Dead Horse Point on a giant scale; a narrow neck of land connects the north side with the "mainland."

If you're really on a tight schedule, it's possible to spend a few hours exploring Arches National Park, then head to Island in the Sky for a drive to the scenic Grand View overlook and a brief hike to Mesa Arch or the Upheaval Dome viewpoint. A one-day visit should include these elements, plus a hike along the Neck Springs Trail. For a longer visit, hikers, mountain bikers, and those with suitable high-clearance 4WD vehicles can drop off the Island in the Sky and descend about 1,300 feet (396 m) to White Rim Road, which follows the cliffs of the White Rim around most of the Island. Plan to spend at least two or three days exploring this 100-mile-long road.

Needles District

Colorful rock spires prompted the name of the Needles District, which is easily accessed from Highway 211 and U.S. 191 south of Moab. Splendid canyons contain many arches, strange rock formations, and archaeological sites. Overlooks and short nature trails can be enjoyed from the paved scenic drive in the park; if you are only here for a day, hike the Cave Spring and Pothole Point Trails. On a longer visit, make a loop of the Big Spring and Squaw Canyon Trails, and hike to Chesler Park. A 10-mile (16-km) round-trip hike will take you to the Confluence Overlook, a great view of the junction of the Green and Colorado Rivers.

Drivers with 4WD vehicles have their own challenging roads through canyons and other highly scenic areas.

Maze District

Few visitors make it over to the Maze District, which is some of the wildest country in the United States. Only the rivers and a handful of 4WD roads and hiking trails provide access. Experienced hikers can explore the maze of canyons on unmarked routes. Plan to spend at least two or three days in this area; even if you're only taking day hikes, it can take a long

---

Previous: Needles District hiking trails; rafters on the Colorado River; Mesa Arch.

Canyonlands in One Day

- Begin your day at the **Island in the Sky visitors center,** which overlooks an 800-foot-deep natural amphitheater.

- After a 6-mile (9.7 km) drive south, you'll find the trail for the easy walk to **Mesa Arch,** which rewards you with one of the most dramatic vistas in Utah: an arch on the edge of an 800-foot (244-m) cliff.

- For lunch, hit the picnic area at **Grand View Point,** another 6 miles (9.7 km) south, for astonishing views over red-rock canyons.

- After lunch, take a longer hike from a trailhead near the visitors center on the **Neck Springs Trail.**

- For dinner, the closest dining is in Moab, 32 miles (52 km) east of the visitors center, where you can quench your thirst and hunger at **Eddie McStiff's** brewpub.

time to get to any destination here. That said, a hike from the Maze Overlook to the Harvest Scene pictographs is a good bet if you don't have a lot of time. If you have more than one day, head to the Land of Standing Rocks area and hike north to the Chocolate Drops.

Horseshoe Canyon Unit

The Horseshoe Canyon Unit, a detached section of the park northwest of the Maze District, is equally remote. It protects the Great Gallery, a group of pictographs left by prehistoric Native Americans. This ancient artwork is reached at the end of a series of long unpaved roads and down a canyon on a moderately challenging hiking trail. Plan to spend a full day exploring this area.

River District

The River District includes long stretches of the Green and the Colorado Rivers. River-running is one of the best ways to experience the inner depths of the park. Boaters can obtain helpful literature and advice from park rangers. Groups planning their own trip through Cataract Canyon need a river-running permit. Flat-water permits are also required. River outfitters based in Moab offer trips ranging from half a day to several days in length.

Exploring the Park

There are four districts and a noncontiguous unit in **Canyonlands National Park** (425/719-2313, www.nps.gov/cany, $30 per vehicle, $25 motorcyclists, $15 bicyclists and pedestrians, good for one week in all districts, no fee to enter Maze or Horseshoe Canyon, $55 Southeast Utah Parks Pass good for Arches and Canyonlands National Parks and Hovenweep and Natural Bridges National Monuments), each affording great views, spectacular geology, a chance to see wildlife, and endless opportunities to explore. You won't find crowds or elaborate park facilities because most of Canyonlands remains a primitive backcountry park. Indeed, bring along a lunch and any other food that you'll need during your stay. There are no restaurants and no accommodations in any unit of the park.

Front-country camping is allowed only in the established Island in the Sky Campground and Needles Campground.

Rock climbing is allowed in some areas of the park. Permits are not required unless the trip involves overnight camping; however, it's always a good idea to check in at district visitors centers for advice and information and to learn where climbing is restricted. Climbing is not allowed within 300 feet (91 m) of cultural sites.

Pets aren't allowed on trails and must be leashed in campgrounds. No firewood collecting is permitted in the park; backpackers must use gas stoves for cooking. Vehicle and boat campers can bring in firewood but must use grills or fire pans.

The best maps for the park are a series of topographic maps by National Geographic/Trails Illustrated; these have the latest trail and road information. For most day hikes, the simple maps issued at park visitors centers will suffice.

VISITORS CENTERS

Because Canyonlands covers so much far-flung territory, separate visitors centers serve each district. One website (www.nps.gov/cany) serves the whole park and is a good source for current information and permit applications. There are visitors centers at the entrances to the **Island in the Sky District** (435/259-4712, 8am-6pm daily late Apr.-late-Sept., 8am-5pm early spring and fall, closed late Dec.-early Mar.) and the **Needles District** (435/259-4711, 8am-6pm daily spring and fall, 8am-5pm daily July-Aug.). The **Hans Flat Ranger Station** (435/259-2652, 8am-4:30pm daily year-round) is on a remote plateau above the even more isolated canyons of the Maze District and the Horseshoe Canyon Unit. The River District is administered out of the **National Park Service Office** (2282 SW Resource Blvd., Moab, 435/719-2313, 8am-4pm Mon.-Fri.). This office can generally handle inquiries for all districts of the park. For backcountry information, or to make backcountry reservations, call 435/259-4351. Handouts from the ranger offices describe natural history, travel, and other aspects of the park.

If you are in Moab, it is most convenient to stop at the **Moab Information Center** (Main St. and Center St., 435/259-8825 or

800/635-6622, 8am-7pm Mon.-Sat., 9am-6pm Sun. mid-Mar.-Nov.), where a national park ranger or volunteers with the Canyonlands Natural History Association are often on duty. All visitors centers have brochures, maps, and books, as well as someone to answer your questions.

TOURS

Rangers lead interpretive programs (Apr.-Oct.) in the Island in the Sky and Needles Districts, and they guide hikers into Horseshoe Canyon (Sat.-Sun. spring and fall), weather permitting. Call the **Hans Flat Ranger Station** (435/259-2652) for details on these hikes.

OUTFITTERS

Outfitters must be authorized by the National Park Service to operate in Canyonlands. Most guides concentrate on river trips, but some can take you on mountain bike trips, including vehicle-supported tours of the White Rim 4WD Trail. Most of the guides operating in Canyonlands are based in Moab. For a complete list of authorized outfitters, visit the park website (www.nps.gov/cany).

Mountain Biking

- **Escape Adventures** (at Moab Cyclery, 391 S. Main St., Moab, 702/596-2953 or 800/596-2953, www.escapeadventures.com)
- **Rim Tours** (1233 S. U.S. 191, Moab, 435/259-5223, www.rimtours.com)
- **Western Spirit Cycling** (478 Mill Creek Dr., Moab, 435/259-8732 or 800/845-2453, www.westernspirit.com)

Rafting

- **Adrift Adventures** (378 N. Main St., Moab, 435/259-8594 or 800/874-4483, www.adrift.net)
- **Sheri Griffith Expeditions** (435/259-8229 or 800/332-2439, www.griffithexp.com)
- **Tag-A-Long Expeditions** (452 N. Main

St., Moab, 435/259-8594 or 800/453-3292, http://tagalong.com)

• **Western River Expeditions** (225 S. Main St., Moab, 801/942-6669 or 866/904-1163, www.westernriver.com)

BACKCOUNTRY EXPLORATION

A complex system of fees is charged for backcountry camping, 4WD exploration, and river rafting. Except for Island in the Sky Campground and Needles Campground, you'll need a **backcountry camping permit.** There is a $30 fee for a backpacking, biking, or 4WD overnight permit. **Day-use permits** (free, but limited in quantity) are required for vehicles, including motorcycles and bicycles on the White Rim Road, Elephant Hill, and a couple of other areas. Each of the three major districts has a different policy for backcountry vehicle camping, so it's a good idea to make sure that you understand the details. Backcountry permits are also needed for any trips with horses or stock; check with a ranger for details.

It's possible to reserve a backcountry permit in advance; for spring and fall travel to popular areas like Island in the Sky's White Rim Trail or the Needles backcountry, this is an extremely good idea. Find application forms on the Canyonlands website (https://canypermits.nps.gov). Forms should be completed and returned at least two weeks in advance of your planned trip. Telephone reservations are not accepted.

Back-road travel is a popular method of exploring the park. Canyonlands National Park offers hundreds of miles of exceptionally scenic jeep roads, favorites both with mountain bikers and 4WD enthusiasts. Park regulations require all motorized vehicles to have proper registration and licensing for highway use, and all-terrain vehicles are prohibited in the park; drivers must also be licensed. Normally you must have a vehicle with both 4WD and high clearance; it must also be maneuverable (large pickup trucks don't work for many places). It's essential for both motor vehicles and bicycles to stay on existing roads to prevent damage to the delicate desert vegetation. Carry tools, extra fuel, water, and food in case you break down in a remote area.

Before making a trip, drivers and cyclists should talk with a ranger to register and to check current road conditions, which can change drastically from one day to the next. The rangers can also tell you where to seek help if you get stuck. Primitive campgrounds are provided on most of the roads, but you'll need a backcountry permit from a ranger. Books on backcountry exploration include Charles Wells's *Guide to Moab, UT Backroads & 4-Wheel Drive Trails,* which includes Canyonlands, and Damian Fagan and David Williams's *A Naturalist's Guide to the White Rim Trail.*

One more thing about backcountry travel in Canyonlands: You may need to pack your poop out of the backcountry. Because of the abundance of slickrock and the desert conditions, it's not always possible to dig a hole, and you can't just leave your waste on a rock until it decomposes (decomposition is a very slow process in these conditions). Check with the ranger when you pick up your backcountry permit for more information.

Island in the Sky District

The main part of this district sits on a mesa high above the Colorado and Green Rivers. It is connected to points north by a narrow land bridge just wide enough for the road, known as "the neck," which forms the only vehicle access to the 40-square-mile (104-sq-km) Island in the Sky. Panoramic views from the "Island" can be enjoyed from any point along the rim; you'll see much of the park and southeastern Utah.

Short hiking trails lead to overlooks and to Mesa Arch, Aztec Butte, Whale Rock, Upheaval Dome, and other features. Longer trails make steep, strenuous descents from the Island to the White Rim Road below. Elevations on the Island average about 6,000 feet (1,829 m).

Although much of the rock within Canyonlands is not suitable for climbing, there are some routes in the Island in the Sky, including Taylor Canyon in the extreme northwest corner of the park, which is reached by lengthy and rugged 4WD roads.

Bring water for all hiking, camping, and travel in Island in the Sky. During the summer, water is available at the visitors center; otherwise, there is no water available in this district of the park.

GETTING THERE

From Moab, drive 10 miles (16 km) north on U.S. 191 and turn left (west) onto Highway 313. If you are coming in from I-70, drive 20 miles (32 km) south on U.S. 191 from exit 182 to reach the junction. Continue on this paved road for 22 miles (35 km) west then south to reach the park entrance. These aren't fast roads: From Moab, allow 45 minutes to reach the park. Note that GPS-based navigation systems don't always provide accurate positioning and mapping in remote areas like the Island in the Sky. Rely on maps and road signs to get you where you want to go, not your sat-nav system.

VISITORS CENTER

Stop here for information about Island in the Sky and to see exhibits on the geology and history of the area. Books and maps are available for purchase, and an audio tour of the park's scenic road is available for purchase or rental. The **visitors center** (435/259-4712, 8am-6pm daily late Apr.-late-Sept., 8:30am-5pm mid-Mar.-mid-April and Oct., 9am-4pm daily Nov.-Dec., 9am-4pm Fri.-Tues. Jan.-Feb., 8am-4pm daily Mar.1-Mar 16) is located just before the neck crosses to Island in the Sky. From Moab, go northwest 10 miles (16 km) on U.S. 191, then turn left and drive 15 miles (24 km) on Highway 313 to the junction for Dead Horse Point State Park. From here, continue straight for 7 miles (11.3 km).

SIGHTS
Shafer Canyon Overlook

Half a mile (0.8 km) past the visitors center is the Shafer Canyon Overlook (on the left, just before crossing the neck). The overlook has good views east down the canyon and onto the incredibly twisting **Shafer Trail Road.** Cattlemen Frank and John Schafer built the trail in the early 1900s to move stock between pastures (the *c* in their name was later dropped by mapmakers). Uranium prospectors upgraded the trail to a 4WD road during the 1950s so that they could reach their claims at the base of the cliffs. Today, Shafer Trail Road connects the mesa top with White Rim Road and Potash Road, 4 miles (6.4 km) and 1,200 vertical feet (366 m) below. High-clearance vehicles should be used on the Shafer. It's also fun to ride this road on a mountain bike. Road conditions can vary considerably, so contact a ranger before starting. Shafer Trail Viewpoint, across the neck,

1: Shafer Canyon Overlook 2: Green River overlook
3: The Island in the Sky is flanked by 800-foot cliffs.

provides another perspective 0.5 mile (0.8 km) farther on.

Back on top of the Island, the paved park road leads south from the neck 6 miles (9.7 km) across Gray's Pasture to a junction. The Grand View Point Overlook road continues south while the road to Upheaval Dome turns west.

Buck Canyon Overlook

As the park road continues south, a series of incredible vistas over the canyons of the Green and Colorado Rivers peek into view. The first viewpoint, 9 miles (14.5 km) south of the visitors center, is the wheelchair-accessible Buck Canyon Overlook, which looks east over the Colorado River canyon. Two miles (3.2 km) farther (11 mi/17.7 km south of the visitor center) is the **Grand View Picnic Area,** a handy lunch stop.

Grand View Point

At the end of the main road, 1 mile (1.6 km) past the Grand View Picnic Area (12 mi/19.3 km south of the visitors center), is the Grand View Point Overlook, perhaps the most spectacular panorama from Island in the Sky. Monument Basin lies directly below, and countless canyons, the Colorado River, the Needles, and mountain ranges are in the distance. The Grand View Point Overlook is wheelchair-accessible, and the easy 1-mile (1.6-km) **Grand View Trail** continues past the end of the road for other vistas from the point.

Return to the main road to explore more overlooks and geological curiosities in the western portion of Island in the Sky.

Green River Overlook

The Green River Overlook is just west of the main junction on a paved road. From this wheelchair-accessible overlook, Soda Springs Basin and a section of the Green River (deeply entrenched in Stillwater Canyon) can be seen below. Small Island in the Sky Campground is on the way to the overlook.

Upheaval Dome Road

At the end of the road, 5.3 miles (8.5 km) northwest of the junction (just over 11 mi/17.7 km from the visitors center), is **Upheaval Dome.** This geologic oddity is a fantastically deformed pile of rock sprawled across a crater about 3 miles (4.8 km) wide and 1,200 feet (366 m) deep. For many years, Upheaval Dome has kept geologists busy trying to figure out its origins. They once assumed that salt of the Paradox Formation pushed the rock layers upward to form the dome. Now, however, strong evidence suggests that a meteorite impact created the structure. The surrounding ring depression, caused by collapse, and the convergence of rock layers upward toward the center correspond precisely to known impact structures. Shatter cones and microscopic analysis also indicate an impact origin. When the meteorite struck, sometime in the last 150 million years, it formed a crater up to 5 miles (8 km) across. Erosion removed some of the overlying rock—perhaps as much as a vertical mile. The underlying salt may have played a role in uplifting the central section.

The easy **Crater View Trail** leads to overlooks on the rim of Upheaval Dome; the first viewpoint is 0.5 mile round-trip, and the second is 1 mile (1.6 km) round-trip. There's also a small **picnic area** here.

★ White Rim Road

This driving adventure follows the White Rim below the sheer cliffs of Island in the Sky. A close look at the light-colored surface reveals ripple marks and cross beds laid down near an ancient coastline. The plateau's east side is about 800 feet (244 m) above the Colorado River. On the west side, the plateau meets the bank of the Green River.

Travel along the winding road presents a constantly changing panorama of rock, canyons, river, and sky. Keep an eye out for desert bighorn sheep. You'll see all three levels of Island in the Sky District, from the high plateaus to the White Rim to the rivers.

Only 4WD vehicles with high clearance

Four-Wheeling in Canyonlands

Canyonlands is a tonic for people who think that just as a dog needs to run free every once in a while, jeeps need to occasionally escape the home-to-work loop.

Each of the park's three main districts has a focal point for 4WD travel. In the Island in the Sky, it's the 100-mile-long **White Rim Road.** Four-wheelers in the Needles head to **Elephant Rock** for the challenging climb to a network of roads. The Maze's **Flint Trail** traverses clay slopes that are extremely slippery when wet. Though all of the park's 4WD roads are rugged, those in the Maze are especially challenging, and this area is by far the most remote.

Drivers should note that ATVs are not permitted in national parks. All vehicles must be street-legal. The most commonly used vehicles are jeeps. Four-wheel drivers should be prepared to make basic road or vehicle repairs and should carry the following items:

Four-wheeling on White Rim Road

- at least one full-size spare tire

- extra gas

- extra water

- a shovel

- a high-lift jack

- chains for all four tires, especially October-April

Also note that towing from any backcountry area of Canyonlands is very expensive: It's not uncommon for bills to top $1,000.

Permits are required for overnight trips; camping is only in designated sites.

can make the trip. With the proper vehicle, driving is mostly easy but slow and winding; a few steep or rough sections have to be negotiated. The 100-mile (161-km) trip takes two or three days. Allow an extra day to travel all the road spurs.

Mountain bikers find this a great trip too; most cyclists arrange an accompanying 4WD vehicle to carry water and camping gear. Primitive campgrounds along the way provide convenient stopping places. Both cyclists and 4WD drivers must obtain **reservations** and a **backcountry permit** ($30) for the White Rim campsites from the Island in the Sky visitors center. Find application forms on the Canyonlands website (https://canypermits.

nps.gov); return the completed application at least two weeks in advance of your planned trip. Questions can be fielded via telephone (435/259-4351, 8am-noon Mon.-Fri.), but no telephone reservations are accepted. Demand exceeds supply during the popular spring and autumn seasons, when you should make reservations as far in advance as possible. No services or developed water sources exist anywhere on the drive, so be sure to have plenty of fuel and water with some to spare. Access points are Shafer Trail Road (from near Island in the Sky) and Potash Road (Hwy. 279 from Moab) on the east and Mineral Bottom Road on the west. White Rim sandstone forms the distinctive plateau crossed on the drive.

Island in the Sky Hikes

Trail	Effort	Distance	Duration
★ Mesa Arch Trail	easy	0.25 mi/0.4 km one-way	15 minutes
White Rim Overlook Trail	easy	0.75 mi/1.2 km one-way	1 hour
Upheaval Dome Viewpoint Trail	easy	1 mi/1.6 km one-way	1.5 hours
★ Grand View Trail	easy	1 mi/1.6 km one-way	1 hour
Whale Rock Trail	easy-moderate	0.5 mi/0.8 km one-way	1 hour
Aztec Butte Trail	moderate	1 mi/1.6 km one-way	1.5 hours
Neck Springs Trail	moderate	5.8-mi/9.3-km loop	3-4 hours
Gooseberry Trail	strenuous	2.5 mi/4 km one-way	5 hours
Syncline Loop Trail	strenuous	8-mi/12.9-km loop	5-7 hours
Murphy Point	strenuous	11-mi/17.7-km loop	5-7 hours
Alcove Spring Trail	strenuous	10 mi/16 km one-way	overnight
Lathrop Trail	strenuous	10.5 mi/16.9 km one-way	Overnight

HIKING

Neck Springs Trail

Distance: 5.8-mile (9.3 km) loop
Duration: 3-4 hours
Elevation change: 300 feet (91 m)
Effort: moderate
Trailhead: Shafer Canyon Overlook

The trail begins near the Shafer Canyon Overlook and loops down Taylor Canyon to Neck and Cabin Springs, formerly used by ranchers (look for the remains of the old cowboy cabin near Cabin Springs). It then climbs back to Island in the Sky Road at a second trailhead 0.5 mile (0.8 km) south of the start. Water at the springs supports maidenhair fern and other plants. Also watch for birds and wildlife attracted to this spot. Bring water with you, as the springs are not potable.

Lathrop Trail

Distance: 10.5 miles (16.9 km) one-way to the Colorado River
Duration: overnight
Elevation change: 2,000 feet (610 m)
Effort: strenuous
Trailhead: on the left, 1.3 miles (2.1 km) past the neck

This is the only marked hiking route going all the way from Island in the Sky to the Colorado River. The first 3 miles (4.8 km) cross Gray's Pasture to the rim, which affords fantastic vistas over the Colorado. From here, the trail descends steeply, dropping 1,600 feet (488 m) over the next 2.5 miles (4 km) to White Rim Road, a little less than 7 miles (11.3 km) from the trailhead. Part of this section follows an old mining road past several abandoned mines, all relics of the uranium boom. Don't enter the shafts; they're in danger of collapse and may contain poisonous gases. From the mining area, the route descends through a wash to White Rim Road, follows the road a short distance south, then goes down Lathrop Canyon Road to the Colorado River, another 4 miles (6.4 km) and 500 vertical feet (152 m). The trail has little shade and can be very hot. Vehicular traffic may be encountered along the White Rim Road portion of the trail. For a long day hike (13.6 mi/21.9 km round-trip), turn around when you reach the White Rim Road and hike back up to the top of the mesa.

★ Mesa Arch Trail

Distance: 0.25 mile (0.4 km) one-way
Duration: 15 minutes
Elevation change: 80 feet (24 m)
Effort: easy
Trailhead: on the left, 5.5 miles (8.9 km) from the neck

This easy trail leads to a spectacular arch on the rim of the mesa. On the way, the trail crosses the arid grasslands and scattered juniper trees of Gray's Pasture. A trail brochure available at the start describes the ecology of the mesa. The rather barren, undramatic trail climbs gently until it suddenly reaches the edge of an 800-foot (244-m) precipice, topped by a sandstone arch. The arch frames views of rock formations below and the La Sal Mountains in the distance. Photographers come here to catch the sun (or moon) rising through the arch.

Murphy Point

Distance: 11-mile (17.7-km) loop
Duration: 5-7 hours
Elevation change: 1,100 feet (335 m)
Effort: strenuous

Trailhead: Murphy Point
Directions: From the Upheaval Dome junction on the main park road, head 3 miles (4.8 km) south. Turn right onto a rough dirt road and follow it 1.7 miles (2.7 km) to Murphy Point.

Murphy Trail starts as a jaunt across the mesa, then drops steeply from the rim down to White Rim Road. This strenuous route forks partway down; one branch follows Murphy Hogback (a ridge) to Murphy Campground on the 4WD road, and the other follows a wash to the road 1 mile (1.6 km) south of the campground.

White Rim Overlook Trail

Distance: 0.75 mile (1.2 km) one-way
Duration: 1 hour
Elevation change: 25 feet (8 m)
Effort: easy
Trailhead: Grand View Picnic Area

Hike east along a peninsula to an overlook of Monument Basin and beyond. There are also good views of White Rim Road and potholes.

Gooseberry Trail

Distance: 2.5 miles (4 km) one-way
Duration: 5 hours
Elevation change: 1,400 feet (427 m)
Effort: strenuous
Trailhead: Grand View Picnic Area

Mesa Arch spans the cliff's edge.

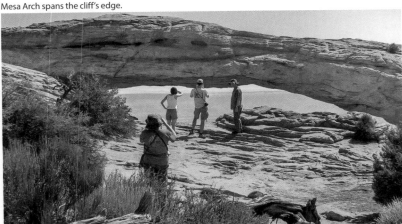

Gooseberry Trail drops off the mesa and makes an extremely steep descent to White Rim Road, just north of Gooseberry Campground. The La Sal Mountains are visible from the trail.

★ Grand View Trail

Distance: 1 mile (1.6 km) one-way
Duration: 1 hour
Elevation change: 50 feet (15 m)
Effort: easy
Trailhead: Grand View Point Overlook

At the overlook, Grand View Trail continues past the end of the road for other vistas from the point, which is the southernmost tip of Island in the Sky. This short hike across the slickrock will really give you a feel for the entire Canyonlands National Park. From the mesa-top trail, you'll see the gorges of the Colorado and Green Rivers come together; across the chasm is the Needles District. Look down to spot vehicles traveling along the White Rim Trail at the base of the mesa.

Aztec Butte Trail

Distance: 1 mile (1.6 km) one-way
Duration: 1.5 hours
Elevation change: 200 feet (61 m)
Effort: moderate
Trailhead: Aztec Butte parking area, 1 mile (1.6 km) northwest of road junction on Upheaval Dome Road

It's a bit of a haul up the slickrock to the top of this sandstone butte, but once you get here, you'll be rewarded with a good view of the Island and Taylor Canyon. Atop the butte a loop trail passes several Ancestral Puebloan granaries. Aztec Butte is one of the few areas in Island in the Sky with Native American ruins; the shortage of water in this area prevented permanent settlement.

Whale Rock Trail

Distance: 0.5 mile (0.8 km) one-way
Duration: 1 hour
Elevation change: 100 feet (30 m)
Effort: easy-moderate
Trailhead: Upheaval Dome Road, on the right, 4.4 miles (7.1 km) northwest of the road junction

A relatively easy trail climbs Whale Rock, a sandstone hump near the outer rim of Upheaval Dome. In a couple of places you'll have to do some scrambling up the slickrock, which is made easier and a bit less scary thanks to handrails. From the top of the rock, there are good views of the dome.

Watch your step along the Grand View Trail.

Grand View Trails

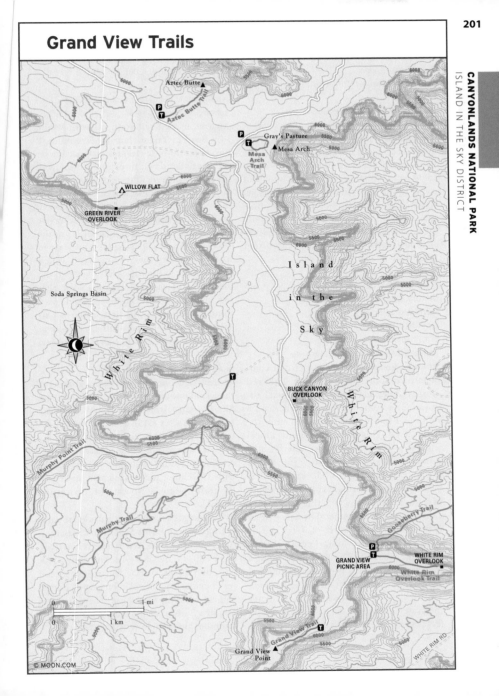

© MOON.COM

Upheaval Dome Viewpoint Trail

Distance: 1 mile (1.6 km) one-way
Duration: 1.5 hours
Elevation change: 150 feet (46 m)
Effort: easy
Trailhead: Upheaval Dome parking area

The trail leads to Upheaval Dome overviews; it's about 0.5 mile (0.8 km) to the first overlook and 1 mile (1.6 km) to the second. The shorter trail leads to the rim with a view about 1,000 feet (305 m) down into the jumble of rocks in the craterlike center of Upheaval Dome. The longer trail descends the slickrock and offers even better views. Energetic hikers can explore this formation in depth by circling it on the Syncline Loop Trail or from White Rim Road below.

Syncline Loop Trail

Distance: 8-mile (12.9-km) loop
Duration: 5-7 hours
Elevation change: 1,200 feet (366 m)
Effort: strenuous
Trailhead: Upheaval Dome parking area

Syncline Loop Trail makes a circuit completely around Upheaval Dome. The trail crosses Upheaval Dome Canyon about halfway around from the overlook; walk east 1.5 miles (2.4 km) up the canyon to enter the crater itself. This is the only nontechnical route into the center of the dome. A hike around Upheaval Dome with a side trip to the crater totals 11 miles (17.7 km), and it is best done as an overnight trip. Carry plenty of water for the entire trip; this dry country can be very hot in summer. The Green River is the only reliable source of water. An alternative approach is to start near Upheaval Campsite on White Rim Road; hike 4 miles (6.4 km) southeast on through Upheaval Canyon to a junction with the Syncline Loop Trail, then go another 1.5 miles (2.4 km) into the crater. The elevation gain is about 600 feet (183 m).

Alcove Spring Trail

Distance: 10 miles (16 km) one-way
Duration: overnight
Elevation change: 1,500 feet (457 m)
Effort: strenuous
Trailhead: 1.5 miles (2.4 km) southeast of the Upheaval Dome parking area

Alcove Spring Trail connects with White Rim Road in Taylor Canyon. Five miles (8 km) of the 10-mile (16-km) distance are on the steep trail down through Trail Canyon; the other 5 miles (8 km) are on a jeep road in Taylor Canyon. One downside of this trail is the 4WD traffic, which can be pretty heavy during the spring and fall. From the Taylor Canyon end of the trail, it is not far to the Upheaval Trail, which heads southeast to its junction with the Syncline Trail, which in turn leads to the Upheaval Dome parking area. Allow at least one overnight if you plan to hike this full loop. Day hikers should plan to turn around after the first 5-mile (8-km) section; this is still a very full day of hiking. Carry plenty of water—the trail is hot and dry.

CAMPGROUNDS

There is only one developed campground in the Island in the Sky District. **Island in the Sky Campground** on Murphy Point Road has only 12 sites ($15), available on a first-come, first-served basis; sites tend to fill up in all seasons except winter. There is one accessible campsite that is reserved for people with disabilities, and a paved path leading to the nearby pit-toilet. No water or services are available.

Camping is available just outside the park at **Dead Horse Point State Park** (reservations 800/322-3770, www.reserveamerica. com, $40 RV, $35 hike-in tent only, $140 yurt, plus $9 reservation fee), which is also very popular, so don't plan on getting a spot without reserving way ahead. There are also primitive Bureau of Land Management (BLM) campsites along Highway 313.

Upheaval Dome Trails

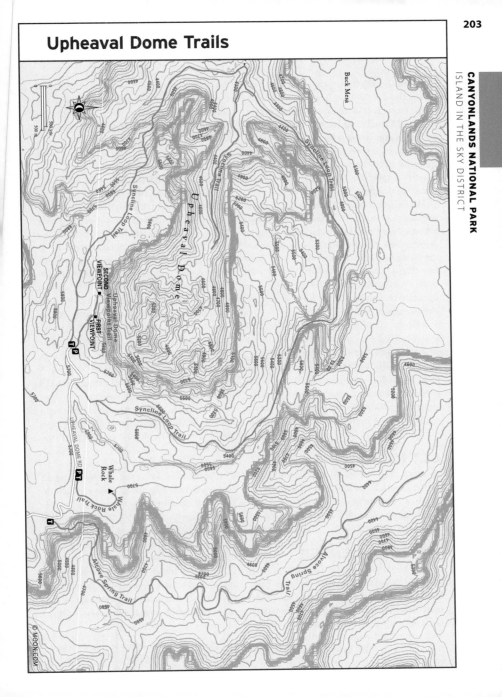

Needles District

The Needles District, named for the area's distinctive sandstone spires, showcases some of the finest rock sculptures in Canyonlands National Park. Spires, arches, and monoliths appear in almost every direction. Prehistoric ruins and rock art exist in greater variety and quantity here than elsewhere in the park. Perennial springs and streams bring greenery to the desert.

While scenic paved Highway 211 leads to the district, this area of the park has only about a dozen miles of paved roads. Needles doesn't have a lot to offer travelers who are unwilling to get out of their vehicles and hike; however, it's the best section of the park for a wide variety of day hikes. Even a short hike opens up the landscape and leads to remarkable vistas and prehistoric sites.

The primary access road to Needles District, Highway 211, also passes through **Indian Creek National Monument,** designated in 2018 by President Donald Trump. Officials at this new monument are in the process of creating its management plan. For current recreational information, contact the BLM office in Monticello (365 N. Main, 435/587-1500).

GETTING THERE

To reach the Needles District, go 40 miles (64 km) south from Moab (or 14 mi/22.5 km north of Monticello) on U.S. 191, turn west onto Highway 211, and continue for 38 miles (61 km).

VISITORS CENTER

Stop at the **visitors center** (west end of Hwy. 211, 435/259-4711, 9am-4pm Fri.-Tues. Jan.-Feb., 8am-4pm daily Mar. 1-mid-Mar., 8am-6pm daily mid-Mar.-Sept., 8:30am-5pm daily Oct., 9am-4pm Nov.-Dec.) for information on hiking, back roads, and other aspects of travel in the Needles, as well as **backcountry permits** (required for all overnight stays in the backcountry) and maps, brochures, and books. Take about 15 minutes to watch the film on the region's geology. When the office isn't open, you'll find information posted outside.

SIGHTS
★ BLM Newspaper Rock Historical Monument

Although not in the park itself, Newspaper Rock lies just 150 feet (46 m) off Highway 211 on Bureau of Land Management (BLM) land on the way to the Needles District. At Newspaper Rock, a profusion of petroglyphs depict human figures, animals, birds, and abstract designs. These represent 2,000 years of human history during which prehistoric people and Ancestral Puebloan, Fremont, Paiute, Navajo, and Anglo travelers passed through Indian Creek Canyon. The patterns on the smooth sandstone rock face stand out clearly, thanks to a coating of dark desert varnish. A short nature trail introduces you to the area's desert and riparian vegetation.

From U.S. 191 between Moab and Monticello, turn west onto Highway 211 and travel 12 miles (19.3 km) to Newspaper Rock.

Indian Creek

The "splitter cracks" in the rock walls around **Indian Creek** offer world-class rock climbing, with close to 1,000 routes. Most routes here are tough, rating 5.10 and above. Fall climbing is best, followed by early spring; summer afternoons are way too hot, and it's dangerous to climb after a rainstorm.

Climbers should track down a copy of *Indian Creek: A Climbing Guide* by David Bloom, which has details and lots of pictures. **Moab Desert Adventures** (415

1: Big Spring Canyon Overlook 2: Pothole Point Nature Trail 3: Newspaper Rock 4: camping at Needles Outpost

N. Main St., Moab, 804/814-3872, www. moabdesertadventures.com) offers guided climbing at Indian Creek.

Indian Creek's climbing walls start on Highway 211, about 15 miles (24 km) west of U.S. 191, and 3 miles (4.8 km) west of Newspaper Rock.

Needles and Anticline Overlooks

Although outside the park, these viewpoints atop the high mesa east of Canyonlands National Park offer magnificent panoramas of the surrounding area. Part of the BLM's Canyon Rims Recreation Area (www. blm.gov), these easily accessed overlooks provide the kind of awe-inspiring vistas over the Needles District that would otherwise require a hike in the park. The turnoff for both overlooks is at milepost 93 on U.S. 191, which is 32 miles (52 km) south of Moab and 7 miles (11.3 km) north of Highway 211. There are also two campgrounds along the access road.

For the Needles Overlook, follow the paved road 22 miles (35 km) west to its end (turn left at the junction 15 mi/24 km in). The BLM maintains a picnic area and interpretive exhibits here. A fence protects visitors from the sheer cliffs that drop off more than 1,000 feet (305 m). You can see much of Canyonlands National Park and southeastern Utah. Look south for the Six-Shooter Peaks and the high country of the Abajo Mountains; southwest for the Needles (thousands of spires reaching for the sky); west for the confluence area of the Green and Colorado Rivers, the Maze District, the Orange Cliffs, and the Henry Mountains; northwest for the lazy bends of the Colorado River canyon and the sheer-walled mesas of Island in the Sky and Dead Horse Point; north for the Book Cliffs; and northeast for the La Sal Mountains. The changing shadows and colors of the canyon country make for a continuous show throughout the day.

For the Anticline Overlook, from U.S. 191, head 15 miles (24 km) west to the junction with the Needles road, then turn right and drive 17 miles (27 km) north on a good gravel road to the fenced overlook at road's end. You'll be standing 1,600 feet (488 m) above the Colorado River. The sweeping panorama over the canyons, the river (and the bright blue evaporation ponds at the potash factory outside Moab), and the twisted rocks of the Kane Creek Anticline is nearly as spectacular as that from Dead Horse Point, only 5.5 miles (8.9 km) west as the crow flies. Salt and other minerals of the Paradox Formation pushed up overlying rocks into the dome visible below. Down-cutting by the Colorado River has revealed the twisted rock layers. Look carefully at the northeast horizon to see an arch in the Windows Section of Arches National Park, 16 miles (26 km) away.

The BLM operates two campgrounds in the Canyon Rims Recreation Area. Hatch Point Campground (10 sites, May-mid-Oct., $15) has a quiet and scenic mesa-top setting just off the road to the Anticline Overlook, about 9 miles (14.5 km) north of the road junction. Closer to the highway in a rock amphitheater is Windwhistle Campground (May-mid-Oct., $15); it's 6 miles (9.7 km) west of U.S. 191 on the Needles Overlook road. Although both of these campgrounds supposedly have water, it wasn't evident when we visited.

Needles Outpost

The Needles Outpost campground (435/979-4007, http://www.needlesoutpost. com, mid-Feb.-mid Dec., $20 tents or RVs, no hookups), just outside the park boundary, is a good place to stay if the campground in the park is full. A general store here has groceries, ice, gas, propane, showers ($3 campers, $6 noncampers), and basic camping supplies. Campsites have a fair amount of privacy and great views onto the park's spires. The turnoff from Highway 211 is one mile before the Needles visitors center.

SCENIC DRIVE

The main paved park road continues 6.5 miles (10.5 km) past the visitors center to Big Spring Canyon Overlook. On the way, you

Needles Hikes

Trail	Effort	Distance	Duration
Roadside Ruin Trail	easy	0.3 mi/0.5 km round-trip	15 minutes
★ Cave Spring Trail	easy	0.6 mi/1 km round-trip	45 minutes
Pothole Point Nature Trail	easy	0.6 mi/1 km round-trip	40 minutes
Slickrock Trail	easy-moderate	2.4 mi/3.9 km round-trip	2 hours
★ Chesler Park	moderate	3 mi/4.8 km one-way	3-4 hours
Squaw Canyon Trail	moderate	3.75 mi/6 km one-way	4 hours
Lost Canyon Trail	moderate-strenuous	3.25 mi/5.2 km one-way	4-5 hours
Big Spring Canyon Trail	moderate-strenuous	3.75 mi/6 km one-way	4 hours
Confluence Overlook Trail	moderate-strenuous	5.5 mi/8.9 km one-way	5 hours
Peekaboo Trail	strenuous	5 mi/8 km one-way	5-6 hours
Druid Arch	strenuous	5.5 mi/8.9 km one-way	5-7 hours
Lower Red Lake Canyon Trail	strenuous	9.5 mi/15.3 km one-way	2 days
Upper Salt Creek Trail	strenuous	12 mi/19.3 km one-way	2 days

can stop at several nature trails or turn onto 4WD roads. The overlook takes in a view of slickrock-edged canyons dropping away toward the Colorado River.

HIKING

The Needles District includes about 60 miles (97 km) of backcountry trails. Many interconnect to provide all sorts of day-hike and overnight opportunities. Cairns mark the trails, and signs point the way at junctions. You can normally find water in upper Elephant Canyon and canyons to the east in spring and early summer, although whatever remains is often stagnant by midsummer. Always ask the rangers about sources of water, and don't depend on its availability. Treat water from all

sources, including springs, before drinking it. Chesler Park and other areas west of Elephant Canyon are very dry; you'll need to bring all your water. Mosquitoes, gnats, and deer flies can be pesky late spring to midsummer, especially in the wetter places, so be sure to bring insect repellent. To plan your trip, obtain the small hiking map available from the visitors center, the National Geographic/Trails Illustrated Needles District map, or USGS topographic maps. Overnight backcountry hiking requires a **permit** ($30 per group). Permits can be hard to get at the last minute during the busy spring hiking season, but you can apply for your permit any time after mid-July for the following spring. Find permit applications on the Canyonlands permitting website (https://canypermits.nps.gov). Note that campers at sites in Chesler Park, Elephant Canyon, and at Peekaboo will be required to pack out their human waste.

Roadside Ruin Trail

Distance: 0.3 mile (0.5 km) round-trip
Duration: 15 minutes
Elevation change: 20 feet (6 m)
Effort: easy
Trailhead: on the left, 0.4 mile (0.6 km) past the visitors center

This is one of two easy hikes near the visitors center. It passes near a well-preserved Ancestral Puebloan granary. A trail guide available at the start tells about the Ancestral Puebloans and the local plants.

★ Cave Spring Trail

Distance: 0.6 mile (1 km) round-trip
Duration: 45 minutes
Elevation change: 50 feet (15 m)
Effort: easy
Trailhead: Cave Spring
Directions: Turn left 0.7 mile (1.1 km) past the visitors center and follow signs about 1 mile (1.6 km) to the trailhead.

Don't miss the Cave Spring Trail, which introduces the geology and ecology of the park and leads to an old cowboy line camp. Pick up the brochure at the beginning. The loop goes clockwise, crossing some slickrock; two ladders assist hikers on the steep sections. Native Americans first used these rock overhangs for shelter, and faint pictographs still decorate the rock walls. Much later—from the late 1800s until the park was established in 1964—cowboys used these open caves as a line camp. The National Park Service has recreated the line camp, just 50 yards in from the trailhead, with period furnishings and equipment. If you're not up for the full hike, or would rather not climb ladders, the cowboy camp and the pictographs are just a five-minute walk from the trailhead.

This trail is a good introduction to hiking on slickrock and using rock cairns to find your way. Signs identify plants along the way.

Pothole Point Nature Trail

Distance: 0.6 mile (1 km) round-trip
Duration: 40 minutes
Elevation change: 20 feet (6 m)
Effort: easy
Trailhead: parking area on the left side of Big Spring Canyon Overlook Scenic Drive, 5 miles (8 km) past the visitors center

Highlights of this hike across the slickrock are the many potholes dissolved in the Cedar Mesa sandstone. A brochure illustrates the fairy shrimp, tadpole shrimp, horsehair worms, snails, and other creatures that spring to life when rain fills the potholes. Desert varnish rims the potholes; it forms when water evaporates, leaving mineral residues on the surface of the rocks. In addition to the potholes, you'll enjoy fine views of distant buttes from the trail.

Slickrock Trail

Distance: 2.4 miles (3.9 km) round-trip
Duration: 2 hours
Elevation change: 150 feet (46 m)
Effort: easy-moderate
Trailhead: parking area on the right side of Big Spring Canyon Overlook Scenic Drive, 6.2 miles (10 km) past the visitors center

The Slickrock Trail leads north to a series of four viewpoints, including a panoramic view over much of southeastern Utah, and overlooks of Big Spring and Little Spring Canyons. As its name indicates, much of the trail is across slickrock, but there are enough pockets of soil to support a good springtime display of wildflowers. The trailhead is almost at the end of the paved road, where **Big Spring Canyon Overlook,** 6.5 miles (10.5 km) past the visitors center, marks the end of the scenic drive but not the scenery.

Confluence Overlook Trail

Distance: 5.5 miles (8.9 km) one-way
Duration: 5 hours
Elevation change: 1,250 feet (381 m)
Effort: moderate-strenuous
Trailhead: Big Spring Canyon Overlook

The Confluence Overlook Trail begins at the

Big Spring Canyon Overlook Trails

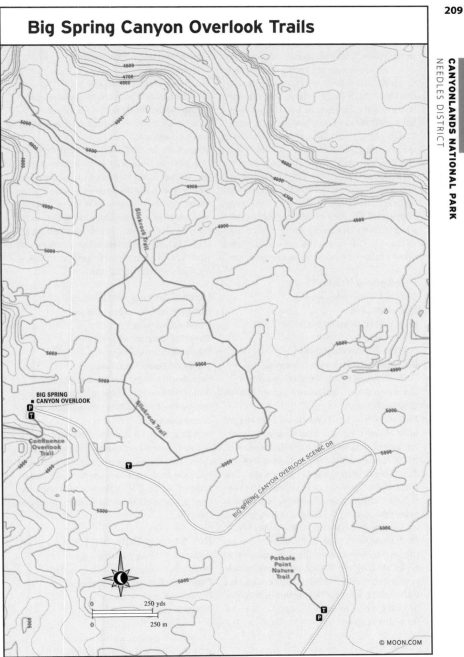

BIG SPRING
CANYON OVERLOOK

Confluence
Overlook
Trail

Slickrock Trail

Slickrock Trail

BIG SPRING CANYON OVERLOOK SCENIC DR

Pothole
Point
Nature
Trail

0   250 yds

0   250 m

© MOON.COM

end of the paved road and winds west to an overlook of the Green and Colorado Rivers 1,000 feet (305 m) below; there's no trail down to the rivers. The trail starts with some ups and downs, crossing Big Spring and Elephant Canyons, and follows a jeep road for a short distance. Much of the trail is through open country, so it can get quite hot. Higher points have good views of the Needles to the south. You might see rafts in the water or bighorn sheep on the cliffs. Except for a few short steep sections, this trail is level and fairly easy; it's the length of this 11-mile (17.7-km) round-trip to the confluence as well as the hot sun that make it challenging. A very early start is recommended in summer because there's little shade. Carry water even if you don't plan to go all the way. This enchanting country has lured many a hiker beyond his or her original goal.

Peekaboo Trail

Distance: 5 miles (8 km) one-way
Duration: 5-6 hours
Elevation change: 550 feet (168 m)
Effort: strenuous
Trailhead: Squaw Flat trailhead
Directions: A road to Needles Campground and Elephant Hill turns left 2.7 miles (4.3 km) past the visitors center. The Squaw Flat trailhead is at the end of campground loop A.

Peekaboo Trail winds southeast over rugged up-and-down terrain, including some steep sections of slickrock (best avoided when wet, icy, or covered with snow) and a couple of ladders. There's little shade, so carry water. The trail follows Squaw Canyon, climbs over a pass to Lost Canyon, then crosses more slickrock before descending to Peekaboo Campground on Salt Creek Road (accessible by 4WD vehicles). Look for Ancestral Puebloan ruins on the way and rock art at the campground. A rockslide took out Peekaboo Spring, which is still shown on some maps. Options on this trail include a turnoff south through Squaw or Lost Canyon to make a loop of 8.75 miles (14.1 km) or more.

Squaw Canyon Trail

Distance: 3.75 miles (6 km) one-way
Duration: 4 hours
Elevation change: 700 feet (213 m)
Effort: moderate
Trailhead: Squaw Flat trailhead
Directions: A road to Needles Campground and Elephant Hill turns left 2.7 miles (4.3 km) past the visitors center. The Squaw Flat trailhead is at the end of campground loop A.

Squaw Canyon Trail follows the canyon south. Intermittent water can often be found until late spring, when there's plenty of greenery. Connect with the Big Spring Canyon Trail to make a great 7.5-mile (12-km) loop. Another possible loop is formed by linking the Squaw Canyon and Lost Canyon Trails, totaling 8.7 miles (14 km). Both of these loops require stiff climbs (with great views) to get over the slickrock hills separating the canyons.

Lost Canyon Trail

Distance: 3.25 miles (5.2 km) one-way
Duration: 4-5 hours
Elevation change: 360 feet (110 m)
Effort: moderate-strenuous
Trailhead: Squaw Flat trailhead
Directions: A road to Needles Campground and Elephant Hill turns left 2.7 miles (4.3 km) past the visitors center. The Squaw Flat trailhead is at the end of campground loop A.

Lost Canyon Trail is reached via Peekaboo or Squaw Canyon Trails and makes a loop with them. Lost Canyon is surprisingly lush, and you may be forced to wade through water. Most of the trail is in the wash bottom, except for a section of slickrock to Squaw Canyon.

Big Spring Canyon Trail

Distance: 3.75 miles (6 km) one-way
Duration: 4 hours
Elevation change: 370 feet (113 m)
Effort: moderate-strenuous
Trailhead: Squaw Flat trailhead

1: Slickrock Trail 2: Big Spring Canyon Trail

Directions: A road to Needles Campground and Elephant Hill turns left 2.7 miles (4.3 km) past the visitors center. The Squaw Flat trailhead is at the end of campground loop A.

Big Spring Canyon Trail crosses an outcrop of slickrock from the trailhead, then follows the canyon bottom to the head of the canyon. It's a lovely springtime hike with lots of flowers, including the fragrant cliffrose. Except in summer, you can usually find intermittent water along the way. At canyon's end, a steep slickrock climb leads to Squaw Canyon Trail and back to the trailhead for a 7.5-mile (12-km) loop. Another possibility is to turn southwest to the head of Squaw Canyon, then hike over a saddle to Elephant Canyon, for a 10.5-mile (16.9-km) loop.

★ Chesler Park

Distance: 3 miles (4.8 km) one-way
Duration: 3-4 hours
Elevation change: 920 feet (280 m)
Effort: moderate
Trailhead: Elephant Hill parking area or Squaw Flat trailhead—increases the round-trip distance by 2 miles/3.2 kilometers
Directions: Drive west 3 miles (4.8 km) past the Needles Campground turnoff (on passable dirt roads) to the Elephant Hill picnic area and trailhead at the base of Elephant Hill.

The Elephant Hill parking area doesn't always inspire confidence: Sounds of racing engines can often be heard from above as vehicles attempt the difficult 4WD road that begins just past the picnic area. However, the noise quickly fades as you hit the trail. Chesler Park is a favorite hiking destination. A lovely desert meadow contrasts with the red and white spires that give the Needles District its name. An old cowboy line camp is on the west side of the rock island in the center of the park. The trail winds through sand and slickrock before ascending a small pass through the Needles to Chesler Park. Once inside, you can take the Chesler Park Loop Trail (5 mi/8 km) completely around the park. The loop includes the unusual 0.5-mile (0.8-km) Joint Trail, which follows the bottom of a very narrow crack. Camping in Chesler Park is restricted to certain areas; check with a ranger.

Druid Arch

Distance: 5.5 miles (8.9 km) one-way
Duration: 5-7 hours
Elevation change: 1,000 feet (305 m)
Effort: strenuous
Trailhead: Elephant Hill parking area or Squaw Flat trailhead—increases the round-trip distance by 2 miles/3.2 kilometers

Chesler Park

Directions: Drive west 3 miles (4.8 km) past the Needles Campground turnoff (on passable dirt roads) to the Elephant Hill picnic area and trailhead at the base of Elephant Hill.

Druid Arch reminds many people of the massive slabs at Stonehenge in England, which are popularly associated with the druids. Follow the Chesler Park Trail 2 miles (3.2 km) to Elephant Canyon, turn up the canyon for 3.5 miles (5.6 km), and then make a steep 0.25-mile (0.4 km) climb, which includes a ladder and some scrambling, to the arch. Upper Elephant Canyon has seasonal water but is closed to camping.

Lower Red Lake Canyon Trail

Distance: 9.5 miles (15.3 km) one-way
Duration: 2 days
Elevation change: 1,000 feet (305 m)
Effort: strenuous
Trailhead: Elephant Hill parking area or Squaw Flat trailhead (increases the round-trip distance by 2 mi/3.2 km)
Directions: Drive west 3 miles (6.4 km) past the Needles Campground turnoff (on passable dirt roads) to the Elephant Hill picnic area and trailhead at the base of Elephant Hill.

Lower Red Lake Canyon Trail provides access to the Colorado River's Cataract Canyon. This long, strenuous trip is best suited for experienced hikers and is ideally completed in two days. Distance from the Elephant Hill trailhead is 19 miles (31 km) round-trip; you'll be walking on 4WD roads and trails. If you can drive Elephant Hill 4WD Road to the trail junction in Cyclone Canyon, the hike is only 8 miles (12.9 km) round-trip. The most difficult trail section is a steep talus slope that drops 700 feet (213 m) in 0.5 mile (0.8 km) into the lower canyon. The canyon has little shade and lacks any water source above the river. Summer heat can make the trip grueling; temperatures tend to be 5-10°F hotter than on other Needles trails. The river level drops between midsummer and autumn, allowing hikers to go along the shore both downstream to see the rapids and upstream to the confluence.

Undertows and strong currents make the river dangerous to cross.

Upper Salt Creek Trail

Distance: 12 miles (19.3 km) one-way
Duration: 2 days
Elevation change: 1,650 feet (503 m)
Effort: strenuous
Trailhead: end of Salt Creek Road
Directions: Drive to the end of the rugged 13.5-mile (21.7-km) 4WD road up Salt Creek to start this hike.

Several impressive arches and many inviting side canyons attract adventurous hikers to the extreme southeast corner of the Needles District. The trail goes south 12 miles (19.3 km) up-canyon to Cottonwood Canyon and Beef Basin Road near Cathedral Butte, just outside the park boundary. The trail is nearly level except for a steep climb at the end. Water can usually be found. Some wading and bushwhacking may be necessary. The famous "All-American Man" pictograph, shown on some topographic maps (or ask a ranger), is in a cave a short way off to the east at about the midpoint of the trail; follow your map and unsigned paths to the cave, but don't climb in—it's dangerous to you, the ruins, and the pictograph inside. Many more archaeological sites are near the trail, but they're all fragile, and great care should be taken when visiting them.

MOUNTAIN BIKING AND 4WD EXPLORATION

Visitors with bicycles or 4WD vehicles can explore the many backcountry roads that lead to the outback. More than 50 miles (81 km) of challenging roads link primitive campsites, remote trailheads, and sites with ancient cultural remnants. Some roads in the Needles District are rugged and require previous experience in handling 4WD vehicles on steep inclines and in deep sand. Be aware that towing charges from this area commonly run over $1,000.

The best route for mountain bikers is the 7-mile-long (11.3 km) Colorado Overlook Road, which starts near the visitors center.

Squaw Flat and Elephant Hill Trails

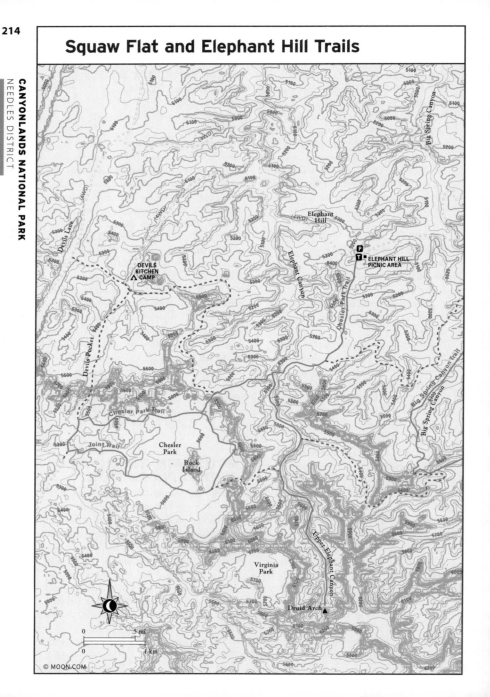

© MOON.COM

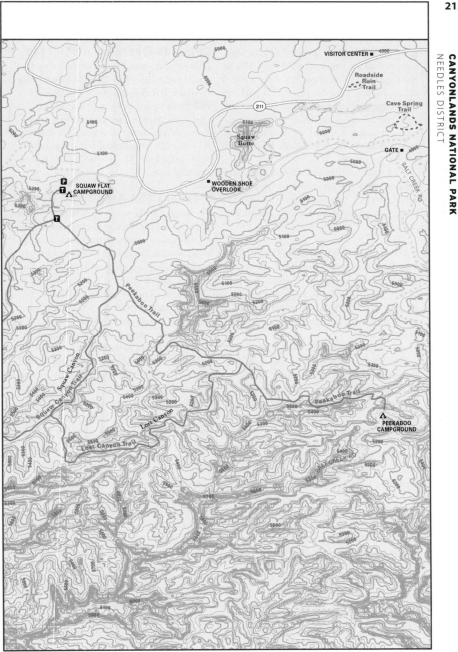

Although very steep for the first stretch and busy with 4WD vehicles spinning their wheels on the hill, Elephant Hill Road is another good bet, with just a few sandy parts. Start here and do a combination ride and hike to the Confluence Overlook. It's about 8 miles (12.9 km) from the Elephant Hill parking area to the confluence; the final 0.5 mile (0.8 km) is on a trail, so you'll have to lock up your bike and walk this last bit. Horse Canyon and Lavender Canyon are too sandy for pleasant biking.

All motor vehicles and bicycles must have a **day-use permit** and remain on designated roads. Overnight backcountry trips with bicycles or motor vehicles require a permit ($30 per group).

Salt Creek Canyon 4WD Road

This rugged route begins near Cave Spring Trail, crosses sage flats for the next 2.5 miles (4 km), and then terminates at Peekaboo Campground. Hikers can continue south into a spectacular canyon on Upper Salt Creek Trail.

Horse Canyon 4WD Road turns off to the left shortly before the mouth of Salt Canyon. The round-trip distance, including a side trip to Tower Ruin, is about 13 miles (21 km); other attractions include Paul Bunyan's Potty, Castle Arch, Fortress Arch, and side canyon hiking. Salt and Horse Canyons can easily be driven in 4WD vehicles. Salt Canyon is usually closed in summer because of quicksand after flash floods and in winter due to shelf ice.

Davis and Lavender Canyons

Both canyons are accessed via Davis Canyon Road off Highway 211; contain great scenery, arches, and Native American historic sites; and are easily visited with high-clearance vehicles. Davis is about 20 miles (32 km) round-trip, while sandy Lavender Canyon is about 26 miles (42 km) round-trip. Try to allow plenty of time in either canyon, because there is much to see and many inviting side canyons to

hike. You can camp on BLM land just outside the park boundaries, but not in the park itself.

Colorado Overlook 4WD Road

This popular route begins beside the visitors center and follows Salt Creek to Lower Jump Overlook. It then bounces across slickrock to a view of the Colorado River, upstream from the confluence. Driving, for the most part, is easy-moderate, although it's very rough for the last 1.5 miles (2.4 km). Round-trip distance is 14 miles (22.5 km). This is also a good mountain bike ride.

Elephant Hill 4WD Loop Road

This rugged backcountry road begins 3 miles (4.8 km) past the Needles Campground turn-off. Only experienced drivers with stout vehicles should attempt the extremely rough and steep climb up Elephant Hill (coming up the back side of Elephant Hill is even worse). The loop is about 10 miles (16 km) round-trip. Connecting roads go to the Confluence Overlook trailhead (the viewpoint is 1 mile/1.6 kilometers round-trip on foot), the Joint trailhead (Chesler Park is 2 miles/3.2 kilometers round-trip on foot), and several canyons. Some road sections on the loop are one-way. In addition to Elephant Hill, a few other difficult spots must be negotiated. The parallel canyons in this area are grabens caused by faulting, where a layer of salt has shifted deep underground.

This area can also be reached by a long route south of the park using Cottonwood Canyon and Beef Basin Road from Highway 211, about 60 miles (97 km) one-way. You'll enjoy spectacular vistas from the Abajo Highlands. Two very steep descents from Pappys Pasture into Bobbys Hole effectively make this section one-way; travel from Elephant Hill up Bobbys Hole is possible but much more difficult than going the other way, and it may require hours of road-building. The Bobbys Hole route may be impassable at times; ask about conditions at the BLM office in Monticello or at the Needles visitors center.

CAMPGROUNDS

The **Needles Campground** (year-round, reservations available and recommended for Loop B only Mar. 15-June 30 and Sept. 1-Oct. 31, $20), formerly known as Squaw Flat Campground, is about 6 miles (9.7 km) from the visitors center. It has water and 26 sites (two of which are accessible), with many snuggled under the slickrock. RVs must be less than 28 feet (8.5 m) long. Rangers present evening programs (spring-autumn) at the campfire circle on Loop A.

If you can't find a space at the Needles Campground—a common occurrence in spring and fall—the private campground at **Needles Outpost** (435/979-4007, https://needlesoutpost.com, Mar.-Nov., $22 tents or RVs, no hookups, showers $3), just outside the park entrance, is a good alternative.

Nearby BLM land also offers a number of places to camp. A string of campsites along **Lockhart Basin Road** are convenient and inexpensive. Lockhart Basin Road heads north from Highway 211 about 5 miles (8 km)

east of the entrance to the Needles District. **Hamburger Rock Campground** (no water, $6) is about 1 mile (1.6 km) up the road. North of Hamburger Rock, camping is dispersed, with many small (no water, free) campsites at turnoffs from the road. Not surprisingly, the road gets rougher the farther north you travel; beyond Indian Creek Falls, it's best to have 4WD. These campsites are very popular with climbers who are here to scale the walls at Indian Creek.

There are two first-come, first-served campgrounds ($15) in the Canyon Rims Special Recreation Management Area (www.blm.gov). **Windwhistle Campground,** backed by cliffs to the south, has fine views to the north and a nature trail; follow the main road from U.S. 191 for 6 miles (9.7 km) and turn left. At **Hatch Point Campground,** in a piñon-juniper woodland, you can enjoy views to the north. Go 24 miles (39 km) in on the paved and gravel roads toward Anticline Overlook, then turn right and continue for 1 mile (1.6 km). It's best to come supplied with water.

The Maze District

Only adventurous and experienced travelers will want to visit this rugged land west of the Green and Colorado Rivers. Vehicle access wasn't even possible until 1957, when mineral-exploration roads first entered what later became Canyonlands National Park. Today, you'll need a high-clearance, low gear-range 4WD vehicle, a horse, or your own two feet to get around, and most visitors spend at least three days in the district. The National Park Service plans to keep this district in its remote and primitive condition. If you can't come overland, an airplane flight provides the only easy way to see the scenic features.

The names of erosional forms describe the landscape—Orange Cliffs, Golden Stairs, the Fins, Land of Standing Rocks, Lizard Rock, the Doll House, Chocolate Drops, the Maze, and Jasper Canyon. The many-fingered

canyons of the Maze gave the district its name; although it is not a true maze, the canyons give that impression. It is extremely important to have a high-quality map before entering this part of Canyonlands. National Geographic/Trails Illustrated makes a good one, called *Canyonlands National Park Maze District, NE Glen Canyon NRA*.

GETTING THERE

Dirt roads to the **Hans Flat Ranger Station** (435/259-2652, 8am-4:30pm daily) and Maze District branch off from Highway 24 (across from the Goblin Valley State Park turnoff) and Highway 95 (take the usually unmarked Hite-Orange Cliffs Road between the Dirty Devil and Hite Bridges at Lake Powell). The easiest way in is the graded 46-mile (74-km) road from Highway 24; it's fast, although sometimes badly corrugated. The 4WD Hite-Orange Cliffs Road is longer, bumpier, and, for some drivers, tedious; it's 54 miles (87 km) from the turnoff at Highway 95 to the Hans Flat Ranger Station via the Flint Trail. All roads to the Maze District cross Glen Canyon National Recreation Area. From Highway 24, two-wheel-drive vehicles with good clearance can travel to Hans Flat Ranger Station and other areas near, but not actually in, the Maze District. From the ranger station it takes at least three hours of skillful four-wheeling to drive into the canyons of the Maze.

One other way of getting to the Maze District is by river. **Tex's Riverways** (435/259-5101 or 877/662-2839, www.texsriverways.com, about $150 pp) can arrange a jet-boat shuttle on the Colorado River from Moab to Spanish Bottom. After the two-hour boat ride, it's 1,260 vertical feet (384 m) uphill in a little over 1 mile (1.6 km) to the Doll House via the Spanish Bottom Trail.

PLANNING AN EXPEDITION

Maze District explorers need a **backcountry permit** ($30) for overnight trips. Note that a backcountry permit in this district is not a reservation. You may have to share a site, especially in the popular spring months. As in the rest of the park, only designated sites can be used for vehicle camping. You don't need a permit to camp in the adjacent Glen Canyon National Recreation Area (NRA) or on BLM land.

There are no developed sources of water in the Maze District. Hikers can obtain water from springs in some canyons (check with a ranger to find out which are flowing) or from the rivers; purify all water before drinking. The Maze District has nine camping areas (two at Maze Overlook, six at Land of Standing Rocks), each with a 15-person, three-vehicle limit.

The National Geographic/Trails Illustrated topographic map of the Maze District describes and shows the few roads and trails here; some routes and springs are marked on

it too. Agile hikers experienced in desert and canyon travel may want to take off on cross-country routes, which are either unmarked or lightly cairned.

Extra care and preparation must be undertaken for travel in both Glen Canyon NRA and the Maze. Always ask rangers beforehand for current conditions. Be sure to leave an itinerary with someone reliable who can contact the rangers if you're overdue returning. Unless the rangers know where to look for you in case of breakdown or accident, a rescue could take weeks.

SIGHTS
★ Land of Standing Rocks

Here in the heart of the Maze District, strangely shaped rock spires stand guard over myriad canyons. Six camping areas offer scenic places to stay (**permit** required). Hikers have a choice of many ridge and canyon routes from the 4WD road, a trail to a confluence overlook, and a trail that descends to the Colorado River near Cataract Canyon.

Getting to the Land of Standing Rocks takes some careful driving, especially on a 3-mile (4.8-km) stretch above Teapot Canyon. The many washes and small canyon crossings here make for slow going. Short-wheelbase vehicles have the easiest time, of course. The turnoff for Land of Standing Rocks Road is 6.6 miles (10.6 km) from the junction at the bottom of the Flint Trail via a wash shortcut (add about 3 miles/4.8 kilometers if driving via the four-way intersection). The lower end of the Golden Stairs foot trail is 7.8 miles (12.6 km) in; the western end of the Ernies Country route trailhead is 8.6 miles (13.8 km) in; the Wall is 12.7 miles (20.4 km) in; Chimney Rock is 15.7 miles (25.2 km) in; and the Doll House is 19 miles (31 km) in, at the end of the road. If you drive from the south on Hite-Orange Cliffs Road, stop at the self-registration stand at the four-way intersection, about 31 miles (50 km) in from Highway 95; you can write your own permit for overnights in the park.

Tall, rounded rock spires near the end of the road reminded early visitors of dolls, hence the name Doll House. The Doll House is a great place to explore, or you can head out on nearby routes and trails.

North Point

Hans Flat Ranger Station and this peninsula, which reaches out to the east and north, are at an elevation of about 6,400 feet (1,950 m). Panoramas from North Point take in the vastness of Canyonlands, including the Maze, Needles, and Island in the Sky Districts. From **Millard Canyon Overlook,** just 0.9 mile (1.4 km) past the ranger station, you can see arches, Cleopatra's Chair, and features as distant as the La Sal Mountains and Book Cliffs. For the best views, drive out to Panorama Point, about 10.5 miles (16.9 km) one-way from the ranger station. A spur road to the left goes 2 miles (3.2 km) to Cleopatra's Chair, a massive sandstone monolith and area landmark.

HIKING
North Canyon Trail

Distance: 7 miles (11.3 km) one-way
Duration: overnight
Elevation change: 1,000 feet (305 m)
Effort: strenuous
Trailhead: on North Point Road
Directions: From Hans Flat Ranger Station, drive 2.5 miles (4 km) east, turn left onto North Point Road, and continue about 1 mile (1.6 km) to the trailhead.

This is just about the only trailhead in the Maze District that two-wheel-drive vehicles can usually reach. The trail leads down through the Orange Cliffs. At the eastern end of the trail, ambitious hikers can follow 4WD roads an additional 6 miles (9.7 km) to the Maze Overlook Trail, then 1 more mile (1.6 km) into a canyon of the Maze. Because North Point belongs to the Glen Canyon NRA, you can camp here without a permit.

Maze Overlook Trail

Distance: 3 miles (4.8 km) one-way (to Harvest Scene)
Duration: 3-4 hours
Elevation change: 550 feet (168 m)
Effort: strenuous

Trailhead: at the end of the road in the Maze District

Here, at the edge of the sinuous canyons of the Maze, the Maze Overlook Trail drops 1 mile (1.6 km) into the South Fork of Horse Canyon; bring a 25-foot-long rope to help lower backpacks through one difficult section. Once in the canyon, you can walk around the Harvest Scene, a group of prehistoric pictographs, or do a variety of day hikes or backpacking trips. These canyons have water in some places; check with the ranger when you get your permit. At least four routes connect with the 4WD road in the Land of Standing Rocks, shown on the Trails Illustrated map. Hikers can also climb Petes Mesa from the canyons or head downstream to explore Horse Canyon, but a dry fall blocks access to the Green River. You can stay at primitive camping areas (**backcountry permit** required) and enjoy the views.

The Golden Stairs

Distance: 2 miles (3.2 km) one-way
Duration: 3 hours
Elevation change: 800 feet (244 m)
Effort: moderate
Trailhead: bottom of Flint Trail, at Golden Stairs camping area
Directions: Drive the challenging Flint Trail, a 4WD route, to its bottom. The top of the Golden Stairs is 2 miles (3.2 km) east of the road junction at the bottom of the Flint Trail.

Hikers can descend this steep foot trail to the Land of Standing Rocks Road in a fraction of the time it takes for drivers to follow the roads. The trail offers good views of Ernies Country, the vast southern area of the Maze District, but it lacks shade or water. The eponymous stairs are not actual steps carved into the rock, but a series of natural ledges.

Chocolate Drops Trail

Distance: 4.5 miles (7.2 km) one-way
Duration: 5 hours
Elevation change: 550 feet (168 m)
Effort: strenuous
Trailhead: Chocolate Drops
Directions: The Land of Standing Rocks turnoff is

6.6 miles (10.6 km) from the junction at the bottom of the Flint Trail. The trailhead is just east of the Wall camping area.

The well-named Chocolate Drops can be reached by a trail from the Wall near the beginning of the Land of Standing Rocks. A good day hike makes a loop from Chimney Rock to the Harvest Scene pictographs; take the ridge route (toward Petes Mesa) in one direction and the canyon fork northwest of Chimney Rock in the other. Follow your topographic map through the canyons, and the cairns between the canyons and ridge. Other routes from Chimney Rock lead to lower Jasper Canyon (no river access) or into Shot and Water Canyons and on to the Green River.

Spanish Bottom Trail

Distance: 1.2 miles (1.9 km) one-way
Duration: 3 hours
Elevation change: 1,260 feet (384 m)
Effort: strenuous
Trailhead: Doll House, near Camp 1, just before the end of the Land of Standing Rocks Road

This trail drops steeply to Spanish Bottom beside the Colorado River; a thin trail leads downstream into Cataract Canyon and the first of a long series of rapids. **Surprise Valley Overlook Trail** branches to the right off the Spanish Bottom Trail after about 300 feet (91 m) and winds south past some dolls to

a T junction (turn right for views of Surprise Valley, Cataract Canyon, and beyond); the trail ends at some well-preserved granaries, after 1.5 miles (2.4 km) one-way. From the same trailhead, the **Colorado-Green River Overlook Trail** heads north 5 miles (8 km) one-way from the Doll House to a viewpoint of the confluence. See the area's Trails Illustrated map for routes, trails, and roads.

4WD EXPLORATION
Flint Trail 4WD Road

This narrow, rough 4WD road connects the Hans Flat area with the Maze Overlook, Doll House, and other areas below. The road, driver, and vehicle should all be in good condition before attempting this route. Winter snow and mud close the road late December-March, as can rainstorms anytime. Check conditions with a ranger before you go. If you're starting from the top, stop at the signed overlook just before the descent to scout for vehicles headed up (the Flint Trail has very few places to pass). The top of the Flint Trail is 14 miles (22.5 km) south of Hans Flat Ranger Station; at the bottom, 2.8 nervous miles later, you can turn left and go 2 miles (3.2 km) to the Golden Stairs trailhead or 12.7 miles (20.4 km) to the Maze Overlook; keep straight 28 miles (45 km) to the Doll House or 39 miles (63 km) to Highway 95.

Horseshoe Canyon Unit

This canyon, a separate section of Canyonlands National Park, contains exceptional prehistoric rock art. Ghostly life-size pictographs in the Great Gallery provide an intriguing look into the past. Archaeologists think that the images had religious importance, although the meaning of the figures remains unknown. The Barrier Canyon Style of these drawings has been credited to an archaic culture beginning at least 8,000 years ago and lasting until about AD 450. Horseshoe Canyon

also contains rock art left by the subsequent Fremont and Ancestral Puebloan people. The relationship between the earlier and later prehistoric groups hasn't been determined.

Call the **Hans Flat Ranger Station** (435/259-2652) to inquire about ranger-led hikes to the Great Gallery (Sat.-Sun. spring, summer, and fall); when staff are available, additional walks may be scheduled. In-shape hikers will have no trouble making the hike on their own, however.

GETTING THERE

Horseshoe Canyon is a noncontiguous unit of Canyonlands and requires quite a bit of driving to reach. It is northwest of the Maze District. The access road turns east from Highway 24 between Hanksville (14 mi/22.5 km south) and I-70 exit 149 (19 mi/31 km north). The access road is signed, but it's also handy to note that the turn is across the road from the entrance to Goblin Valley State Park. Once on this graded dirt road, travel 30 miles (48 km) east to Horseshoe Canyon, keeping left at the Hans Flat Ranger Station and Horseshoe Canyon turnoff 25 miles (40 km) in. In good weather, the road is passable to most passenger cars, though the road has many washboard sections and blowing sand can be a hazard. If you have questions, call Hans Flat Ranger Station (435/259-2652) or another of the park's visitors centers. Allow an hour to make the journey in from Highway 24 to the canyon and the Great Gallery trailhead.

HIKING
★ Great Gallery Trail

Distance: 3.5 miles (5.6 km) one-way
Duration: 4-6 hours
Elevation change: 800 feet (244 m)
Effort: moderate-strenuous
Trailhead: parking area on the canyon's west rim

From the rim and parking area, the trail descends 800 feet (244 m) in 1 mile (1.6 km) on an old jeep road, which is now closed to vehicles. At the canyon bottom, turn right and go 2 miles (3.2 km) upstream to the Great Gallery. The sandy canyon floor is mostly level; trees provide shade in some areas.

Look for other rock art along the canyon walls on the way to the Great Gallery. Take care not to touch any of the drawings, because they're fragile and irreplaceable—the oil from your hands will remove the paints. Horseshoe Canyon also offers pleasant scenery and spring wildflowers. Carry plenty of water. Neither camping nor pets are allowed in the canyon, although horses are OK. Camping is permitted on the rim. Contact the Hans Flat Ranger Station (435/259-2652) or the Moab Information Center (435/259-8825 or 800/635-6622) for road and trail conditions.

Horseshoe Canyon can also be reached via primitive roads from the east. A 4WD road runs north 21 miles (34 km) from Hans Flat Ranger Station and drops steeply into the canyon from the east side. The descent on this road is so rough that most people prefer to park on the rim and hike the last mile of road. A vehicle barricade prevents driving right up to the rock-art panel, but the 1.5-mile (2.4-km) walk is easy.

The River District

The River District is the name of the administrative unit of the park that oversees conservation and recreation for the Green and Colorado Rivers.

Generally speaking, there are two boating experiences on offer in the park's River District. First are the relatively gentle paddling and rafting experiences on the Colorado and Green Rivers above their confluence. After these rivers meet, deep in the park, the resulting Colorado River then tumbles into Cataract Canyon, a white-water destination par excellence with abundant Class III-V rapids.

While rafting and canoeing enthusiasts can plan their own trips to any section of these rivers, by far the vast majority of people sign on with outfitters, often located in Moab, and let them do the planning and work. Do-it-yourselfers must start with the knowledge that permits are required for most trips but are not always easily procured; because these rivers flow through rugged and remote canyons, most trips require multiple days and can be challenging to plan.

No matter how you execute a trip through the River District, there are several issues

to think about beforehand. There are no designated campsites along the rivers in Canyonlands. During periods of high water, camps can be difficult to find, especially for large groups. During late summer and fall, sandbars are usually plentiful and make ideal camps. There is no access to potable water along the river, so river runners either need to bring along their own water or be prepared to purify river water.

While it's possible to fish in the Green and Colorado Rivers, these desert rivers don't offer much in the way of species that most people consider edible. You'll need to bring along all your foodstuffs.

The park requires all river runners to pack out their solid human waste. Specially designed portable toilets that fit into rafts and canoes can be rented from most outfitters in Moab.

RIVER-RUNNING ABOVE THE CONFLUENCE

The Green and Colorado Rivers flow smoothly through their canyons above the confluence of the two rivers. Almost any shallow-draft boat can navigate these waters: Canoes, kayaks, rafts, and powerboats are commonly used. Any travel requires advance planning because of the remoteness of the canyons and the scarcity of river access points. No campgrounds, supplies, or other facilities exist past Moab on the Colorado River or the town of Green River on the Green River. All river runners must follow park regulations, which include carrying life jackets, using a fire pan for fires, and packing out all garbage and solid human waste. The river flow on both the Colorado and the Green Rivers averages a gentle 2-4 mph (7-10 mph at high water). Boaters typically do 20 miles (32 km) per day in canoes and 15 miles (24 km) per day on rafts.

The Colorado has one modest rapid, called the Slide (1.5 mi/2.4 km above the confluence), where rocks constrict the river to one-third of its normal width; the rapid is roughest during high water levels in May-June. This is the only difficulty on the 64 river miles (103 km) from Moab. Inexperienced canoeists and rafters may wish to portage around it. The most popular launch points on the Colorado are the Moab Dock (just upstream from the U.S. 191 bridge near town) and the Potash Dock (17 mi/27 km downriver on Potash Rd./ Hwy. 279).

On the Green River, boaters at low water need to watch for rocky areas at the mouth of Millard Canyon (33.5 mi/54 km above the confluence, where a rock bar extends across the river) and at the mouth of Horse Canyon (14.5 mi/23.3 km above the confluence, where a rock and gravel bar on the right leaves only a narrow channel on the left side). The trip from the town of Green River through Labyrinth and Stillwater Canyons is 120 miles (193 km). Launch points include Green River State Park (in the town of Green River) and Mineral Canyon (52 mi/84 km above the confluence and reached on a fair-weather road from Hwy. 313). Boaters who launch at Green River State Park pass through Labyrinth Canyon; a free interagency permit is required for travel along this stretch of the river. **Permits** are available from the BLM office (82 Dogwood Ave., Moab, 435/259-2100, 7:45am-4:30pm Mon.-Fri.), the Canyonlands National Park headquarters (2282 SW Resource Blvd., Moab, 435/719-2313, 8am-4pm Mon.-Fri.), Green River State Park in Green River, or the John Wesley Powell River History Museum (1765 E. Main St., Green River, 435/564-3427, 9am-5pm Mon.-Sat.). A permit can also be downloaded from the BLM website (www.blm.gov).

No roads go to the confluence. The easiest return to civilization for nonmotorized craft is a pickup by jet boat from Moab by **Tex's Riverways** (435/259-5101, www.tex-sriverways.com) or **Tag-A-Long Tours** (800/453-3292, www.tagalong.com). A far more difficult way out is hiking either of two trails just above the Cataract Canyon Rapids to 4WD roads on the rim. Don't plan to attempt this unless you're a very strong hiker and have a packable watercraft.

1: the Great Gallery 2: the Colorado River

National park rangers require that boaters above the confluence obtain a backcountry permit ($30) from the **Moab National Park Service office** (2282 SW Resource Blvd., Moab, 435/719-2313, 8am-4pm Mon.-Fri.).

Notes on boating the Green and Colorado Rivers are available on request from the National Park Service's Moab office (435/259-3911). Bill and Buzz Belknap's *Canyonlands River Guide* has river logs and maps pointing out items of interest on the Green River below the town of Green River and all of the Colorado River from the upper end of Westwater Canyon to Lake Powell.

★ RIVER-RUNNING THROUGH CATARACT CANYON

The Colorado River enters Cataract Canyon at the confluence and picks up speed. The rapids begin 4 miles (6.4 km) downstream and extend for the next 14 miles (22.5 km) to Lake Powell. Especially in spring, the 26 or more rapids give a wild ride equal to the best in the Grand Canyon. The current zips along at up to 16 mph and forms waves more than 7 feet (2.1 m) high. When the excitement dies down, boaters have a 34-mile (55-km) trip across Lake Powell to Hite Marina; most people either carry a motor or arrange for a powerboat to pick them up. Depending on water levels, which can vary wildly from year to year, the dynamics of this trip and the optimal take-out point can change. Depending on how much motoring is done, the trip through Cataract Canyon takes 2-5 days.

Because of the real hazards of running the rapids, the National Park Service requires boaters to have proper equipment and a **permit** ($30). Many people go on commercial trips with Moab outfitters on which everything has been taken care of. Private groups must contact the **Canyonlands River Unit of the National Park Service** (435/259-3911, www.nps.gov/cany) far in advance for permit details.

Arches National Park

A concentration of rock arches of marvelous variety has formed within the maze of sandstone fins at Arches National Park, one of the most popular national parks in the United States. Balanced rocks and tall spires add to the splendor.

Paved roads and short hiking trails provide easy access to some of the more than 1,500 arches in the park. If you're short on time, a drive to the Windows Section (23.5 mi/38 km round-trip) affords a look at some of the largest and most spectacular arches. To visit all the stops and hike a few short trails takes a full day.

Although Native Americans were in the area for thousands of years and left rock art, most of the early settlers and cowboys who passed through the Arches area paid little attention to the scenery.

Highlights

Look for ★ to find recommended sights, activities, dining, and lodging.

★ **See Balanced Rock:** Rising 128 feet (39 m) from the desert, this unbelievable spire-upon-spire balancing act will give your camera a warm-up (page 230).

★ **Explore the Windows Section:** The park's largest must-see arches are here, drawing large crowds. Escape them by hiking the more primitive trail behind the North Window (page 230).

★ **Trek the Delicate Arch Trail:** Beautiful from afar, Delicate Arch is mystical up close. It's worth the tough 1.5-mile (2.4-km) hike that leads to its base (page 236).

★ **Tour the Fiery Furnace Trail:** Take a ranger-led expedition of this wonderland of rock mazes, fins, and turrets (page 237).

★ **Hike the Devils Garden Loop:** The park's best day hike is on this 7.2-mile (11.6-km) trail through a landscape of bizarre rock fins (page 241).

★ **Discover Tower Arch Trail:** This trail leads to a spire in the backcountry, one of the park's most beautiful but neglected sights (page 241).

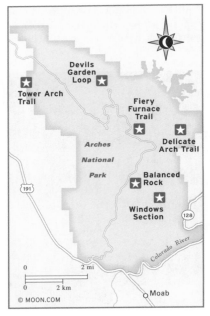

Devils Garden Loop ★

Tower Arch Trail ★

Fiery Furnace Trail ★

Delicate Arch Trail ★

Arches National Park

Balanced Rock ★

Windows Section ★

191

128

Colorado River

0   2 mi

0   2 km

© MOON.COM

Moab

Arches National Park

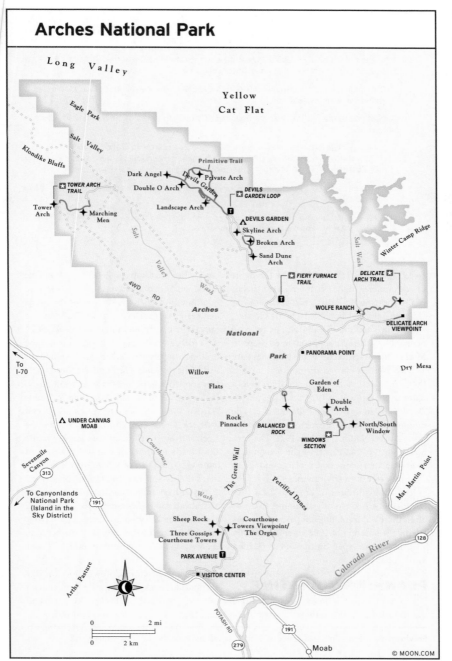

Long Valley

Yellow
Cat Flat

Eagle Park

Salt Valley

Klondike Bluffs

Primitive Trail

TOWER ARCH TRAIL

Dark Angel
Devils Garden
Private Arch
Double O Arch
DEVILS GARDEN LOOP
Landscape Arch

Tower Arch
Marching Men

DEVILS GARDEN

Skyline Arch

Broken Arch

Sand Dune Arch

Salt Valley Wash

Winter Camp Ridge

Salt Wash

4WD RD

FIERY FURNACE TRAIL

DELICATE ARCH TRAIL

Arches

National

WOLFE RANCH

DELICATE ARCH VIEWPOINT

Park

PANORAMA POINT

Dry Mesa

To I-70

Willow

Flats

Garden of Eden

Double Arch

Sevenmile Canyon

UNDER CANVAS MOAB

Rock Pinnacles

BALANCED ROCK

WINDOWS SECTION

North/South Window

Mat Martin Point

313

To Canyonlands National Park (Island in the Sky District)

Courthouse Wash

The Great Wall

Petrified Dunes

191

Sheep Rock
Three Gossips
Courthouse Towers

Courthouse Towers Viewpoint/ The Organ

PARK AVENUE

128

Arths Pasture

VISITOR CENTER

Colorado River

0   2 mi
0   2 km

POTASH RD

279

191

Moab

© MOON.COM

Arches in One Day

- Get to the park early to avoid lines at the entrance station. Stop at the visitors center to learn about the natural and human history of the park.

- Drive 11 miles (17.7 km) to the Windows trailhead, where a number of easy trails lead to arches carved into fins of rock.

- Continue to the Delicate Arch trailhead to hike up to the iconic arch before the day gets too hot.

- Enjoy a picnic lunch and views from the picnic area at Devils Garden trailhead, 7 miles (11.3 km) north of the Windows (18 mi /29 km from the park entrance). Then explore a bit of the trail: Tunnel and Pine Tree Arches are less than a mile in from the trailhead.

- If you still have some time, stop on the way back out of the park and take a stroll on the Park Avenue Trail.

- There are no dining facilities in the park, so enjoy a refined meal at the Desert Bistro in Moab, 6 miles (9.7 km) south of the park entrance.

In 1923, however, a prospector by the name of Alexander Ringhoffer interested officials of the Rio Grande Railroad in the scenic attractions at what he called Devils Garden, now known as Klondike Bluffs. The railroad people liked the area and contacted Stephen Mather, the first director of the National Park Service. Mather started the political process that led to designating two small areas as a national monument in 1929, but Ringhoffer's Devils Garden wasn't included until later. The monument grew in size over the years and became Arches National Park in 1971. The park now comprises 76,519 acres—small enough to be appreciated in one day, yet large enough to warrant extensive exploration.

Thanks to unrelenting erosion, the arches themselves are constantly changing. Every so often there's a dramatic change, as there was during the summer of 2008 when Wall Arch, a 71-foot (22-m) span on the Devils Garden Trail, collapsed.

PLANNING YOUR TIME

If you only have part of the day to explore, drive the 18-mile (29-km) length of the main park road with a brief stop at Balanced Rock and the Windows Section, where short trails lead to enormous arches in the skyline. At the road's end, set out on the Devils Garden Trail, but take only the trip to Tunnel and Pine Tree Arches.

A full day in the park allows plenty of time to stop at the visitors center and then hike the full Delicate Arch Trail and explore Devils Garden. Energetic hikers may want to do the entire 7.2-mile (11.6-km) loop in Devils Garden; those who want less of a workout can walk the 1-mile (1.6-km) trail to Landscape Arch. Often overlooked, the Park Avenue Trail leads to views of massive towers and hoodoos, and it's an easy 1-mile (1.6-km) hike that's fine even if you're not totally in shape.

If you have more than one day to spend, plan ahead and register online for a ranger-led hike into the Fiery Furnace area of the park. This takes about half a day; for the other half, head out via car or mountain bike to Tower Arch Trail.

Although Arches is known more for day hiking than backpacking, park rangers can help you put together a backpacking trip and issue the required backcountry permit.

Previous: the Delicate Arch Trail; Windows Section; sandstone towers in the Fiery Furnace.

Exploring the Park

The entrance to **Arches National Park** (435/719-2299, www.nps.gov/arch, $30 per vehicle for seven days, $25 motorcyclists, $15 bicyclists and pedestrians, $50 annual Southeast Utah Parks Pass) is 5 miles (8 km) north of downtown Moab on U.S. 191. With less than 30 miles (48 km) of paved road in the entire park, the traffic can be heavy in the spring and summer high seasons.

Come prepared with a picnic lunch; there are no accommodations and no restaurants inside the park.

VISITORS CENTER

Located just past the park entrance booth, the expansive **visitors center** (8am-5pm daily Mar.- Oct., 9am-4pm daily Nov.-mid-Mar.) provides a good introduction to what you can expect ahead. A short film on the geology of the park runs regularly, and exhibits identify the rock layers, describe the geologic and human history, and illustrate some of the wildlife and plants of the park. A large outdoor plaza is a good place to trawl for information when the visitors center is closed.

Staff members are available to answer your questions and check you in for a ranger-led tour in the Fiery Furnace area of the park.

Look for the posted list of special activities; rangers host campfire programs and lead a wide variety of **guided walks** (Apr.-Sept.). You'll find checklists, pamphlets, books, maps, posters, postcards, and T-shirts available for purchase. An audio tour of the park's scenic main road is also available for rent or purchase. An audio version of the park brochure is available on CD (or can be downloaded from www.nps.gov/arch), and you may also request large-print or braille publications at the visitors center. See the rangers for advice and the **free backcountry permit** required for overnight trips.

Desert bighorn sheep frequent the area around the visitors center and can sometimes be seen from U.S. 191 just south of the park entrance. A sheep crossing about 3 miles (4.8 km) north of the visitors center is also a good place to scan the steep talus slopes for these nimble animals.

If your plans include visiting Canyonlands National Park plus Hovenweep and Natural Bridges National Monuments, consider the **Southeast Utah Parks Pass** ($50), which buys annual entry to all of these federal preserves. Purchase the pass at any of the park or national monument entrances.

Sights

MOAB FAULT

The park road begins a long but well-graded climb from the visitors center up the cliffs to the northeast. A pullout on the right after 1.1 miles (1.8 km) offers a good view of Moab Canyon and its geology. The rock layers on this side of the canyon have slipped down more than 2,600 feet (792 m) in relation to the other side. This movement took place about six million years ago along the Moab Fault, which follows the canyon floor. Rock layers at the top of the far cliffs are nearly the same age as those at the bottom on this side. If you could stack the rocks of this side on top of rocks on the other side, you'd have a complete stratigraphic column of the Moab area—more than 150 million years' worth.

PARK AVENUE

The South Park Avenue overlook and trailhead are on the left 2.1 miles (3.4 km) from the visitors center. Great sandstone slabs form a skyline on each side of this dry wash. A trail goes north 1 mile (1.6 km) down the wash to the North Park Avenue trailhead (1.3 mi /2.1 km ahead by road). Arrange to be picked up there, or backtrack to your starting point. The large rock monoliths of Courthouse Towers rise north of Park Avenue. Only a few small arches exist now, although major arches may have formed there in the past. One striking feature, visible from the road and the trail, is the group of sandstone towers forming the Three Gossips.

★ BALANCED ROCK

This gravity-defying formation is on the right, 8.5 miles (13.7 km) from the visitors center. A boulder more than 55 feet (17 m) high rests precariously atop a 73-foot (22-m) pedestal. Chip Off the Old Block, a much smaller version of Balanced Rock, stood nearby until it collapsed in the winter of 1975-1976. For a closer look at Balanced Rock, take the 0.3-mile (0.5-km) trail encircling it. There's a picnic area across the road. Author Edward Abbey lived in a trailer near Balanced Rock for a season as a park ranger in the 1950s; his journal became the basis for the classic *Desert Solitaire*.

TOP EXPERIENCE

★ WINDOWS SECTION

The Windows Section of Arches is located 2.5 miles (4 km) past Balanced Rock, on a paved road to the right. Short trails (0.25-1 mi /0.4-1.6 km one-way) lead from the road's end to some massive arches. The Windows trailhead is the start for North Window (an opening 51 ft/16 m high and 93 ft/28 m wide), South Window (66 ft/20 m high and 105 ft/32 m wide), and Turret Arch (64 ft/20 m high and 39 ft/12 m wide). Cut across the parking area for the trail to Double Arch, an unusual pair of arches. The larger opening—105 feet (32 m) high and 163 feet (50 m) wide—is best appreciated by walking inside. The smaller opening is 61 feet (19 m) high and 60 feet (18 m) wide. Together, the two arches frame a large opening overhead.

Garden of Eden Viewpoint, on the way back to the main road, promises a good panorama of Salt Valley to the north. Under the valley floor, the massive body of salt and gypsum that's responsible for the arches comes close to the surface. Far-off Delicate Arch can be seen across the valley on a sandstone ridge. Early visitors to the Garden of Eden saw rock formations resembling Adam (with an apple) and Eve. Two other viewpoints of the Salt Valley area lie farther north on the main road.

1: the aptly named Balanced Rock 2: a ranger-led hike in the Windows Section 3: Delicate Arch

DELICATE ARCH AND WOLFE RANCH

A bit of pioneer history survives at Wolfe Ranch, 2.5 miles (4 km) north on the main road from the Windows junction (turn right and drive 1.8 mi/2.9 km to the parking area). John Wesley Wolfe came to this spot in 1888, hoping the desert climate would provide relief for health problems related to a Civil War injury. He found a good spring high in the rocks, grass for cattle, and water in Salt Wash to irrigate a garden. The ranch that he built provided a home for him and some of his family for more than 20 years, and cattlemen later used it as a line ranch. Then sheepherders brought in their animals, which so overgrazed the range that the grass has yet to recover. A trail guide available at the entrance tells about the Wolfe family and the features of their ranch. The weather-beaten cabin built in 1906 still survives. A short trail leads to petroglyphs above Wolfe Ranch; figures of horses indicate that Ute people, rather than earlier inhabitants, did the artwork. Park staff can give directions to other rock-art sites; great care should be taken not to touch the fragile artwork.

Delicate Arch stands in a magnificent setting atop gracefully curving slickrock. Distant canyons and the La Sal Mountains lie beyond. The span is 45 feet (14 m) high and 33 feet (10 m) wide. A moderately strenuous 3-mile (4.8 km) round-trip hike leads to the arch. Another perspective on Delicate Arch can be obtained by driving 1.2 miles (1.9 km) beyond Wolfe Ranch. Look for the small arch high above. A short wheelchair-accessible trail and a slightly longer, steeper trail (0.5 mi/0.8 km round-trip) provide views onto the arch.

FIERY FURNACE

The Fiery Furnace Viewpoint and trailhead are 3 miles (4.8 km) from the Wolfe Ranch junction, on the right side of the main road. The Fiery Furnace gets its name from sandstone fins that turn flaming red on occasions when thin cloud cover at the horizon reflects the warm light of sunrise or sunset. The shady recesses beneath the fins provide a cool respite from the hot summer sun.

Closely packed sandstone fins form a maze of deep slots, with many arches and at least one natural bridge inside. Both for safety reasons (it's easy to get a bit lost in here) and to reduce human impact on this sensitive area, which harbors several species of rare plants, hikers are encouraged to join a ranger-led hike. The hike is moderately strenuous and involves steep ledges, squeezing through narrow cracks, a couple of jumps, and hoisting yourself up off the ground. There is no turning back once the hike starts, so make sure you're physically prepared and properly equipped.

Rangers offer two different guided hikes into the Fiery Furnace (May-Sept.). Ranger-led loop hikes are roughly three hours long and cover 2 miles/3.2 kilometers ($16 adults, $8 ages 5-12), while ranger-led out-and-back hikes ($10 adults, $5 ages 5-12) are about 2.5 hours long and cover about 1.25 miles (2 km). Tours are offered both in the morning and in the afternoon; only the morning tours are reservable in advance. The afternoon tickets are only sold in person at the visitors center up to a week in advance.

Group size is limited to about 20 people, and children under age five are not allowed. An adult must accompany children 12 and under. Morning walks often fill weeks in advance. Make reservations for the morning hikes online at www.recreation.gov. To visit the Fiery Furnace without a ranger, visitors must obtain a **permit** at the visitors center ($10 adults, $5 ages 5-12). Several Moab outfitters also lead hikes into the Fiery Furnace; these cost considerably more, but there's usually space available.

SKYLINE ARCH

This arch is on the right, 1 mile (1.6 km) past the Sand Dune/Broken Arch trailhead. In desert climates, erosion can proceed imperceptibly for centuries until a cataclysmic event happens. In 1940 a giant boulder fell from the

Why Are There Arches?

The park's distinctive arches are formed by an unusual combination of geologic forces. About 300 million years ago, evaporation of inland seas left behind a salt layer more than 3,000 feet (915 m) thick in the Paradox Basin of this region. Sediments, including those that later became the arches, then covered the salt. Unequal pressures caused the salt to gradually flow upward in places, bending the overlying sediments as well. These upfolds, or anticlines, later collapsed when groundwater dissolved the underlying salt.

The faults and joints caused by the uplift and collapse opened the way for erosion to carve hundreds of thin freestanding formations that look like shark fins. Alternate freezing and thawing action and exfoliation (flaking caused by expansion when water or frost penetrates the rock) continued to peel away more rock until holes formed in some of the fins. Rockfalls within the holes helped enlarge the arches. Nearly all arches in the park eroded out of Entrada sandstone. The towering stone walls of **Courthouse Towers** and the **Fin Canyon** section of Devils Garden are good examples of complete rock fins, while **Turret Arch,** in the Windows Section, is an example of a smaller arch being formed within a rock fin.

Eventually all the present arches will collapse, as Wall Arch did in 2008, but there should be plenty of new ones by the time that happens. The fins' uniform strength and hard upper surfaces have proved ideal for arch formation. Not every hole in the rock is considered an arch. To qualify, the opening must be at least 3 feet (0.9 m) in one direction, and light must be able to pass through. Although the term *windows* often refers to openings in large walls of rock, windows and arches are really the same.

Water seeping through the sandstone from above has created a second type of arch—the pothole arch. **Pothole Arch,** near Balanced Rock off Windows Road, and **Ring Arch** are good examples. (You can see them from the Courthouse Wash trail, accessible from a parking lot off U.S. 191 just north of the Colorado River Bridge near Moab.) You may also come across a few natural bridges cut from the rock by perennial water runoff. Rock bridges are different from arches as they have water flowing through them at least part of the year.

A succession of rock layers is on display at Arches. The rocks on top of the salt beds—the rocks you actually see at Arches—are mostly Entrada sandstone, which is a pretty general category of rock. Within this Entrada Formation are three distinct types of sandstone. The formation's dark red base layer is known as the Dewey Bridge Member. It's softer than the formation's other sandstones and erodes easily. Dewey Bridge rocks are topped by the pinkish-orange Slick Rock Member, the park's most visible rocks. The Slick Rock layer is much harder than the Dewey Bridge, and the combination of the two layers—softer rocks overlaid by harder—is responsible for the differential erosion that forms hoodoos and precariously balanced rocks. The thin top layer of Entrada sandstone, a white rock similar to Navajo sandstone, is called the Moab Tongue.

SIGHTS

ARCHES NATIONAL PARK

opening of Skyline Arch, doubling the size of the arch in seconds. The hole is now 45 feet (14 m) high and 69 feet (21 m) wide. A short trail leads to the base of the arch.

DEVILS GARDEN

The Devils Garden trailhead, picnic area, and campground are all near the end of the main park road. Devils Garden offers fine scenery and more arches than any other section of the park. The hiking trail leads past large sandstone fins to Landscape and six other named arches. Carry water, even if you think you're just going for a short stroll; this is an area where it's tempting to keep on hiking! Adventurous hikers could spend days exploring the maze of canyons among the fins.

KLONDIKE BLUFFS AND TOWER ARCH

Relatively few visitors come to the spires, high bluffs, and fine arch in this northwestern section of the park. A fair-weather dirt road turns off the main drive 1.3 miles (2.1 km) before Devils Garden trailhead, winds down into Salt Valley, and heads northwest. After 7.5 miles (12 km), turn left on the road to Klondike Bluffs and proceed 1 mile (1.6 km) to the Tower Arch trailhead. These roads may have washboards, but they are usually passable by cars in dry weather; don't drive on them if storms threaten. The trail to Tower Arch winds past the Marching Men and other rock formations (3 mi/4.8 km round-trip). Alexander Ringhoffer, who discovered the arch in 1922, carved an inscription on the south column. The area can also be fun to explore off-trail with a map and compass or a GPS receiver. Those with 4WD vehicles can drive close to the arch on a separate jeep road. Tower Arch has an opening 34 feet (10 m) high by 92 feet (28 m) wide. A tall monolith nearby gave the arch its name.

4WD ROAD

A rough road near Tower Arch in the Klondike Bluffs turns southeast past **Eye of the Whale Arch** in Herdina Park to Balanced Rock on the main park road, 10.8 miles (17.4 km) away. The road isn't particularly difficult for 4WD enthusiasts, although normal backcountry precautions should be taken. A steep sand hill north of Eye of the Whale Arch is difficult to climb for vehicles coming from Balanced Rock; it's better to drive from the Tower Arch area instead. (Trust us and don't try this road in a big pickup truck, even one with 4WD!)

Recreation

Because of its great popularity and proximity to Moab, Arches sees a lot of visitors (about 1.8 million people visit the park yearly). Most are content, however, to drive the parkways and perhaps saunter to undemanding viewpoints. You can quickly leave the crowds behind by planning a hike to more outlying destinations. Arches' outback offers magnificent rewards for hikers willing to leave the pavement behind and get dusty on a backcountry trail.

HIKING

Established hiking trails lead to many fine arches and overlooks that can't be seen from the road. You're free to wander cross-country too, but stay on rock or in washes to avoid damaging the fragile cryptobiotic soils. Wear good walking shoes with rubber soles for travel across slickrock. The summer sun can be especially harsh on the unprepared hiker—don't forget water, a hat, and sunscreen. The desert rule is to carry at least one gallon of water per person for an all-day hike. Take a map and compass or a map and GPS unit for off-trail hiking. Be cautious on the slickrock, as the soft sandstone can crumble easily. Also,

remember that it's easier to go up a steep slick-rock slope than it is to come back down.

You can reach almost any spot in the park on a day hike, although you'll also find some good overnight camping possibilities. Areas for longer trips include Courthouse Wash in the southern part of the park and Salt Wash in the eastern part. All backpacking is done off-trail. A **backcountry permit** must be obtained from a ranger before camping in the backcountry.

Backcountry regulations prohibit fires and pets, and they allow camping only out of sight of any road (at least 1 mi/1.6 km away), or trail (at least 0.5 mi/0.8 km away), and at least 300 feet (91 m) from a recognizable archaeological site or nonflowing water source.

Park Avenue

Distance: 1 mile (1.6 km) one-way
Duration: 30 minutes one-way; 1 hour round-trip
Elevation change: 320 feet (98 m)
Effort: easy-moderate
Trailheads: Park Avenue or North Park Avenue trailhead

Get an eyeful of massive stone formations and a feel for the natural history of the park

Arches Hikes

Trail	Effort	Distance	Duration
Broken and Sand Dune Arches	easy	1 mi/1.6 km round-trip	45 minutes
The Windows	easy	1 mi/1.6 km round-trip	1 hour
Landscape Arch	easy	2 mi/3.2 km round-trip	1 hour
Delicate Arch Viewpoint	easy-moderate	0.5 mi/0.8 km round-trip	15-30 minutes
Park Avenue	easy-moderate	1 mi/1.6 km one-way	30 minutes
★ Fiery Furnace Trail	moderate-strenuous	2 mi/3.2 km round-trip	3 hours
★ Delicate Arch Trail	moderate-strenuous	3 mi/4.8 km round-trip	2 hours
★ Tower Arch Trail	moderate-strenuous	3.4 mi/5.5 km round-trip	2.5 hours
★ Devils Garden Loop	strenuous	7.2 mi/11.6 km round-trip	4 hours

on the easy-moderate Park Avenue Trail. The Park Avenue trailhead, just past the crest of the switchbacks that climb up into the park, is the best place to start. The vistas from here are especially dramatic: Courthouse Towers, the Three Gossips, and other fanciful rock formations loom above a natural amphitheater. The trail drops into a narrow wash before traversing the park highway at the North Park Avenue trailhead. Hikers can be dropped off at one trailhead and picked up 30 minutes later at the other.

The Windows

Distance: 1 mile (1.6 km) round-trip
Duration: 1 hour
Elevation change: 140 feet (43 m)
Effort: easy
Trailhead: end of Windows Road
Ten miles (16 km) into the park, just past the impossible-to-miss Balanced Rock, follow signs and a paved road to the Windows Section. A 1-mile (1.6-km) loop along a sandy trail leads to the Windows—a cluster of enormous arches that are impossible to see from the road. Highlights include the **North** and **South Windows** and **Turret Arch.** Unmarked trails lead to vistas and scrambles along the stone faces that make up the ridge. If this easy loop leaves you eager for more exploration in the area, a second trail starts from just across from the Windows parking area and goes to **Double Arch.** This 0.5-mile (0.8-km) trail leads to two giant spans that are joined at one end. These easy trails are good for family groups because younger or more ambitious hikers can scramble to their hearts' content along rocky outcrops.

Delicate Arch Viewpoint

Distance: 0.5 mile (0.8 km) round-trip
Duration: 15-30 minutes
Elevation change: 100 feet (30 m)
Effort: easy-moderate
Trailhead: 1.2 miles (1.9 km) past Wolfe Ranch, at the end of Wolfe Ranch Road

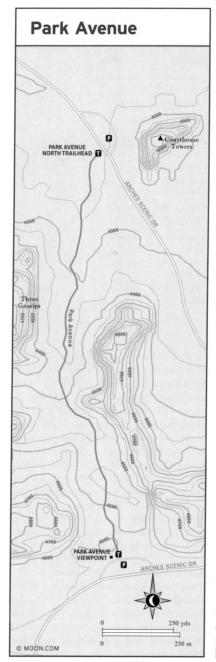

Park Avenue

If you don't have the time or the endurance for the relatively strenuous hike to Delicate Arch, you can view the astonishing arch from a distance at the Delicate Arch Viewpoint. From the viewing area, hikers can scramble up a steep trail to a rim with views across Cache Valley. Even though this is a short hike, it's a good place to wander around the slickrock for a while. It's especially nice to linger around sunset, when the arch captures the light and begins to glow. If you'd rather not scramble around on the slickrock, a short wheelchair-accessible path leads about 100 yards from the parking area to a decent view of the arch.

TOP EXPERIENCE

★ Delicate Arch Trail

Distance: 3 miles (4.8 km) round-trip
Duration: 2 hours
Elevation change: 500 feet (152 m)
Effort: moderate-strenuous
Trailhead: Wolfe Ranch

For those who are able, the hike to the base of Delicate Arch is one of the park's highlights. Shortly after the trail's start at Wolfe Ranch, a spur trail leads to some petroglyphs depicting horses and their riders and a few bighorn sheep. Horses didn't arrive in the area until the mid-1600s, so these petroglyphs are believed to be the work of the Ute people.

The first stretch of the main trail is broad, flat, and not especially scenic, except for a good display of spring wildflowers. After about half an hour of hiking, the trail climbs steeply up onto the slickrock and the views open up across the park to the La Sal Mountains in the distance.

Just before the end of the trail, walk up to the small, decidedly indelicate Frame Arch for a picture-perfect view of the final destination. The classic photo of Delicate Arch is taken late in the afternoon or in the evening when the sandstone glows with golden hues. Standing at the base of Delicate Arch is a magical moment: The arch rises out of the barren, almost lunar, rock face, yet it seems ephemeral. Views

The Windows

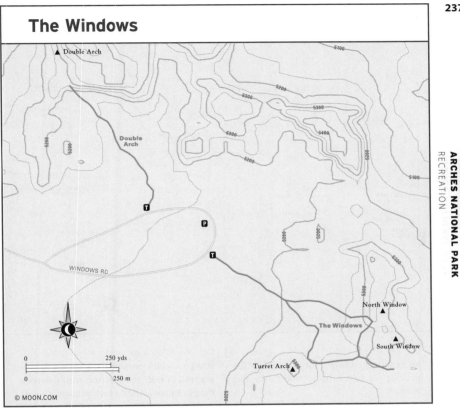

from the arch over the Colorado River valley are amazing.

★ Fiery Furnace Trail

Distance: 2-mile (3.2-km) loop
Duration: 3 hours
Elevation change: 250 feet (76 m)
Effort: moderate-strenuous
Trailhead: Fiery Furnace Viewpoint

The Fiery Furnace area is open only to hikers with **permits** ($6 adults, $3 ages 5-12) or to those joining a ranger-led hike. From May through September there are two daily hike options: Ranger-led **loop hikes** are roughly three hours long and cover 1.5 miles/2.4 kilometers ($16 adults, $8 ages 5-12), while ranger-led **out-and-back hikes** ($10 adults, $5 ages 5-12) are about 2.5 hours long and cover 1.25

miles (2 km). Tours are offered both in the morning and in the afternoon; only the morning tours are reservable in advance online at www.recreation.gov. The afternoon tickets are only sold in person at the visitors center up to a week in advance. These hikes are popular and are often booked weeks in advance, so plan accordingly.

Hiking in the Fiery Furnace is not along a trail; hikers navigate a maze of narrow sandstone canyons. The route through the area is sometimes challenging, requiring hands-and-knees scrambling up cracks and ledges. Navigation is difficult: Route-finding can be tricky because what look like obvious paths often lead to dead ends. Drop-offs and ridges make straight-line travel impossible. It's easy to become disoriented. Even if you're

Delicate Arch

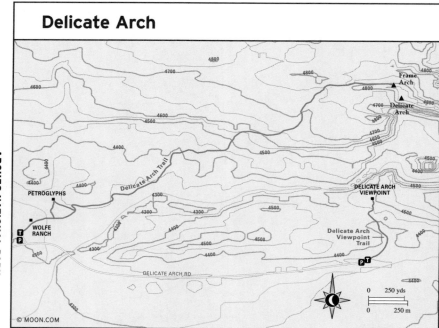

an experienced hiker, the ranger-led hikes provide the best introduction to the Fiery Furnace.

If you're not able to get in on a ranger-led hike and aren't strapped for cash, several Moab outfitters, including **Canyonlands By Night** (1861 N. U.S. 191, Moab, 435/259-2628 or 800/394-9978, www.canyonlandsbynight. com, $89 adults, $67 ages 5-15) offer guided tours in the Fiery Furnace.

Broken and Sand Dune Arches

Distance: 1 mile (1.6-km) round-trip
Duration: 45 minutes
Elevation change: 140 feet (43 m)
Effort: easy
Trailhead: on the right side of the road, 2.4 miles (3.9 km) past the Fiery Furnace turnoff

A short, sandy trail leads to small Sand Dune Arch (its opening is 8 ft/2.4 m high and 30

ft/9.1 m wide), tucked within fins. A longer trail (1 mi/1.6 km round-trip) crosses a field to Broken Arch, which you can also see from the road. The opening in this arch is 43 feet (13 m) high and 59 feet (18 m) wide. Up close, you'll see that the arch isn't really broken. These arches can also be reached by a trail across from campsite 40 at Devils Garden Campground. Another beautiful arch, **Tapestry Arch,** requires a short detour off the trail between the campground and Broken Arch.

Look for low-growing Canyonlands biscuit root, found only in areas of Entrada sandstone, colonizing in the sand dunes. Hikers can protect the habitat of the biscuit root and other fragile plants by keeping to washes or rock surfaces.

1: Delicate Arch **2:** sandstone towers in the Fiery Furnace **3:** Broken Arch isn't really broken, it's just wearing a little thin on top.

1

2

3

Devils Garden Loop

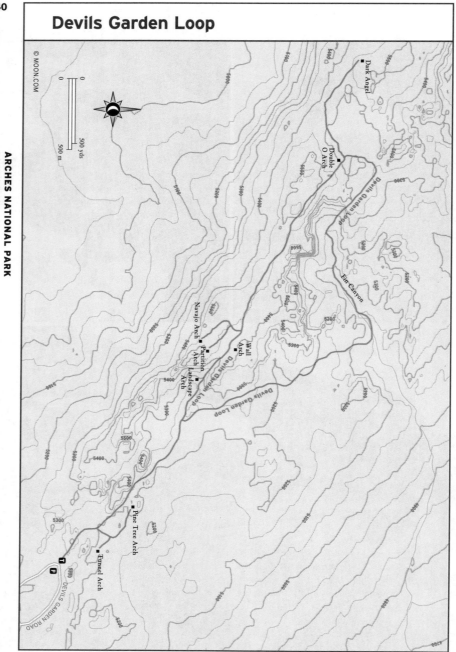

© MOON.COM

Dark Angel

Double O Arch

Devils Garden Loop

Fin Canyon

Navajo Arch

Partition Arch

Wall Arch

Landscape Arch

Devils Garden Loop

Devils Garden Loop

Pine Tree Arch

Tunnel Arch

DEVILS GARDEN ROAD

0   500 yds
0   500 m

★ Devils Garden Loop

Distance: 7.2 miles (11.6 km) round-trip
Duration: 4 hours
Elevation change: 350 feet (107 m)
Effort: strenuous
Trailhead: Devils Garden trailhead

From the end of the paved park road, a full tour of Devils Garden leads to eight named arches and a vacation's worth of scenic wonders. This is one of the park's most popular areas, with several shorter versions of the full loop hike that make the area accessible to nearly every hiker. Don't be shocked to find quite a crowd at the trailhead—it will most likely dissipate after the first two or three arches.

The first two arches are an easy walk from the trailhead and are accessed via a short side trail to the right. **Tunnel Arch** has a relatively symmetrical opening 22 feet (6.7 m) high and 27 feet (8.3 m) wide. The nearby **Pine Tree Arch** is named for a piñon pine that once grew inside; the arch has an opening 48 feet (15 m) high and 46 feet (14 m) wide.

Continue on the main trail to **Landscape Arch.** The trail narrows past Landscape Arch and continues to the remains of **Wall Arch,** which collapsed in August 2008. A short side trail branches off to the left beyond the stubs of Wall Arch to **Partition Arch** and **Navajo Arch.** Partition was so named because a piece of rock divides the main opening from a smaller hole. Navajo Arch is a rock-shelter type; prehistoric Native Americans may have camped here.

The main trail climbs up slickrock, offering great views of the La Sal Mountains and Fin Canyon. At the Fin Canyon viewpoint, the trail curves left (watch for rock cairns) and continues northwest, ending at **Double O Arch** (4 mi/6.4 km round-trip from the trailhead). Double O has a large oval-shaped opening (45 ft/14 m high and 71 ft/22 m wide) and a smaller hole underneath. **Dark Angel** is a distinctive rock pinnacle 0.25 mile (0.4 km) northwest; cairns mark the way. Another primitive trail loops back to Landscape Arch via **Fin Canyon.** This route goes through a different part of Devils Garden but adds about 1 mile (1.6 km) to your trip (3 mi/4.8 km back to the trailhead instead of 2 mi/3.2 km). Pay careful attention to the trail markers to avoid getting lost.

Landscape Arch

Distance: 2 miles (3.2 km) round-trip
Duration: 1 hour
Elevation change: 60 feet (18 m)
Effort: easy
Trailhead: Devils Garden trailhead

Landscape Arch, with an incredible 306-foot (93-m) span—6 feet (1.8 m) longer than a football field—is one of the longest unsupported rock spans in the world. It's also one of the park's more precarious arches to observe up close. The thin arch looks ready to collapse at any moment. Indeed, a spectacular rockfall from the arch on September 1, 1991, accelerated its disintegration, which is the eventual fate of every arch. Now the area directly underneath the arch is fenced off; when you look at the photos of the 1991 rockfall, you'll be happy to stand back a ways.

On the way to Landscape Arch, be sure to take the short side trails to Tunnel and Pine Tree Arches.

★ Tower Arch Trail

Distance: 3.4 miles (5.5 km) round-trip
Duration: 2.5 hours
Elevation change: 450 feet (137 m)
Effort: moderate-strenuous
Trailhead: Klondike Bluffs parking area
Directions: From the main park road, take Salt Valley Road (a dirt road; usually fine for passenger cars but not for RVs) west 7.5 miles (12 km) to the Klondike Bluffs turnoff.

Most park visitors don't venture into this area of sandstone fins and big dunes. It's a bit like Devils Garden, but without the crowds.

After a short but steep climb, the trail levels out and opens up to views of Arches' distinctive sandstone fins and, in the distance, the La Sal and Abajo Mountains. The trail drops down to cross a couple of washes, then climbs onto the fin-studded slickrock

Klondike Bluffs. Tower Arch is actually both an arch and a tower, and there's no mistaking the tower for just another big sandstone rock.

Because of the dirt-road access to this hike, it's best to skip it if there has been recent rain or if rain is threatening.

BIKING

Cyclists are required to keep to established roads in the park; there is no single-track or trail riding allowed. You'll also have to contend with heavy traffic on the narrow paved roads and dusty washboard surfaces on the dirt roads. Beware of deep sand on the 4WD roads, traffic on the main park road, and summertime heat wherever you ride.

One good, not-too-hard ride is along the Willow Springs Road. Allow two to three hours for an out-and-back, starting from the Balanced Rock parking area and heading west.

Perhaps the best bet for relatively fit mountain bikers is the 24-mile (39-km) ride to Tower Arch and back. From the Devils Garden parking area, ride out the **Salt Valley Road,** which can be rough. After about 7.5 miles (12 km), turn left onto a jeep road that leads to the "back door" to Tower Arch.

Nearby, Bureau of Land Management and Canyonlands National Park areas offer world-class mountain biking.

CLIMBING

Rock climbers should stop by a kiosk outside the visitors center for a **free permit** (also available online at https://archespermits.nps.gov). Groups are limited to five climbers, and Balanced Rock, the "Arches Boulders," and all arches with openings greater than 3 feet (0.9 m) are closed to climbing. Check at the visitors center or online for temporary closures, often due to nesting raptors. Slacklining and BASE jumping are prohibited in the park. There are still plenty of long-standing routes for advanced climbers to enjoy, although the rock in Arches is sandier and softer than in other areas around Moab.

Several additional climbing restrictions are in place. No new permanent climbing hardware may be installed in any fixed location. If an existing bolt or other hardware item is unsafe, it may be replaced. This effectively limits all technical climbing to existing routes or new routes not requiring placement of fixed anchors. Other restrictions are detailed on the park's website.

The most commonly climbed areas are along the sheer stone faces of **Park Avenue.**

Devils Garden Campground

Another popular destination is Owl Rock, the small, owl-shaped tower located in the Windows Section of the park. For more information on climbing in Arches, consult *Desert Rock* by Eric Bjørnstad or *High on Moab* by Karl Kelley, or ask for advice at Pagan Mountaineering (59 S. Main St., Moab, 435/259-1117, www.paganclimber.com), a climbing and outdoor-gear store.

CAMPGROUNDS

Devils Garden Campground (elev. 5,355 ft/1,632 m, year-round, $25) is near the end of the 18-mile (29-km) main park road. It's an excellent place to camp, with some sites tucked under rock formations and others offering great views, but it's extremely popular. The well-organized traveler must plan accordingly and reserve a site in advance for March to October. Reservations (www.recreation. gov) must be made no less than 4 days and no more than 240 days in advance. All campsites can be reserved, so during the busy spring, summer, and fall seasons, campers without reservations are pretty much out of luck. In winter, sites 1-24 are available first come, first served. There are two accessible sites, close to an accessible bathroom, for people with limited physical mobility. A camp host is on-site, firewood is for sale ($5), and water is available, but there are no other services or amenities.

If you aren't able to score a coveted Arches campsite, all is not lost. There are many Bureau of Land Management (BLM) campsites within an easy drive of the park. Try the primitive BLM campgrounds on Highway 313, just west of U.S. 191 and on the way to Canyonlands National Park's Island in the Sky District. Another cluster of BLM campgrounds is along the Colorado River on Highway 128, which runs northeast from U.S. 191 at the north end of Moab.

Getting There

Arches National Park is 26 miles (42 km) south of I-70 and 5 miles (8 km) north of Moab, both off U.S. 191. If you're driving from Moab, allow 15 minutes to reach the park, as there is often slow-moving RV traffic along the route. If you're on a bike, a paved bike path parallels the highway between Moab and the park.

Moab

Located near the Colorado River in a green val-

ley enclosed by high red sandstone cliffs, Moab makes an excellent base for exploring the surrounding canyon country. The biblical Moab was a kingdom at the edge of Zion; early settlers must have felt themselves at the edge of their world too.

Today, Moab (pop. 5,000, elev. 4,025 ft/1,225 m) is the largest town in southeastern Utah. Its existence on the fringe of Mormon culture and its sizable young non-Mormon population give it a unique character. The town's first boom came during the 1950s, when vast deposits of uranium, important fuel for the atomic age, were discovered. By the 1970s the uranium mines were largely abandoned, but all the rough roads that had been built to access the mines set the stage for exploration with

Highlights

Look for ★ to find recommended sights, activities, dining, and lodging.

★ **Camp at Dead Horse Point State Park:** Set up camp on this peninsula of land perched 2,000 feet (610 m) above the Colorado River to enjoy spectacular views and mountain bike trails for the whole family (page 250).

★ **Hike Corona Arch and Bowtie Arch Trail:** Three arches are visible from this short, easy trail, including 140-foot-wide Corona Arch (page 259).

★ **Wander through Fisher Towers:** These thin rock columns reach nearly 1,000 feet (305 m) into the desert sky. Hiking trails loop through the unworldly landscape, leading to views of rugged Onion Creek Canyon (page 261).

★ **Bike down the Gemini Bridges Trail:** Skip the pros and poseurs at the Slickrock Trail and have some real fun on this mostly downhill ride (page 263).

★ **Go high:** You really grasp the scale of Moab's canyon country by getting an eagle's eye view on an **air tour** (page 269).

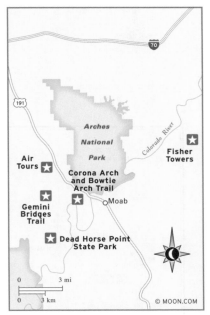

Moab

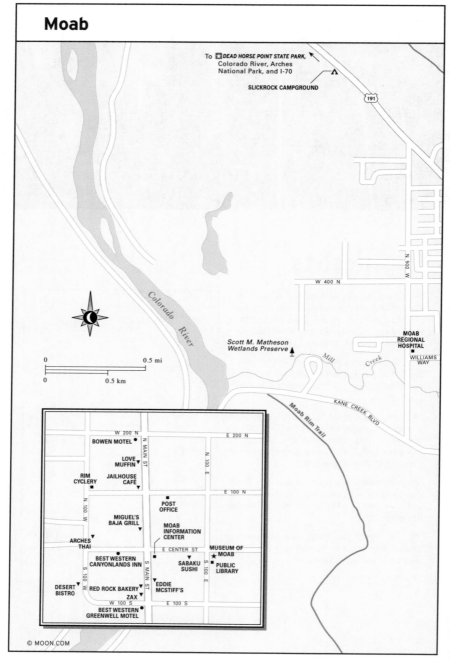

To ✚ DEAD HORSE POINT STATE PARK, Colorado River, Arches National Park, and I-70

SLICKROCK CAMPGROUND

191

N 500 W

W 400 N

Colorado River

Scott M. Matheson Wetlands Preserve

Mill Creek

MOAB REGIONAL HOSPITAL

WILLIAMS WAY

KANE CREEK BLVD

Moab Rim Trail

0   0.5 mi
0   0.5 km

W 200 N   E 200 N

BOWEN MOTEL

N MAIN ST

N 100 E

LOVE MUFFIN

RIM CYCLERY

JAILHOUSE CAFÉ

E 100 N

N 100 W

POST OFFICE

MIGUEL'S BAJA GRILL

MOAB INFORMATION CENTER

ARCHES THAI

E CENTER ST

MUSEUM OF MOAB

BEST WESTERN CANYONLANDS INN

SABAKU SUSHI

PUBLIC LIBRARY

S 100 E

S MAIN ST

S 100 W

DESERT BISTRO

RED ROCK BAKERY

EDDIE MCSTIFF'S

ZAX

W 100 S   E 100 S

BEST WESTERN GREENWELL MOTEL

© MOON.COM

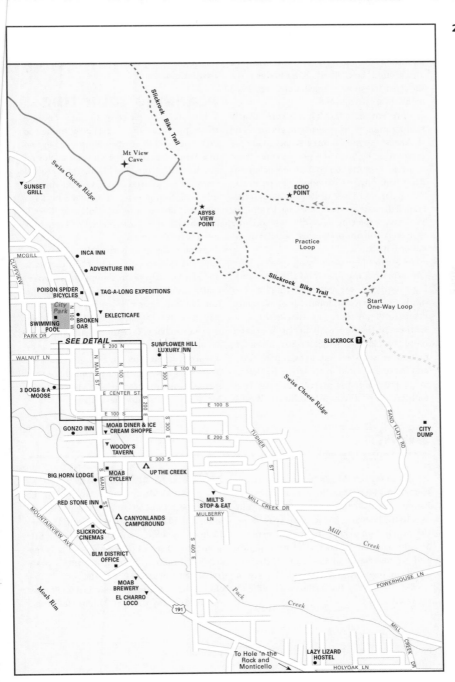

jeeps, ATVs, and mountain bikes. Another legacy of the uranium boom can be seen along the highway at the north end of town, where the area around the Colorado River bridge is the site of a massive environmental cleanup, slated to take years to complete.

In recent years Moab has become nearly synonymous with mountain biking. The slickrock canyon country seems made for exploration by bike, and people come from all over the world to pedal the backcountry. River trips on the Colorado River are nearly as popular, and a host of other outdoor recreational diversions—from horseback riding to 4WD jeep exploring to skydiving—combine to make Moab one of the most popular destinations in Utah.

As Moab's popularity has grown, so have concerns that the town and the surrounding countryside are simply getting loved to death. On a busy day, hundreds of mountain bikers form queues to negotiate the trickier sections of the famed Slickrock Trail, and more than 20,000 people crowd into town on peak-season weekends to bike, hike, float, and party. As noted in an article in *Details* magazine, "Moab is pretty much the Fort Lauderdale of the intermountain West."

Whether this old Mormon town and the delicate desert environment can endure such an onslaught of popularity is a question of increasing concern.

PLANNING YOUR TIME

While many people come to Moab because of what it's near, there's certainly enough to do in the town to justify adding a day or two to a park-focused itinerary just for exploring Moab and environs. The hiking trails around town are varied and beautiful (and you can hike with your pooch). Or pay a few bucks to take a jet-boat tour on the Colorado River, a horseback ride in Castle Valley, or a jeep tour into the backcountry.

Moab is the most hospitable town in this part of Utah, so don't blow right through. Spend a hot afternoon shopping for books, crafts, and outdoor gear. The quality of the food and beer has its own appeal, particularly after several days of hiking or driving the Utah outback. Take time to stop and enjoy Moab's quirky charms. However, be forewarned that the adrenaline (or is it testosterone?) level reaches a fever pitch here during spring break, so don't plan a quiet weekend in Moab anytime around Easter.

Sights

It's fair to say that Moab doesn't tempt travelers with a lot of traditional tourism establishments, but all you have to do is raise your eyes to the horizon. The locale is so striking that you'll want to get outdoors and explore, and the astonishing sights of Canyonlands and Arches National Parks are just minutes from town. And there's nothing wrong with just enjoying the enthusiastic vibe of the town.

MUSEUM OF MOAB

The regional **Museum of Moab** (118 E. Center St., 435/259-7985, www.moabmuseum.org, 10am-6pm Mon.-Sat. Apr. 15-Oct. 15, noon-5pm Mon.-Sat. Oct. 16-Apr. 14, $10 adults, $7.50 seniors, $5 ages 5-14) tells the story of Moab and Grand County's past, from prehistoric and Ute artifacts to the explorations of Spanish missionaries. Photos and tools show pioneer Moab life, much of which centered on ranching or mining. You'll also find displays of rocks and minerals as well as the bones of huge dinosaurs, including the backbone of a sauropod found by a rancher just outside town.

HOLE 'N THE ROCK

Twelve miles (19.3 km) south of Moab, Albert Christensen worked 12 years to excavate his dream home within a sandstone monolith. When he died in 1957, his wife, Gladys, worked another eight years to complete the 5,000-square-foot house, called **Hole 'n the Rock** (11037 S. U.S. 191, 435/686-2250, www.theholeintherock.com, 9am-5pm daily, House tours $6.50 6 and older, exotic zoo $4.25 2 and older). It's now a full-on roadside attraction. The interior has notable touches like a 65-foot chimney drilled through the rock ceiling, paintings, taxidermy exhibits, and a lapidary room. The 14-room home is open for 12-minute-long guided tours and offers a gift shop, a petting zoo, exotic animals, a picnic area, and a snack bar.

MILL CANYON DINOSAUR TRAIL

The 0.5-mile (0.8-km) **Mill Canyon Dinosaur Trail**, with numbered stops, identifies the bones of dinosaurs that lived in the wet climate that existed here 150 million years ago. You'll see fossilized wood and dinosaur footprints too. Pick up the brochure from the **Moab Information Center** (25 E. Center St., at Main St., 435/259-8825, www.discovermoab.com) or at the trailhead.

To reach the dinosaur bone site, drive 15 miles (24 km) north of Moab on U.S. 191, then turn left (west) at an intersection just north of milepost 141. Cross the railroad tracks; after 0.6 mile (1 km), turn left at the Y intersection; after another 0.5 mile (0.8 km), turn right and proceed 0.6 mile (1 km) on a rough dirt road (impassable when wet) to the trailhead. On the way to the trailhead, you'll pass another trailhead, where a short trail leads to dinosaur tracks.

You'll find many other points of interest nearby. A copper mill and tailings dating from the late 1800s are across the canyon. The ruins of Halfway Stage Station, where travelers once stopped on the Thompson-Moab run, are a short distance down the other road fork. Jeepers and mountain bikers explore the nearby Monitor and Merrimac Buttes; a sign just off U.S. 191 has a map and details.

Hole 'n the Rock is a popular roadside attraction.

COPPER RIDGE DINOSAUR TRACKWAYS

Apatosaurus, aka brontosaurus, and theropod tracks crisscross an ancient riverbed at the **Copper Ridge Dinosaur Trackways** site. It's easy to make out the two-foot-wide hind footprints of the brontosaurus, but its small front feet didn't leave much of a dent in the sand. Three-toed tracks of the carnivorous theropods, possibly *Allosaurus,* are 8-15 inches long, and some show an irregular gait—perhaps indicating a limp.

The Copper Ridge tracks are 23 miles (37 km) north of Moab on U.S. 191; turn right (east) 0.75 mile (1.2 km) north of milepost 148. Cross the railroad tracks and turn south onto the dirt road, following signs 2 miles (3.2 km) to the tracks. It's a short walk to the trackway. A network of mountain bike trails, the "Dino-Flow" trails, can also be accessed from the parking area.

MOAB GIANTS

If you (or your kids) want a more commercial take on the local dinosaurs, visit **Moab Giants** (112 W. Hwy. 313, 435/355-0228, www.moabgiants.com, 10am-6pm Thurs.-Tues.) There are two experiences and ticket prices. The outdoor Dino Pass ($16 adults, $12 ages 4-15, $50 family) lets you walk a well-executed 0.5-mile (0.8-km) outdoor trail flanked by more than 100 life-size dinosaur replicas. The Discovery Pass ($22 adult, $16 ages 4-15, $70 family) includes the outdoor dino exhibits plus a museum with a focus on fossil footprints and a movie theater with two 3-D films on ancient local life. This large complex is at the corner of U.S. 191 and the road to Dead Horse Point.

★ DEAD HORSE POINT STATE PARK

Just east of Canyonlands National Park's Island in the Sky District and a short drive northwest of Moab is one of Utah's most spectacular state parks. At **Dead Horse Point** (435/259-2614, www.stateparks.utah.gov,

day use $20 per vehicle), the land drops away in sheer cliffs, and 2,000 feet (610 m) below, the Colorado River twists through a gooseneck on its long journey to the sea. The river and its tributaries have carved canyons that reveal a geologic layer cake of colorful rock formations. Even in a region with impressive views around nearly every corner, Dead Horse Point stands out for its exceptionally breathtaking panorama. You'll also see below you, along the Colorado River, the result of powerful underground forces: Salt, under pressure, has pushed up overlying rock layers into an anticline. This formation, the Shafer Dome, contains potash that is being processed by the Moab Salt Plant. You can see the mine buildings, processing plant, and evaporation ponds, which are tinted blue to hasten evaporation.

A narrow neck of land only 30 yards wide connects the point with the rest of the plateau. Cowboys once herded wild horses onto the point, then placed a fence across the neck to make a 40-acre corral. They chose the desirable animals from the herd and let the rest go. According to one tale, a group of horses left behind after such a roundup became confused by the geography of the point. They couldn't find their way off and circled repeatedly until they died of thirst within sight of the river below. You may also hear other stories of how the point got its name.

Besides the awe-inspiring views, the park also has a **visitors center** (9am-5pm daily), a very popular campground, a picnic area, a group area, a nature trail, hiking trails, and great mountain biking on the **Intrepid Trail System.** Spectacularly scenic hiking trails run along the east and west rims of the park; hikers are also allowed to use the Intrepid trails. Rangers lead hikes during the busy spring season and on some evenings during the summer, including monthly full-moon hikes. Whether you're visiting for the day or camping at Dead Horse Point, it's best to bring

1: walk in the footsteps of dinosaurs at the Copper Ridge Dinosaur Trackways **2:** Fremont style of rock art at Sego Canyon **3:** Dead Horse Point State Park

Moab's Mining Boom and Bust

Moab is within the Paradox Salt Basin, a geologic formation responsible for the area's famous arch formations and accumulations of valuable minerals relatively near the surface. In addition to significant mineral wealth, mining and oil exploration have provided the region with some of its liveliest history and most colorful characters. French scientist Marie Curie, who discovered the element radium in uranium ore in 1898, visited the Moab area in 1899 to inspect a uranium-processing operation near the Dolores River.

Oil exploration in the 1920s caused some excitement in Moab, but nothing like that of the uranium boom that began in 1952. A down-on-his-luck geologist from Texas named Charles Steen struck it rich at his Mi Vida claim southeast of Moab. Steen's timing was exquisite: Uranium was highly sought-after by the federal government, primarily for use in Cold War-era atomic weapons and in nuclear power plants. An instant multimillionaire, Steen built a large mansion overlooking Moab and hosted lavish parties attended by Hollywood celebrities (his home is now the Sunset Grill restaurant). The Mi Vida mine alone would ultimately be worth more than $100 million, and it put Moab on the map.

By the end of 1956, Moab was dubbed "The Richest Town in the USA" and "The Uranium Capital of the World." In the wake of Steen's discovery, thousands of prospectors, miners, laborers, and others descended on the area, hoping to cash in on the mother lode. Moab's population tripled in just three years as eager prospectors swarmed into the canyons.

By the mid-1960s, the boom had died out. As the uranium played out, however, mining operations began in 1965 in one of the largest potash deposits in the world, on the Colorado River between Moab and Dead Horse Point, and work continues there today. Other valuable materials mined in the Moab area over the years include vanadium (used in steel processing), lead, gold, copper, and silver, along with helium, natural gas, and oil.

Cleanup of 16 million tons of uranium tailings is now underway near the U.S. 191 Colorado River crossing. The toxic tailings are being hauled 30 miles (48 km) north to a disposal site near I-70. As of April 2019, 9.5 million tons of radioactive tailings had been transported from the former uranium mill site, with roughly 6.5 million tons remaining.

plenty of water. Although water is available here, it is trucked in.

Dead Horse Point is easily reached by paved road, either as a destination itself or as a side trip on the way to the Island in the Sky District of Canyonlands National Park. From Moab, head northwest 10 miles (16 km) on U.S. 191, then turn left and travel 22 miles (35 km) on Highway 313. The drive along Highway 313 climbs through a scenic canyon and tops out on a ridge with panoramas of distant mesas, buttes, mountains, and canyons. There are several rest areas along the road.

SCENIC DRIVES

Each of the following routes is at least partly accessible to standard low-clearance highway vehicles. If you have a 4WD vehicle, you have the option of additional off-road exploring.

You'll find detailed travel information on these and other places in Charles Wells's *Guide to Moab, UT Backroads & 4-Wheel Drive Trails*, which, along with a good selection of maps, is available at the **Moab Information Center** (25 E. Center St., at Main St., 435/259-8825 or 800/635-6622, www.discovermoab.com). Staff at the info center usually know current road and trail conditions.

Utah Scenic Byway 279

Highway 279 goes downstream along the west side of the Colorado River Canyon, across the river from Moab. Pavement extends 16 miles (26 km) past fine views, prehistoric rock art, arches, and hiking trails. A potash plant marks the end of the highway; a rough dirt road continues to Canyonlands National Park. From Moab, head north 3.5 miles (5.6 km) on U.S. 191, then turn left onto

Highway 279. The highway enters the canyon at the "portal," 2.7 miles (4.3 km) from the turnoff. Towering sandstone cliffs rise on the right, and the Colorado River drifts along just below on the left.

Stop at a signed pullout on the left, 0.6 mile (1 km) past the canyon entrance, to see **Indian Ruins Viewpoint,** small prehistoric Native American ruins tucked under a ledge across the river. The stone structure was probably used for food storage.

Groups of **petroglyphs** cover cliffs along the highway 5.2 miles (8.4 km) from U.S. 191, which is 0.7 mile (1.1 km) beyond milepost 11. Look across the river to see the Fickle Finger of Fate among the sandstone fins of Behind the Rocks. A petroglyph of a bear is 0.2 mile (0.3 km) farther down the highway. Archaeologists think that the Fremont people and the later Utes did most of the artwork in this area.

A signed pullout on the right, 6.2 miles (10 km) from U.S. 191, points out **dinosaur tracks** and petroglyphs visible on rocks above. Sighting tubes help locate the features. It's possible to hike up the steep hillside for a closer look.

Ten miles (16 km) west of the highway turnoff is the trailhead for the **Corona Arch Trail** (3 mi/4.8 km round-trip).

The aptly named **Jug Handle Arch,** with an opening 46 feet (14 m) high and 3 feet (1 m) wide, is close to the road on the right, 13.6 miles (21.9 km) from U.S. 191. Ahead the canyon opens up where underground pressure from salt and potash has folded the rock layers into an anticline.

At the **Moab Salt Plant,** mining operations inject water underground to dissolve potash and other chemicals, then pump the solution to evaporation ponds. The ponds are dyed blue to hasten evaporation, which takes about a year. You can see these colorful ponds from Dead Horse Point and Anticline Overlook on the canyon rims.

High-clearance vehicles can continue on the unpaved road beyond the plant. The road passes through varied canyon country,

with views overlooking the Colorado River. At a road junction in Canyonlands National Park's Island in the Sky District, you have a choice of turning left for the 100-mile (161-km) White Rim Trail (4WD vehicles only past Musselman Arch), continuing up the steep switchbacks of the Shafer Trail Road (4WD recommended) to the paved park road, or returning the way you came.

Utah Scenic Byway 128

Highway 128 turns northeast from U.S. 191 just south of the Colorado River bridge, 2 miles (3.2 km) north of Moab. This exceptionally scenic canyon route follows the Colorado for 30 miles (48 km) upstream before crossing at Dewey Bridge and turning north to I-70. The entire highway is paved and passes many campsites and trailheads. The Lions Park picnic area at the turnoff from U.S. 191 is a pleasant stopping place. Big Bend Recreation Site is another good spot 7.5 miles (12 km) up Highway 128.

The rugged scenery along this stretch of the Colorado River has been featured in many films—mostly Westerns, but also *Thelma & Louise*—and commercials. If you're intrigued, stop by the free **Film Museum** at Red Cliffs Ranch, a resort near milepost 14.

The paved and scenic **La Sal Mountains Loop Road,** with viewpoints overlooking Castle Valley, Arches and Canyonlands National Parks, Moab Rim, and other scenic features, has its northern terminus at Castle Valley. From here, this route climbs high into the La Sals, and then loops back to Moab. Vegetation along the drive runs the whole range from the cottonwoods, sage, and rabbitbrush of the desert to forests of aspen, fir, and spruce. The 62-mile (100-km) loop road can easily take a full day with stops for scenic overlooks, a picnic, and a bit of hiking or fishing. Because of the high elevations, the loop's season usually lasts May to October. Before venturing off the Loop Road, it's a good idea to check current back-road conditions with the **Moab Ranger District** (62 E. 100 N., 435/259-7155, www.fs.usda.gov/mantilasal).

MOAB
SIGHTS

Rock Art Around Moab

The fertile valley around Moab has been home to humans for thousands of years. Prehistoric Fremont and Ancestral Puebloan people once lived and farmed in the bottoms of the canyons around Moab. Their rock art, granaries, and dwellings can still be seen here. Nomadic Utes had replaced the earlier groups by the time the first nonnative settlers arrived. They left fewer signs of settlement but added their artistry to the area's rock-art panels. You don't need to travel far to see excellent examples of Native American pictographs and petroglyphs.

Sego Canyon: If you approach Moab along I-70, consider a side trip to one of the premier rock-art galleries in Utah. Sego Canyon is about 5 miles (8 km) north of I-70; take exit 187, the Thompson Springs exit. Drive through the slumbering little town and continue up the canyon behind it (BLM signs also point the way). A side road leads to a parking area where the canyon walls close in. Sego Canyon is a showcase of prehistoric rock art—it preserves rock drawings and images that are thousands of years old. The Barrier Canyon Style drawings may be 8,000 years old; the more recent Fremont Style images were created in the last 1,000 years. Compared to these ancient pictures, the Ute etchings are relatively recent: Experts speculate that they may have been drawn in the 1800s, when Ute villages still lined Sego Canyon. The newer petroglyphs and pictographs are more representational than the older ones. The ancient Barrier Canyon figures are typically horned ghostlike beings that look like aliens from early Hollywood sci-fi thrillers. The Fremont Style images depict stylized human figures made from geometric shapes; the crudest figures are the most recent. The Ute images are of bison and hunters on horseback.

Potash Road (Hwy. 279): From U.S. 191 just north of the Colorado River bridge, take Highway 279 west along the river 5.2 miles (8.4 km) to these easily accessed petroglyphs. There's even a sign ("Indian Writing") to guide you to them.

Golf Course Rock Art: Take U.S. 191 south to the Moab Golf Course, which is about 4 miles (6.4 km) from the corner of Main and Center Streets in downtown Moab. Turn left and proceed to Spanish Trail Road. Approximately 1 mile (1.6 km) past the fire station, turn right onto Westwater Drive. Proceed 0.5 mile (0.8 km) to a small pullout on the left side of the road. An area approximately 30 feet by 90 feet (9 m by 27 m) is covered with human and animal figures, including "Moab Man" and what is popularly referred to as the "reindeer and sled."

Kane Creek Boulevard: Kane Creek Boulevard (south of downtown Moab; watch for the McDonald's) follows the Colorado River and leads to a number of excellent rock-art sites.

You can also ask at the **Moab Information Center** (25 E. Center St., at Main St., 435/259-8825, www.discovermoab.com, 8am-4pm daily) for a road log of sights and side roads. The turnoff from Highway 128 is 15.5 miles (25 km) up from U.S. 191.

A graded county road, **Onion Creek Road,** turns southeast off Highway 128 about 20 miles (32 km) from U.S. 191 and heads up Onion Creek, crossing it many times. Avoid this route if storms threaten. The unpleasant-smelling creek contains poisonous arsenic and selenium. Colorful rock formations of dark red sandstone line the creek. After about 8 miles (12.9 km), the road climbs steeply out of Onion Creek to upper Fisher Valley and a junction with Kokopelli's Trail, which follows a jeep road over this part of its route.

Some of the area's most striking sights are the gothic spires of **Fisher Towers,** which soar as high as 900 feet (275 m) above Professor Valley. Supposedly, the name Fisher is not that of a pioneer but a corruption of the geologic term *fissure* (a narrow crack). In 1962, three climbers from Colorado made the first ascent of Titan Tower, the tallest of the three towers. The almost vertical rock faces, overhanging bulges, and sections of rotten rock made for an exhausting 3.5 days of climbing; the party descended to the base for two of the nights. Their final descent from the summit took only six hours. More recently, slackliners have walked a rope strung between

From the junction with U.S. 191, turn west and proceed 0.8 mile (1.3 km) to the intersection of Kane Creek Drive and 500 West. Keep left and continue along Kane Creek Drive approximately 2.3 miles (3.7 km) to the mouth of Moon Flower Canyon. Along the rock cliff just beyond the canyon, you will see a rock-art panel behind a fence. Continue another 1.2 miles/1.9 kilometers (3.5 mi/5.6 km from 500 West) to another rock-art panel, where a huge rock surface streaked with desert varnish is covered with images of bighorn sheep, snakes, and human forms. For a unique rock-art image, continue on Kane Creek Boulevard past the cattle guard, where the road turns from pavement to graded gravel road. About 1.4 miles (2.3 km) from the cattle guard, just past the second sign for the Amasa Back trail, 5.5 miles (8.9 km) from the intersection of Kane Creek Drive and 500 West, watch for two small pullouts. Down the slope from the road is a large boulder with rock art on all four sides. The most amazing image is of a woman giving birth.

One of the Kane Creek petroglyphs depicts a woman giving birth.

Courthouse Wash: Although this site is located within Arches National Park, it is accessed from a parking lot off U.S. 191 just north of the Colorado River bridge, 1 mile (1.6 km) north of Moab. A 0.5-mile (0.8-km) hike leads to the panel, which is almost 19 feet (5.8 m) high and 52 feet (15.9 m) long. It has both pictographs and petroglyphs, with figures resembling ghostly humans, bighorn sheep, scorpions, and a large beaked bird. This panel, which was vandalized in 1980, was restored by the National Park Service; restoration work revealed older images underneath the vandalized layer.

A Rock Art Auto Tour brochure is available at the **Moab Information Center** (25 E. Center St., at Main St., Moab, 435/259-8825, www.discovermoab.com, 8am-4pm daily).

the two tallest towers, and visitors to the towers can frequently see climbers. The Bureau of Land Management (BLM) has a small campground and picnic area nearby, and a hiking trail skirts the base of the three main towers. An unpaved road turns southeast off Highway 128 near milepost 21, which is 21 miles (34 km) from U.S. 191, and continues 2 miles (3.2 km) to the picnic area.

The existing **Dewey Bridge,** 30 miles (48 km) up the highway, replaced a picturesque wood-and-steel suspension bridge built in 1916, which burned in 2008. Here, the BLM has built the Dewey Bridge Recreation Site, with a picnic area, a trailhead, a boat launch, and a small campground.

Upstream from Dewey Bridge are the wild rapids of **Westwater Canyon.** The Colorado River cut this narrow gorge into dark metamorphic rock. You can raft or kayak down the river in one day or a more leisurely two days; many local outfitters offer trips. Camping is limited to a single night. Unlike most desert rivers, this section of the Colorado River also offers good river-running at low water levels in late summer and autumn. Westwater Canyon's inner gorge, where boaters face their greatest challenge, is only about 3.5 miles (5.6 km) long; however, you can enjoy scenic sandstone canyons both upstream and downstream.

The rough 4WD **Top-of-the-World Road** climbs to an overlook with outstanding views of Fisher Towers, Fisher Valley, Onion Creek, and beyond. Pick up a map at the **Moab Information Center** (25 E. Center St., at Main St., 435/259-8825, www.discovermoab.com) to guide you to the rim. The elevation here is 6,800 feet (2,073 m), nearly 3,000 feet (915 m) higher than the Colorado River.

Kane Creek Scenic Drive

Kane Creek Road heads downstream along the Colorado River on the same side as Moab. The 4 miles (6.4 km) through the Colorado River Canyon are paved, followed by 6 miles (9.7 km) of good dirt road through Kane Springs Canyon. This route also leads to the **Matheson Wetland Preserve** (934 W. Kane Creek Blvd.), which is a Nature Conservancy site, as well as great rock art, several hiking trails and campgrounds, and some modern-day **cave dwellings.** People with high-clearance vehicles or mountain bikes can continue across Kane Springs Creek to Hurrah Pass and an extensive network of 4WD trails. From Moab, drive south on Main Street (U.S. 191) for 1 mile (1.6 km) and then turn right onto Kane Creek Boulevard, which becomes Kane Creek Road.

Recreation

Moab is at the center of some of the most picturesque landscapes in North America. Even the least outdoorsy visitor will want to explore the river canyons, natural arches, and mesas. Mountain biking, four-wheeling, and river tours are the recreational activities that get the most attention in the Moab area, although hikers, climbers, and horseback riders also find plenty to do. If you're less physically adventurous, you can explore the landscape on scenic flights or follow old mining roads in a jeep to remote backcountry destinations.

It's easy to find outfitters and sporting goods rental operations in Moab; it's the largest business segment in town. There's a remarkable cohesion to the town's operations: It seems that everyone markets everyone else's excursions and services, so just ask the closest outfitter for whatever service you need, and chances are excellent you'll get hooked up with what you want.

Make the **Moab Information Center** (25 E. Center St., at Main St., 435/259-8825, www.discovermoab.com, 8am-4pm daily) your first stop in town. It's an excellent source for information about the area's recreational options. The center is staffed by representatives of the National Park Service, the BLM, the U.S. Forest Service, and the Canyonlands Field Institute; they can direct you to the adventure of your liking. The center also has literature, books, and maps for sale. BLM officials can point you to the developed and undeveloped designated campsites near the Moab Slickrock Bike Trail, up Kane Creek, and along the Colorado River; you must use the designated sites in these areas.

To reach most of Moab's prime hiking trails requires a short drive to trailheads. For more options, head to nearby Arches and Canyonlands National Parks. For small groups, **Canyonlands Field Institute** (435/259-7750 or 800/860-5262, http://cfi-moab.org) leads day hikes (mid-Apr.-mid-Oct., $480 for up to six people, includes transportation and park admission) at various locations near Moab; join one to really learn about the area's natural history. The institute also offers rafting trips down the Colorado and multiday trips with an archaeological and natural history focus.

HIKING KANE CREEK SCENIC DRIVE AND U.S. 191 SOUTH

The high cliffs just southwest of town provide fine views of the Moab Valley, the highlands of Arches National Park, and the La Sal Mountains.

Vicinity of Moab

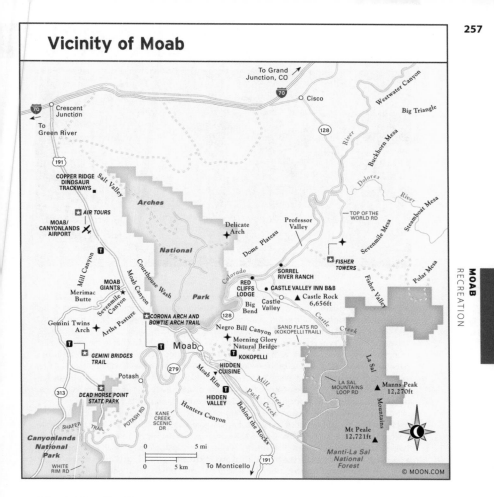

Moab Rim Trail

Distance: 6 miles (9.7 km) round-trip
Duration: 4 hours
Elevation change: 940 feet (287 m)
Effort: moderate
Trailhead: Kane Creek Boulevard, 2.6 miles (4.2 km) northwest of its intersection with U.S. 191 in Moab

If you're hiking, expect to share this route with mountain bikers and 4WD enthusiasts. The trail climbs northeast 1.5 miles (2.4 km) along tilted rock strata of the Kayenta Formation to the top of the plateau west of Moab, with the first of several great views over town and the Spanish Valley. Once on top, hikers can follow jeep roads southeast to Hidden Valley Trail, which descends to U.S. 191 south of Moab—a 5.5-mile (8.9-km) trip one-way. Experienced hikers can also head south from the rim to Behind the Rocks, a fantastic maze of sandstone fins.

Hidden Valley Trail

Distance: 2.3 miles (3.7 km) round-trip to Behind the Rocks overlook
Duration: 3 hours
Elevation change: 680 feet (207 m)

Odd Formations Behind the Rocks

the Behind the Rocks formations

A look at a topographic map will show that something strange is going on in the area called **Behind the Rocks.** Massive fins of Navajo sandstone, 100-500 feet (30-152 m) high, 50-200 feet (15-61 m) thick, and up to 0.5 mile (0.8 km) long cover a large area. Narrow vertical cracks, sometimes only a few feet wide, separate the fins. The concentration of arches in the area is similar to that in Arches National Park, with more than 20 major named arches. Where canyon drainages penetrate the sandstone, pour-offs form into 400-1,000-foot-deep sheer-walled canyons, often exposing perennial springs at the bottom. Behind the Rocks was inhabited extensively by the Ancestral Puebloan and Fremont peoples, the two cultures apparently overlapping here. Petroglyph panels, habitation caves, stone ruins, and middens abound throughout the area.

No maintained trails exist, and some routes require technical climbing skills. The maze offers endless routes for exploration. If you get lost, which is very easy to do, remember that the fins are oriented east-west; the rim of the Colorado River canyon is reached by going west, and Spanish Valley is reached by going east. Bring plenty of water, a topographic map (Moab 7.5-minute), and a compass. Access routes are the **Moab Rim** and **Hidden Valley Trails** (from the north and east) and **Pritchett Canyon** (from the west and south). Although it is only a couple of miles from Moab, Behind the Rocks seems a world away.

Effort: moderate

Trailhead: 3 miles (4.8 km) south of Moab on U.S. 191. Turn right onto Angel Rock Road. After two blocks, turn right onto Rimrock Road and drive to the parking area.

You'll see not only a hidden valley from this trail, but also panoramas of the Moab area and the Behind the Rocks area. The trail ascends a series of steep switchbacks to a broad shelf below the Moab Rim, then follows the shelf (hidden valley) to the northwest. It then crosses a low pass and follows a second shelf in the same direction. Near the end of the second shelf, the trail turns left to a divide, where you can see a portion of the remarkable fins of Behind the Rocks. The trail continues 0.3 mile (0.5 km) from the divide down to the end of the Moab Rim Trail, with the possibility of hiking on loop trails. Instead of turning left to the divide, you can make a short side trip (no trail) to the right for views of Moab.

Hunter Canyon

Distance: 4 miles (6.4 km) round-trip
Duration: 4 hours
Elevation change: 240 feet (73 m)
Effort: moderate
Trailhead: on Kane Creek Scenic Drive, 7.5 miles (12 km) west of its intersection with U.S. 191. Hunters Canyon is on the left, 1 mile (1.6 km) beyond the switchbacks.
Directions: To reach the trailhead from Moab, drive 8 miles (12.9 km) on Kane Creek Boulevard along the Colorado River and up Kane Creek Canyon. The road is asphalted where it fords Hunter Creek, but the asphalt is usually covered with dirt washed over it by the creek.

A rock arch and other rock formations in the canyon walls and the lush vegetation along the creek are highlights of a Hunter Canyon hike. Off-road vehicles have made tracks a short way up; you'll be walking mostly along the creek bed. Short sections of trail lead around thickets of tamarisk and other water-loving plants. Look for Hunter Arch on the right, about 0.5 mile (0.8 km) up. Most of the water in Hunter Canyon comes from a deep pool surrounded by hanging gardens of maidenhair ferns. A dry fall and a small natural bridge are above the pool. This pretty spot marks the hike's turnaround point and an elevation gain of 240 feet (73 m).

HIKING HIGHWAY 279
Portal Overlook Trail

Distance: 4 miles (6.4 km) round-trip
Duration: 3 hours
Elevation change: 980 feet (300 m)
Effort: moderate
Trailhead: JayCee Park Recreation Site, Highway 279, 4.2 miles (6.8 km) west of the Highway 279-U.S. 191 junction

The Portal Overlook Trail switchbacks up a slope, then follows a sloping sandstone ledge of the Kayenta Formation for 2 miles (3.2 km) to an overlook. A panorama (the "portal") takes in the Colorado River, Moab Valley, Arches National Park, and the La Sal Mountains. This trail is a twin of the Moab Rim Trail across the river. Expect to share it with mountain bikers.

★ Corona Arch and Bowtie Arch Trail

Distance: 3 miles (4.8 km) round-trip
Duration: 2 hours
Elevation change: 200 feet (61 m)
Effort: moderate
Trailhead: Highway 279, 10 miles (16 km) west of the Highway 279-U.S. 191 junction

If you have time for only one hike in the Moab area, this one is especially recommended. The trail leads across slickrock country to two impressive arches. You can't see them from the road, although a third arch—Pinto—is visible. The trail climbs 1.5 miles (2.4 km) from the parking area, crosses railroad tracks, and follows a jeep road and a small wash to an ancient gravel bar. Pinto Arch, also called Gold Bar Arch, stands to the left, but there's no trail to it. Follow rock cairns to Corona and Bowtie Arches. Handrails and a ladder help in the few steep spots.

Despite being only a few hundred yards apart, each arch has a completely different character and history. Bowtie formed when a pothole in the cliffs above met a cave underneath. It used to be called Paul Bunyan's Potty before that name was appropriated for an arch in Canyonlands National Park. The hole is about 30 feet (9 m) in diameter. Corona Arch, reminiscent of the larger Rainbow Bridge, eroded out of a sandstone fin. The graceful span is 140 feet (43 m) long and 105 feet (32 m) high. Both arches are composed of Navajo sandstone.

HIKING HIGHWAY 128
Grandstaff Canyon

Distance: 4 miles (6.4 km) round-trip
Duration: 3-4 hours
Elevation change: 330 feet (100 m)
Effort: easy-moderate
Trailhead: Highway 128, 3 miles (4.8 km) east of the Highway 128-U.S. 191 junction

One of the most popular hiking destinations in the Moab area, the Grandstaff Canyon trail follows a lively stream dammed by beavers and surrounded by abundant greenery and sheer cliffs. The high point of the hike is

Morning Glory Natural Bridge, the sixth-longest natural rock span in the country at 243 feet (74 m).

The trail is named after William Grandstaff, the first African American to live in the area from about 1877 to 1881. The trailhead and a large parking area are on the right just after crossing a concrete bridge 3 miles (4.8 km) from U.S. 191. The Grandstaff Campground, run by the BLM, is on the banks of the Colorado River just across the road from the trailhead.

The trail follows the creek up the canyon, with numerous stream crossings. Although the crossings are not difficult, hikers must be comfortable with stepping from rock to rock.

To see Morning Glory Natural Bridge, head 2 miles (3.2 km) up the main canyon to the second side canyon on the right, then follow a good but fairly steep side trail for 0.5 mile (0.8 km) up to the long, slender bridge. The spring and small pool underneath keep the air cool even in summer; ferns, columbines, and abundant poison ivy grow here.

★ Fisher Towers

Distance: 4.4 miles (7.1 km) round-trip
Duration: 4 hours
Elevation change: 670 feet (204 m)
Effort: moderate
Trailhead: off Highway 128; 21 miles (34 km) east of the Highway 128-U.S. 191 junction, turn right and go 2.2 miles (3.5 km) on an improved dirt road to a parking lot

These spires of dark red sandstone rise 900 feet (274 m) above Professor Valley. You can hike around the base of these needle rocks on a trail accessed by a short flight of stairs from the BLM picnic area. The trail follows a small slickrock-covered ridge leading away from the main cliffs; when the ridge narrows, go left into the ravine through a small cut in the ridge. From the bottom of the ravine, the trail heads steeply up and then begins to wind directly beneath the Fisher Towers. After

skirting around the largest tower, the Titan, the trail ascends and ends after 2.2 miles (3.5 km) on a ridge with a panoramic view. The Fisher Towers attract many very good rock climbers, and hikers may find that they linger along the trail to watch some spectacular climbing exploits. Carry plenty of water, as much of the trail is exposed and is frequently quite hot.

BIKING

The first mountain bikes came to Moab in 1982, when they were used to herd cattle. That didn't work out so well, but within a decade or so, Moab had become the West's most noted mountain bike destination. In addition to riding the famed and challenging slickrock trails (slickrock is the exposed sandstone that composes much of the land's surface here, and despite its name, bike tires grab it quite nicely) that wind through astonishing desert landscapes, cyclists can pedal through alpine meadows in the La Sal Mountains or take nearly abandoned 4WD tracks into the surrounding backcountry. Beware: The most famous trails—like the Slickrock Bike Trail—are not for beginners. Other trails are better matched to the skills of novices. A good online resource for trails and advice is the Moab Bike Patrol (www.moabbikepatrol.com).

It's a good idea to read up on Moab-area trails before planning a trip; heaps of books and pamphlets are available. You can also hire an outfitter to teach you about the special skills needed to mountain bike in slickrock country, or join a guided tour. The Moab Information Center's website (www.discovermoab.com) also has good information about bike trails.

Most people come to Moab to mountain bike mid-March to late May, and then again in the fall mid-September to the end of October. Unless you are an early riser, summer is simply too hot for extended bike touring in these desert canyons. Be prepared for crowds, especially in mid-March during spring break. The Slickrock Trail alone has been known to attract more than 150,000 riders per year.

1: Bowtie Arch **2:** Morning Glory Natural Bridge **3:** the trail up Grandstaff Canyon **4:** Fisher Towers

Mountain Bike Etiquette

When mountain biking in the Moab area, don't expect an instant wilderness experience. Because of the popularity of the routes, the fragile desert environment is under quite a bit of stress, and you'll need to be considerate of the thousands of other people who share the trails. By keeping these rules in mind, you'll help keep Moab from being loved to death.

- **Ride only on open roads and trails.** Much of the desert consists of extremely fragile plant and animal ecosystems, and riding recklessly through cryptobiotic soils can destroy desert life and lead to erosion. If you pioneer a trail, chances are someone else will follow the tracks, leading to ever more destruction. When riding on slickrock, brake carefully to avoid leaving skid marks on the rocks.

- **Protect and conserve scarce water sources.** Don't wash, swim, walk, or bike through potholes, and camp well away from isolated streams and water holes. The addition of your insect repellent, body oils, suntan lotion, or bike lubrication can destroy the thriving life of a pothole. Camping right next to a remote stream can deprive shy desert wildlife of life-giving water access.

- **Leave all Native American sites and artifacts as you find them.** First, it's against the law to disturb antiquities; second, it's stupid. Enjoy looking at rock art, but don't touch the images—body oils hasten their deterioration. Don't even think about taking potsherds, arrowheads, or artifacts from where you find them. Leave them for others to enjoy or for archaeologists to interpret.

- **Dispose of solid human waste thoughtfully.** The desert can't easily absorb human fecal matter. Desert soils have few microorganisms to break down organic material, and, simply put, mummified turds can last for years. Be sure to bury solid waste at least 6 to 12 inches deep in sand and at least 200 feet (61 m) away from streams and water sources. Pack out toilet paper in plastic bags. Check regulations; in some areas human waste disposal bags are required.

- **Check before riding power-assisted bikes on trails.** At the current moment, pedal-assist or e-bikes are prohibited on some singletrack bike paths and trails in Moab, while other trails, even the famed Slickrock Trail, are now open to e-bike riders. Check the status of your trail at the Moab Information Center before heading out.

If you've never biked on slickrock or in the desert, here are a few basic guidelines. Take care if venturing off a trail—it's a long way down some of the sheer cliff faces. A trail's steep slopes and sharp turns can be tricky, so a helmet is a must. Knee pads and riding gloves also protect from scrapes and bruises. Fat bald tires work best on the rock; partially deflated knobby tires do almost as well. Carry plenty of water—one gallon in summer, half a gallon in cooler months. Tiny plant associations, which live in fragile cryptobiotic soil, don't want you tearing through their homes; stay on the rock and avoid the crusty black cryptobiotic soil.

Dozens of trails thread through the Moab area; one good place for beginners to start is on the **Intrepid Trail System** at Dead Horse Point State Park. Descriptions of several local trails follow.

MOAB Brand Trails

The interconnected loops and spur trails (named for cattle brands that spell out M-O-A-B) form a trail system with several options that are especially good for beginners or riders who are new to slickrock. The 7-mile (11.3-km) **Bar-M** loop is easy and makes a good family ride, although you might share the packed-dirt trail with motor vehicles; try **Circle O** (no motor vehicles) for a good 3-mile (4.8-km) initiation to slickrock riding. More experienced slickrock cyclists can find some challenges on the **Deadman's Ridge, Long Branch,** and **Killer-B** routes at the southern end of the trail system.

To reach the trailhead for all these rides, head about 8 miles (12.9 km) north of town on U.S. 191 to the parking lot for the Bar M Chuckwagon (now closed), and park at the south end of the lot.

Slickrock Bike Trail

Undulating slickrock in the Sand Flats Recreation Area just east of Moab challenges even the best mountain bike riders; this is not an area in which to learn riding skills. Originally, motorcyclists laid out this route, although now most riders rely on leg and lung power. The 2-mile (3.2 km) practice loop near the trail's beginning allows first-time visitors a chance to get a feel for the slickrock. The "trail" consists only of painted white lines. Riders following it have less chance of getting lost or finding themselves in hazardous areas. Plan on about five hours to do the 10.5-mile (16.9-km) main loop, and expect to do some walking.

Side trails lead to viewpoints overlooking Moab, the Colorado River, and arms of Grandstaff Canyon. Panoramas of the surrounding canyon country and the La Sal Mountains add to the pleasure of biking.

To reach the trailhead from Main Street in Moab, turn east and go 0.4 mile (0.6 km) on 300 South, turn right and go 0.1 mile (0.2 km) on 400 East, turn left (east) and go 0.5 mile (0.8 km) on Mill Creek Drive, then turn left and go 2.5 miles (4 km) on Sand Flats Road. The Sand Flats Recreation Area, where the trail is located, charges $5 for an automobile day pass, $2 for a bicycle or motorcycle. Camping ($15) is available, but there is no water—bring plenty with you!

Farther up Sand Flats Road, the quite challenging, often rock-strewn **Porcupine Rim Trail** draws motorcyclists, jeeps, and mountain bikers; after about 11 miles (17.7 km), the trail becomes single-track, and four-wheelers drop out. The whole trail is about 15 miles (24 km) long.

★ Gemini Bridges Trail

This 14-mile (22.5-km) one-way trail passes tremendous twin rock arches (the bridges) and the slickrock fins of the Wingate Formation, making this one of the most scenic of the trails in the Moab area; it's also one of the more moderate trails in terms of necessary skill and fitness. The trail begins 12.5 miles (20.1 km) up Highway 313, just before the turnoff to Dead Horse Point State Park. It's a stiff 21-mile (33.8-km) uphill ride from Moab to reach the trailhead; consider shortening the ride by parking at the MOAB Brand parking area or taking a shuttle from town. Several companies, including **Coyote Shuttle** (435/260-2097, www.coyoteshuttle.com, $25), provide this service, enabling cyclists to concentrate on the fun, mostly downhill ride back toward Moab. The Gemini Bridges Trail, which is shared with motorcycles and 4WD vehicles, ends on U.S. 191 just north of town.

Intrepid Trail System

Mountain bikers, including novices, should bring their rides to Dead Horse Point, where the Intrepid Trail System offers about 15 miles (24 km) of slickrock and sand single-track trails in three loops that range from a 1-mile (1.6-km) beginner's loop to a more challenging 9-mile (14.5-km) loop. All routes start at the visitors center and have great views into the canyon country. To reach Dead Horse Point State Park (435/259-2614, $20) from Moab, take U.S. 191 north 9 miles (14.5 km), then turn west onto Highway 313 and follow it 23 miles (37 km) to the park entrance.

Lower Monitor and Merrimac Trail

A good introduction to the varied terrains of the Moab area, the 7.5-mile (12-km) Lower Monitor and Merrimac Trail includes lots of slickrock riding and a bit of sand. Reach the trailhead by traveling 15 miles (24 km) north of Moab on U.S. 191 and turning west (left) onto Mill Canyon Road, just past milepost 141. Make sure to go on the lower trail, not the Monitor and Merrimac Jeep Trail. After your ride, explore the nearby Mill Canyon Dinosaur Trail (foot traffic only).

Sovereign Single Track

Not every bike trail here is over slickrock; the challenging single-track Sovereign Trail is good to ride in hot weather. The trail, which contains rocky technical sections, a bit of slickrock, and more flowing single-track, is shared with motorcycles. Several trailheads access this trail; a popular one is from Willow Springs Road. From Moab, travel 11 miles (17.7 km) north on U.S. 191 and turn right onto Willow Springs Road, following this sandy road 2.5 miles (4 km) to the trailhead. To best see the options, pick up a map at a local bike store.

Kokopelli's Trail

Mountain bikers have linked a 142-mile (229-km) series of back roads, paved roads, and bike trails through the magical canyons of eastern Utah and western Colorado. The trail is usually ridden from east to west, starting in Loma, Colorado, and passing Rabbit Valley, Cisco Boat Landing, Dewey Bridge, Fisher Valley, and Castle Valley before landing on Sand Flats Road in Moab. Lots of optional routes, access points, and campsites allow for many possibilities. This multiday trip requires a significant amount of advance planning; **Bikerpelli Sports** (www.bikerpelli.com) is a good place to start this process.

Moab Canyon Pathway (Road Biking)

Although the Moab area is great for biking, riding along busy U.S. 191 is no fun. The Moab Canyon Pathway starts at the pedestrian and bike bridge over the Colorado River on Highway 128 at the north end of town and closely parallels the highway north to Arches National Park. From the entrance to the park, the path, which is separated from the road, continues north, climbing to the junction of U.S. 191 and Highway 313, the road to Dead Horse Point State Park and Canyonlands' Island in the Sky District.

From this intersection, the bike path is on a relatively wide shoulder; it's a 35-mile (56-km) ride to Canyonlands' Grand View Point, or a mere 24-mile (39-km) uphill chug to Dead Horse Point.

The paved route provides easy cycling access to the MOAB Brand mountain bike trails just off U.S. 191 and a more challenging ride to the Intrepid trails in Dead Horse Point State Park and the Gemini Bridges Trail, which starts just outside the park.

Bike Tours

Most of the bicycle rental shops in Moab offer daylong mountain bike excursions, while outfitters offer multiday tours that vary in price depending on the difficulty of the trail and the degree of comfort involved. The charge for these trips is usually around $200-250 per day, including food and shuttles. Be sure to inquire whether rates include bike rental.

Rim Tours (1233 S. U.S. 191, 435/259-5223 or 800/626-7335, https://rimtours.com) is a well-established local company offering several half-day (around $105-135 pp for 2-3 cyclists), full-day (around $150-165 pp for 2-3 cyclists), and multiday trips, including a five-day bike camping trip in Canyonlands' Maze District ($1,250). **Magpie Cycling** (800/546-4245, http://magpieadventures.com) is a small local business that runs day trips, which include instruction on mountain biking techniques and overnight rides, mostly in Canyonlands, including a three-day tour of the White Rim Trail ($875).

Western Spirit Cycling (478 Mill Creek Dr., 435/259-8732, www.westernspirit.com) offers mountain and road bike tours in the western United States, with about one-third of them in Utah. Moab-area trips include the White Rim, the Maze, and Kokopelli's Trail (5 days, $1,260). Another Moab-based company with tours all over the West is **Escape Adventures** (local base at Moab Cyclery, 391 S. Main St., 435/259-7423 or 800/596-2953, www.escapeadventures.com), which leads multiday mountain bike trips, including a five-day "Best of Moab" tour of mountain bike trails ($1,195 camping, $1,995 inn accommodations); some of the tours combine cycling with rafting, climbing, hiking, or plane rides.

Rentals and Repairs

Rim Cyclery (94 W. 100 N., 435/259-5333, www.rimcyclery.com, 8am-6pm daily) is Moab's oldest bike and outdoor gear store, offering both road and mountain bike sales, rentals, and service. Mountain bike rentals are also available at **Poison Spider Bicycles** (497 N. Main St., 435/259-7882 or 800/635-1792, www.poisonspiderbicycles.com, 8am-7pm daily spring and fall, 9am-6pm daily winter and summer) and **Chile Pepper** (702 S. Main St., 435/259-4688 or 888/677-4688, www.chilebikes.com, 8am-5pm daily). **Moab Cyclery** (391 S. Main St., 435/259-7423 or 800/559-1978, www.moabcyclery.com, 8am-6pm daily) offers rentals, tours, shuttles, and gear. Expect to pay about $60-80 per day to rent a mountain bike, a little less for a road bike; e-bike rentals are around $100 a day. If you just want to tool around a bit, rent a basic townie ($35) at **Bike Fiend** (69 E. Center St., 435/315-0002, www.moabbikefiend.com, 8am-6pm daily).

Shuttle Services

Several of the Moab area's best mountain bike trails are essentially one-way, and unless you want to cycle back the way you came, you'll need to arrange a shuttle service to pick you up and bring you back to Moab or your vehicle. Also, if you don't have a vehicle or a bike rack (available at most shops when you rent a bike), you will need to use a shuttle service to get to more distant trailheads. **Coyote Shuttle** (435/260-2097, www.coyoteshuttle.com) and **Whole Enchilada Shuttle** (435/260-2534, https://wholeenchiladashuttles.com) both operate shuttle services; depending on distance, the usual fare is $15-30 per person. Both companies also shuttle hikers to trailheads and pick up rafters.

RAFTING AND BOATING

Even a visitor with a tight schedule can get out and enjoy the canyon country on rafts and other watercraft. Outfitters offer both laid-back and exhilarating day trips, which usually require little advance planning. Longer multiday trips include gentle canoe paddles along the placid Green River and thrilling expeditions down the Colorado River.

You'll need to reserve well in advance for most of the longer trips: The BLM and the National Park Service limit trips through the backcountry, and space, especially in high season, is at a premium. Experienced rafters can also plan their own unguided trips, although you'll need a **permit** for all areas except for the daylong Fisher Towers float upstream from Moab.

The rafting season runs April to September, and jet-boat tours run February to November. Most do-it-yourself river-runners obtain their permits by applying in January-February for a March drawing; the Moab Information Center's BLM ranger (25 E. Center St., at Main St., 435/259-8825) can advise on this process and provide the latest information about available cancellations.

Rafting and Kayaking Trips

For most of the following trips, full-day rates include lunch and beverages, while part-day trips include just lemonade and soft drinks. On overnight trips, you'll sleep in tents in backcountry campgrounds.

The **Colorado River** offers several exciting options. The most popular day run near Moab starts upstream near Fisher Towers and bounces through several moderate rapids on the way back to town. Full-day raft trips ($85-110 pp adults) run from Fisher Towers to near Moab. Half-day trips ($60-75 pp adults) run over much the same stretch of river but don't usually include lunch.

Several outfitters offer guided **stand-up paddling** trips (half day about $75-85) on quiet stretches of the Colorado River near the border of Arches National Park.

For a more adventurous rafting trip, the

Colorado's rugged **Westwater Canyon** offers lots of white water and several Class III-IV rapids near the Utah-Colorado border. These long day trips are more expensive, typically around $180-200 per day. The Westwater Canyon is also often offered as part of multiday adventure packages.

The **Cataract Canyon** section of the Colorado River, which begins south of the river's confluence with the Green River and extends to the backwater of Lake Powell, usually requires four days of rafting to complete. However, if you're in a hurry, some outfitters offer time-saving trips that motor rather than float through placid water and slow down only to shoot rapids, enabling these trips to conclude in as little as one day. This is the wildest white water in the Moab area, with big boiling Class III-IV rapids. Costs range $485-1,650, depending on what kind of craft, the number of days, and whether you fly, hike, or drive out at the end of the trip.

The **Green River** also offers Class II-III rafting and canoeing or kayaking opportunities, although they are milder than those on the Colorado. Trips on the Green make good family outings. Most trips require five days, leaving from the town of Green River, paddling through **Labyrinth Canyon** and taking out at Mineral Bottom, just before Canyonlands National Park. Costs range $950-1,750 for a five-day rafting trip.

Rafting or Kayaking on Your Own

The Class II-III **Fisher Towers** section of the Colorado River is gentle enough for amateur rafters to negotiate on their own. A popular one-day raft trip with mild rapids begins from the Hittle Bottom Recreation Site (Hwy. 128, 23.5 mi/38 km north of Moab, near Fisher Towers) and ends 14 river miles (22.5 km) downstream at Take-Out Beach (Hwy. 128, 10.3 mi/16.6 km north of U.S. 191). You can rent rafts and the mandatory life jackets in Moab, and you won't need a permit on this section of river.

Experienced white-water rafters can run the Whitewater Canyon of the Colorado River on their own. Obtain **permits** ($10) by calling 435/259-7012 up to two months prior to launch date; it's important to plan well in advance. The usual put-in is at the Westwater Ranger Station 9 miles (14.5 km) south of I-70 exit 227; another option is the Loma boat launch in Colorado. A start at Loma adds a day or two to the trip along with the sights of Horsethief and Ruby Canyons. Normal takeout is at Cisco, although it's possible to continue 16 miles (26 km) on slow-moving water through open country to Dewey Bridge.

Wild West Voyages (422 Kane Creek Blvd., 435/35-0776 or 866/390-3994, www.canyonvoyages.com) and **Navtec Expeditions** (321 N. Main St., 435/259-7983 or 800/833-1278, www.navtec.com) are two local rafting companies that rent rafts (from $120-140 per day). Both companies also rent kayaks ($40-65 per day) and stand-up paddleboards ($55-65) for those who would rather organize their own river adventures.

Rafting Outfitters

Moab is full of river-trip companies, and most offer a variety of day and multiday trips; in addition, many will combine raft trips with biking, horseback riding, hiking, or 4WD excursions. Check out the many websites at www.discovermoab.com. The following list includes major outfitters offering a variety of rafting options. Most lead trips to the main river destinations on the Colorado and Green Rivers as well as other rivers in Utah and the West. Red River Adventures runs trips in smaller self-paddled rafts and inflatable kayaks. Inquire about natural history or petroglyph tours if these specialty trips interest you.

- **Adrift Adventures** (378 N. Main St., 435/259-8594 or 800/874-4483, www.adrift.net)

- **Canyonlands Field Institute** (1320 S. Hwy. 191, 435/259-7750 or 800/860-5262, http://cfimoab.org)

1: mountain biker riding on slickrock **2:** paddling into the Labyrinth Canyon

1

2

- **Wild West Voyages** (422 Kane Creek Blvd., 435/355-0776, www.wildwestvoyages.com)

- **Moab Adventure Center** (225 S. Main St., 435/259-7019 or 866/904-1163, www.moabadventurecenter.com)

- **Navtec Expeditions** (321 N. Main St., 435/259-7983 or 800/833-1278, www.navtec.com)

- **Red River Adventures** (1140 S. Main St., 435/259-4046 or 877/259-4046, www.redriveradventures.com)

- **Sheri Griffith Expeditions** (2231 S. Hwy. 191, 503/259-8229 or 800/332-2439, www.griffithexp.com)

- **Tag-A-Long Expeditions** (378 N. Main St., 435/259-8594 or 800/874-4483, www.tagalong.com)

Canoeing

Canoeists can also sample the calm waters of the Green River on multiday excursions with **Moab Rafting and Canoe Company** (420 Kane Creek Blvd., 435/259-7722, www.moabrafting.com), which runs scheduled guided trips ($999 for a four-day trip) to four sections of the Green and to calmer stretches of the Colorado River. They also rent canoes ($40-50 per day), including the necessary equipment.

Another good source for DIY canoe and kayak trips on the Green River is **Tex's Riverways** (691 N. 500 West, 435/259-5101 or 877/662-2839, www.texsriverways.com), which specializes in rentals, shuttles, and support for self-guided trips.

Jet Boats and Motorboats

Canyonlands by Night & Day (435/259-5261 or 800/394-9978, www.canyonlandsbynight.com, Apr.-mid-Oct., $79 adults, $69 ages 4-12, includes dinner, $69 adult, $59 ages 4-12 boat only) tours leave at sunset in an open tour boat and go several miles upstream on the Colorado River; a guide points out canyon features. The sound and light show begins on the way back. Music and historical narration accompany the play of lights on the canyon walls. Reservations are a good idea because the boat fills up fast. This company also offers a selection of daytime jet-boat tours, including a three-hour trip ($109 adults, $99 children) to the Colorado River canyon downstream from Moab. Trips depart from the Spanish mission-style office just north of Moab, across the Colorado River.

4WD EXPLORATION

Road tours offer visitors a special opportunity to view unique canyon-country arches and spires, Indigenous rock art, and wildlife. An interpretive brochure and map at the **Moab Information Center** (25 E. Center St., at Main St., 435/259-8825, www.discovermoab.com) outlines Moab-area 4WD trails: four rugged 15-54-mile (24-87-km) loop routes through the desert that take 2.5-4 hours to drive. Those who left their trusty four-by-fours and off-road-driving skills at home can take an off-road jeep tour with a private operator. Most Moab outfitters offer jeep or Hummer tours, often in combination with rafting or hiking options. The **Moab Adventure Center** (452 N. Main St., 435/259-7019 or 866/404-1163, www.moabadventurecenter.com) runs two-hour ($89 adults, $59 youths) and half-day ($185 adults, $135 youths) guided Hummer safaris. The Adventure Center, which can book you on any number of trips, can also arrange jeep rentals (from $260 per day).

Jeep and other 4WD-vehicle rentals are also available at a multitude of other Moab outfits, including **Twisted Jeep Rentals** (446 S. Main St., 435/259-0335, www.twistedjeeps.com) and **Cliffhanger Jeep Rentals** (40 W. Center St., 435/259-0889, www.cliffhangerjeeprental.com). Expect to pay at least $225 per day.

ATVS AND DIRT BIKES

As an alternative to four-by-four touring in the backcountry, there's all-terrain vehicle (ATV) and motorcycle "dirt biking," typically but not exclusively geared toward youngsters and families. Although youths ages 8-15 may operate an ATV, provided they possess an Education Certificate issued by Utah State Parks and Recreation or an equivalent certificate from their home state, parents should research ATV safety before agreeing to such an outing. Much of the public land surrounding Moab is open to ATV exploration, with many miles of unpaved roads and existing trails on which ATVs can travel. However, ATV and dirt bike riding is not allowed within either Arches or Canyonlands National Parks.

One particularly popular area for ATVs is **White Wash Sand Dunes,** with many miles of dirt roads in a strikingly scenic location. It is 48 miles (77 km) northwest of Moab, reached by driving 13 miles (21 km) south from I-70 exit 175, just east of Green River. The dunes are interspersed with large cottonwood trees and bordered by red sandstone cliffs. In addition to the dunes, White Wash is a popular route around three sides of the dunes.

ATVs and dirt bikes are available from a number of Moab-area outfitters, including **High Point Hummer** (281 N. Main St., 435/259-2972 or 877/486-6833, www.highpointhummer.com) and **Moab Tour Company** (427 N. Main St., 435/259-4080 or 877/725-7317, www.moabtourcompany.com). A half-day dirt bike or ATV rental starts at around $299.

★ AIR TOURS

You'll have a bird's-eye view of southeastern Utah's incredible landscape from Moab's Canyonlands Field with **Redtail Aviation** (435/259-7421, https://flyredtail.com). A 30-minute flight over Arches National Park is $109 per person; add Canyonlands and the rate is $229 per person. Longer tours are also available, and flights operate year-round.

SKYDIVING

If you think the Arches and Canyonlands area looks dramatic from an airplane, imagine the excitement of parachuting into the desert landscape. **Skydive Moab** (Canyonlands Fields Airport, U.S. 191, 16 miles (26 km) north of Moab, 435/259-5867, www.skydivemoab.com) offers jumps for both first-time and experienced skydivers. First-timers receive 30 minutes of ground schooling, followed by a half-hour flight before a tandem parachute jump with an instructor from 10,000 feet (3,048 m). Tandem skydives, including instruction and equipment, start at $169; equipment and parachutes are available for rent.

ATV rentals aren't hard to find in Moab.

CLIMBING

Just outside town, the cliffs along Highway 279 and Fisher Towers attract rock climbers. For world-class crack climbing, head south to Indian Creek, near the Needles District of Canyonlands National Park.

Moab Desert Adventures (39 E. Center St., 804/814-3872 or 877/765-6622, www.moabdesertadventures.com) offers rock-climbing and canyoneering lessons, both for beginners and experienced climbers; families are welcome. A half-day of basic climbing instruction is $185 for a private lesson; rates are lower for groups of two to four students. Head out for a climbing or canyoneering trip with **Moab Cliffs & Canyons** (253 N. Main St., 435/259-3317 or 877/641-5271, www.cliffsand-canyons.com). A day of climbing rock crags will cost $250 for one person, $195 per person for two.

Moab has a couple of stores with rock climbing gear and informative staff: **Gearheads** (1040 S. Main St., 435/259-4327, 8am-8pm daily) and **Pagan Mountaineering** (59 S. Main St., 435/259-1117, www.paganclimber.com, 9am-8pm daily).

HORSEBACK RIDING

Head up the Colorado River to the Fisher Towers area, where **Moab Horses** (Hauer Ranch, Hwy. 128, milepost 21, 435/259-8015, www.moabhorses.com, half-day $90 for two or more riders) runs guided trail rides. Also along Highway 128, **Red Cliffs Lodge** (Hwy. 128, milepost 14, 435/259-2002 or 866/812-2002, www.redcliffslodge.com) and **Sorrel River Ranch** (Hwy. 128, milepost 17, 435/259-4642 or 877/317-8244, www.sorrel-river.com) both offer trail rides.

GOLF

The **Moab Golf Club** (2705 E. Bench Rd., 435/259-6488, https://moabgolfcourse.com, $42-58) is an 18-hole par-72 public course in a well-watered oasis amid stunning red-rock formations. To get here from Moab, go south 5 miles (8 km) on U.S. 191, turn left onto Spanish Trail Road and follow it 2 miles (3.2 km), then go right on Murphy Lane and follow it to Bench Road and the golf course.

LOCAL PARKS

The **City Park** (181 W. 400 N.) has shaded picnic tables and a playground. It's also home to the **Moab Recreation and Aquatic Center** (374 Park Ave., 435/259-8226), a very nice community center with indoor and outdoor swimming pools, a weight room, and group exercise classes.

Two miles (3.2 km) north of town, **Lions Park** (U.S. 191 and Hwy. 128) offers picnicking along the Colorado River. **Rotary Park** (Mill Creek Dr.) is family-oriented and has lots of activities for kids.

Entertainment and Events

For a town of its size, Moab puts on a pretty good nightlife show, with lots of hikers, bikers, and rafters reliving their daily conquests in bars and brewpubs. There are also notable seasonal music events, ranging from folk to classical.

NIGHTLIFE

A lot of Moab's nightlife focuses on the well-loved **Eddie McStiff's** (57 S. Main St., 435/259-2337, www.eddiemcstiffs.com, 11:30am-close daily), right downtown, with abundant beers on draft, cocktails, two outdoor seating areas, and live music on a regular basis.

Woody's Tavern (221 S. Main St., 435/259-9323, www.woodystavernmoab.com, 2pm-1am Mon.-Sat., 11am-1am Sun.), a classic dive bar, has pool and live bands on the weekend—you might hear bluegrass, rock, or jam bands. Come for some barbecue and stay for the blues (or vice versa; both are good) at **Blu Pig** (811 S. Main St., 435/259-3333, 11:30am-10pm daily).

For a more family-friendly evening out, cruise the Colorado with **Canyonlands by Night** (435/259-5261, www.canyonlandsby-night.com, Apr.-mid-Oct., $79 adults, $69 ages 4-12, includes dinner). The evening cruise ends with a sound-and-light presentation along the sandstone cliffs. Dinner packages are available; children under age four are not permitted, per Coast Guard regulations.

EVENTS

To find out about local happenings, contact the Moab Information Center (25 E. Center St., at Main St., 435/259-8825, www.discovermoab.com) or browse *Moab Happenings*, available free around town or online (www.moabhappenings.com). Unsurprisingly, Moab offers quite a few annual biking events. The **Moab Skinny Tire Festival**, held in mid-March, and the **Moab Century Tour**, held in late September or early October, are both sponsored road bike events that benefit the fight against cancer. For information on both, visit www.skinnytireevents.com or call 435/260-8889. The bike demo event **OuterBike** (www.outerbike.com) is held in early October, and the **Moab Ho-Down Mountain Bike and Film Festival** (http://moabhodown.com) in late October offers silly competitions, endurance races, jump contests, skills camps and other fun events (costume party!), plus an evening of bike-themed films.

Other major annual athletic events include a number of running events organized by **Mad Moose Events** (www.madmooseevents.com). These include the **Canyonlands Half Marathon and Five Mile Run,** held the third Saturday in March, and a women's half marathon held in early June, the **Thelma and Louise Half Marathon.**

Moab's most popular annual event, more popular than anything celebrating two wheels, is the **Easter Jeep Safari** (www.rr4w.com), which is the Sturgis or Daytona Beach of recreational four-wheeling. Upward of 2,500 4WD vehicles (it's not exclusively for jeeps, although ATVs are not allowed) converge on Moab for ten days' worth of organized backcountry trail rides. "Big Saturday" (the day before Easter) is the climax of the event, when all participating vehicles parade through Moab. Plan well ahead for lodging if you are planning to visit Moab during this event, as hotel rooms are often booked a year in advance.

Memorial Day weekend brings artists, musicians, and art cars to the city park for the **Moab Arts Festival** (435/259-2742, www.moabartsfestival.org).

The dust gets kicked up at the Spanish Trail Arena (3641 S. U.S. 191, just south of Moab) with the professional **Canyonlands PRCA Rodeo** (www.moabcanyonlandsrodeo.com), held the last weekend in May or first weekend in June, with a rodeo, a parade, a dance, horse racing, and a 4-H gymkhana.

The **Moab Music Festival** (435/259-7003, www.moabmusicfest.org) is first and foremost a classical chamber music festival, but every year a few jazz, bluegrass, or folk artists are included in the lineup. More than 30 artists are currently involved in the festival, held in late August and early September. Many of the concerts are held in dramatic outdoor settings. The **Moab Folk Festival** (www.moabfolkfestival.com) is the town's other big annual musical event, attracting top-notch acoustic performers to Moab the first weekend of November.

SHOPPING

Main Street, between 200 North and 200 South, has nearly a dozen galleries and gift shops with T-shirts, outdoor apparel, Native American art, and other gifts. **Back of Beyond Books** (83 N. Main St., 435/259-5154, 9am-10pm daily) features an excellent selection of regional books and maps. Pick up those missing camping items at **Gearheads**

(1040 S. Main St., 435/259-4327, 8am-8pm daily), an amazingly well-stocked outdoor store. If you're heading out to camp or hike in the desert, Gearheads is a good place to fill your water jugs with free filtered water.

Moab's largest grocery store, **City Market** (425 S. Main St., 435/259-5181, 6am-11pm daily), is a good place to pick up supplies; it has a pharmacy and a gas station.

Stop by the **Moonflower Community Cooperative** (39 E. 100 N., 435/259-5712, 8am-8pm daily) for natural-food groceries.

Food

Moab has the largest concentration of good restaurants in Southern Utah. No matter what else the recreational craze has produced, it has certainly improved the food. Several Moab-area restaurants are closed for vacation in February, so call ahead if you're visiting in winter.

CASUAL DINING

Food isn't limited to muffins at ★ **Love Muffin** (139 N. Main St., 435/259-6833, http://lovemuffincafe.com, 6:30am-1pm daily, $7-9), but if you decide to skip the breakfast burritos or tasty rainbow quinoa, the Shake Yo Peaches muffin may be just what you need. While you're eating breakfast, order a Cubano sandwich to pack along for lunch.

Another good option for a tasty but healthy breakfast or lunch is ★ **Eklectica Coffee and Collectables** (352 N. Main St., 435/259-6896, 7am-2:30pm daily, $5-10), a charming and busy little café serving delicious organic and vegetarian dishes. For a more traditional breakfast, try the **Jailhouse Café** (101 N. Main St., 435/259-3900, 7am-noon Wed.-Mon., $8-11), a Moab classic.

Dense, chewy bagels and good sandwiches make the **Red Rock Bakery** (74 S. Main St., 435/259-5941, 7am-noon daily, $3-7) worth a visit.

Two Moab diners have an old-fashioned ambience and really good food. At the **Moab Diner & Ice Cream Shoppe** (189 S. Main St., 435/259-4006, http://moabdiner.com, 6am-9pm daily, $7-15), the breakfasts are large, with a Southwestern green chili edge to much of the food. The house-made ice cream is delicious. Another spot with great burgers and shakes is ★ **Milt's Stop & Eat** (356 Millcreek Dr., 435/259-7424, www.miltssto-pandeat.com, 11am-8pm Tues.-Sun., $5-8)—it's a local classic, and just the place to stop and sprawl under the big tree out front after a day of biking or hiking.

For good Mexican food in a friendly, un-fussy strip-mall setting, head south of downtown to tiny **El Charro Loco** (812 S. Main St., 435/355-0854, 11am-10pm daily, $7-20). Don't miss the pastries here—they're a special treat. No alcohol is served. A more upscale Mexican restaurant is **Miguel's Baja Grill** (51 N. Main St., 435/259-6546, www.miguelsbajagrill.net, 5pm-10pm daily, $10-26), with well-prepared Baja-style seafood, including good fish tacos. It's a busy place, so make a reservation or be prepared to wait.

Zax (96 S. Main St., 435/259-6555, www.zaxmoab.com, 11am-10pm daily, $10-15) is a busy restaurant in the heart of downtown with something for everyone. If you're with fussy eaters, this might be the ticket for sandwiches, steaks, pasta, pizza, or salad, and there's an all-you-can-eat pizza, soup, and salad bar ($15).

Get away from high-volume assembly-line restaurants at **Sabaku Sushi** (90 E. Center St., 435/259-4455, www.sabakusushi.com, 5pm-9:30pm Tues.-Sun., rolls $6-16), which offers surprisingly good sushi with a few innovations (seared elk meat is featured in one roll).

In a pretty building a block off the main drag, **Arches Thai** (60 N. 100 W., 435/355-0533, http://archesthai.com, 11am-10pm daily,

Moab Wineries

Southern Utah is not exactly the first place you think of when you envision fine wine, but for a handful of wine pioneers, the Moab area is the *terroir* of choice. Actually, conditions around Moab are similar to parts of Spain and the eastern Mediterranean, where wine grapes have flourished for millennia. The area's first wine grapes were planted in the 1970s through the efforts of the University of Arizona and the Four Corners Regional Economic Development Commission. The results were positive, as the hot days, cool nights, and deep sandy soil produced grapes of exceptional quality and flavor. A fruit-growing cooperative was formed in Moab to grow wine grapes, and by the 1980s the co-op was producing wine under the Arches Winery label. As teetotal Utah's first winery, Arches Winery was more than a novelty—its wines were good enough to accumulate nearly 40 prizes at national wine exhibitions.

Arches Winery was a true pioneer, and now two wineries produce wine in the Moab area, both open for wine tasting. In addition, many of Moab's fine restaurants offer wine from these local wineries.

Castle Creek Winery (Red Cliffs Lodge, Hwy. 128, 14 miles (22.5 km) east of Moab, 435/259-3332, www.castlecreekwinery.com, 11am-6pm Mon.-Sat.), formerly Arches Winery, produces merlot, cabernet sauvignon, chenin blanc, chardonnay, and a number of blended wines.

Spanish Valley Vineyards and Winery (4710 Zimmerman Lane, 6 mi/9.7 km south of Moab, 435/259-8134, www.moab-utah.com/spanishvalleywinery, noon-6pm Mon.-Sat. Mar.-Oct., noon-5pm Mon.-Sat. Feb. and Nov.) produces riesling, gewürztraminer, cabernet sauvignon, and syrah.

$13-21) has surprisingly good Thai food. It's a pleasant place if you're not in a hurry.

The **Broken Oar** (53 W. 400 N., 435/259-3127, 5pm-10pm Mon.-Sat., closed Dec., $11-29) is just north of downtown in a large log building that looks like a ski lodge. In addition to burgers, pasta, and steaks, the restaurant offers a selection of meats from its smoker. The beer and wine menu veers toward local producers.

About 3 miles (4.9 km) south of downtown, ★ **Hidden Cuisine** (2740 S. Hwy. 191, 425/259-7711, www.hidden-cuisine.com, 8am-2pm Tues.-Wed., 8am-2pm and 5:30pm-9:30pm Thurs.-Sun., $13-27) is that rare thing in Utah: a restaurant specializing in South African food. While you can get a good burger here, try the delicious South-African-style ribs or the *babotie* (a ground beef stew baked with savory custard) for a meal out of the ordinary. For lunch, the citrus quinoa salad is especially tasty.

BREWPUBS

After a hot day out on the trail, who can blame you for thinking about a cold brew and a hearty meal? Luckily, Moab has two excellent pubs to fill the bill. ★ **Eddie McStiff's** (57 S. Main St., 435/259-2337, www.eddiemcstiffs.com, 11:30am-close daily, $9-19) is an extremely popular place to sip a cool beer or a mojito, eat standard pub food (the pizza is a good bet), and meet other travelers; in good weather there's seating in a nice courtyard. You'd have to try hard not to have fun here.

There's more good beer and perhaps better food at the **Moab Brewery** (686 S. Main St., 435/259-6333, www.themoabbrewery.com, 11:30am-10pm Sun.-Thurs., 11:30am-11pm Fri.-Sat., $8-21), although it doesn't attract the kind of scene you'll find at Eddie McStiff's. The atmosphere is light and airy, and the food is good—steaks, sandwiches, burgers, and a wide selection of salads. Try the spinach salad with smoked salmon ($13) or the smoked tri-tip beef ($19). There's deck seating when weather permits. Immediately next door, the same folks operate the Moab Distillery; though there's no tasting room, you can sample their gin and vodka in the brewery.

FINE DINING

Just off Main Street, the ★ **Desert Bistro** (36 S. 100 W., 435/259-0756, www.desertbistro. com, reservations recommended, 5pm-10pm daily, $22-50) is housed in a lovely renovated building that was, when it was built in 1892, Moab's first dance hall. Today, it's a longtime favorite for regional fine dining. Its seasonal, sophisticated Southwest-meets-continental cuisine features local meats and game plus fresh fish and seafood. The patio dining is some of the nicest in Moab, and the indoor dining rooms are pretty and peaceful.

The **River Grill** (Sorrel River Ranch, Hwy. 128, 17 mi/27 km northeast of Moab, 435/259-4642, www.sorrelriver.com, 7am-2pm and 6pm-9pm daily Apr.-Oct., 7am-10am and 6pm-9pm daily Nov.-Mar., $34-48) has a lovely dining room and riverside patio that overlooks spires of red rock and the dramatic cliffs of the Colorado River. The scenery is hard to top, and the food is good, with a focus on prime beef and continental specialties. Dinner reservations are strongly recommended.

The **Sunset Grill** (900 N. U.S. 191, 435/259-7146, www.moab-utah.com/sunsetgrill, 5pm-9:30pm Mon.-Sat., $14-35) is in uranium king Charlie Steen's mansion, situated high above Moab, with sweeping million-dollar views of the valley. Choose from steaks, fresh seafood, and a selection of pasta dishes—what you'll remember is the road up here and the view. The grill now offers a free shuttle from most Moab locations; call 435/259-7777 to request a ride during regular restaurant hours.

Accommodations

Moab has been a tourism destination for generations and offers a wide variety of lodging choices, ranging from older motels to new upscale resorts. U.S. 191 is lined with all the usual chain motels, but we tend to go for the smaller local operations that are within walking distance of downtown restaurants and shopping, and that's mostly what you'll find listed here. Check with hotel booking sites for chain motel rooms farther out of town.

Moab Property Management (435/259-5125 or 800/505-5343, www.moabutahlodging.com) can make bookings at area vacation homes, which include some relatively inexpensive apartments. Another handy tool is www.moab-utah.com, which has a complete listing of lodging websites for the Moab area.

The only time Moab isn't busy is in the dead of winter, November to February. At all other times, be sure to make reservations well in advance. Summer room rates are listed here; in winter rates typically drop 40 percent, and in the busy spring break season, they tend to rise, especially during Easter weekend, when jeepers fill the town.

UNDER $50

The **Lazy Lizard Hostel** (1213 S. U.S. 191, 435/259-6057, www.lazylizardhostel.com) costs just $16 (cash preferred) for simple dorm-style accommodations. You won't need a hostel membership to stay at this casual classic Moab lodging. All guests share access to a hot tub, kitchen, barbecue, coin-operated laundry, and a common room with cable TV. Showers for nonguests ($3) and private guest rooms ($39 for 2 people) are also offered. Log cabins can sleep two ($45-47) to six ($62) people. If you're traveling in a large group, the hostel also offers a number of group houses that can sleep from 12 to 30 people under one roof. The Lazy Lizard is 1 mile (1.6 km) south of town, behind A-1 Storage; the turnoff is about 200 yards south of Moab Lanes.

$50-100

A couple of older but well-cared-for motels just north of downtown have clean, unfussy guest rooms starting at about $75-90: the **Adventure Inn** (512 N. Main St., 435/662-2466 or 866/662-2466, www.

adventureinnmoab.com) and the **Inca Inn** (570 N. Main St., 435/259-7261 or 866/462-2466, www.incainn.com), with a pool.

In the heart of town but off the main drag, the **Rustic Inn** (120 E. 100 S., 435/259-6477, www.moabrusticinn.com, $90-100) offers basic motel rooms, a guest laundry room, and a pool. If you want something more spacious, there are also apartments ($149-169). They have two bedrooms, a living room, and a kitchen. The apartments are popular, so book well in advance.

$100-150

Another simple but quite adequate place is the **Bowen Motel** (169 N. Main St., 435/259-7132 or 800/874-5439, www.bowenmotel.com, $118-152), a homey motel with an outdoor pool. The Bowen offers a variety of room types, including three-bedroom family suites and an 1,800-square-foot three-bedroom house with a full kitchen.

A few blocks south of downtown, the **Red Stone Inn** (535 S. Main St., 435/259-3500 or 800/772-1972, www.moabredstone.com, $139-149) is a one-story knotty-pine-sided motel; all guest rooms have efficiency kitchens. Other amenities include a bicycle maintenance area, a covered patio with a gas barbecue grill, a hot tub, and guest laundry. Motel guests have free access to the hotel pool next door at the Red Stone's sister property, the sprawling **Big Horn Lodge** (550 S. Main St., 435/259-6171 or 800/325-6171, www.moabbighorn.com, $109-119), which has similar knotty-pine guest rooms equipped with microwaves and fridges as well as a pool and a steak restaurant. If you want seclusion in a quiet community 18 miles (29 km) east of Moab, stay at the **Castle Valley Inn** (424 Amber Lane, Castle Valley, 435/259-6012 or 888/466-6012, www.castlevalleyinn.com, $145-235). The B&B-style inn adjoins a wildlife refuge in a stunning landscape of red-rock mesas and needle-pointed buttes. You can stay in one of the main house's four guest rooms, in a cabin, or in one of the three bungalows that have kitchens. Facilities include a hot tub. To reach Castle Valley Inn,

follow Highway 128 east from Moab for 16 miles (26 km), turn south, and continue 2.3 miles (3.7 km) toward Castle Valley.

OVER $150

The ★ **Best Western Canyonlands Inn** (16 S. Main St., 435/259-2300 or 800/649-5191, www.canyonlandsinn.com, $257-299) is at the heart of Moab, with suites, a pool, a fitness room and spa, a better-than-average complimentary breakfast, and a bike storage area. This is the best address in the downtown area if you're looking for upscale amenities.

At the heart of downtown Moab, **Best Western Greenwell Motel** (105 S. Main St., 435/259-6151 or 800/528-1234, www.bestwesternmoab.com, $175-224) has a pool, fitness facilities, an on-premises restaurant, and some kitchenettes.

One of the most interesting accommodations options in Moab is the ★ **Gonzo Inn** (100 W. 200 S., 435/259-2515 or 800/791-4044, www.gonzoinn.com, $203-249). With a look somewhere between an adobe inn and a post-modern warehouse, the Gonzo doesn't try to appear anything but hip. Expect large guest rooms with vibrant colors and modern decor, a pool, and a friendly welcome.

Located in a lovely and quiet residential area, the ★ **Sunflower Hill Luxury Inn** (185 N. 300 E., 435/259-2974 or 800/662-2786, www.sunflowerhill.com, $257-337) offers high-quality accommodations. Choose from a guest room in one of Moab's original farmhouses, a historic ranch house, or a garden cottage. All 12 guest rooms have private baths, air-conditioning, and queen beds; there are also two suites. Guests share access to an outdoor swimming pool and a hot tub, bike storage, patios, and large gardens. Children over age seven are welcome, and the inn is open year-round.

Families or groups might want to rent a condo at **Moab Springs Ranch** (1266 N. U.S. 191, 435/259-7891 or 888/259-5759, www.moabspringsranch.com, $225-365, 2-night minimum), located on the north end of town on the site of Moab's oldest ranch.

The townhomes have a parklike setting with a swimming pool and a hot tub, and they sleep up to 10. Book well in advance.

A cluster of four charming and pet-friendly cottages dubbed **3 Dogs & a Moose** (171 and 173 W. Center St., 435/260-1692, www.3dogsandamoosecottages.com) is just off the main drag. The two smaller cottages ($140-205) are perfect for couples, and the larger cottages ($320-330) sleep up to six. Booking is through Airbnb; follow links from the website.

A short drive from Moab along the Colorado River's red-rock canyon is the region's most upscale resort, the **Sorrel River Ranch** (Hwy. 128, 17 mi/27 km northeast of Moab, 435/259-4642 or 877/317-8244, www.sorrelriver.com, $770-1,069, minimum two-night stay required). The ranch sits on 240 acres in one of the most dramatic landscapes in the Moab area—just across the river from Arches National Park and beneath the soaring mesas of Castle Valley. Accommodations are in a series of beautifully furnished wooden lodges, all tastefully fitted with Old West-style furniture and kitchenettes. Horseback rides are offered into the arroyos behind the ranch, and kayaks and bicycles are available for rent. The ranch's restaurant, the **River Grill** (435/259-4642, 7am-2pm and 6pm-9pm daily Apr.-Oct., 7am-10am and 6pm-9pm daily Nov.-Mar., $34-48), has some of the best views in Utah.

Sharing a similar view of the Colorado River and Castle Valley but 3 miles (4.8 km) closer to Moab is the sprawling **Red Cliffs Lodge** (Hwy. 128, milepost 14, 435/259-2002 or 866/812-2002, www.redcliffslodge.com, $289), which houses guests in "mini suites" in the main lodge building and in a number of riverside cabins that can sleep up to six ($379). The lodge offers the Cowboy Grill bar and restaurant, horseback rides, and mountain bike rentals and will arrange river raft trips. The lodge is also the headquarters for Castle Creek Winery and the site of the free **Moab Museum of Film & Western Heritage,** which displays a collection of movie memorabilia from Westerns filmed in the area.

CAMPGROUNDS
Moab Campgrounds

It's really easy and comfy to camp at ★ **Up the Creek** (210 E. 300 S., 435/260-1888, www.moabupthecreek.com, mid-Mar.-Oct., $26 for 1 person, $33 for 2, $40 for 3), a walk-in, tents-only campground tucked into a residential neighborhood near downtown Moab. The shady campground, with a bathhouse and showers, picnic tables, and a few propane grills (campfires are prohibited), is right alongside a bike path.

RV parks cluster at the north and south ends of town. **Moab Valley RV Resort** (1773 N. U.S. 191, at Hwy. 128, 2 mi /3.2 km north of Moab, 435/259-4469, www.moabvalleyrv.com, $37-48 tents, from $58 RVs) is open year-round; it has showers, a pool, a playground, and free wireless Internet access. Pets are allowed only in RVs. Although this place is convenient to town and Arches, it is pretty close to a large ongoing environmental cleanup project involving removal of radioactive mine tailings (according to the Environmental Protection Agency, it's safe to camp here). **Moab KOA** (3225 S. U.S. 191, 435/259-6682 or 800/562-0372, http://moab-koa.com, Mar.-Nov., $50-57 tents, from $56 RVs with hookups, $109-189 cabins), barely off the highway 4 miles (6.4 km) south of town, has showers, a laundry room, a store, miniature golf, and a pool.

More convenient to downtown, **Canyonlands RV Resort and Campground** (555 S. Main St., 435/259-6848 or 800/522-6848, www.sunrvresorts.com, $39-44 tents, $52-57 RVs, $99 cabins) is open year-round; it has showers, a laundry room, a store, a pool, and two-person air-conditioned cabins—bring your own bedding. One mile (1.6 km) north of Moab, **Slickrock Campground** (1301½ N. U.S. 191, 435/259-7660 or 800/448-8873, http://slickrockcampground.com, $39-49 tents or RVs without hookups, $62-72 with hookups, $79 cabins

---

1: Up the Creek campground 2: BLM campground near Moab

with air-conditioning and heat but no bath or kitchen) remains open year-round; it has nice sites with some shade as well as showers, a store, an outdoor café, and a pool.

You'll also find campgrounds farther out at Arches and Canyonlands National Parks, Dead Horse Point State Park, Canyon Rims Recreation Area, and east of town in the cool La Sal Mountains.

For something a little less rugged, **Under Canvas Moab** (13748 N. U.S. 191, 801/895-3213, www.undercanvas.com/camps/moab, open mid-Mar.-Oct.) offers a luxury safari tent experience on 40 acres near the entrance to Arches National Park. Lodging is in a variety of large wall tents, some with private en suite bathrooms, and all fitted with fine bedding and furniture. In other words, this isn't exactly roughing it. Tent accommodations that sleep four start at $219 per night, with modern plumbing and bathroom facilities in group shower houses. Adventure packages are also available that customize outdoor activities to your preferences, and also include three camp-cooked meals a day.

BLM Campgrounds

There are 26 BLM campgrounds (most $10-15) in the Moab area. Although these spots can't be reserved, sites are abundant enough that campers are rarely unable to find a spot.

The campgrounds are concentrated on the banks of the Colorado River—along Highway 128 toward Castle Valley, along Highway 279 toward the potash factory, and along Kane Creek Road—and at the Sand Flats Recreation Area near the Slickrock Trail. Only a few of these campgrounds can handle large RVs, none have hookups, and few have piped water. For a full list of BLM campground and facilities, visit www.discovermoab.com.

Dead Horse Point State Park Campground

Soak in Dead Horse Point's spectacular scenery at the park's **Kayenta Campground** (reservations 800/322-3770, www.reserveamerica.com, $35 hike-in tent camping, $40 RVs, $140 yurts, plus $10 reservations fee), just past the visitors center, which offers sites with water and electric hookups but no showers. The campground nearly always fills up during the main season, so it's almost essential to reserve well in advance. Winter visitors may camp at the park; no hookups are available, but the restrooms have water.

If you aren't able to secure a spot inside the park, try the BLM's **Horsethief Campground** (no drinking water, $15) on Highway 313 a few miles east of the state park entrance. It has nearly 60 sites, all first come, first served, so it's usually possible to find a site.

Information and Services

Moab is a small town, and people are generally friendly. Between the excellent Moab Information Center and the county library—and the friendly advice of people in the street—you'll find it easy to assemble all the information you need to have a fine stay.

INFORMATION

The **Moab Information Center** (25 E. Center St., at Main St., 435/259-8825, www.discovermoab.com, 8am-4pm daily) is the place to start for nearly all local and area information. The

National Park Service, the BLM, the U.S. Forest Service, the Grand County Travel Council, and the Canyonlands Natural History Association are all represented here. Visitors who need help from any of these agencies should start at the information center rather than at the agency offices. Free literature is available, the selection of books and maps for sale is large, and the staff is knowledgeable. The center's website is also well organized and packed with information. In addition, the center screens a high-definition 4K film, *Welcome to Moab,* which introduces visitors to the wonders of the surrounding area.

The **BLM district office** (82 E. Dogwood Ave., 435/259-2100, 7:45am-4:30pm Mon.-Fri.) is on the south side of town behind Comfort Suites. Some land-use maps are sold here, and this is the place to pick up **river-running permits**.

SERVICES

The **Grand County Public Library** (257 E. Center St., 435/259-1111, 9am-8pm Mon.-Fri., 9am-5pm Sat.) is a good place for local history and general reading.

The **post office** (50 E. 100 N., 435/259-7427) is downtown. **Moab Regional Hospital** (450 W. Williams Way, 435/719-3500) provides medical care. For ambulance, sheriff, police, or fire emergencies, dial 911.

Dogs can spend a day or board at **Karen's Canine Campground** (435/259-7922, https://karensk9campground.wordpress.com) while their people hike the no-dog trails in Arches and Canyonlands.

Getting There

SkyWest, associated with United Airlines (800/335-2247, www.united.com), provides daily scheduled air service between **Canyonlands Field** (CNY, U.S. 191, 16 miles (26 km) north of Moab, 435/259-4849, www.moabairport.com) and Denver. Grand Junction, Colorado, is 120 miles (193 km) east of Moab via I-70 and has better air service; Salt Lake City is 240 miles (385 km) northwest of Moab.

Moab Express (435/260-9289, https://moabexpress.com) runs shuttles between Moab and Canyonlands Field ($25 pp, must book in advance). Moab Express shuttles also link to the Grand Junction airport in Colorado.

Enterprise (711 S. Main St., 435/259-8505, www.enterprise.com) rents cars at the airport.

The Southeastern Corner

Although Arches and Canyonlands capture

more attention, Utah's southeastern corner contains an incredible wealth of scenic and culturally significant sites. Round out your trip to this part of Utah with a tour of Ancestral Puebloan ruins, remote desert washes, soaring natural bridges, snowy mountain peaks, and a vast reservoir in a red-rock desert.

U.S. 191 runs south from Moab between Canyonlands National Park and the surprisingly tall Abajo Mountains to the west and the La Sal Mountains to the east. In the heat of the summer, these mountains are cool refuges. Also east of the highway, near the Colorado border, is Hovenweep National Monument, an Ancestral Puebloan site with an astounding collection of masonry buildings. Here the Ancestral Puebloans

Highlights

Look for ★ to find recommended sights, activities, dining, and lodging.

★ **Visit Edge of the Cedars State Park Museum:** Archaeological exhibits provide a good introduction to Ancestral Puebloan, Ute, Navajo, and Anglo history (page 285).

★ **Float the San Juan River:** Ignore the rest of the world by paddling through deep canyons and down Class III rapids (page 287).

★ **Go back in Time:** An impressive collection of masonry dwellings can be found at **Hovenweep National Monument** (page 289).

★ **Hike in Natural Bridges National Monument:** Three spectacular natural bridges are your reward on this 8.6-mile (13.8-km) loop hike. A 9-mile (14.5-km) drive with short hikes to each bridge will also do the trick (page 298).

★ **Roam Goblin Valley State Park:** Wander amid sandstone oddities—big mushroom-shaped rock formations, some with eroded "eyes" (page 307).

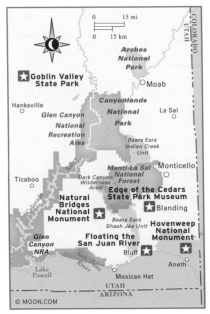

The Southeastern Corner

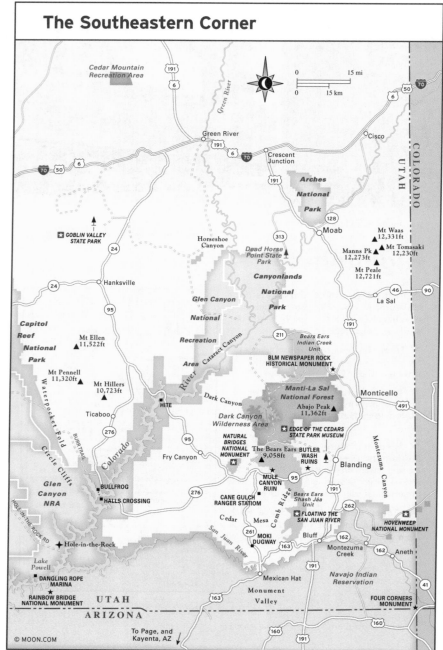

© MOON.COM

lived in what was more or less a city until they suddenly departed about 900 years ago.

The San Juan River runs across the southern tier of the region, with Cedar Mesa to the north and Monument Valley and Navajo Nation land to the south. Bluff, a charming village that's the put-in for many river trips on the San Juan, was settled in 1880 by Mormon pioneers who made the incredible wagon train trip from Escalante through steep canyons, including Hole-in-the-Rock.

Cedar Mesa is a place to explore on foot; canyons here often shelter Ancestral Puebloan ruins. To the west of the mesa, Natural Bridges National Monument is often overlooked, probably because it's rather remote. But its soaring stone bridges (carved by streams and spanning a streambed) are beautiful, even elegant, and a night in the campground will allow you to see stars in one of the nation's darkest places.

At Lake Powell the Colorado River is backed up by the Glen Canyon Dam. Lake Powell draws boaters—including visitors who rent houseboats to motor to the huge reservoir's remote inlets and canyons—but for a quick look, the car ferry across the lake is far less expensive. The surrounding Glen Canyon National Recreation Area encompasses the rugged canyons that drop down toward Lake Powell; before the dam was built, Glen Canyon was considered the equal of the Grand Canyon for drama and beauty, and in low-water years, a few peeks into the past are possible. A popular side trip—usually visited via tour boats from one of the lake's marinas—is to Rainbow Bridge National Monument, where the enormous stone bridge spans an arm of the lake.

On the northwestern edge of the region, about 25 miles (40 km) south of I-70, Goblin Valley State Park has rock formations that would be worthy of national park status if they weren't so close to Arches. Here you can hike among hoodoos, spires, and balancing rocks, many with wind-carved "eyes" that explain the area's supernatural moniker.

Remember that this is remote country: Fill your gas tank when you have the opportunity. Hanksville and Blanding are good places to check your gauge; if it's showing less than half a tank, definitely fill up. Likewise, pack a lunch and plenty of water when exploring remote areas such as Cedar Mesa, Hovenweep, or Glen Canyon.

PLANNING YOUR TIME

Although it's possible to spend many days exploring the backcountry of Cedar Mesa, floating the San Juan River, houseboating to remote reaches of Lake Powell, or really getting to understand the ancient dwellings at Hovenweep National Monument, most travelers will, at least initially, just pass through. Be sure to allow a day to visit Hovenweep and the Edge of the Cedars Museum in Blanding. From there, if you are short on time, head west across Cedar Mesa to Natural Bridges National Monument and north through Hanksville to Goblin Valley State Park.

Although there are motels in all the towns included in this chapter, you'll have more flexibility if you are camping. There are many campgrounds and even more de facto primitive campsites where you can make your own camp; however, be certain that you have the necessary permits before camping in the Cedar Mesa area.

Previous: the ruins at Hovenweep; the San Juan River; Twin Rocks Cafe in Bluff.

South of Moab

U.S. 191 runs south out of Moab, with the La Sal Mountains to the east and Canyonlands National Park to the west. A string of small towns—Monticello, Blanding, and Bluff—offer places to stop for a meal or a motel room as well as opportunities to explore mountains, desert, rivers, and archaeological sites.

MONTICELLO

This small Mormon town (pop. 2,000) is about 50 miles (81 km) south of Moab and pretty much its polar opposite. Quiet and relatively untouristed, it's the best place to stay if you're visiting the Needles District of Canyonlands National Park and don't want to camp. Monticello (mon-tuh-SELL-o) is at an elevation of 7,069 feet (2,155 m), just east of the Abajo Mountains. It is 46 miles (74 km) east of the entrance to the Needles District.

Food

A great addition to otherwise sleepy Monticello, the ★ **Granary Bar and Grill** (64 S. 300 W., 435/587/2597, www. granarybargrill.com, 7am-10pm, 11am-4pm, and 5pm-10pm daily, dinner $9-27) offers good food and craft cocktails in a converted grain silo with a Prohibition-era speakeasy atmosphere. The Granary is part of the Grist Mill Inn, and with a wide menu of pasta, burgers, steaks and other well-prepared main courses, this is the best place to eat within miles.

Accommodations

Monticello has a number of comfortable and affordable motels. The **Inn at the Canyons** (533 N. Main St., 435/587-2458, www. monticellocanyonlandsinn.com, $115-125) is nicely renovated and has an indoor pool, a pretty basic continental breakfast, and microwaves and fridges in the guest rooms. The **Monticello Inn** (164 E. Central St.,

435/587-2274, www.themonticelloinn.com, $75-89) is a well-maintained older motel with a pleasant in-town setting.

The local B&B, the **Grist Mill Inn** (64 S. 300 E., 435/587-2597, www.oldgristmillinn. com, $119-149), is indeed housed in an old flour mill. But rest assured, you won't be sleeping under an old millstone: The seven guest rooms are all furnished in typical B&B fashion, and all have private baths and TVs. An additional four rooms are found in the Cottage, a separate but adjacent building; the inn also rents two large homes for groups. The adjacent Granary Bar and Grill is the best place to eat in Monticello.

CAMPING

Campgrounds in the nearby Manti-La Sal National Forest include **Buckboard** and **Dalton Springs** (435/587-2041, $10). Buckboard, 7 miles (11.3 km) west of town on Blue Mountain Road (Forest Rd. 105), is at 8,600 feet (2,621 m) elevation, so it's not your best bet early in the spring. But when the rest of southeastern Utah swelters in the summer, this shady campground is perfect. Dalton Springs is along the same road, a couple of miles closer to town, at 8,200 feet (2,500 m). An abandoned ski area nearby is a good place for mountain biking.

Information and Services

Stop at the **Southeastern Utah Welcome Center** (216 S. Main St., 435/587-3401, www. monticelloutah.org, 9am-6pm daily Mar.-Oct., 9am-3pm Wed.-Sun. Nov.-Feb.) for information about southeastern Utah, including Canyonlands National Park.

The **San Juan Hospital** (364 W. 100 N., 435/587-2116) is friendly and small, and it's a good place to have any camping-related injuries repaired.

BLANDING

The largest town in San Juan County, Blanding (pop. 3,500, elev. 6,105 ft/1,860 m) is also a handy, if not exactly compelling, stop for travelers. The restaurant scene here is especially dire; if you're staying here, you might opt to picnic. Blanding is one the few "dry" towns in Utah, meaning alcohol cannot be sold inside the municipality. In 2017, locals had a chance to vote for the first time in more than 80 years to allow beer and wine sales in town. Blanding overwhelmingly voted to keep the anti-alcohol restrictions in place. In this environment, few restaurants of note take root.

If you're heading east toward Hovenweep or west into the Cedar Mesa area, check your gas gauge. Blanding is a good place to gas up—it's a long way between gas stations in this corner of Utah.

TOP EXPERIENCE

★ Edge of the Cedars State Park Museum

One mile (1.6 km) north of present-day Blanding, Ancestral Puebloan people built at least six groups of pueblo structures between AD 700 and 1220. The **Edge of the Cedars State Park Museum** (660 W. 400 N., 435/678-2238, www.stateparks.utah.gov, 10am-4pm Mon.-Sat., $5 adults, $3 children) features an excellent array of pottery, baskets, sandals, jewelry, and stone tools. The pottery collection on the second floor stands out for its rich variety of styles and decorative designs. This is the top museum in Utah if you're interested in the history and art of the Ancestral Puebloans, and it serves as a marvelous introduction to the ruins at nearby Hovenweep National Monument. The museum also has exhibits and artifacts of the people who followed the Ancestral Puebloans—the Utes and Navajo and the early Anglo pioneers.

A short trail behind the museum leads past a ruin that has been excavated and partly restored to suggest the village's appearance when the Ancestral Puebloans lived here.

You may enter the kiva by descending a ladder through the restored roof; the walls and interior features are original.

The Dinosaur Museum

The Dinosaur Museum (754 S. 200 W., 435/678-3454, www.dinosaur-museum.org, 9am-1pm Mon.-Sat. Apr. 15-Oct. 15, $4.50 adults, $3.50 seniors, $3 children) showcases the prehistoric plant and animal life of this corner of Utah. Exhibits include life-size models of dinosaurs (including the dino model used in the original King Kong movie) as well as fossils and skeletons. Don't miss the models of feathered dinosaurs.

Food

Blanding is not a center of gastronomy. In fact, restaurants seem to have trouble even staying open in this alcohol-free town. Only the fast-food joints are open on Sunday. Though **The Patio Drive In** (95 Grayson Pkwy., 435/678-2177, 11am-8pm Mon.-Thurs., 11am-9pm Fri.-Sat., $7-10) has a big local reputation as a drive-in restaurant, there are also a handful of tables and booths in the diner. **The Homestead** (121 E. Center St., 435/678-3456, 11am-9pm Mon.-Fri., 4pm-9pm Sat., $11-30) is the local steak house, with typical American fare and pizza, plus Navajo tacos.

Accommodations

With one exception, Blanding's motels are all pretty generic. That exception is ★ **Stone Lizard Lodge** (88 W. Center St., 435/678-3323, www.stonelizardlodging.com, $124-175), an older motel with remodeled but homey guest rooms, including a two-bedroom suite ($149). There's also a good breakfast. The motel also offers a pleasant garden area in the back with comfortable seating. The **Four Corners Inn** (131 E. Center St., 435/678-3257 or 800/574-3150, www.fourcornersinnblanding.com, $76-90), which has a restaurant next door, a simple continental breakfast, and several pet-friendly rooms, is a fine enough place to spend a night.

CAMPGROUNDS

At the south edge of town, **Blue Mountain RV Park** (1930 S. Main St., 435/678-7840, www.bluemountainrvpark.com, $26 tents, $35 RVs) is also home to a trading post with some high-quality Native American rugs, jewelry, and baskets. Although tent campers are welcome at the RV park, **Devil's Canyon Campground** (reservations 877/444-6777, www.recreation.gov, $10, plus $9 reservation fee), at an elevation of 7,100 feet (2,164 m) in the Manti-La Sal National Forest, is a better bet for tents. It has sites with water early May to late October, and no water or fees off-season. A 0.25-mile (0.4 km) nature trail begins at the far end of the campground loop. From Blanding, go north 8 miles (12.9 km) on U.S. 191, then turn west onto a paved road for 1.3 miles (2.1 km); the turnoff from U.S. 191 is between mileposts 60 and 61.

BLUFF

Bluff, a sleepy community of about 300 inhabitants, is nestled in a striking physical location. In the past few years, Bluff has become a rather unlikely mecca for recreationists and escapees from urban congestion. The quality of lodging is better than that of almost any other town of this size in the state, and local outfitters make it easy to get out and enjoy the remarkable scenery hereabouts.

Bluff is the oldest non-Native American community in southeastern Utah; it was settled in 1880 by Mormon pioneers who had traveled the excruciatingly difficult Hole-in-the-Rock Trail from the town of Escalante down into what's now Lake Powell. When the Mormon settlers finally got to the San Juan River valley, they founded **Bluff Fort,** which has been reconstructed (550 E. Black Locust St., 435/672-9995, 9am-5pm Mon.-Sat., free).

Spend an afternoon poking around local washes or examining a large pictograph panel, found along the cliff about 0.3 mile

(0.5 km) downstream from the Sand Island Campground. The visitors center, located in the Bluff Fort complex, is worth a stop; the staff can give you detailed directions for good informal hikes in the nearby washes.

If you want a guided trip into the backcountry of southeastern Utah, **Far Out Expeditions** (425/672-2294, www.faroutexpeditions.com) is a local company with lots of experience leading day trips and overnights in the area. **Wild Expeditions** (435/672-2244, www.riversandruins.com) leads half-day, full-day, and multiday trips to many of the destinations in southeastern Utah, including the Bears Ears area, with your choice of hiking, canyoneering, off-road vehicles, or 4WD touring.

★ Floating the San Juan River

From the high San Juan Mountains in southern Colorado, the San Juan River winds its way into New Mexico, enters Utah near Four Corners, and twists through spectacular canyons before ending at Lake Powell. Most boaters put in at Sand Island Campground near Bluff and take out at the town of Mexican Hat, 26 river miles (42 km) downstream. This trip combines ancient Native American ruins, rock art, and a trip through Monument Upwarp and the Upper Canyon, with some Class III rapids for thrills and weirdly buckled geology to ponder. This portion of the San Juan River can be done as a day trip or a more leisurely multiday trip. Longer trips continue through the famous Goosenecks, the "entrenched meanders" carved thousands of feet below the desert surface, and through more Class III rapids on the way to Clay Hills Crossing or Paiute Farms (not always accessible) on Lake Powell. Allow at least four days for the full trip, though more time will allow for exploration of side canyons and visits to Ancestral Puebloan sites. Rafts, kayaks, and canoes can be used. The season usually lasts March to October despite arid summer conditions because of adequate water flow from Navajo Reservoir upstream.

1: Edge of the Cedars State Park **2:** the Stone Lizard Lodge in Blanding **3:** Bluff Fort **4:** rafting the San Juan River

Several commercial river-running companies offer San Juan trips. If you go on your own, you should have river-running experience or be with someone who does. Private groups need to obtain **permits** ($10-30 pp) from the **Bureau of Land Management's San Juan Resource Area office** (435/587-1544, www.blm.gov); permits are issued through a preseason lottery (via www.recreation.gov), although boaters with flexible schedules can usually get permits close to their time of travel. Permit fees vary depending on how far you're floating.

Some people also like to run the river between Montezuma Creek and Sand Island, a leisurely trip of 20 river miles (32 km). The solitude often makes up for the lack of scenery. It's easy to get a river permit for this section because no use limits or fees apply.

If you're looking for a guided trip on the San Juan River, contact local **Wild Expeditions** (2625 S. U.S. 191, 435/672-2244, www.riversandruins.com), which offers both day and multiday trips out of Bluff; trips run daily in summer, and only a day's notice is usually needed to join a float. On eight-hour, 26-mile (42-km) day excursions to Mexican Hat ($199 adults, $133 under age 15), motors may be used if the water level is low. This highly recommended trip includes lunch plus stops at Ancestral Puebloan ruins and rock-art panels.

Food

A longtime local hangout and a good place for a meal and a friendly vibe is the **Twin Rocks Cafe** (435/672-2341, www.twinrockscafe.com, 8am-8pm Mon.-Sat., $8-20), next to the trading post just below the impossible-to-miss Twin Rocks. Here you can dine on Navajo tacos (fry bread with chili) or Navajo pizza (fry bread with pizza toppings) as well as more standard fare. Be sure to visit the trading post for high-quality Native American crafts, many of them produced locally by Navajo artisans.

Settle in under the big cottonwood tree for a flame-grilled steak dinner at the **Cottonwood Steakhouse** (Main St. and 4th St. E., 435/672-2282, www.cottonwoodsteakhouse.com, 5:30pm-9:30pm daily spring-fall, call for winter hours, $15-26). Dinners come with salad, beans, and potatoes; for $10 you can split an entrée with someone else and get full servings of side dishes. Indoor dining is also an option. Homemade pies are a specialty.

★ **Comb Ridge Eat and Drink** (680 S. U.S. 191, 435/485-5555, 3pm-8:30pm Tues.-Fri., 11:30am-8:30pm Sat.-Sun., $8-15), an artsy café housed in a historic trading post, has lots of character and surprisingly delicious food. Although the menu items are simple (burgers and pub grub), the quality is high. Where else in this part of Utah are you going to find a tabouli bowl? There are several good options for vegetarians here.

On the premises of the Desert Rose Inn find **Duke's** (701 W. Main St., 735/672-2303, www.desertroseinn.com, 5pm-9pm Mon.-Sat., Mar.-Oct., $13-32), with very good burgers and steaks, an attractive dining room, and a lovely patio (but no alcohol).

Accommodations

Attractive ★ **Desert Rose Inn** (701 W. Main St., 735/672-2303 or 888/475-7673, www.desertroseinn.com, $149-230) is one of the nicest lodgings in this corner of the state. The large lodge-like log structure has two-story wraparound porches and guest rooms furnished with pine furniture, quilts, and Southwestern art. An additional wing has an indoor pool and spa, and a handsome restaurant has been added. At the edge of the property are a number of handsome one-bedroom log cabins. This is definitely a class act.

Another classy place to stay is **La Posada Pintada** (239 N. 7th E./Navajo Twins Dr., 435/459-2274, www.laposadapintada.com, $155-175), a stylish, recently built boutique inn with 11 spacious rooms (one a pioneer cabin) and a serious breakfast buffet. This is a refined place: all rooms come with flat screen TVs, Wi-Fi, fridges and microwaves, private patios, large bathrooms, and high-end linens and amenities.

Another great place to stay is **Recapture Lodge** (220 E. Main St., 435/672-2281, www.recapturelodge.com, $98-119). For many years the heart and soul of Bluff, this rustic, comfortable lodge is operated by longtime outfitters and the staff can help you plan an outdoor adventure. Besides guest rooms and kitchenettes, Recapture Lodge has trails out the back door, a swimming pool, a hot tub, and a coin laundry. The Recapture also rents a couple of fully equipped homes in Bluff for families and groups.

Bluff's newest lodging is ★ **Bluff Dwellings Resort and Spa** (2625 S. Hwy. 191, 435/672-2477, www.bluffdwellings.com, $189-289), a large complex centered around a welcoming pool and patio area. The rooms are in a series of structures designed to echo the ancient stone dwellings tucked into local cliffs but with every modern amenity. All rooms have private decks or balconies; some offer kitchenettes. The onsite Hozho Spa offers a number of massage, body, and beauty treatments by appointment.

CAMPGROUNDS

Sand Island Recreation Area (435/587-1500, www.blm.gov, $15) is a Bureau of Land Management (BLM) camping area along the San Juan River, 3 miles (4.8 km) south of town, with piped water. Large cottonwood trees shade this pretty spot, but tenters need to watch for thorns in the grass. River-runners often put in at the campground, so it can be a busy place. Two RV parks are right in town: **Cadillac Ranch RV Park** (U.S. 191, 435/672-2262 or 800/538-6195, www.cadillacranchrv.com, year-round, $22-30) is in the center of town, and **Cottonwood R.V. Park** (U.S. 191, 435/672-2287, http://cottonwoodrvpark.blogspot.com, Mar.-Nov. 15, $35) is at the west end of Bluff.

★ HOVENWEEP NATIONAL MONUMENT

Delve into the region's cultural history and architecture at remote **Hovenweep National Monument** (970/562-4283, www.nps.gov/hove, free), where the Ancestral Puebloans built many impressive masonry buildings during the early-mid-1200s, near the end of their 1,300-year stay in the area. A drought that began in 1274 and lasted 25 years probably hastened their migration from this area. Several centuries of intensive farming, hunting, and woodcutting had already taken a toll on the land. Archaeologists believe the inhabitants retreated south in the late 1200s to sites in northwestern New Mexico and northeastern Arizona. The Ute word *hovenweep* means "deserted valley," an appropriate name for the lonely high-desert country they left behind. The Ancestral Puebloans at Hovenweep had much in common with the Mesa Verde culture, although the Dakota sandstone here doesn't form large alcoves suitable for cliff-dweller villages. Ruins at Hovenweep remain essentially unexcavated.

The Ancestral Puebloan farmers had a keen interest in the seasons because of their need to know the best time for planting crops. Astronomical stations (alignments of walls, doorways, and tiny openings) allowed the sun priests to determine the equinoxes and solstices with an accuracy of one or two days. This precision also may have been necessary for a complex ceremonial calendar. Astronomical stations at Hovenweep have been discovered at Hovenweep Castle, House of Square Tower Ruins, and Cajon Ruins.

Planning Your Time

Hovenweep National Monument protects six groups of villages left behind by the Ancestral Puebloans. The sites are near the Colorado border, southeast of Blanding. **Square Tower Ruins Unit,** where the visitors center is located, has the most ruins and the most varied architecture. In fact, you can find all the Hovenweep architectural styles here. There are other ruins that are good to visit if you'd like to spend more time in the area; you'll need a map and directions from a ranger to find them because they aren't signed. One group, the Goodman Point, near Cortez, Colorado, offers relatively little to see except unexcavated mounds.

Visitors Center

The **visitors center** (970/562-4282, 5am-5pm daily Apr.-Oct., 9am-4pm daily Nov.-Mar.) has a few exhibits on the Ancestral Puebloans, photos of local wildlife, and a small bookstore. A ranger can answer your questions, provide brochures and handouts about various aspects of the monument, and give directions for visiting the other groups of ruins.

Square Tower Ruins

This extensive group of Ancestral Puebloan towers and dwellings lines the rim and slopes of Little Ruin Canyon, located a short walk from the visitors center. Obtain a trail-guide booklet from the ranger station. You can take easy walks of less than 0.5 mile (0.8 km) on

the rim. Combine all the trails for a loop of about 2 miles (1.2 km) with only one up-and-down section in the canyon. The booklet has good descriptions of Ancestral Puebloan life and architecture and of the plants growing along the trail. You'll see towers (D-shaped, square, oval, and round), cliff dwellings, surface dwellings, storehouses, kivas, and rock art. Keep an eye out for the prairie rattlesnake, a subspecies of the western rattlesnake, which is active at night in summer and during the day in spring and fall. And stay on the trail: Don't climb the fragile walls of the ruins or walk on rubble mounds.

Holly Ruins

Holly Ruins group is noted for its Great House, Holly Tower, and Tilted Tower. Most of Tilted Tower fell away after the boulder on which it sat shifted. Great piles of rubble mark the sites of structures built on loose ground. Look for remnants of farming terraces in the canyon below the Great House. A hiking trail connects the campground at Square Tower Ruins with Holly Ruins; the route follows canyon bottoms and is about 8 miles (12.9 km) round-trip. Ask a ranger for a map and directions. Hikers can also continue to Horseshoe Ruins (1 mi/1.6 km farther) and Hackberry

The ruins at Hovenweep National Monument date from the 1200s.

Ruins (just beyond Horseshoe). All of these are just across the Colorado border and about 6 miles (9.7 km) one-way by road from the visitors center.

Horseshoe and Hackberry Ruins

Horseshoe Ruins and Hackberry Ruins are best reached by an easy trail (1 mi/1.6 km round-trip) off the road to Holly Ruins. Horseshoe House, built in a horseshoe shape similar to Sun Temple at Mesa Verde, has exceptionally good masonry work. Archaeologists haven't determined the purpose of the structure. An alcove in the canyon below contains a spring and a small shelter. A round tower nearby on the rim has a strategic view. Hackberry House has only one room still intact. Rubble piles and wall remnants abound in the area. The spring under an alcove here still has a good flow and supports lush growths of hackberry and cottonwood trees along with smaller plants.

Cutthroat Castle Ruins

Cutthroat Castle Ruins were remote even in Ancestral Puebloan times. The ruins lie along an intermittent stream rather than at the head of a canyon like most other Hovenweep sites. Cutthroat Castle is a large multistory structure with both straight and curved walls. Three round towers stand nearby. Look for wall fragments and the circular depressions of kivas. High-clearance vehicles can get close to the ruins, about 11.5 miles (18.5 km) one-way from the visitors center. Visitors with cars can drive to a trailhead and then walk to the ruins, 1.5 (2.4 km) miles round-trip on foot.

Cajon Ruins

Cajon Ruins are at the head of a little canyon on Cajon Mesa on the Navajo Reservation in Utah, about 9 miles (14.5 km) southwest of the visitors center. The site has a commanding view across the San Juan Valley as far as Monument Valley. Buildings include a large multiroom structure, a round tower, and a tall square tower. An alcove just below has a spring and some rooms. Look for pictographs, petroglyphs, and grooves in the rock used for tool grinding. Farming terraces were located on the canyon's south side.

Camping

A small **campground** (no reservations, $15, no credit cards) near the visitors center has 31 sites geared toward tent campers, although a few sites will accommodate RVs up to 36 feet (11 m) long. Running water is available only during summer, when five gallons are allotted to each camper. Like Hovenweep's ancient inhabitants, campers are often treated to excellent stargazing; the monument is far from light pollution, and the dark night skies are frequently clear.

Getting There

One approach is from U.S. 191 between Blanding and Bluff; head east 9 miles (14.5 km) on Highway 262, continue straight 6 miles (9.7 km) on a small paved road to Hatch Trading Post, and then follow the signs for 16 miles (74 km). A good way in from Bluff is to go east 21 miles (34 km) on paved Highway 162 to Montezuma Creek and Aneth, then follow the signs north for 20 miles (32 km). A scenic 58-mile (93-km) route through Montezuma Canyon begins 5 miles (8 km) south of Monticello and follows unpaved roads to Hatch and on to Hovenweep; you can stop at the BLM's Three Turkey Ruin on the way. From Colorado, take a partly paved road west and north 41 miles (66 km) from U.S. 491 (the turnoff is 4 miles (6.4 km) south of Cortez).

Don't expect your cell phone to work in this remote area.

Cedar Mesa and Vicinity

Head way off the beaten track to explore ancient ruins and stunning geography in the area west of U.S. 191 and east of Glen Canyon and Lake Powell. Experienced hikers can wander deep into this rugged area; those with less experience or fortitude may want to focus on the trails at Natural Bridges National Monument.

CEDAR MESA

Just south of Blanding, Highway 95—here labeled Trail of the Ancients National Scenic Byway—heads west across a high plateau toward the Colorado River, traversing Comb Ridge, Cedar Mesa, and many canyons. This is remote country, so fill up with gas before leaving Blanding; you can't depend on finding gasoline until Hanksville, 122 miles (196 km) away. Hite and the other Lake Powell marinas do have gas and supplies, but their hours are limited.

Cedar Mesa and its canyons have an exceptionally large number of prehistoric Ancestral Puebloan sites. Several ruins are just off the highway, and hikers will discover many more Cedar Mesa is also home to **Bears Ears Buttes,** two distinctive outcrops that are visible for miles across southeastern Utah. Native Americans in the area consider just about all of southeastern Utah to be a sacred place, and the Bears Ears have come to represent it. In 2016, 1.35 million acres in this part of the state were designated the Bears Ears National Monument by the Obama administration, to protect the cultural resources of local Native Americans. In 2018, the Trump administration shrank the monument by 85 percent, reopening much of this land to mineral and oil-and-gas extraction. In place of the original Bears Ears monument, the Trump administration designated two smaller monuments: the 71,896-acre Indian Creek National Monument and the 129,980-acre Shash Jaa National Monument.

If you would like to explore the Cedar Mesa and Bears Ears area, be sure to drop in at the BLM's **Kane Gulch Ranger Station** (435/587-1532, www.blm.gov, 8am-noon daily spring and fall), at the west end of Cedar Mesa, 4 miles (6.4 km) south of Highway 95 on Highway 261. BLM staff issue the permits required to explore the Cedar Mesa backcountry for day-use ($5) and for overnight stays ($15 pp) in Grand Gulch, Fish Creek Canyon, and Owl Creek Canyon. The number of people permitted to camp at a given time is limited, so call ahead. BLM staff will also tell you about archaeological sites and their historic value, current hiking conditions, and where to find water. Cedar Mesa is managed for more primitive recreation, so hikers in the area should have good route-finding skills and come prepared with food and water.

If you'd rather leave the logistics to the professionals, the friendly folks at **Wild Expeditions** (435/672-2244, www.riversandruins.com) offer multiday guided trips into the Cedar Mesa and Bears Ears area, and also offer rentals and support for personalized trips into this remote area.

Butler Wash Ruins

Well-preserved pueblo ruins left by the Ancestral Puebloans are tucked under an overhang across the wash. Find the trailhead 11 miles (17.7 km) west of U.S. 191, on the north side of Highway 95, between mileposts 111 and 112. Follow cairns for 0.5 mile (0.8 km) through juniper and piñon pine woodlands and across slickrock to the overlook, where you can see four kivas and several other structures. Parts have been reconstructed, but most of the site is about 900 years old.

Comb Ridge

Geologic forces have squeezed up the earth's crust in a long ridge running 80 miles (129 km) south from the Abajo Peaks into Arizona.

Sheer cliffs plunge 800 feet (244 m) into Comb Wash on the west side. Engineering the highway down these cliffs took considerable effort. A parking area near the top of the grade offers expansive panoramas across Comb Wash. Side roads along the east side of Comb Ridge access a number of Ancestral Puebloan rock-art sites and village ruins. Contact the **Kane Gulch Ranger Station** (435/587-1532, www. blm.gov/visit/kane-gulch-ranger-station) for information about these sites.

Arch Canyon

This tributary canyon of Comb Wash has spectacular scenery and many Native American ruins. Much of the canyon can be seen on a day hike, but 2-3 days are required to explore the upper reaches. (Many visitors shorten the trip by driving a 4WD rig up the canyon for a few miles.) The main streambeds usually have water, but you should purify it before drinking it. To reach the trailhead, turn north onto Comb Wash Road (between mileposts 107 and 108 on Hwy. 95) and go 2.5 miles (4 km) on the dirt road, past a house and a water tank. Park in a grove of cottonwood trees before a stream. The mouth of pretty Arch Canyon is just to the northwest (it's easy to miss). Look for a Native American ruin about 0.25 mile (0.4 km) up Arch Canyon on the right. More ruins are tucked under alcoves farther up-canyon; the canyon's three arches are past the 7-mile (11.3-km) point.

Arch Canyon Overlook

A road and a short trail to the rim of Arch Canyon provide a beautiful view into the depths. Turn north onto Texas Flat Road (County Rd. 263) from Highway 95, between mileposts 102 and 103. Continue 4 miles (6.4 km) and park just before the road begins a steep climb, and then walk east on an old jeep road to the rim. This is a fine place for a picnic, although there are no facilities or guardrails. Texas Flat Road is dirt but passable when dry for cars with good clearance. Trucks can continue up the steep hill to other viewpoints of Arch and Texas Canyons.

Mule Canyon Ruin

Archaeologists have excavated and stabilized this Ancestral Puebloan village on the gentle slope of Mule Canyon's South Fork. A stone kiva, circular tower, and 12-room structure are all visible, and all were originally connected by tunnels. Cave Towers, 2 miles (3.2 km) southeast, would have been visible from the top of the tower here. Signs describe the ruins and periods of Ancestral Puebloan development. Turn north from Highway 95 between mileposts 101 and 102 and continue 0.3 mile (0.5 km) on a paved road. The ruin is right here—no hiking required! Hikers can explore other ruins in the North and South Forks of Mule Canyon; check with the Kane Gulch Ranger Station for advice and directions. You might see pieces of pottery and other artifacts in this area. Federal laws prohibit the removal of artifacts. Leave every piece in place so that future visitors can enjoy the discovery. Be sure to have a BLM day-hiking permit when exploring this area.

Shash Jaa National Monument

This national monument, established in 2018, protects 129,980 acres of striking geologic features, juniper forests, canyons, and a cultural and historical legacy that includes an abundance of Ancestral Puebloan ruins and rock art. In addition to the Bears Ears Buttes area, Shash Jaa also protects a long tail of land extending south along Comb Ridge to the San Juan River, another area also rich in ancient remains. The monument includes two tiny satellite units that protect Doll House and Moon House ruins. For recreational information on Shash Jaa, contact **Kane Gulch Ranger Station** (435/587-1532, www.blm. gov/visit/kane-gulch-ranger-station).

GRAND GULCH PRIMITIVE AREA

Within this twisting canyon system are some of the most captivating scenery and largest concentrations of Ancestral Puebloan ruins in southeastern Utah. The main canyon

The Future of Bears Ears

The Bears Ears area is home to two national monuments.

Bears Ears National Monument was established in 2016 in the waning weeks of the Obama administration. It was divided into two much smaller national monuments by President Trump. President Biden has moved to re-instate the original boundaries.

The two new Utah national monuments are the 71,896-acre **Indian Creek National Monument** and the 129,980-acre **Shash Jaa National Monument**. The Indian Creek monument is essentially an eastern annex to the Needles District of Canyonlands National Park and includes noted rock-climbing cliffs and Newspaper Rock, famous for its petroglyphs. Shash Jaa monument protects the area that includes Bears Ears Buttes, parts of Mule and Arch Canyons, and the drainages of Comb Ridge, a sacred landscape for many Indigenous people and an area rich in Ancestral Puebloan ruins and rock art. Notably, this redrawn monument eliminates the earlier designation's protection for Cedar Mesa, another region with a wealth of Ancestral Puebloan remains—and uranium deposits.

The acreage comprising these two new national monuments is a mix of Forest Service, Bureau of Land Management (BLM), state, and private land, and a management plan to administer to these units has been developed but has not been approved. Meanwhile, a number of lawsuits from Native American and environmentalist groups that dispute the legality of the original monument's reduction are making their way through federal court. All publicly accessible sites are expected to remain open in the interim. Specific questions should be directed to the **Kane Gulch Ranger Station** (Hwy. 261, four miles south of Hwy. 95, 435/587-1532, www.blm.gov/visit/kane-gulch-ranger-station), the **BLM field office** in Monticello (365 N. Main St., 435/587-1510, www.blm.gov/programs/recreation/permits-and-passes/lotteries-and-permit-systems), or the **Blanding Visitor Center** (12 N. Grayson Pkwy., 435/678-3662, www.blanding-ut.gov/visitor-s-center.html).

begins only about 6 miles (9.7 km) southeast of Natural Bridges National Monument. From an elevation of 6,400 feet (1,950 m), Grand Gulch cuts deeply into Cedar Mesa on a tortuous path southwest to the San Juan River, dropping 2,700 feet (823 m) in about 53 miles (85 km). Sheer cliffs, alcoves, pinnacles, Ancestral Puebloan cliff dwellings, rock-art sites, arches, and a few natural bridges line Grand Gulch and its many tributaries.

From the Kane Gulch Ranger Station, a trail leads 4 miles (6.4 km) down Kane Gulch to the upper end of Grand Gulch, where a camping area is shaded by cottonwood trees. **Junction Ruin,** a cave dwelling, is visible from here, and less than 1 mile (1.6 km) farther into Grand Gulch are more ruins and an arch.

Kane Gulch and Bullet Canyon provide access to the upper end of Grand Gulch from the east side. A popular loop hike using these canyons is 23 miles (37 km) long (3-4 days); arrange a 7.5-mile (12-km) car shuttle or hitch. Ask at the ranger station if a shuttle service is available. Collins Canyon, reached from the Collins Spring trailhead, leads into lower Grand Gulch from the west side. The hike between the Kane Gulch and Collins Spring trailheads is 38 miles (61 km) one-way (5-7 days). A car shuttle of about 29 miles (47 km), including 8 miles (12.9 km) of dirt road, is required. Be sure to visit the BLM's **Kane Gulch Ranger Station** (435/587-1532, www.blm. gov, 8am-noon daily spring and fall) or the BLM Monticello office for a permit and information. You must have a day-use ($5) or overnight camping permit ($15) to enter the area.

MEXICAN HAT

South of the Kane Gulch Ranger Station, Highway 261 loses its pavement at the Moki Dugway, a series of steeply banked switchbacks incised into the sheer face of Cedar Mesa. Even if you're not given to vertigo, this road will get your attention. Slow down and take this stretch of road (with 1,100 feet/335 meters of elevation change and 5-10 percent grades) at 5-10 mph. About 10 miles (16 km) south of the Dugway is the town of Mexican Hat, a modest trade and tourism center.

Spectacular geology surrounds this tiny community perched on the north bank of the San Juan River. Dramatic folded layers of red and gray rock stand out. Alhambra Rock, a jagged remnant of a volcano, marks the southern approach to Mexican Hat. Another rock, which looks just like an upside-down sombrero, gave Mexican Hat its name; you'll see this formation from U.S. 163, 2 miles (3.2 km) north of town. Monument Valley, Valley of the Gods Scenic Drive, Goosenecks State Park, and Grand Gulch Primitive Area are only short drives away. The riverbanks near town can be a busy place in summer as river-runners on the San Juan put in, take out, or just stop for ice and beer.

Goosenecks State Park

The San Juan River winds through a series of incredibly tight bends 1,000 feet (305 m) below this park. So closely spaced are the bends that the river takes 6 miles (9.7 km) to cover an air distance of only 1.5 miles (2.4 km). The bends and exposed rock layers form exquisitely graceful curves. Geologists know the site as a classic example of entrenched meanders, caused by gradual uplift of a formerly level plain. Signs at the overlook explain the geologic history and identify the rock formations. **Goosenecks State Park** (435/678-2238, http://stateparks.utah.gov, $5 per vehicle) is an undeveloped area with a few picnic tables and vault toilets. A **campground** ($10) is available but has no water. From the junction of U.S. 163 and Highway 261, 4 miles (6.4 km) north of Mexican Hat, go 1 mile (1.6 km) northwest on Highway 261, then turn left and go 3 miles (4.8 km) on Highway 316 to its end.

Muley Point Overlook

One of the great views in the Southwest is just a short drive from Goosenecks State Park and more than 1,000 feet (305 m) higher in elevation. Although the view of the Goosenecks below is less dramatic than at the state park, the 6,200-foot elevation provides a magnificent panorama across the Navajo Reservation to Monument Valley and countless canyons and mountains. To get here, travel northwest 9 miles (14.5 km) on Highway 261 from the Goosenecks turnoff. At the top of the Moki Dugway switchbacks, turn left (southwest) and go 5.3 miles (8.5 km) on gravel County Road 241 (the turnoff may not be signed), and follow it toward the point. This road is not suitable for wet-weather travel.

Food and Accommodations

The **San Juan Inn and Trading Post** (U.S. 163 and San Juan River Rd., 435/683-2220 or 800/447-2022, www.sanjuaninn.net, $98-140), just west of town at a dramatic location above the river, offers clean guest rooms without extras, a few yurts, Native American trade goods, and a restaurant, the **Olde Bridge Grill** (435/683-2322, 7am-10pm daily, $8-15), serving American, Mexican, and Navajo food. **Hat Rock Inn** (120 U.S. 163, 435/683-2221, www.hatrockinn.com, $145-169) offers the nicest guest rooms in town and a swimming pool. **Mexican Hat Lodge** (100 N. Main St., 435/683-2222, www.mexicanhat.net, $84-160) offers guest rooms, a pool, and a fun but somewhat expensive restaurant (lunch and dinner daily) with grilled steaks and burgers.

Valle's Trading Post and RV Park (435/683-2226, year-round, $35) has tent and RV sites with hookups. The camping area is pretty basic, but great scenery surrounds it. The trading post offers crafts, groceries, showers, vehicle storage, and car shuttles. **Goosenecks State Park** has camping ($10) with great views but no amenities.

Valley of the Gods

Great sandstone monoliths, delicate spires, and long rock fins rise from the broad valley. This strange red-rock landscape resembles better-known Monument Valley but on a smaller scale. A 17-mile (27-km) dirt road winds through the spectacular scenery. Cars can usually travel the road at low speeds if the weather is dry (the road crosses washes). Allow 1-1.5 hours for the drive; it's studded with viewpoints, and you'll want to stop at all of them. The east end of the road connects with U.S. 163 at milepost 29 (7.5 mi/12 km northeast of Mexican Hat, 15 mi/24 km southwest of Bluff); the west end connects with Highway 261 just below the Moki Dugway switchbacks (4 mi/6.4 km north of Mexican Hat on U.S. 163, then 6.6 mi/10.6 km northwest on Hwy. 261).

If you're looking to really get away from it all, book a room at the **Valley of the Gods B&B** (970/749-1164, www.valleyofthegodsbandb.com, $175-195), a pretty Southwestern-style solar- and wind-powered ranch house with no TVs.

MONUMENT VALLEY

Towering buttes, jagged pinnacles, and rippled sand dunes make this area along the Utah-Arizona border an otherworldly landscape. Changing colors and shifting shadows during the day add to the enchantment. Most of the natural monuments are remnants of sandstone eroded by wind and water. Agathla Peak and some lesser summits are the roots of ancient volcanoes, whose dark rock contrasts with the pale yellow sandstone of the other formations. The valley is at an elevation of 5,564 feet (1,695 m) in the Upper Sonoran Life Zone; annual rainfall averages about 8.5 inches.

In 1863-1864, when Kit Carson was ravaging Canyon de Chelly in Arizona to round up the Navajo, Chief Hoskinini led his people to the safety and freedom of Monument Valley.

Hollywood movies made the splendor of Monument Valley widely known to the outside world. *Stagecoach*, filmed here in 1938 and directed by John Ford, became the first in a series of Westerns that has continued to the present.

The Navajo have preserved the valley as a park with a scenic drive, visitors center, and campground. From Mexican Hat, drive 22 miles (35 km) southwest on U.S. 163, then turn left and go 3.5 miles (5.6 km) to the visitors center. At the turnoff on U.S. 163 is a village's worth of outdoor market stalls and a modern complex of enclosed shops where you can stop to buy Navajo art and crafts.

Visitors Center

At the entrance to the **Monument Valley Navajo Tribal Park** is a **visitors center** (435/727-5874, www.navajonationparks.org,

1: Ancestral Puebloan village along Comb Wash **2:** Mexican Hat's namesake rock formation **3:** the San Juan River winding through Goosenecks State Park **4:** Monument Valley

6am-8pm daily Apr.-Sept., 8am-5pm daily Oct.-Mar., $20 per vehicle with up to 4 people; $6 pp for additional people in the same vehicle) with exhibits and crafts. This is a good place to get a list of Navajo tour guides to lead you on driving or hiking trips into the monument. Lots of folks along the road will also offer these services.

Tours

Take one of several guided tours leaving daily year-round from the visitors center to visit sites such as a hogan, a cliff dwelling, and petroglyphs in areas beyond the self-guided drive. The trips last 1.5-4 hours and cost $55-100 per person. Guided horseback rides from near the visitors center cost around $90 for two hours; longer day and overnight trips can be arranged too. If you'd like to hike in Monument Valley, you must hire a guide. Hiking tours of two hours to a full day or more can be arranged at the visitors center.

Monument Valley Drive

A 17-mile (27-km) **self-guided scenic drive** (6am-8pm daily Apr.-Sept., 8am-4:30pm daily Oct.-Mar.) begins at the visitors center and loops through the heart of the valley. Overlooks provide sweeping views from different vantage points. The dirt road is normally OK for cautiously driven cars. Avoid stopping or you may get stuck in the loose sand that sometimes blows across the road. Allow 90 minutes for the drive. No hiking or driving is allowed off the signed route. Water and restrooms are available only at the visitors center.

Accommodations

Don't be surprised to find that lodgings at Monument Valley are expensive; they're also extremely popular, so be sure to book well ahead.

The Navajo-owned ★ **View Hotel** (435/727-5555, www.monumentvalleyview.com, $119-339) provides the only lodging in Monument Valley Tribal Park. Views are terrific from this stylish newer hotel; reserve a room well in advance. Secluded cabins ($209-279) and camping ($23 tents, $45 RVs) are also available.

★ **Goulding's Lodge and Trading Post** (435/727-3231, www.gouldings.com, $239-317) is another great place to stay in the Monument Valley area. Harry Goulding and his wife, Mike, opened this dramatically located trading post in 1924. It's a large complex tucked under the rimrocks 2 miles (3.2 km) west of the U.S. 163 Monument Valley turnoff, just north of the Arizona-Utah border. Modern motel rooms offer incredible views of Monument Valley. Guests can use a small indoor pool; meals are available in the dining room. A gift shop sells a wide range of souvenirs, books, and Native American crafts. The nearby store has groceries and gas pumps, a restaurant is open daily for all meals, and tours and horseback rides are available. The lodge stays open year-round, and rates drop in winter and early spring. Goulding's Museum, in the old trading post building, displays prehistoric and modern artifacts, movie photos, and memorabilia of the Goulding family. The Gouldings' **campground** ($34-48 without hookups, $55-60 with hookups) is pleasant and well managed.

There are a handful of less costly hotels about 30 minutes south in Kayenta, Arizona. The adobe-style **Hampton Inn** (U.S. 160, 520/697-3170 or 800/426-7866, $199) is the nicest place in town, and it's only a little more expensive than its Kayenta neighbors.

TOP EXPERIENCE

★ NATURAL BRIDGES NATIONAL MONUMENT

Streams in White Canyon and its tributaries cut deep canyons, then formed three impressive bridges, now protected as **Natural Bridges National Monument** (435/692-1234, www.nps.gov/nabr, $20 per vehicle, $15 motorcyclists, $10 cyclists and pedestrians, $55 annual Southeast Utah Parks Pass also includes entrance to Arches and Canyonlands National Parks). When the sun sets, Natural Bridges becomes one of the darkest places in the United States. In fact, the International Dark Sky Association has named this the world's first **dark-sky park**. Come here for some serious **stargazing!**

Silt-laden floodwaters sculpted the bridges by gouging tunnels between closely spaced loops in the meandering canyons. You can distinguish a natural bridge from an arch because the bridge spans a streambed and was initially carved out of the rock by flowing water. In the monument, these bridges illustrate three different stages of development, from the massive, newly formed Kachina Bridge to the middle-aged Sipapu Bridge to the delicate and fragile span of Owachomo. All three natural bridges will continue to widen and eventually collapse under their own weight. A 9-mile (14.5-km) scenic drive has overlooks of the picturesque bridges, Ancestral Puebloan ruins, and twisting canyons. You can follow short trails down from the rim to the base of each bridge or hike through all three bridges on an 8.6-mile (13.8-km) loop.

Ruins, artifacts, and rock art indicate a long occupation by Native Americans, ranging from archaic groups to the Ancestral Puebloans. Many fine cliff dwellings built by the Ancestral Puebloans still stand. In 1883, prospector Cass Hite passed on tales of the huge stone bridges that he had discovered on a trip up White Canyon. Adventurous travelers, including those on a 1904 National Geographic expedition, visited this isolated region to marvel at the bridges. The public's desire for protection of the bridges led President Theodore Roosevelt to proclaim the area a national monument in 1908. Federal administrators then changed the original bridge names from Edwin, Augusta, and Caroline to the Hopi names used today. Although the Hopi never lived here, the Ancestral Puebloans of White Canyon very likely have descendants in the modern Hopi villages in Arizona.

Visitors Center

From the signed junction on Highway 95, it is 4.5 miles (7.2 km) on Highway 275 to the **visitors center** (435/692-1234, 9am-5pm daily April-mid-Oct., 9am-5pm mid-Oct.-Mar. Thurs-Mon.), at an elevation of 6,505 feet (1,983 m). Exhibits and a short film introduce the people who once lived here, as well as the area's geology, wildlife, and plants. Outside, labels identify native plants of the monument.

The Bridge View Drive is always open, except after heavy snowstorms. A winter visit can be very enjoyable; ice or mud often close the steep Sipapu and Kachina Trails, but the short trail to Owachomo Bridge usually stays open. Pets aren't allowed on the trails or in the backcountry at any time.

Other than the small but popular campground at the national monument, the nearest accommodations are 40 miles (64 km) east near Blanding or a slow 40 miles (64 km) south in Mexican Hat.

Bridge View Drive

This 9-mile (14.5-km) drive begins its one-way loop just past the campground. Allow about 1.5 hours for a quick trip around. To make all the stops and do a bit of leisurely hiking takes about half a day. The cross-bedded sandstone of the bridges and canyons is part of the 265-million-year-old Cedar Mesa Formation.

Sipapu Bridge viewpoint is 2 miles (3.2 km) from the visitors center. The Hopi name refers to the gateway from which their ancestors entered this world from another world below. Sipapu Bridge has reached its mature or middle-age stage of development. The bridge, with a span of 268 feet (82 m) and a height of 220 feet (67 m), is the largest in the monument and, after Rainbow Bridge in Glen Canyon, the second largest in the world. Another view and a trail to the base of Sipapu are 0.8 mile (1.3 km) farther. The viewpoint is about halfway down on an easy trail; allow half an hour. A steeper and rougher trail branches off the viewpoint trail and winds down to the bottom of White Canyon, which is probably the best place to fully appreciate the bridge's size. The total round-trip distance is 1.2 miles (1.9 km), with an elevation change of 600 feet (183 m).

Horse Collar Ruin, built by the Ancestral Puebloans, looks as though it has been abandoned for just a few decades, not 800 years. A short trail leads to an overlook 3.1 miles (5 km) from the visitors center (bring binoculars for a good look). The name comes from the shape of the doorway openings in two storage rooms. Other groups of Ancestral Puebloan dwellings can also be seen in or near the monument; ask a ranger for directions.

The **Kachina Bridge** viewpoint and trailhead are 5.1 miles (8.2 km) from the visitors center. The massive bridge has a span of 204 feet (62 m) and a height of 210 feet (64 m). A trail, 1.5 miles (2.4 km) round-trip, leads to the canyon bottom next to the bridge; the elevation change is 650 feet (198 m). Look for pictographs near the base of the trail. Some of the figures resemble Hopi kachinas (spirits) and inspired the bridge's name. Armstrong Canyon joins White Canyon just downstream from the bridge. Floods in each canyon abraded opposite sides of the rock fin that later became Kachina Bridge.

The **Owachomo Bridge** viewpoint and trailhead are 7.1 miles (11.4 km) from the visitors center. An easy walk leads to Owachomo's base—0.5 mile (0.8 km) round-trip with an elevation change of 180 feet (55 m). Graceful Owachomo spans 180 feet (55 m) and is 106 feet (32 m) high. Erosive forces have worn the venerable bridge to a thickness of only nine feet (2.7 m). Unlike the other two bridges, Owachomo spans a smaller tributary stream instead of a major canyon. Two streams played a role in the bridge's formation. Floods coming down the larger Armstrong Canyon surged against a sandstone fin on one side while floods in a small side canyon wore away the rock on the other side. Eventually a hole formed, and waters flowing down the side canyon took the shorter route through the bridge. The word *owachomo* means "flat-rock

mound" in the Hopi language; a large rock outcrop nearby inspired the name. Toward the end of the one-way loop drive, stop at the **Bears Ears Overlook** to see the twin mesas in the distance.

Natural Bridges Loop Trail

Distance: 8.6 miles (13.8 km) round-trip
Duration: 5-6 hours
Elevation change: 500 feet (152 m)
Effort: moderate-strenuous
Trailhead: Sipapu Bridge

A canyon hike through all three bridges can be the highlight of a visit to the monument. Unmaintained trails make a loop in White and Armstrong Canyons and cross a wooded plateau. The trip is easier if you start from Sipapu and come out on the relatively gentle grades at Owachomo. A path cuts through the center of the driving loop to shorten the return trip to the car; however, you can save 2.5 miles (4 km) by arranging a car shuttle between the Sipapu and Owachomo trailheads. Another option is to go in or out on the Kachina Bridge Trail midway to cut the hiking distance to 5.4 miles (8.7 km). As you near Owachomo Bridge from below, a small sign points out the trail, which bypasses a deep pool. The canyons remain in their wild state; you'll need some hiking experience, water, proper footwear, a compass, and a map (the handout available at the visitors center is adequate).

When hiking in the canyons, keep an eye out for natural arches and Native American writing. Try not to step on midget faded rattlesnakes or other living entities (including the fragile cryptobiotic soil). And beware of flash floods, especially if you see big clouds billowing in the sky in an upstream direction. You don't need a hiking permit, although it's a good idea to talk beforehand with a ranger to find out current conditions. Overnight camping within the monument is permitted only in the campground.

1: Kachina Bridge **2:** Horse Collar Ruin
3: Owachomo Bridge

Campgrounds

The **Natural Bridges Campground** (first come, first served, year-round, $15) is in a forest of piñon pine and juniper. Obtain water from a faucet in front of the visitors center. Rangers give talks several evenings each week during the summer season. The campground is often full, but there is a rather grim designated overflow area near the intersection of Highways 95 and 261. RVs and trailers longer than 26 feet (8 m) must use this parking area. To reach the campground, drive 0.3 mile (0.5 km) past the visitors center and turn right.

Lake Powell and Glen Canyon

Lake Powell is at the center of the **Glen Canyon National Recreation Area** (520/608-6404, www.nps.gov/glca, always open, $30 per vehicle, $25 motorcycles, $15 cyclists and pedestrians, no charge for passing through Page, Arizona, on U.S. 89), a vast preserve covering 1.25 million acres in Arizona and Utah. When the Glen Canyon Dam was completed in 1964, conservationists deplored the loss of the remote and beautiful Glen Canyon of the Colorado River beneath the lake's waters. In terms of beauty and sheer drama, Glen Canyon was considered the equal of the Grand Canyon. Today, we have only words, pictures, and memories to remind us of its wonders. On the other hand, the 186-mile-long lake now provides easy access to an area most had not even known existed. Lake Powell is the second-largest artificial lake in the United States. Only Lake Mead, farther downstream, has a greater water-storage capacity. Lake Powell, however, has three times more shoreline—1,960 miles/3,154 kilometers—and when full, it holds enough water to cover the state of Pennsylvania one foot deep. Just a handful of roads approach the lake, so access is basically limited to boats—bays and coves offer nearly limitless opportunities for exploration by boaters—as well as long-distance hiking trails.

NATURAL BRIDGES TO BULLFROG MARINA BY FERRY

Eight miles (12.9 km) west of the entrance to Natural Bridges National Monument, travelers must make a decision: whether to continue on Highway 95 to cross the Colorado by bridge at Hite or to follow Highway 276 to the Halls Crossing Marina and cross the river, at this point tamed by the Glen Canyon Dam and known as Lake Powell, by car ferry.

Obviously, the ferry is the more exotic choice, and both Halls Crossing and Bullfrog Marinas offer lodging and food, a relative scarcity in this remote area. Crossing the Colorado on the ferry also makes it easy to access Bullfrog-Notom Road, which climbs for 60 miles (97 km) through dramatic landscapes on its way to Capitol Reef National Park's otherwise remote Waterpocket Fold. The road ends at Notom, just 4 miles (6.4 km) from the eastern entrance to Capitol Reef National Park on Highway 24. Drivers can also turn west on the Burr Trail and follow back roads to Boulder, near the Escalante River Canyon.

Halls Crossing and Bullfrog Ferry

At the junction of Highways 95 and 276, a large sign lists the departure times for the ferry; note that these may be different from the times listed in the widely circulated flyer or on the website. Confirm the departure times (435/893-4747, www.udot.utah.gov) before making the 42-mile (68-km) journey to Halls Crossing.

The crossing time for the 3-mile (4.8 km) trip from Halls Crossing to Bullfrog is 27 minutes. Fares are $25 for cars, which includes the driver and all passengers, $10 for bicycles and foot passengers, and $15 for motorcycles. Vehicles longer than 20 feet (6 m) pay $1.50 per foot.

Ferry service runs late April-early October, and there's a trip every other hour daily beginning with the 8am boat from Halls Landing, which then leaves Bullfrog at 9am. In summer high season, the final ferry from Halls Crossing departs at 6pm, and the final ferry from Bullfrog departs at 7pm. The ferry does not run early October-late April.

If drought or downstream demand lowers the level of Lake Powell beyond a certain point, there may not be enough water for the ferry to operate. If this is the case, there will be notices about the ferry's status at just about every park visitors center in Southern Utah.

For reservations and information regarding lodging, camping, tours, boating, and recreation at both Halls Crossing and Bullfrog Marina, contact **Lake Powell Resorts & Marinas** (888/896-3829, www.lakepowell.com).

Arriving at Halls Crossing by road, you'll first reach a small store offering three-bedroom units in trailer houses and an RV park. Continue for 0.5 mile (0.8 km) on the main road to the boat ramp and **Halls Crossing Marina** (435/684-7008). The marina has a larger store (groceries and fishing and boating supplies), a boat-rental office (fishing, waterskiing, and houseboats), a gas dock, slips, and storage. The **ranger station** is nearby, although rangers are usually out on patrol; look for their vehicle in the area if the office is closed.

On the western side of the lake, **Bullfrog Marina** is more like a small town (albeit one run by Aramark), with a **visitors center** (435/684-7423, hours vary May-early Oct.), a clinic, stores, a service station, and a handsome hotel and restaurant. The marina rents boats ranging from kayaks ($50 per day) and paddleboards ($90 per day) to eight-person powerboats ($500 per day) to houseboats ($2,079-10,649 per week), but for guided boat tours of Lake Powell, you'll have to go to the Wahweap Marina near Page, Arizona.

Defiance House Lodge (888/896-3829, www.lakepowell.com, $150-176) offers comfortable lake-view accommodations and the **Anasazi Restaurant** (8am-10am, 11am-1pm, 5pm-9pm daily Apr.-Oct., $12-28). The front desk at the lodge also handles family lodging units (well-equipped trailers, about $270 per night) and an RV park ($46). Showers, a laundry room, a convenience store, and a post office are at **Trailer Village.** Ask the visitors center staff or rangers for directions to primitive camping areas with vehicle access elsewhere along Bullfrog Bay.

Bullfrog Marina can be reached from the north via paved Highway 276. It is 40 miles (64 km) between Bullfrog and the junction with Highway 95. Ticaboo, 20 miles (32 km) north of Bullfrog, has another good lodging option. The **Ticaboo Lodge** (435/788-2110 or 800/842-2267, http://ticaboo.com, $129-151) is a hotel with a swimming pool, a restaurant, and a service-station complex that pretty much constitutes all of Ticaboo.

NATURAL BRIDGES TO LAKE POWELL VIA HIGHWAY 95

If the Lake Powell ferry schedule doesn't match your travel plans, Highway 95 will quickly get you across the Colorado River to the junction with Highway 24 at Hanksville.

Hite

In 1883 Cass Hite came to Glen Canyon in search of gold. He found some at a place later named Hite City, which set off a small gold rush. Cass and a few of his relatives operated a small store and post office, which were the only services for many miles. Travelers who wanted to cross the Colorado River here had the difficult task of swimming their animals across. Arthur Chaffin, a later resident, put through the first road and opened a ferry service in 1946. The Chaffin Ferry served uranium prospectors and adventurous motorists until the lake backed up to the spot in 1964. A steel bridge now spans the Colorado River upstream from Hite Marina. Cass Hite's store and the ferry site are underwater about 5 miles (8 km) down the lake from Hite Marina.

Beyond Hite, on the tiny neck of land between the Colorado River bridge and the Dirty Devil bridge, an unmarked dirt road turns north. Called Hite Road, or Orange Cliffs Road, this long and rugged road eventually links up with backcountry routes—including the Flint Trail—in the Maze District of Canyonlands National Park.

The uppermost marina on Lake Powell, Hite is 141 lake miles (227 km) from Glen Canyon Dam. It is hit hard when water levels drop in Lake Powell, which has been most of the time in recent years. When water is available, boats can continue up the lake to the mouth of Dark Canyon in Cataract Canyon at low water or into Canyonlands National Park at high water. During times of low water, the boat ramp is often high above the lake and the place is pretty desolate. Facilities include a small **store** with gas and a primitive **campground** (free) with no drinking water. Primitive camping is also available nearby, off Highway 95 at Dirty Devil, Farley Canyon, White Canyon, Blue Notch, and other locations. A **ranger station** (435/684-2457) is occasionally open; look for the ranger's vehicle at other times.

PAGE, ARIZONA

Although the town of Page is hot, busy, and not particularly appealing, it is the largest community anywhere near Lake Powell, and it offers travelers a number of places to stay and eat and access to boat tours. The town overlooks Lake Powell and Glen Canyon Dam.

The largest resort in the Glen Canyon National Recreation Area, **Wahweap Resort and Marina** (100 Lakeshore Dr., 928/645-2433, www.lakepowell.com), is just 6 miles (9.7 km) northwest of Page off U.S. 89. Wahweap is a major center for all manner of water sports, including houseboats (from $3,939 for five days in high summer season; they sleep up to 10), kayaks (from $50 per day), and paddleboards ($90 per day). Wahweap also offers an extensive range of boat tours and boat-assisted hiking, among other recreational activities. Wahweap's Lake Powell Resort, a hotel and restaurant complex, offers some of the most comfortable rooms in the area.

Tours

From Wahweap, board a tour boat to really see the special areas of Glen Canyon still visible from Lake Powell. A 1.5-hour tour (10:30am, 2:30pm, and 4:15pm daily Apr.-Oct., $48 adults, $33 children) into the mouth of 10-mile-long **Antelope Canyon** leaves from the Wahweap Marina (928/645-2433). During summer, a 6:15pm tour is added; in the winter, a 10:30am tour runs if there is sufficient demand. Another popular boat tour from Wahweap motors to **Rainbow Bridge National Monument** (Wahweap Marina, 928/645-2433, 7:30am daily April-Oct., with an additional tour at 12:30pm June-Sept. 15, $126 adults, $79 children). This tour, which takes around six hours and includes a 1.25-mile (2 km) round trip hike, cruises 50 miles (81 km) of shoreline to reach Rainbow Bridge, one of the largest known natural bridges in the world, at 290 feet (88 m) high and spanning 275 feet (84 m). If the price seems too stiff, or the boat ride too tame, a couple of rugged 17-mile-long trails leave from Page and travel across Navajo lands to the bridge. See the monument's website (www.nps.gov/rabr) for details on these trails.

Quite a different Antelope Canyon is the focus of a land-based tour to a famed slot canyon east of Page, beloved by multitudes of photographers seeking to capture the canyon's supple curves and pink-gold hues. Travel to Upper Antelope Canyon by truck with **Antelope Canyon Tours** (22 S. Lake Powell Blvd., 928/645-9102, www.antelopecanyon. com, $54-67). Tours last about 1.5 hours and run several times a day year-round.

Food

If you've been traveling through remote rural Utah for a while, dipping into Page, Arizona, can seem like a gastronomic mecca. The

Ranch House Grill (819 N. Navajo Dr., 928/645-1420, 6am-3pm daily, $7-15) serves breakfast all day plus sandwiches, burgers, steaks, and chops during the day. After a few days of abstemious travel in Southern Utah, Blue Wine Bar (644 N. Navajo Dr., 928/608-0707, 6pm-11pm Tues.-Sat., $5-12) is a real treat. The tapas and small plates are excellent, as is the wine selection. In the same Dam Plaza complex, the stylish Blue Buddha (644 N. Navajo Dr., 928/608-0707, 5pm-9pm Tues.-Sat., $10-20) serves cocktails and Japanese food, including sushi. For steaks and Italian food, Bonkers Restaurant (810 N. Navajo Dr., 928/645-2706, 4pm-9pm Tues.-Sat., $19-44) is a small but classy operation with good salads, pasta and old-time favorites like chicken Marsala. Fiesta Mexicana (125 S. Lake Powell Blvd., 928/645-4082, 11am-9pm Sun.-Thurs., 11am-10:30pm Fri.-Sat., $9-15) is a busy but friendly little Mexican place (and here in Arizona, it's easy to get a margarita).

Accommodations

Nearly all Page motels are on or near Lake Powell Boulevard (U.S. 89L), a 3.25-mile (5.2-km) loop that branches off the main highway. Page is a busy place in summer, however, and a call ahead is a good idea if you don't want to chase around town looking for vacancies. Expect to pay top dollar for views of the lake. The summer rates listed here drop in winter (Nov.-Mar.).

In a way, the most appealing lodgings are in the small apartments-turned-motels on and around 8th Avenue, a quiet residential area two blocks off Lake Powell Boulevard. These apartments date back to 1958-1959, when they housed supervisors for the dam construction project. One such place is the Lake Powell Motel (750 S. Navajo Dr., 480/452-9895, https://lakepowellmotel.net, $99-159), a nicely remodeled property with standard motel rooms and stylish one- and two-bedroom apartments with kitchenettes. Another vintage motel that's been freshly updated, the Red Rock Motel (114 8th Ave., 928/645-0062, https://redrockmotel.com, $69-139) offers everything from small basic rooms to two-bedroom apartments with kitchens and living rooms. All rooms have private patios, some with BBQs.

If you prefer the standard comforts of chain motels, a quick search of hotel booking websites will reveal that Page has all the usual suspects, plus some upscale resorts if you're looking for luxury. Courtyard Page (600 Clubhouse Dr., 928/645-5000, www.marriott.com, $209-239) is a good option in a great setting, with views, a restaurant, pool, spa, an exercise room, and an adjacent 18-hole golf course.

If you want to play in the water, there's no better spot to spend the night than the Lake Powell Resort at Wahweap Marina (6 mi/9.7 km north of Page off U.S. 89 at 100 Lakeshore Dr., 928/645-2433, www.lakepowell.com, $229-309), with access to lake recreation, tours and a lively drinking and dining scene right out your front door.

West of Canyonlands

It's a lonely road that leads north from the Glen Canyon National Recreation Area and Lake Powell to I-70, just west of the town of Green River. The crossroads town of Hanksville is a good place to gas up (don't expect any bargains on fuel) and grab a burger, and Goblin Valley State Park and Little Wild Horse Canyon are worthwhile detours. Highway 24 north of Hanksville also provides access to Canyonlands National Park's Maze District and the incredible rock art in the park's Horseshoe Canyon Unit.

HANKSVILLE

Even by Utah standards, tiny Hanksville (pop. just over 200) is pretty remote. Ebenezer Hanks and other Mormon settlers founded this out-of-the-way community in 1882 along the Fremont River, then known as the Dirty Devil River. The isolation attracted polygamists like Hanks and other fugitives from the law. Butch Cassidy and his gang found refuge in the rugged canyon country of "Robbers' Roost," east of town. Several houses and the old stone church on Center Street, one block south of the highway, survive from the 19th century.

Travelers exploring this scenic region find Hanksville a handy if lackluster stopover; Capitol Reef National Park is to the west, Lake Powell and the Henry Mountains are to the south, the remote Maze District of Canyonlands National Park is to the east, and Goblin Valley State Park is to the north. Because Hanksville is a true crossroads, the few lodgings here are often booked up well in advance, so plan ahead.

Wolverton Mill

E. T. Wolverton built this ingenious mill during the 1920s at his gold-mining claims in the Henry Mountains. A 20-foot waterwheel, still perfectly balanced, powered ore-crushing machinery and a sawmill. Owners of claims at the mill's original site didn't like a steady stream of tourists coming through to see the mill, so it was moved to the BLM office at Hanksville. Drive south 0.5 mile (0.8 km) on 100 West to see the mill and some of its original interior mechanism.

Food

Hanksville's restaurants cluster at the south end of town; don't expect anything fancy. **Stan's Burger Shack** (150 S. Hwy. 95, 435/542-3330, 10am-10pm Mon.-Sat., noon-10pm Sun., $5-9), at the Chevron station, is full of locals and a step up from the chains. The classiest spot for dinner is **Duke's Slickrock Grill** (275 Hwy. 24, 435/542-3235, 7am-10pm daily, $9-28), with steaks, barbecue, and burgers.

Accommodations

Hanksville is a busy crossroads with just two lodging options, so rooms go fast. Book in advance if your plans call for spending a night here, even though accommodations are pretty basic. At **Whispering Sands Motel** (90 S. Hwy. 95, 435/542-3238, $99-129) you'll have a choice of rooms in the motel or in "cabins" that look a lot like garden sheds. Never mind—by the time you arrive, you'll be glad to see them. Though most people would call this a motel, **OYO Hotel** (280 E. 100 N., 435/542-3471, www.oyorooms.com/us, $89-122) is the other option, also basic but serviceable.

In the center of town, behind Duke's Slickrock Grill, is **Duke's Slickrock Campground & RV Park** (275 Hwy. 24, 435/542-3235 or 800/894-3242, mid-Mar.-Oct., $15-20 tents, $35 RVs) has showers and a laundry, and also a number of new cabins that are easily the nicest places to stay in Hanksville. Each of the cabins has two queen beds, private bath, and a porch with a table and chairs.

It's also good to know about the **Rodeway Inn Capitol Reef** (25 E. Hwy. 24, 435/456-9900, www.choicehotels.com, $94-99), 15 miles (24 km) west of Hanksville in Caineville, another pleasant but standard lodging, but note that the nearest actual restaurant is in Hanksville. Fortunately, there's a small breakfast served; even better, the Mesa Farm Market is nearby on the road to Capitol Reef National Park with excellent homemade bread and cheese.

Information and Services

The **Bureau of Land Management** (435/542-3461, www.blm.gov) has a field station 0.5 mile (0.8 km) south of Highway 24 on 100 West, with information on road conditions, hiking, camping, and the buffalo herd in the Henry Mountains.

★ GOBLIN VALLEY STATE PARK

Thousands of rock formations, many with goblin-like "faces," inhabit **Goblin Valley State Park** (435/275-4584, reservations 800/322-3770, www.reserveamerica.com, year-round, $20 per vehicle day use, $30 camping, $100 yurts). All of these so-called goblins have weathered out of the Entrada Formation, here a soft red sandstone and even softer siltstone. The **Carmel Canyon Trail** (1.5-mi/2.4-km loop) begins at the northeast side of the parking lot at road's end, then drops down to the desert floor and a strange landscape of goblins, spires, and balanced rocks. Just wander around at your whim; this is a great place for the imagination. A 1.3-mile (2.1-km) trail connects the campground and the goblin-studded Carmel Canyon Trail.

Curtis Bench Trail begins on the road between the parking lot and the campground and goes south to a viewpoint of the Henry Mountains; cairns mark the 1.5-mile/2.4-kilometer (one-way) route.

The turnoff from Highway 24 is at milepost 137, which is 21 miles (34 km) north of Hanksville and 24 miles (39 km) south of I-70; follow signs west 5 miles (8 km) on a paved road, then south 7 miles (11.3 km) on a gravel road.

Although there are off-road vehicle and motorcycle riding areas just west of the park, bicycling is limited to the park's roads. However, 12 miles (19.3 km) north, the **Temple Mountain Bike Trail** traverses old mining roads, ridges, and wash bottoms. Popular hikes near the state park include the Little Wild Horse and Bell Canyons Loop, Chute and Crack Canyons Loop, and Wild Horse Canyon. The park is also a good base for exploring the **San Rafael Swell** area to the northwest.

Camping at Goblin Valley is a real treat; the late-evening and early-morning sun makes the sandstone spires glow. If you're not much of a camper, consider booking one of the park's two yurts ($100). They're tucked back among the rock formations, and each is equipped with bunk beds and a futon, a swamp cooler, and propane stove. There are only 26 camping sites, so it's best to reserve well in advance.

LITTLE WILD HORSE CANYON

About 6 miles (9.7 km) west of Goblin Valley, Little Wild Horse is a good slot canyon hike for people without technical experience, though obstacles do require a little scrambling. Hike in as far as you like and turn around to exit or make a loop with Bell Canyon. Hiking is best in spring and fall; avoid the area when there's a chance of rain, which is often the case in August. Reach the trailhead by traveling west on Goblin Valley Road; turn right on Wild Horse Road before you reach the Goblin Valley State Park entrance.

GREEN RIVER

Green River (population about 950) is, except for a handful of motels and a lively tavern, pretty run-down, but it's the only real settlement on the stretch of I-70 between Salina and the Colorado border. Travelers can stop for a night or a meal, set off on a trip down the Green River, or use the town as a base for exploring the scenic San Rafael Swell country nearby.

Green River is known for its melons. In summer, stop at roadside stands and partake of wondrous cantaloupes and watermelons. The blazing summer heat and ample irrigation water make such delicacies possible. **Melon Days** (3rd weekend in Sept.) celebrate the harvest with a parade, a city fair, music, a canoe race, games, and lots of melons.

John Wesley Powell River History Museum

Stop by the fine **John Wesley Powell River History Museum** (1765 E. Main St., 435/564-3427, http://johnwesleypowell.com, 9am-5pm Mon.-Sat., $6 adults, $2 ages 3-12) to learn about Powell's daring expeditions down the Green and Colorado Rivers in 1869 and 1871-1872. An excellent multimedia presentation about both rivers uses narratives from Powell's trips. Historic riverboats on display include a replica of Powell's *Emma Dean.*

Labyrinth and Stillwater Canyons

The Green River's Labyrinth and Stillwater Canyons are downstream, between the town of Green River and the river's confluence with the Colorado River in Canyonlands National Park. Primarily a canoeing or kayaking river, the Green River at this point is calm and wide as it passes into increasingly deep, rust-colored canyons. This isn't a wilderness river; regular powerboats can also follow the river below town to the confluence with the Colorado River and head up the Colorado to Moab, two or three days and 186 river miles (300 km) away.

The most common trip on this portion of the Green River begins just south of town and runs south through the Labyrinth Canyon, ending at Mineral Bottom (68 river mi/109 km). **Moab Rafting and Canoe Company** (420 Kane Creek Blvd., Moab, 435/259-7722, http://moab-rafting.com, four-day guided trip from $999 pp, depending on group size) offers this trip in canoes and offers unguided raft rentals too. **Tex's Riverways** (691 N. 500 West, Moab, 435/259-5101, www.texsriverways.com) offers canoe and touring kayak rentals and all the other equipment you need to outfit a self-guided multiday trip, plus shuttle services to and from the river. Permits are required to paddle in Labyrinth Canyon; they're free and available to download from the BLM website (www.blm.gov) or can be picked up in town at the John Wesley Powell Museum (1765 E. Main St.) or Green River State Park (150 S. Green River Blvd.).

Crystal Geyser

With some luck, you'll catch the spectacle of this cold-water geyser on the bank of the Green River. The carbon-dioxide-powered gusher occasionally shoots as high as 60 feet (18 m), but it's pretty unpredictable, so you may just see burbles. This isn't a natural geothermal geyser; it was created by an oil drill in the 1930s, and water shoots out from a rusty pipe.

Even if the geyser is only putting out a few little spurts, its setting is beautiful. Colorful travertine terraces around the opening and down to the river make this a pretty spot, even if the geyser is quiet.

Crystal Geyser is 10 miles (16 km) south of Green River by road; boaters should look for the geyser deposits on the left, about 4.5 river miles (7.2 km) downstream from Green River. From downtown, drive east 1 mile (1.6 km) on Main Street, turn left, and go 3 miles (4.8 km) on signed Frontage Road (near milepost 4), then turn right and go 6 miles (9.7 km) on a narrow paved road just after going under a railroad overpass. The road goes under I-70; keep right at a fork near some power lines. Some washes must be crossed, so the drive isn't recommended after rains. When the weather is fair, cars shouldn't have a problem.

1: Little Wild Horse Canyon **2:** Goblin Valley State Park **3:** eroded mudstone spires near Hanksville

Food

Other than motel restaurants and fast food, the one really notable place to eat in Green River is ★ **Ray's Tavern** (25 S. Broadway, 435/564-3511, 11am-9pm daily, $8-27). Ray's doesn't look like much from the outside, but inside you'll find a friendly welcome, tables made from tree trunks, and some of the best steaks, chops, and burgers in this part of the state. Don't expect haute cuisine, but the food is good, and the atmosphere is truly Western; beer drinkers will be glad for the selection of regional microbrews after a long day navigating the river or driving desert roads.

Grab a taco from **La Pasadita** (215 E. Main St., 435/564-8159, 8am-10pm Sun.-Thurs., 9am-10pm Fri.-Sat., $6-10), a taco truck in the parking lot of an old gas station. The food is tasty, and the scene is convivial at the picnic tables set up for diners.

Directly adjacent to the River Terrace hotel is a decent American-style restaurant, **The Tamarisk** (1710 E. Main St., 435/564-8109, 7am-10pm daily, $12-19), with riverfront views.

Accommodations

Green River has a few rather shabby older motels as well as newer chain motels to choose from. Unless noted, each of the following has a swimming pool—a major consideration in this often-sweltering desert valley.

If you're on a budget, try the basic **Robber's Roost Motel** (325 W. Main St., 435/564-3452, www.rrmotel.com, $44-58), which is right in the center of town; it does not

have a pool. Green River's newer motels are on the east end of town. The **Super 8** (1248 E. Main St., 435/564-8888 or 800/888-8888, $63-75), out by I-70 exit 162, is a good value, with spacious, comfortable guest rooms.

The nicest place to stay in town is the ★ **River Terrace** (1740 E. Main St., 435/564-3401 or 877/564-3401, www.river-terrace.com, $140-150), with somewhat older but large guest rooms, some of which overlook the Green River and some with balconies. Breakfast is included, with a restaurant adjacent to the hotel. The very pleasant outdoor pool area is flanked by patios, gardens, and shaded tables.

CAMPGROUNDS

Several campgrounds, all with showers, offer sites for tents and RVs year-round. **Green River State Park** (150 S. Green River Blvd., 435/564-3633 or 800/322-3770, www.reserveamerica.com, year-round, $7 day use, $35 with hookups, $75 cabins) has a great setting near the river; it's shaded by large cottonwoods and has a boat ramp and a nine-hole golf course. **Shady Acres RV Park** (350 E. Main St., 435/564-8290 or 800/537-8674, www.shadyacresrv.com, year-round, $25-30 tents, $43-47 with hookups, $55 cabins) is not all that shady and may be a bit too close to the noisy road for tent campers; it has a store, showers, and a laundry. **Green River KOA** (235 S. 1780 E., 435/564-3651, $29 tents, $50-68 with hookups, $71-81 cabins) has campsites and cabins (bring sleeping bags) across from the John Wesley Powell Museum and next to the Tamarisk restaurant.

Background

The Landscape

Southeastern Utah's five national parks and its preserves of public land are all part of the **Colorado Plateau,** a high, broad physiographic province that includes Southern Utah, northern Arizona, southwestern Colorado, and northwestern New Mexico. This roughly circular plateau, nearly the size of Montana, also contains the Grand Canyon, the Navajo Nation, and the Hopi Reservation.

Created by a slow but tremendous uplift and carved by magnificent rivers, the plateau is mostly between 3,000 and 6,000 feet elevation (915-1,830 m), with some peaks reaching nearly 13,000 feet (3,962 m).

Although much of the terrain is gently rolling, the Green and Colorado Rivers have sculpted remarkable canyons, buttes, mesas, arches, and badlands. Isolated uplifts and folds have formed such features as the San Rafael Swell, Waterpocket Fold, and Circle Cliffs. The rounded Abajo, Henry, La Sal, and Navajo Mountains are examples of intrusive rock—an igneous layer that is formed below the earth's surface and later exposed by erosion.

The Colorado Plateau province is broken down into six physiographic sections: the Grand Canyon, Datil, Navajo, Uinta Basin, Canyon Lands, and High Plateaus. Utah's national parks are spread across the High Plateaus and Canyon Lands sections. The westernmost parks, Zion and Bryce, are in the High Plateaus; Capitol Reef, Arches, and Canyonlands are, not surprisingly, in the Canyon Lands section; and the Escalante River forms the dividing line between the two sections.

The High Plateaus (the Paunsaugunt, Markagunt, and Aquarius Plateaus) are lava-topped uplands reaching above the main height of the Colorado Plateau, then dropping off to the south in a series of steps known as the Grand Staircase. Exposed layers range from the relatively young rocks of the Black Cliffs (lava flows) in the north to the increasingly older Pink Cliffs (visible at Bryce), Gray Cliffs (which include the Straight Cliffs of Grand Staircase-Escalante), White Cliffs (Zion's Navajo sandstone), and Vermilion Cliffs (surrounding Kanab, Utah) toward the south.

The Canyon Lands section is noted for its synclines, anticlines, and folds—nongeologists can picture the rock layers as blankets on a bed, and then imagine how they look before the bed is made in the morning. This warping, which goes on deep beneath the earth's surface, has affected the overlying rocks, permitting the development of deeply incised canyons.

GEOLOGY

When you visit any one of Utah's national parks, the first things you're likely to notice are rocks. Vegetation is sparse and the soil is thin, so there's not much to hide the geology here. Particularly stunning views are found where rivers have carved deep canyons through the rock layers.

The clean, orderly stairsteps from the young rocks in Bryce Canyon to the much older Grand Canyon show off the clearly defined layers of rock. Weird crenellations, hoodoos, and arches occur as a result of the way erosion acted on the various rocks that make up this big Colorado Plateau layer cake.

Sedimentation

Water made this desert what it is today. Back before the continents broke apart and began drifting to their present-day locations, Utah was near the equator, just east of a warm ocean. Ancient seas washed over the land, depositing sand, silt, and mud. Layer upon layer, the soils piled up and were—over time—compressed into sandstones, limestones, and shales.

The ancestral Rocky Mountains rose to the east of the ocean, and, just to their west, a trough-like basin formed and was intermittently flushed with sea water. Evaporation caused salts and other minerals to collect on the basin floor; when the climate became wetter, more water rushed in.

As the ancestral Rockies eroded, their bulk washed down into the basin. The sea level rose, washing in more mud and sand. When the seas receded, dry winds blew sand across the region, creating enormous dunes.

Over time, the North American continent drifted north, away from the equator, but this region remained near the sea and was regularly washed by tides, leaving more sand and silt. Just inland, freshwater lakes filled, then dried, and the lakebeds consolidated into shales. During wet periods, streams coursed

---

Previous: capturing the view from Bryce Point

The Colorado Plateau

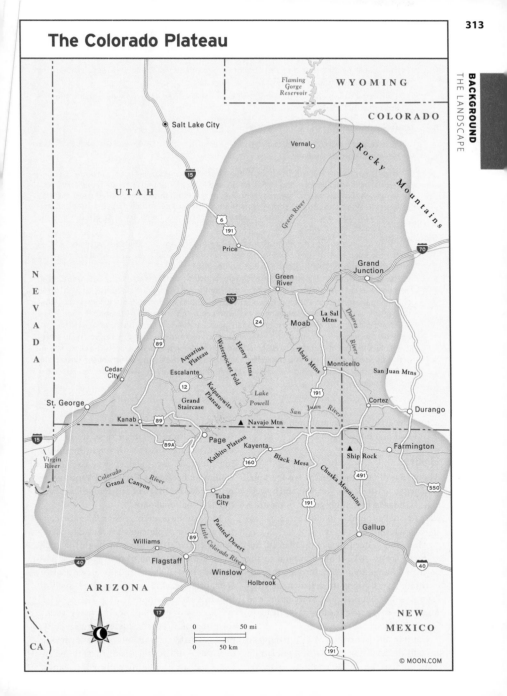

Flaming Gorge Reservoir

WYOMING

COLORADO

Salt Lake City

Vernal

Rocky Mountains

UTAH

Green River

15

6
191

Price

Green River

Grand Junction

70

NEVADA

70

24

Moab

La Sal Mtns

Dolores River

89

Aquarius Plateau

Waterpocket Fold

Henry Mtns

Abajo Mtns

Monticello

San Juan Mtns

Cedar City

Escalante

12

Kaiparowits Plateau

Lake Powell

191

Cortez

Durango

St. George

Grand Staircase

San Juan River

Kanab

89

▲ Navajo Mtn

15

89A

Page

Kaibito Plateau

Kayenta

▲ Ship Rock

Farmington

Virgin River

160

Black Mesa

Chuska Mountains

491

550

Colorado River

Grand Canyon

Tuba City

191

Gallup

Williams

89

Little Colorado River

Painted Desert

40

Flagstaff

Winslow

Holbrook

40

ARIZONA

CA

17

NEW MEXICO

191

0   50 mi

0   50 km

© MOON.COM

Nature's Palette

In Utah, you'll get used to seeing a lot of colorful rock formations. The color gives you clues to the composition and geologic history of the rock. In general:

- **Red rocks** are stained by rusty iron-rich sediments washed down from mountains, and they are a clue that erosion has occurred.

- **Gray or brown rocks** were deposited by ancient seas.

- **White rocks** are colored by their "glue," the limey remains of dissolved seashells that leach down and harden sandstones.

- **Black rocks** are volcanic in origin, though not all volcanic, or igneous, rocks are black. Igneous rocks are present in the La Sal, Abajo, and Henry Mountains near Canyonlands. These mountains are "laccoliths," formed by molten magma that pushed through the sedimentary layers, leaking deeper into some layers than others and eventually forming broad dome-shaped protuberances, which were eroded into soft peaks, then carved by glaciers into the sharp peaks we see today.

A layer of lava also caps the Paunsaugunt, Markagunt, and Aquarius Plateaus, which have lifted above the main level of the Colorado Plateau. This mostly basalt layer was laid down about 37 million years ago, before the Colorado Plateau began to uplift.

The dark-colored vertical stripes often seen on sandstone cliff faces across the Colorado Plateau are known as **desert varnish.** They're mostly composed of very fine clay particles, rich in iron and manganese. It's not entirely known how these streaks are formed, but it seems likely that they're at least partly created by mineral-rich water coursing down the cliffs along the varnished areas and wind-blown clay dust sticking to cliff faces. Bacteria and fungi on the rock's surface may help this process along by absorbing manganese and iron from the atmosphere and precipitating it as a black layer of manganese oxide or reddish iron oxide on the rock surfaces. The clay particles in this thin layer of varnish help shield the bacteria against the drying effects of the desert sun. Prehistoric rock artists worked with desert varnish, chipping away the dark surface to expose the lighter underlying rocks.

across the area, carrying and then dropping their loads of mud, silt, and sand.

Uplift

About 15 million years ago, the sea-level plateau began to lift slowly, steadily, and by geologic standards, incredibly gently. Some areas were hoisted as high as 10,000 feet (3,048 m) above sea level.

Along the western edge of the plateau, underlying faults—like those common in the Basin and Range area—shot through the sedimentary layers. Along these faults, the High Plateaus—the Paunsaugunt, Markagunt, and Aquarius—rose above the height of the main Colorado Plateau.

Uplift is still occurring. A 1992 earthquake just outside Zion National Park was one strong reminder that the plateau continues to move.

Erosion

As the Colorado Plateau rose, its big rivers carved deep gorges through the uplifting rocks. Today, these rivers—the Green, Colorado, Escalante, Paria, and Virgin—are responsible for much of the dramatic scenery in Utah's national parks.

More subtle forms of erosion have also contributed to the plateau's present-day form. Water percolating down through the rock layers is one of the main erosive forces, washing away loose material and dissolving ancient salts, often leaving odd formations, such as thin fins of resistant rock.

The many layers of sedimentary rocks forming the Colorado Plateau are all composed of different minerals and have varying densities, so it's not surprising that erosion affects each layer a bit differently. For instance, sandstones and limestones erode more readily than the harder mudstones or shales.

Erosion isn't limited to the force of water against rock. Rocks may be worn down or eaten away by a variety of forces, including wind, freezing and thawing, exfoliation (when sheets of rock peel off), oxidation, hydration and carbonation (chemical weathering), plant roots or animal burrows, and dissolving of soft rocks. Rockfalls in Zion, the ever-deepening channel of the Colorado River through Canyonlands, and the slow thinning of pedestals supporting Arches' balanced rocks are all clues that erosion continues unabated.

CLIMATE

The main thing for Southern Utah travelers to remember is that they're in the desert.

The high-desert country of the Colorado Plateau lies mostly between 3,000 and 6,000 feet (915-1,830 m) in elevation. Annual precipitation ranges from an extremely dry 3 inches in some areas to about 10 inches in others. Mountainous regions between 10,000 and 13,000 feet (3,048-3,962 m) receive abundant rainfall in summer and heavy snows in winter.

Sunny skies prevail through all four seasons. Spring comes early to the canyon country, with weather that's often windy and rapidly changing. Summer can make its presence known in April, although the real desert heat doesn't set in until late May-early June. Temperatures then soar into the 90s and 100s at midday, although the dry air makes the heat more bearable. Early morning is the choice time for travel in summer. A canyon seep surrounded by hanging gardens or a mountain meadow filled with wildflowers provides a refreshing contrast to the parched desert; other ways to beat the heat include hiking in the mountains and river rafting.

Summer thunderstorm season begins anywhere mid-June-August; huge billowing thunderstorm clouds bring refreshing rains and coolness. During this season, canyon hikers should be alert for flash flooding.

Fall begins after the rains cease, usually in October, and lasts into November or even December; days are bright and sunny with ideal temperatures, but nights become cold. In all of the parks, evenings will be cool even in midsummer. Although the day may be baking hot, you'll need a jacket and a warm sleeping bag for the night.

Elevation matters: Bryce Canyon National Park is at 8,000 feet (2,438 m) and is significantly cooler than nearby Zion, at about 4,000 feet (1,291 m). Bryce is the only park regularly covered with enough snow for cross-country skiing or snowshoeing. It's also where, during early spring, a motel room will seem like a good idea to all but the most hardy tent campers. Winter lasts only about two months at the lower elevations. Light snows on the canyon walls add new beauty to the rock layers. Nighttime temperatures commonly dip into the teens, which is too cold for most campers. Otherwise, winter can be a fine time for travel. Heavy snows rarely occur below 8,000 feet (2,438 m).

Flash Floods

Rainwater runs quickly off the rocky desert surfaces and into gullies and canyons. A summer thunderstorm or a rapid late-winter snowmelt can send torrents of mud and boulders rumbling down dry washes and canyons. Backcountry drivers, horseback riders, and hikers need to avoid hazardous locations when storms threaten or unseasonably warm winds blow on the winter snowpack.

Flash floods can sweep away anything in their path, including boulders, cars, and campsites. Do not camp or park in potential flash flood areas. If you come to a section of flooded roadway—a common occurrence on desert roads after storms—wait until the water goes down before crossing (it shouldn't take long). Summer lightning causes forest and brush fires, posing a danger to hikers who are foolish enough to climb mountains when storms threaten.

The bare rock and loose soils so common in the canyon country do little to hold back the flow of rain or meltwater. In fact, slickrock is

Mormon Tea

Although it's not the showiest wildflower in the desert, Mormon tea (*Ephedra viridis*) is widespread across Southern Utah, and it's particularly common in Arches National park. This broom-like plant is remarkably well adapted to the desert, and many desert-dwelling humans have adapted themselves to enjoy drinking it as a tea.

The plant's branches contain chlorophyll and are able to conduct photosynthesis. The leaves are like tiny scales or bracts; their small size reduces the amount of moisture the plant loses to transpiration. Male and female flowers grow on separate plants.

Native Americans used this plant medicinally as a tea for stomach and bowel disorders as well as for colds, fever, and headaches. Some used it to control bleeding and as a poultice for burns.

Mormon tea is related to ma huang, a Chinese herb that is traditionally used to treat hay fever. All parts of the plant contain a small amount of ephedrine, a stimulant that in large concentrations can be quite harmful. Pioneers in Southern Utah were mostly Mormons, who are forbidden to drink coffee or similar stimulants. When they learned that drinking the boiled stems of *Ephedra viridis* gave them a mild lift, they approached Brigham Young, the head of the Latter-Day Saints. Young gave the tea his stamp of approval, and the plant's common name grew out of its widespread use by Mormons. In Utah it's also sometimes called Brigham tea.

The tea itself is yellowish and, as one local puts it, tastes something like what she imagines boiled socks would taste like. To increase the tea's palatability, it's often mixed with mint, lemon, and sugar or honey. Pioneers liked to add strawberry jam to their Mormon tea.

If you are tempted to try this tea for yourself, make certain not to harvest plants in a national park. Women who are pregnant or nursing and people with high blood pressure, heart disease, diabetes, glaucoma, or other health problems should definitely avoid even the small amounts of ephedrine present in Mormon tea.

effective at shedding water as fast as it comes in contact. Logs and other debris wedged high on canyon walls give proof enough of past floods.

PLANTS

Within the physiographic province of the Colorado Plateau, several different life zones are represented.

In the low desert, shrubs eke out a meager existence. Climbing higher, you'll pass through grassy steppe, sage, and piñon-juniper woodlands to ponderosa pine. Of all these zones, the piñon-juniper is most common.

But it's not a lockstep progression of plant A at elevation X and plant B at elevation Z. Soils are an important consideration, with sandstones being more hospitable than shales. Plants will grow wherever the conditions will support them, and Utah's parks have many microenvironments that can lead to surprising plant discoveries. Look for different plants in these different habitats: slickrock (where cracks can gather enough soil to host a few plants), riparian (moist areas with the greatest diversity of life), and terraces and open space (the area between riverbank and slickrock, where shrubs dominate). With more than 800 native species, Zion has the greatest plant diversity of any of Utah's parks.

How Plants Survive in the Desert

Most of the plants you'll see in Utah's national parks are well adapted to desert life. Many are succulents, which have their own water storage systems in their fleshy stems or leaves. Cacti are the most obvious succulents; they swell with stored moisture during the spring, then slowly shrink and wrinkle as the stored moisture is used.

Other plants have different strategies for making the most of scarce water. Some, such as yucca, have deep roots, taking advantage of what moisture exists in the soil. The leaves of desert plants are often spiny, exposing less surface area to the sun. Leaves may also have very small pores, slowing transpiration, or stems coated with a resinous substance, which also slows water loss. Hairy or light-colored leaves help reflect sunlight.

Most desert wildflowers are annuals. They bloom in the spring when water is available, form seeds that can survive the dry, hot summer, and then die. A particularly wet spring means a bumper crop of wildflowers.

Even though mosses aren't usually thought of as desert plants, they are found growing in seeps along canyon walls and in cryptobiotic soils. When water is unavailable, mosses dry up; when the water returns, the moss quickly plumps up again.

Junipers have a fairly drastic way of dealing with water shortage: self-pruning. During a prolonged dry spell, a juniper tree can shut off the flow of water to one or more of its branches, sacrificing these branches to keep the tree alive.

Hanging Gardens

Look along Zion's Virgin River canyon for clumps of ferns and mosses lit with maidenhair ferns, shooting stars, monkey flowers, columbine, orchids, and bluebells. These unexpectedly lush pockets are called "hanging gardens," gemlike islands of plant life nestled into canyon walls.

Hanging gardens take advantage of a unique microclimate created by the meeting of two rock layers: Navajo sandstone and Kayenta shale. Water percolates down through porous sandstone and, when it hits the denser shale layer, travels laterally along the top of the harder rock and emerges at cliff's edge. These little springs support lush plant life.

Tamarisk

One of the Colorado Plateau's most common trees, the nonnative tamarisk is also one of the peskiest. Imported from the Mediterranean and widely planted along the Colorado River to control erosion, the tamarisk has spread wildly, and its dense stands have crowded out native trees such as cottonwoods. Tamarisks are notoriously thirsty trees, sucking up vast amounts of water, but they give back little in the way of food or habitat for local wildlife. Their thick growth also increases the risk of fire. State and federal agencies are taking steps to control tamarisk; tamarisk beetles, imported from Kazakhstan and China, have been released in sites in Southern Utah as a biocontrol agent.

Cryptobiotic Soil

Over much of the Colorado Plateau, the soil is alive. What looks like a grayish-brown crust is actually a dense network of filament-forming blue-green algae intertwined with soil particles, lichens, moss, green algae, and microfungi. This slightly sticky, crusty mass holds the soil together, slowing erosion. Its sponge-like consistency allows it to soak up water and hold it. Plants growing in cryptobiotic soil have a great advantage over plants rooted in dry sandy soil.

Cryptobiotic soils take a long time to develop and are extremely fragile. Make every effort to avoid stepping on them—stick to trails, slickrock, or rocks instead.

ANIMALS

Although they're not thought of as great "wildlife parks" like Yellowstone or Denali, Utah's national parks are home to plenty of animals. Desert animals are often nocturnal and unseen by park visitors.

Rodents

Rodents include squirrels, packrats, kangaroo rats, chipmunks, and porcupines, most of which spend their days in burrows.

One of the few desert rodents out foraging during the day is the white-tailed antelope squirrel, which looks much like a chipmunk. Its white tail reflects the sunlight, and when it needs to cool down a bit, an antelope squirrel smears its face with saliva (yes, that probably would work for you too, but that's why you have sweat glands). The antelope squirrel lives at lower elevations; higher up you'll see golden-mantled ground squirrels.

Look for rabbits—desert cottontails and jackrabbits—at dawn and dusk. If you're rafting the Green or Colorado Rivers, keep an eye out for beavers.

Kangaroo rats are particularly well adapted to desert life. They spend their days in cool burrows, eat only plants, and never drink water. Instead, a kangaroo rat metabolizes dry food in a way that produces water.

Utah prairie dogs have been given a new lease on life in Bryce National Park. In 1973 the animals were listed as an endangered species and reintroduced to Bryce. Today, nearly 200 animals live in the park—the largest protected population of Utah prairie dogs. Prairie dogs live together in social groups called colonies or towns, which are laced with burrows, featuring a network of entrances for quick pops in and out of the ground. Prairie dogs are preyed on by badgers, coyotes, hawks, and snakes, so a colony will post lookouts that are constantly searching for danger. When threatened, the lookouts "bark" to warn the colony. Utah prairie dogs hibernate during the winter and emerge from their burrows to mate furiously in early April.

Porcupines are common in Capitol Reef and Zion; although they prefer to live in forested areas, especially the piñon-juniper zone, they sometimes forage in streamside brush. These nocturnal creatures have also been known to visit campsites, where they like to gnaw on sweaty boots or backpack straps.

Bats

As night falls in canyon country, bats emerge from the nooks and crannies that protect them from the day's heat and begin to feed on mosquitoes and other insects. The tiny gray western pipistrelle is common. It flies early in the evening, feeding near streams, and can be spotted by its somewhat erratic flight. The pallid bat spends a lot of its time creeping across the ground in search of food and is a late-night bat; look for it after 10pm in the summer at Capitol Reef. Another common bat

here and across the United States is the prosaically named big brown bat.

Large Mammals

Mule deer are common in all of the parks, as are coyotes. Other large mammals include predators such as mountain lions and coyotes. If you're lucky, you'll get a glimpse of a bobcat or a fox.

If you're hiking the trails of Bryce Canyon early in the morning and see something that looks like a small dog in a tree, it's probably a gray fox. These small (5-10 pounds) foxes live in forested areas and have the catlike ability to climb trees. They're most commonly seen on the connecting trail between the Queen's Garden and Navajo Loop Trails. Kit foxes, which are even tinier than gray foxes, with prominent ears and a big bushy tail, are common in Arches and Canyonlands. Red foxes also live throughout the plateau.

Desert bighorn sheep live in Arches, Canyonlands, and Capitol Reef; look for them trotting across steep, rocky ledges. In Arches, they're frequently sighted along U.S. 191 south of the visitors center. They also roam the talus slopes and side canyons near the Colorado River. Desert bighorns have been reintroduced in Zion and can occasionally be spotted in steep, rocky areas on the park's east side.

Reptiles

Reptiles are well suited to desert life. As cold-blooded, or ectothermic, animals, their body temperature depends on the environment, rather than on internal metabolism, and it's easy for them to keep warm in the desert heat. When it's cold, reptiles hibernate or drastically slow their metabolism.

The western whiptail lizard is common in Arches. You'll recognize it because its tail is twice as long as its body. Also notable is the western collared lizard, with a bright green body set off by a black collar.

Less flashy but particularly fascinating are the several species of parthenogenetic lizards. All of these lizards are female, and they

Mountain Lion Encounters

Imagine hiking down a trail and suddenly noticing fresh large paw prints. Mountain lion or Labrador retriever? Here's the way to tell the difference: Mountain lions usually retract their claws when they walk. Dogs, of course, can't do this. So if close inspection of the print reveals toenails, it's most likely from a canine's paw.

But about those mountain lions: In recent years, incidents of mountain lion-human confrontations have increased markedly and received much publicity. These ambush hunters usually prey on sick or weak animals but will occasionally attack people, especially children and small adults. When hiking or camping with children in mountain lion territory—potentially all of Utah's national parks—it is important to keep them close to the rest of the family.

If you are stalked by a mountain lion, make yourself look big by raising your arms, waving a big stick, or spreading your coat. Maintain direct eye contact with the animal, and do not turn your back to it. If the mountain lion begins to approach, throw rocks and sticks, and continue to look large and menacing as you slowly back away. In the case of an attack, fight back; do not "play dead."

To put things in perspective, it's important to remember that mountain lions are famously elusive. If you do see one, it will probably be a quick glimpse of the cat running away from you.

reproduce by laying eggs that are clones of themselves. Best known is the plateau striped whiptail, but 6 of the 12 species of whiptail present in the area are all-female.

The northern plateau lizard is common at altitudes of about 3,000-6,000 feet (915-1,830 m). It's not choosy about its habitat—juniper-piñon woodlands, prairies, riparian woodlands, and rocky hillsides are all perfectly acceptable. This is the lizard you'll most often see scurrying across your campsite in Zion or Capitol Reef.

Rattlesnakes are present across the area, but given a chance, they'll get out of your way rather than strike. (Still, they're another good reason to wear sturdy boots.) The midget faded rattlesnake, a small subspecies of the western rattlesnake, lives in burrows and rock crevices and is mostly active at night. Although this snake has especially toxic venom, full venom injections occur in only one-third of all bites.

Amphibians

Although they're not usually thought of as desert animals, a variety of frogs and toads live on the Colorado Plateau. Tadpoles live in wet springtime potholes as well as in streams and seeps. If you're camping in a canyon, you may be lucky enough to be serenaded by a toad chorus.

Bullfrogs are not native to the western United States, but since they were introduced in the early 1900s, they have flourished at the expense of native frogs and toads, whose eggs and tadpoles they eat.

The big round toes of the small spotted canyon tree frog make it easy to identify—that is, if you can see this well-camouflaged frog in the first place. These frogs are most active at night, spending their days on streamside rocks or trees.

Toads present in Utah's parks include the Great Basin spadefoot, red spotted toad, and western woodhouse toad.

Birds

Have you ever seen a bird pant? Believe it or not, that's how desert birds expel heat from their bodies. They allow heat to escape by drooping their wings away from their bodies, exposing thinly feathered areas (sort of like pulling up your shirt and using it to fan your torso).

The various habitats across the Colorado Plateau, such as piñon-juniper, perennial streams, dry washes, and rock cliffs, allow many species of bird to find homes. Birders will find the greatest variety of birds near rivers and streams. Other birds, such as golden eagles, kestrels (small falcons), and peregrine falcons nest high on cliffs and patrol open areas for prey. Commonly seen hawks include the red-tailed hawk and northern harrier; late-evening strollers may see great horned owls. California condors were reintroduced in 1996 to Zion, and can now be seen in the Lava Point, Canyon Overlook, and Angels Landing areas.

People usually detect the canyon wren by its lovely song; this small, long-beaked bird nests in cavities along cliff faces. The related rock wren is—as its name implies—a rock collector: It paves a trail to its nest with pebbles, and the nest itself is lined with rocks. Another canyon bird, the white-throated swift, swoops and calls as it chases insects and mates, rather dramatically, in flight. Swifts are often seen near violet-green swallows, which are equally gymnastic fliers, in Canyonlands, Arches, and the Grand Staircase-Escalante region.

The chukar—a chunky game bird introduced for the benefit of hunters in the 1930s—is common at Capitol Reef, where it is often seen on or near the ground, foraging in low-lying shrubs and grasses.

Several species of hummingbird (mostly black-chinned, but also broad-tailed and rufous) are often seen in the summer. Woodpeckers are also common, including the northern flicker and red-naped sapsucker, and flycatchers like Say's phoebe, western kingbird, and western wood pewee can be spotted too. Two warblers—the yellow and the yellow-rumped—are common in the summer, and Wilson's warbler stops in during spring and fall migrations. Horned larks are present year-round.

Mountain bluebirds are colorful, easy for a novice to identify, and common in Canyonlands and Arches. Look for the American dipper along the Virgin River in Zion. This small gray bird distinguishes itself from other similar birds by its habit of plunging headfirst into the water in search of insects.

Both the well-known scrub jay and its local cousin, the piñon jay, are noisy visitors to almost every picnic. Other icons of Western avian life—the turkey vulture, the raven, and the magpie—are widespread and easily spotted.

Fish

Obviously, deserts aren't particularly known for their aquatic life, and the big rivers of the Colorado Plateau are now dominated by nonnative species such as channel catfish and carp. Many of these fish were introduced as game fish. Native fish, like the six-foot, 100-pound Colorado pikeminnow, are now uncommon.

Spiders and Scorpions

Tarantulas, black widow spiders, and scorpions all live across the Colorado Plateau, and all are objects of many a visitor's phobias. Although the black widow spider's venom is toxic, tarantulas deliver only a mildly toxic bite (and they rarely bite humans), and a scorpion's sting is about like that of a bee.

ENVIRONMENTAL ISSUES

Utah's national parks have generally been shielded from the environmental issues that play out in the rest of the state, which has always been business-oriented, with a heavy emphasis on extractive industries such as mining and logging.

The main environmental threats to the parks are the consequences of becoming too popular. During the summer, auto and RV traffic can clog park roads, with particularly bad snarls at viewpoint parking areas. Both Zion and Bryce have made attempts to control park traffic by running shuttle buses along scenic drives. At Zion, it's mandatory to ride the bus (or your bike) during the summer high season, and that has made a significant difference.

Hikers also have an impact, especially when they tread on fragile cryptobiotic soil. Killing this living soil crust drastically

Edward Abbey: "Resist Much, Obey Little"

Edward Abbey spent two summers in the late 1950s living in a trailer in Arches National Park. From this experience, he wrote *Desert Solitaire*, which, when it was published in 1968, introduced many readers to the beauties of Utah's slickrock country and to the need to preserve it. In the introduction to this book, he gives a word of caution to slickrock pilgrims:

> Do not jump into your automobile next June and rush out to the Canyon country hoping to see some of that which I have attempted to evoke in these pages. In the first place you can't see anything from a car; you've got to get out of the goddamned contraption and walk, better yet crawl, on hands and knees, over the sandstone and through the ... cactus. When traces of blood begin to mark your trail you'll see something, maybe.

This sense of letting the outdoors affect you—right down to the bone—pervades Abbey's writing. He advocated responding to assaults on the environment in an equally raw, gutsy way. Convinced that the only way to confront rampant development in the American West was by preserving its wilderness, he was a pioneer of radical environmentalism, a "desert anarchist." Long before Earth First!, Abbey's fictional characters blew up dams and created a holy environmentalist ruckus in *The Monkey Wrench Gang*. Some of his ideas were radical, others reactionary, and he seemed deeply committed to raising a stir. Abbey's writing did a lot to change the way people think about the American West, its development, and staying true to values derived from the natural world.

Two biographies, *Edward Abbey: A Life*, by James M. Cahalan (Tucson: University of Arizona Press, 2001), and the less academic *Adventures with Ed*, by Abbey's good friend Jack Loeffler (Albuquerque: University of New Mexico Press, 2002), help readers see the person behind the icon.

increases erosion in an already easily eroded environment.

Redrawing Utah National Monuments

The 1.9 million-acre Grand Staircase-Escalante National Monument (GSENM) was designated by President Bill Clinton in 1996; the 1.35 million-acre Bears Ears National Monument was created by President Barack Obama in 2016. Both monuments were slashed in size and divided into smaller units in 2018 by the Donald Trump administration. The GSENM lost nearly half of its acreage and is now divided into three units: the Grand Staircase, Kaiparowits Plateau, and Escalante Canyons units. The lands removed from national monument protection include areas known to be rich in coal deposits. The Bears Ears monument lost 85 percent of its land and was divided into two new monuments, Indian Creek and Shash Jaa. Some of the delisted land, particularly on Cedar Mesa, is rich in uranium deposits.

President Biden has moved to re-instate the original boundaries in support of environmental concerns.

ATV Overkill

Off-road vehicles, or ATVs (all-terrain vehicles), have gone from being the hobby of a small group of enthusiasts to being one of the fastest-growing recreational markets in the country. Although use of ATVs is prohibited in the national parks, these dune buggies on steroids are having a huge impact on public lands adjacent to the parks and on Bureau of Land Management (BLM) lands that are currently under study for designation as wilderness. The scope of the issue is easy to measure: In 1979 there were 9,000 ATVs registered in Utah; in 2018 there were over 202,000. In addition, the power and dexterity of the machines has greatly increased. Now essentially military-style machines that can climb near-vertical cliffs and clamber over any kind of terrain, ATVs are the new "extreme sports" toy of choice, and towns like

Moab are now seeing more visitors coming to tear up the backcountry on ATVs than to mountain bike. The problem is that ATVs are extremely destructive to the delicate natural environment of the Colorado Plateau deserts and canyon lands, and the more powerful, roaring, exhaust-belching machines put even the most remote and isolated areas within reach of large numbers of potentially destructive revelers.

Between the two camps—one that would preserve the public land and protect the ancient human artifacts found in remote canyons, the other that sees public land as a playground to be zipped over at high speed—is the BLM. The Moab BLM office has seemed to favor the ATV set, abdicating its role to protect the land and environment for all. Groups like Southern Utah Wilderness Alliance (SUWA, www.suwa.org) are constantly strategizing to force the BLM to comply with its responsibility for environmental stewardship of public land.

Nonnative Species

Nonnative species don't respect park boundaries, and several nonnative animals and plants have established strongholds in Utah's national parks, altering the local ecology by outcompeting native plants and animals.

Particularly invasive plants include tamarisk (salt cedar), cheatgrass, Russian knapweed, and Russian olive. Tamarisk is often seen as the most troublesome invader. This thirsty Mediterranean plant was imported in the 1800s as an ornamental shrub and was later planted by the Department of Agriculture to slow erosion along the banks of the Colorado River in Arizona. It rapidly took hold, spreading upriver at roughly 12 miles (19.3 km) per year, and is now firmly established on all of the Colorado's tributaries, where it grows in dense stands. Tamarisk consumes a great deal of water and rarely provides the food and shelter necessary for the survival of wildlife. It also outcompetes cottonwoods because tamarisk shade inhibits the growth of cottonwood seedlings.

Courthouse Wash in Arches is one of several sites where the National Park Service has made an effort to control tamarisk. Similar control experiments have been established in nearby areas, mostly in small tributary canyons of the Colorado River.

History

The landscape isn't the only vivid aspect of Southern Utah—the area's human history is also noteworthy. This part of the West has been inhabited for over 10,000 years, and there are remnants of ancient villages and panels of mysterious rock art in now-remote canyons. More recently, colonization by Mormon settlers and the establishment of the national parks have brought attention to the human history in this dramatic corner of the Colorado Plateau.

PREHISTORY

Beginning about 15,000 years ago, nomadic groups of Paleo-Indians traveled across the Colorado Plateau in search of game animals and wild plants, but they left few traces.

Nomadic bands of hunter-gatherers roamed the Colorado Plateau for at least 5,000 years. The climate was probably cooler and wetter when these first people arrived, with both food plants and game animals more abundant than today.

Agriculture was introduced from the south about 2,000 years ago and brought about a slow transition to a settled village life. The Fremont culture emerged in the northern part of the region, including present-day Capitol Reef and Arches National Parks and Grand Staircase-Escalante National Monument, and the Ancestral Puebloans resided in the southern part (there was a settlement in present-day Zion National Park). In some areas, including Escalante and Arches, the groups lived contemporaneously. Although both groups made pots, baskets, bowls, and jewelry, only the Ancestral Puebloans constructed masonry villages. Thousands of stone dwellings, ceremonial kivas, and towers built by the Ancestral Puebloans still stand. Both groups left behind intriguing rock art, either pecked in (petroglyphs) or painted (pictographs).

The Ancestral Puebloans and Fremont people departed from this region about 800 years ago, perhaps because of drought, warfare, or disease. Some of the Ancestral Puebloans moved south and joined the Pueblo people of present-day Arizona and New Mexico. The fate of the Fremont people remains a mystery.

After the mid-1200s and until white settlers arrived in the late 1800s, small bands of nomadic Ute and Paiute moved through Southern Utah. The Navajo began to enter Utah in the early 1800s. None of the three groups established firm control of the region north of the San Juan River, where the present-day national parks are located.

SPANISH ARRIVAL

In 1776, Spanish explorers of the Dominguez-Escalante Expedition were the first Europeans to visit and describe the region. They had given up partway through a proposed journey from Santa Fe to California and returned to Santa Fe along a route passing through the sites of present-day Cedar City and Hurricane, crossing the Colorado River in a place that is now covered by Lake Powell.

The Old Spanish Trail, used from 1829 to 1848, ran through Utah to connect New Mexico with California, crossing the Colorado River near present-day Moab. Fur trappers and mountain men, including Jedediah Smith, also traveled Southern Utah's canyons in search of beaver and other animals during the early 1800s; inscriptions carved into the sandstone record their passage. In 1859

the U.S. Army's Macomb Expedition made the first documented description of what is now Canyonlands National Park. Major John Wesley Powell's pioneering river expeditions down the Green and Colorado Rivers in 1869 and 1871-1872 filled in many blank areas on the maps.

MORMON SETTLEMENT

In 1849-1850, Mormon leaders in Salt Lake City took the first steps toward colonizing Southern Utah. Parowan, now a sleepy community along I-15, became the first Mormon settlement in Southern Utah, and Cedar City the second—both were established in 1851. In 1855 a successful experiment in growing cotton along Santa Clara Creek near present-day St. George aroused considerable interest among the Mormons. New settlements soon arose in the Virgin River Valley. Poor roads hindered development, and floods, droughts, and disease, and resistance from the local Indigenous people discouraged some Mormon settlers, but many of those who stayed prospered by raising food crops and livestock.

Also in 1855, the Elk Ridge Mission was founded near present-day Moab, but it lasted only a few months. Conflict with the local Ute people resulted in three deaths and led the Mormon settlers to abandon the mission. Church members later had greater success in the Escalante area in 1876 before returning to Moab in 1877.

For sheer exertion and endurance, the efforts of the Hole-in-the-Rock Expedition of 1879-1880 are remarkable. Sixty families with 83 wagons and more than 1,000 head of livestock crossed some of the West's most rugged canyon country in an attempt to settle at Montezuma Creek on the San Juan River. They almost didn't make it: A journey expected to take six weeks turned into a six-month ordeal. The exhausted company arrived on the banks of the San Juan on April 5, 1880. Too tired to continue just 20 easy miles (32 km) to Montezuma Creek, they stayed and founded

Anasazi or Ancestral Puebloan?

As you travel through the Southwest, you may hear reference to the Anasazi, otherwise known as Ancestral Puebloans. The word *anasazi* is actually a Navajo term that archaeologists chose, thinking it meant "old people." A more literal translation is "enemy ancestors." For this reason, some consider the name inaccurate or even offensive. The terminology is in flux, and which name you hear depends on whom you're talking to or where you are. The National Park Service now uses the more descriptive term Ancestral Puebloan, and that's the term we've chosen to use in this book. These prehistoric people built masonry villages and eventually moved south to Arizona and New Mexico, where their descendants, such as the Acoma, Cochiti, Santa Clara, Taos, and Hopi Mesas, live in modern-day pueblos.

the town of Bluff. The Mormons also established other towns in southeastern Utah, relying on ranching, farming, and mining for their livelihoods. None of the communities in the region ever reached a large size; Moab is the biggest, with a current population of 5,500.

NATIONAL PARK MOVEMENT IN UTAH

In the early 1900s, people other than Native Americans, Mormon settlers, and explorers began to notice that Southern Utah was a remarkably scenic place and that it might be developed for tourism.

In 1909, President William Howard Taft issued an executive order designating Mukuntuweap (now Zion) a national monument in Zion Canyon. Roads were built to improve access, and by 1917 a tent camping resort was operating in the canyon. Two years later, Congress passed a bill forming Zion National Park. In the 1920s, the Union Pacific Railroad completed a rail line to Cedar City and Zion; Zion Lodge was built; and the technically challenging construction of the Zion-Mt. Carmel Highway, including its impressive 1.1-mile (1.8-km) tunnel, began.

Early homesteaders around Bryce took visiting friends and relatives to see the incredible rock formations, and pretty soon they found themselves in the tourism business. In 1923, when Warren G. Harding created Bryce Canyon National Monument, the Union Pacific Railroad took over the fledgling tourist camp and began building Bryce Lodge.

Tours of the hoodoos proved to be spectacularly popular, and Bryce became a national park in 1928.

Like Bryce and Zion, Arches was also helped along by railroad executives looking to develop their own businesses. In 1929 President Herbert Hoover signed the legislation creating Arches National Monument.

Capitol Reef became a national monument in 1937, under President Franklin Roosevelt, and for years it was loved passionately by a handful of Utah archaeology buffs but largely ignored by the federal government, which put it under the administrative control of Zion National Park.

During the 1960s the National Park Service responded to a huge increase in park visitation nationwide by expanding facilities, spurring Congress to change the status of several national monuments to national parks. Canyonlands became a national park in the 1960s, and after a spate of uranium prospecting in the nuclear-giddy 1950s, Capitol Reef and Arches gained national park status in 1971.

As visitors continued to flood the parks during the 1980s and 1990s, park managers realized they needed to develop strategies to deal with the crowds, especially the traffic. New trails, campgrounds, and visitors centers were built, and Zion and Bryce have both made attempts to control traffic on their scenic roads.

In 1996, President Bill Clinton used provisions of the Antiquities Act to establish the Grand Staircase-Escalante National

Monument, a sudden announcement that angered many locals, as it limited possible development in these areas. This vast tract, which totaled nearly 1.9 million acres, was the largest national monument land grouping in the Lower 48, bringing together Department of the Interior management land previously administered by the Bureau of Land Management, the U.S. Forest Service, and the State of Utah.

President Barack Obama used similar provisions in 2016 to create the Bears Ears National Monument to protect 1.35 million acres of land rich in ancient Ancestral Puebloan sites. Both these national monuments were greatly reduced in size and divided into much smaller units under executive orders issued by President Donald Trump in 2018.

The People

One of the oddest statistics about Utah is that it's the most urban state in the country. According to 2015 statistics from the U.S. Census Bureau, 88.4 percent of Utah's nearly 3 million residents live in cities and towns rather than unincorporated areas. That means that there aren't many people in remote Southern Utah. With the exception of St. George, Cedar City, Kanab, and Moab, there are no sizable communities in this part of the state. Even the undaunted Mormon settlers found this a forbidding place to settle during their 19th-century agrarian colonization of Utah.

Moab is known as a youthful and dynamic town, and its mountain bikers set the civic tone more than the Mormon Church. However, outside Moab, most small ranching communities in southeastern Utah are still deeply Mormon. It's a good idea to develop an understanding of Utah's predominant religion if you plan on spending any time here outside the parks.

LATTER-DAY SAINTS

One of the first things to know is that the term *Mormon* is rarely used by church members themselves. The church's proper title is the Church of Jesus Christ of Latter-Day Saints, and members prefer to be called Latter-Day Saints, Saints (usually this term is just used among church members), or LDS. While calling someone a Mormon isn't wrong, it's not quite as respectful.

The religion is based in part on the Book of Mormon, the name given to a text derived from a set of golden plates found by Joseph Smith in 1827 in western New York State. Smith claimed to have been led by an angel to the plates, which were covered with a text written in "reformed Egyptian." A farmer by upbringing, Smith translated the plates and published an English-language version of the Book of Mormon in 1830.

The Book of Mormon tells the story of the lost tribes of Israel, which, according to Mormon teachings, migrated to North America and became the ancestors of today's Native Americans. According to the Book of Mormon, Jesus also journeyed to North America, and the book includes teachings and prophecies that Christ supposedly gave to the ancient Native Americans.

The most stirring and unifying aspect of Mormon history is the incredible westward migration made by the small, fiercely dedicated band of Mormon pioneers in the 1840s. Smith and his followers were persecuted in New York and then in their newly founded utopian communities in Ohio, Missouri, and Illinois. After Smith was murdered near Carthage, Illinois, in 1844, the group decided to press even farther westward toward the frontier, led by church president Brigham Young. The journey across the then very Wild West to the Great Salt Lake basin was made by horse, wagon, or handcart—hundreds of Mormon pioneers pulled their belongings across the Great Plains in small carts. The first group of Mormon pioneers reached what is now the Salt Lake City area in 1847. The bravery and tenacity of the group's two-year migration forms the basis of many Utah residents' fierce pride in their state and their religion.

Most people know that LDS members are clean-living, family-focused people who eschew alcohol, tobacco, and stimulants, including caffeine. This can make it a little tough for visitors to feed their own vices, and indeed, it may make what formerly seemed like a normal habit feel a little more sinister. But Utah has loosened up a lot in the last couple decades, and it's really not too hard to find a place to have a beer with dinner, although you may have to make a special request. Towns near the national parks are particularly used to hosting non-Mormons, and residents attach virtually no stigma to others waking up with a cup of coffee or winding down with a glass of wine.

SOUTHERN UTAH'S NATIVE AMERICANS

It's an oddity of history that most visitors to Utah's national parks will see much more evidence of the state's ancient Indigenous residents—in the form of eerie rock art, stone pueblos, and storehouses—than they will of today's remaining Native Americans. The prehistoric residents of the canyons of southeastern Utah left their mark on the land but largely moved on. The fate of the ancient Fremont people has been lost to history, and the abandonment of Ancestral Puebloan villages is a mystery still being unearthed by archaeologists. When the Mormons arrived in the 1840s, isolated bands of Native Americans lived in the river canyons. Federal reservations were granted to several of these groups.

Ute

Several bands of Utes, or Núuci, ranged over large areas of central and eastern Utah

and adjacent Colorado. Originally hunter-gatherers, they acquired horses around 1800 and became skilled raiders. Customs adopted from Plains people included the use of rawhide, tepees, and the travois, a sled used to carry goods. The discovery of gold in southern Colorado and the pressures of farmers there and in Utah forced the Utes to move and renegotiate treaties many times. They now have the large Uintah and Ouray Indian Reservation in northeast Utah, the small White Mesa Indian Reservation in southeast Utah, and the Ute Mountain Indian Reservation in southwest Colorado and northwest New Mexico.

Southern Paiute

Six of the 19 major bands of Southern Paiutes, or Nuwuvi, lived along the Santa Clara, Beaver, and Virgin Rivers and in other parts of southwest Utah. Historically, extended families hunted and gathered food together. Fishing and the cultivation of corn, beans, squash, and sunflowers supplemented the diet of most of the communities. Today, Utah's Paiutes have their headquarters in Cedar City and scattered small parcels of reservation land. Southern Paiutes also live in southern Nevada and northern Arizona.

Navajo

Calling themselves Diné, the Navajo moved into the San Juan River area around 1600. The Navajo have proved exceptionally adaptable to learning new skills from other cultures: Many Navajo crafts, clothing, and religious practices have come from Native American, Spanish, and Anglo neighbors. The Navajo were the first in the area to move away from hunting and gathering lifestyles, relying instead on the farming and shepherding techniques they had learned from the Spanish. The Navajo are one of the largest Native American groups in the country, with 16 million acres of exceptionally scenic land in southeast Utah and adjacent Arizona and New Mexico. The Navajo Nation's headquarters is at Window Rock, Arizona.

Essentials

Getting There

If you're driving from other points in North America, Utah is easy to reach. The parks are east of I-15, which runs parallel to the Rocky Mountains from Montana to Southern California. And they're south of I-70, which links Denver to I-15.

International travelers flying into the region have numerous options. Salt Lake City is convenient as a terminus for travelers who want to make a road-trip loop tour through all of Utah's parks. For other travelers, Utah's national parks may be best seen as part of a longer U.S. road trip. Many European travelers fly into Denver, rent vehicles

or RVs, cross the Rocky Mountains, and explore the parks of Southern Utah and perhaps the Grand Canyon on the way to Las Vegas, whence they return. Las Vegas is also handy as an air hub, particularly if travelers are focused on Zion and Bryce parks.

Public transportation, except for regularly scheduled flights, is almost nonexistent in Southern Utah and the parks; you'll need your own vehicle to explore the area.

FROM SALT LAKE CITY

Many tours of Utah's national parks begin in Salt Lake City. Its busy airport and plethora of hotels make it an easy place to begin and end a trip.

Airport

Salt Lake City is a hub for Delta Airlines, and all other major airlines have regular flights into Salt Lake City International Airport (SLC, 776 N. Terminal Dr., 801/575-2400, https://slcairport.com). The airport is an easy 7 miles (11.3 km) west of downtown; reach it via I-80 or North Temple Boulevard or take the Green Line TRAX light rail train operated by the Utah Transit Authority (UTA, www.rideuta.com).

SkyWest Airlines (800/453-9417, www.skywest.com), Delta's and United's commuter partner, flies to Cedar City and St. George in Utah and to towns in adjacent states. SkyWest also offers flights between Canyonlands Field (CNY, U.S. 191, 16 mi/25.7 km north of Moab, 435/259-4849) and Denver.

The Salt Lake City airport has three terminals; in each you'll find a ground transportation information desk, restaurants, motel and hotel courtesy phones, and car rentals (all the major companies are either on-site or a short shuttle ride away). Terminal 2 houses Zion's First National Bank for currency exchange. Terminal 3 is dedicated to international arrivals and departures.

Train

The only passenger train through Salt Lake City is Amtrak's California Zephyr, which heads west to Reno and Oakland and east to Denver and Chicago three times a week. Amtrak (station 340 S. 600 W., 800/872-7245, www.amtrak.com) prices tickets as airlines do, with special seasonal fares and advance-booking and other discounts. Amtrak office hours are irregular and timed to meet the trains, so call first.

Long-Distance Bus

Salt Lake City is at a crossroads of several major highways and has good bus service from Greyhound (160 W. South Temple St., 801/355-9579 or 800/231-2222, www.greyhound.com). Generally speaking, buses run north and south along I-15 and east and west along I-80; you won't be able to take the bus to any of Utah's national parks.

Car

From Salt Lake City, it's a long 238-mile drive to Moab, the center for exploring Arches and Canyonlands National Parks. The fastest route takes you south from Salt Lake City on I-15, cutting east at Spanish Fork on U.S. 6/89 to Price, south to Green River and I-70, and then to Moab on U.S. 191. Dramatic scenery highlights the entire length of this four-hour drive. To get to Zion and Bryce, simply take I-15 south from Salt Lake City; driving time is about four hours.

You'll find all of the major car rental companies at the Salt Lake City airport (www.slcairport.com).

RV and Motorcycle Rentals

Expect to pay $1,200-1,800 per week to rent an RV, depending on the season and the size of the vehicle; small travel trailers are less expensive but are frequently unavailable.

Access RV Rental (2240 S. State St., Salt Lake City, 801/936-1200 or 800/327-6910,

Utah Driving Distances

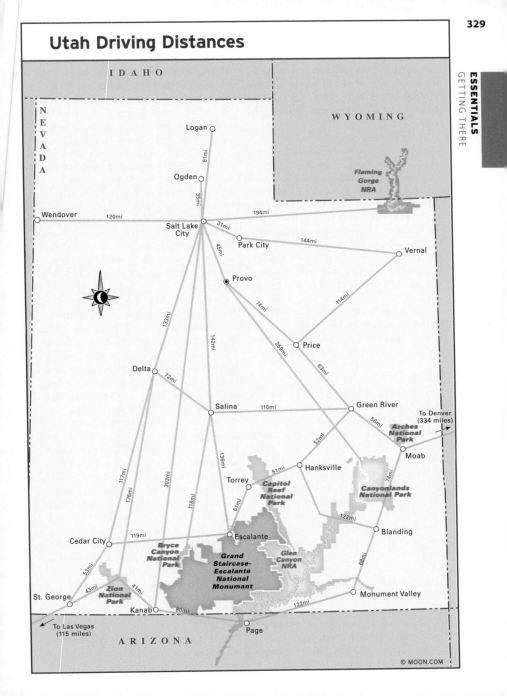

© MOON.COM

http://accessrvrental.com) is a local company with relatively good rates on RV rentals. **Cruise America** (4125 S. State St., Salt Lake City, 801/288-0930, www.cruiseamerica.com) is a larger company with RV rentals available. **El Monte RV** (3490 W. 1820 S., Salt Lake City, 888/337-2214, www.elmonterv.com) also provides rentals.

For automobile campers not quite ready to join the RV set, a popular option is the camper van experience. Camper vans are smaller than RVs and can be parked in regular tent parking spots in most campgrounds, with artfully designed sleeping spaces within the body of the van. These vans typically come with bedding, a propane stove, cooking gear, and camp chairs. **Basecamper Vans** (423 E. 600 S., Salt Lake City, 801/938-4433, www.basecampervans.com) offers several lines of camper vans, with prices starting at $99 per day.

Rent a motorcycle from **EagleRider/ Harley-Davidson of Salt Lake City** (2900 S. State St., Sandy, 385/831-7253, www.eaglerider.com, from $99 per day).

Food

If you're going to be camping on your trip through southeastern Utah's national parks, you may want to pick up some provisions in Salt Lake City before hitting the road south. Just east of I-15, off I-80 in the Sugar House district, **Whole Foods Market** (1131 E. Wilmington Ave., 801/359-7913) has a good deli, lots of organic produce, bulk foods, and good bread (likely the last you'll see for a while). It's in a complex that also contains some good restaurants, a camping supply store, and the brightest, shiniest tattoo parlor you'll ever lay eyes on.

Downtown, stop at **Tony Caputo Market & Deli** (308 W. Broadway, 801/531-8669, www.caputosdeli.com, 9am-7pm Mon.-Sat., 10am-5pm Sun.), an old-style Italian deli brimming with delicious sausages, cheeses, and olives. Don't forget to get a sandwich to go.

Red Iguana (736 W. North Temple St., 801/322-1489, www.rediguana.com,

11am-10pm Mon.-Thurs., 11am-11pm Fri., 10am-11pm Sat., 10am-9pm Sun., $8-22), on the way in from the airport, is one of the city's favorite Mexican restaurants and offers excellent south-of-the-border cooking with a specialty in Mayan and regional foods. Best of all, the flavors are crisp, fresh, and earthy. The Red Iguana is very popular, so arrive early—especially at lunch—to avoid the lines.

The Copper Onion (111 E. Broadway, 801/355-3282, http://thecopperonion.com, 4pm-9pm Wed.-Sun., $12-29) always gets a mention when people talk about the best restaurant in Salt Lake City. Emphasizing full-flavored New American cooking, the Copper Onion offers a choice of small and large plates, with such delights as a pork chop with farro, wild mushrooms and pumpkin seed vinaigrette. For the quality, the prices are very reasonable.

In the Hotel Monaco, **Bambara** (202 S. Main St., 801/363-5454, www.bambara-slc.com, 5pm-9pm Tues.-Sat., $20-25) has a menu that emphasizes the freshest and most flavorful local meats and produce, with preparations in a wide-awake New American style that is equal parts tradition and innovation.

Utah's oldest brewpub is **Squatters Pub Brewery** (147 W. Broadway, 801/363-2739, www.squatters.com, noon-8pm Sun.-Wed., noon-9pm Thurs., noon-10pm Fri.-Sat., $8-18). In addition to fine beers and ales, the pub serves sandwiches, burgers, and other light entrées in a handsome old warehouse. In summer there's seating on the back deck. Another popular brewpub is the **Red Rock Brewing Company** (254 S. 200 W., 801/521-7446, www.redrockbrewing.com, 11:30am-8pm Sun.-Thurs., 11:30am-10pm Fri.-Sat., $10-20), offering pasta, salads, and sandwiches, including an excellent variation on the hamburger, baked in a wood-fired oven inside a bread pocket.

Accommodations

Salt Lake City has many hotel rooms across all price categories. We've included a few of our favorites here. Although most aren't airport hotels, the airport is pretty easy to get to from all of them.

If you're driving into town and just want to find a hotel room fast, head south and west of downtown, where chain hotels proliferate. The area around 600 South and 200 West is especially fertile ground for mid-priced hotels.

UNDER $50

The Avenues Hostel (107 F St., 801/363-3855, www.saltlakehostel.com, $27-47, only half have private baths), 1 mile (1.6 km) east of Temple Square, offers lodging with the use of a kitchen, a TV room, and laundry. Information-packed bulletin boards list city sights and goings-on, and you'll meet travelers from all over the world. Reservations (with first night's deposit) are advised in the busy summer travel and winter ski seasons. From downtown, head east on South Temple Street to F Street, then turn north and go two blocks.

$50-100

One of the most affordable lodging options in central Salt Lake City is the **Metropolitan Inn** (524 S. West Temple St., 801/531-7100, www.metropolitaninn.com, $72-110), with clean simple rooms, an outdoor pool, guest laundry, and buffet breakfast.

$100-150

If you're looking for comfortable rooms without breaking the bank, the ★ **Little America Hotel and Towers** (500 S. Main St., 801/363-6781 or 800/304-8970, http://saltlake.littleamerica.com, $110-269) is a great place to stay. This large lodging complex, with nearly 850 guest rooms, offers three types of rooms: Courtside rooms and garden suites are scattered around the hotel's nicely manicured grounds, with most guest rooms overlooking a pool or a fountain. Tower suites are executive-level suites in a 17-story block offering some of SLC's best views. All guests share the hotel's elegant public areas, two pools, health club, and workout facility. The restaurant is better than average, and there is free airport transfer.

Another of the nicer-for-the-money hotels in this part of Salt Lake City is the **Crystal Inn** (230 W. 500 S., 801/328-4466 or 800/366-4466, www.crystalinnsaltlake.com, $146-191). Guest rooms are very large and nicely furnished; all come with fridges and microwaves. There's a free hot breakfast buffet for all guests. For recreation, there's an indoor pool, an exercise room, a sauna, and a hot tub.

On the campus of the University of Utah, the **University Guest House and Conference Center** (110 S. Ft. Douglas Blvd., 801/587-1000 or 888/416-4075, www.universityguesthouse.com, $155-186) is a good choice if you want a comfortable room, free parking, and nice walks in the neighborhood (check out the Red Butte Garden). Good restaurants are nearby, and downtown is a short drive or light-rail trip away.

At the **DoubleTree by Hilton SLC Airport** (5151 Wiley Post Way, 801/539-1515 or 800/999-3736, www.hilton.com, $95-179), guest rooms are spacious and nicely furnished, and facilities include two pools, a putting green, a sports court, and an exercise room and whirlpool. The hotel even has its own lake. Practically next door to the airport terminal is the **Ramada Salt Lake City Airport** (5575 W. Amelia Earhart Dr., 801/537-7020 or 800/272-6232, www.ramada.com, $79-109), with a pool and a spa.

OVER $150

If you really want to do Salt Lake City in style, two downtown hotels are good places to splurge. **Hotel Monaco** (15 W. 200 S., 801/595-0000 or 877/294-9710, www.monaco-saltlakecity.com, $236-305) occupies a grandly renovated historic office building in a convenient spot in the middle of downtown; on the main floor is Bambara, one of the most sophisticated restaurants in Utah. Guest rooms are sumptuously furnished with real élan. Facilities include an on-site fitness center, meeting rooms, and concierge and valet services. Pets are welcome, and if you forgot your own pet, the hotel will deliver a companion goldfish to your room.

The gigantic **Grand America Hotel and Suites** (75 E. 600 S., 800/533-3525, www. grandamerica.com, $339-414) is Salt Lake City's take on the Vegas fantasy hotel. A block square (that's 10 acres in this land of long blocks), its 24 stories contain 775 guest rooms, more than half of them suites. Guest rooms have luxury-level amenities; expect all the perks and niceties that modern hotels can offer. On the campus of the University of Utah, the **Salt Lake City Marriott University Park Hotel** (480 Wakara Way, 801/581-1000 or 800/637-4390, www.marriott. com, $200-256) is one of the city's best-kept secrets for luxurious lodgings in a lovely setting. You can't miss with the views: All guest rooms either overlook the city or look onto the soaring peaks of the Wasatch Range, directly behind the hotel. Guest rooms are very nicely appointed—the suites are some of the best in the city. All guest rooms have minibars, fridges, and coffeemakers; there's an exercise room, and bicycles are available for rent.

Camping

Of the several commercial campgrounds around the periphery of Salt Lake City, **Salt Lake City KOA** (1400 W. North Temple St., 801/328-0224, www.koa.com, year-round, from $37 tents, from $64-84 RVs) is the most convenient, located between downtown and the airport. It offers showers, a swimming pool, a game room, a playground, a store, and laundry. From I-15 northbound, take exit 311 for I-80; go west 1.3 miles (2.1 km) on I-80, exit north for 0.5 mile (0.8 km) on Redwood Road (Hwy. 68), then turn right and continue another 0.5 mile (0.8 km) on North Temple Street. From I-15 southbound, take exit 313 and go south 1.5 miles (2.4 km) on 900 West, then turn right and drive less than 1 mile (1.6 km) on North Temple Street. From I-80, either take the North Temple exit or the one for Redwood Road (Hwy. 68).

There are two good U.S. Forest Service campgrounds in Big Cottonwood Canyon, about 15 miles (24. km) southeast of downtown Salt Lake City, and another two in Little Cottonwood Canyon, about 19 miles (31 km) southeast of town. All have drinking water, and all prohibit pets because of local watershed regulations; rates range $19-23, and some can be reserved (877/444-6777, www. recreation.gov, reservation fee $9 online, $10 phone). In Big Cottonwood Canyon, **Spruces Campground** (9.1 mi/14.7 km up the canyon, elevation 7,400 ft/2,253 m) is open early June-mid-October. The season at **Redman Campground** (elev. 8,300 ft/2,530 m, first come, first served) is mid-June-early October. It's between Solitude and Brighton, 14 mi/22.5 km up Big Cottonwood Canyon. Little Cottonwood Canyon's **Tanners Flat Campground** (4.3 mi/6.9 km up the canyon, elev. 7,200 ft/2,195 m, first come, first served) is open mid-May-mid-October. **Albion Basin Campground** (elev. 9,500 ft/2,895 m), first come, first served) is high in the mountains a few miles past Alta Ski Area and is open early July-late September; go 11 miles (17.7 km) up the canyon (the last 2.5 mi/4 km are gravel).

FROM LAS VEGAS

Just because you're going to the Southern Utah national parks, don't assume it's best to fly into Salt Lake City. If you're traveling to Zion, Bryce, or the Grand Staircase-Escalante region, consider flying into Las Vegas rather than Salt Lake City. Not only is it closer to these parks, but car rentals are usually about $100 a week cheaper. Even if you have absolutely no interest in gambling, many casino hotels have good midweek rates.

Airport

McCarran International Airport (LAS, 5757 Wayne Newton Blvd., 702/261-5743, www.mccarran.com) is just a few minutes east of the Strip (aka Las Vegas Blvd. S.), the 6-mile (9.7-km) stretch of casinos and hotels.

Las Vegas is well served by major domestic airlines, and also by smaller or "no-frills" carriers such as **Frontier Airlines** (800/432-1359, www.frontierairlines.com), **Spirit Airlines** (800/772-7117, www.spirit.com), and **Southwest Airlines** (800/435-9792, www.

southwest.com), whose bargain prices keep the other airlines competitive.

The airport has two terminals—Terminal 1 has most of the domestic traffic, while the massive new high-tech Terminal 3 serves international and charter flights. Exchange foreign currency in Terminal 3; find full-service banking and check-in for some of the larger casino hotels in Terminal 1. Slot machines, of course, are everywhere.

Long-Distance Bus

Greyhound (220 S. Main St., 702/383-9792, www.greyhound.com) serves communities along I-15, including St. George.

Car

From Las Vegas, it's just 120 miles (193 km) northeast on I-15 to St. George, with Zion just 43 miles (69 km) farther.

It's relatively inexpensive to rent a car in Las Vegas; an economy car will run about $140 per week, before taxes. At the airport, find **Avis** (702/261-5591 or 800/331-1212), **Budget** (800/922-2899), **Dollar** (702/739-8403 or 800/800-4000), **Hertz** (702/736-4900 or 800/654-3131), **National** (702/261-5391 or 800/227-7368), **Payless** (702/736-6147 or 800/729-5377), **Alamo** (800/462-5266), and **Thrifty** (702/896-7600 or 800/367-2277).

Rent a campervan from **Escape Campervan** (5875 Service Ct., 877/270-8267, www.escapecampervans.com) or **JUCY** (5895 Boulder Hwy., 800/650-4180, www.jucyusa. com, $60-177 per day).

RV Rentals

Rent an RV from **Cruise America** (551 N. Gibson Rd., Henderson, 888/980-8282, www. cruiseamerica.com). **El Monte RV** (3800 Boulder Hwy., 702/269-8000 or 888/337-2214, www.elmonterv.com) is another good bet. Rates typically start at about $1,200 a week.

Food

As celebrity chefs from around the country have established outposts in various upscale casinos, Las Vegas has become a destination for fine dining. Nearly every casino hotel has multiple restaurants, and sometimes multiple fine-dining restaurants. For instance, at the MGM Grand (3799 Las Vegas Blvd. S., 702/891-7374, www.mgmgrand.com), there's both **Craftsteak** for the high-end steak house experience, courtesy of Tom Colicchio, and **Joel Robuchon,** the eponymous restaurant of the renowned French chef. And talk about an embarrassment of riches—at the Venetian Hotel (3355 Las Vegas Blvd. S., 702/414-3737, www.venetian.com), Emeril Lagasse owns the **Delmonico,** a steak house that goes well above and beyond your basic rib eye; Thomas Keller has **Bouchon,** promising high-end Napa Valley dining; and Wolfgang Puck operates **CUT.**

Expect main courses at all of these restaurants to be $30-40 and up. Dine less expensively on a selection of appetizers.

Accommodations

For its sheer number of hotel rooms, Las Vegas can't be beat. Even if you have no desire to visit Vegas, it may make sense to spend the first or final night of your trip here. During the week, it's relatively easy to find a good rate at a casino hotel. However, beware of weekends if you're watching your pennies: on Saturday night, rooms often cost triple what they cost during the week. Reservation services, such as **Las Vegas Convention and Visitor Authority** (702/892-0711, www.lasvegas. com), may be able to help you find a good deal on a room. Most of the major casino hotels (Caesar's Palace, New York New York, the Venetian, and others) have guest rooms for over $200, but specials in the $60-80 range are easy to find. You'll find them listed on reservation services, which makes it easy to locate a room that suits your taste and budget.

For budget rooms, about 1 mile (1.6 km) from the airport, and not too far off the south end of the Strip, find the **Ambassador Strip Travelodge** (5075 Koval Lane, 702/736-3600 or 888/844-3131, $48 weekdays, $90 weekends). This motel, with an outdoor pool and continental breakfast included, is a good alternative to a casino hotel. Just a little more expensive and also off the Strip near the airport is the **Best Western McCarran Inn** (4970 Paradise Rd., 702/798-5530 or 800/626-7575, www.bestwestern.com, $98-128 weekdays, $107-138 weekends).

FROM DENVER

Although it may not seem intuitive to start your tour of Utah's national parks in Denver, that's exactly what works best for many folks, especially those who fly from European capital cities to Denver International Airport. From there, it's easy to rent a car or RV and begin a tour that typically includes Rocky Mountain National Park, Utah's five national parks, and the Grand Canyon before terminating at Las Vegas.

Airport

Locals joke that **Denver International Airport** (DEN, 8500 Peña Blvd., 303/342-2000, www.flydenver.com), often referred to as DIA, is in Kansas; it's actually 23 miles (37 km) northeast of downtown Denver on Highway 470, north of I-70. Major airlines using DIA include American, British Airways, Delta, and United.

DIA's Jeppesen Terminal has a giant atrium and three concourses connected by a light-rail train. Car-rental counters are in the central terminal atrium between security screening areas.

Car

To drive from Denver to the parks, follow I-70 west, up over the Continental Divide along the Rocky Mountains, and down to the Colorado River. Cross into Utah and take I-70 exit 212 at Cisco. From Denver to Cisco is 297 miles (478 km), all on the freeway. From Cisco, follow Highway 128 for 37 highly scenic miles (60 km) through red-rock canyons to Moab. Allow 5.5 hours of driving time between Moab and Denver.

All major car rental agencies have facilities near DIA.

RV Rentals

Regional corporations with offices in Denver include **Cruise America** (8950 N. Federal Blvd., Denver, 303/650-2865, www.cruiseamerica.com) and **El Monte RV** (5989 Main St., Louviers, 303/426-7998 or 888/337-2214, www.elmonterv.com).

Food

Denver has a large Hispanic population, so it's no surprise that there are lots of Latin American restaurants, and these are often good and reliable places for inexpensive meals. Indeed, some of Denver's most exciting restaurants are Nuevo Latin American restaurants—where familiar tacos, tortillas, and enchiladas are updated into zippy fine dining. One of the best is **Lola** (1575 Boulder St., 720/570-8686, www.loladenver.com, 4pm-10pm Mon.-Thurs., 4pm-11pm Fri., 10am-11pm Sat., 10am-9pm Sun., entrées under $25), a hip and happening restaurant with over 150 tequilas to choose from and main courses like grilled pork with habanero sauce. Guacamole is prepared table-side. More upscale is **Tamayo** (1400 Larimer St., 720/946-1433, www.richardsandoval.com, noon-8pm Tues.-Thurs., noon-10pm Fri., 11am-10pm Sat., 11am-8pm Sun., entrées $20-28), a hybrid of French refinement and zesty Mexican flavors. Views from this rooftop dining room overlook Larimer Square and the Rockies, making it a top spot for margaritas and appetizers, particularly the excellent shrimp tacos.

The **Barolo Grill** (3030 E. 6th Ave., 303/393-1040, http://barologrilldenver.com, 5:30pm-9:30pm Tues.-Thurs., 5pm-10pm Fri.-Sat., $15-30) is a comfortable northern Italian restaurant with good salads and pasta as well as grilled fish, game, and chicken main courses. The wine list is outstanding. Denver is known for its steak houses, and one of the best is the **Capital Grille** (1450 Larimer St., 303/539-2500, www.thecapitalgrille.com, 11am-10pm Mon.-Thurs., 11am-11pm Fri., 4:30pm-11pm Sat., 4pm-9pm Sun., $19-40), with swank surroundings, an attentive staff, and excellent steaks, prime rib, and chops. For a lighter meal, go to **Falling Rock Tap House** (1919 Blake St., 303/293-8338, http://fallingrocktaphouse.com, 5pm-10pm Thurs., 5pm-11pm Fri., noon-11pm Sat., noon-8pm Sun., $8-20), one of Denver's top regional beer pubs, with over 75 brews on tap and tasty pub grub.

Accommodations

Chain hotels have set up shop in the area surrounding DIA. Almost all offer shuttles to and from the airport.

For budget travelers, the **11th Avenue Hotel and Hostel** (1112 N. Broadway, 303/861-7777, http://innkeeperrockies.com, $33 dorm, $66-99 pp private rooms) is a 1903 hotel on the edge of downtown that's

now a blend of hotel and hostel. Facilities include laundry, Internet access, and cable TV. There's no kitchen, but guests have access to a barbecue grill, microwave, and toaster oven.

The closest lodgings to DIA are about 6 miles (10 km) from the airport. The **DIA Microtel Inn** (18600 E. 63rd Ave., 303/371-8300 or 800/771-7171, www.microtelinn.com, $109-179) includes breakfast. The **Quality Inn** (6890 Tower Rd., 303/371-5300 or 877/424-6423, www.qualityinn.com, $85-189) is easy to find north of I-70 exit 286. About 12 miles (19 km) south of the airport, near the intersection of I-70 and Peña Boulevard, is a cluster of chain motels, including **Red Lion Inn and Suites** (16921 E. 32nd Ave., 303/367-5000, www.redlion.com, $109-139).

Getting Around

For most travelers, getting around Southern Utah requires using some form of automobile. Public transportation is nonexistent between the parks, and distances are great—although the parks cover a relatively compact area, the geography of the land is so contorted that there are few roads that connect the dots. For instance, from Moab to the Arizona border, nearly 130 miles (209 km), only one bridge crosses the Colorado River once it drops into its canyon. Cars are easily rented in gateway cities, and in towns like Moab there is a plethora of jeep and Humvee rentals as well.

Bicycle touring is certainly an excellent option, but cyclists need to be in good shape and be prepared for intense heat during summer trips. For detailed information on cycling Utah, read the classic *Bicycle Touring in Utah* by Dennis Coello, now out of print but available from libraries and used from online sources.

becomes intuitive. A city's address grid will generally have its temple at the center, with blocks numbered by hundreds out in every direction. For instance, 100 West is one block west of the center of town, then comes 200 West, and so on. In conversation, you may hear the shorthand "4th South," "3rd West," and so on to indicate 400 South or 300 West.

While this street-numbering system is a picture of precision, it's also confusing at first. All addresses have four parts: When you see the address 436 North 100 West, for instance, the system tells you that the address will be found four blocks north of the center of town, on 100 West. One rule of thumb is to remember that the last two segments of an address (300 South, 500 East, 2300 West) are the street's actual name—the equivalent of a single street signifier such as Oak Street or Front Avenue.

STREET NUMBERING AND GRID ADDRESSES

Many towns founded by Mormon settlers share a street-numbering scheme that can be confusing to first-time visitors but quickly

TRAVELING BY RV

Traveling the Southwest's national parks in an RV is a time-honored tradition, and travelers will have no problem finding RV rentals in major cities like Denver, Salt Lake City, and Las Vegas, which serve as gateways to the parks of Southern Utah. The parks have good campgrounds, and towns like Moab and Springdale have some very spiffy campground options with extras like swimming pools and fine-dining cookouts. Note that some parks limit RV access—during high season, no vehicles are allowed in Zion, where shuttle buses have replaced private vehicles along the scenic Zion Canyon Road. In Bryce, vehicles measuring 20 feet/6 meters or longer are restricted from the Bryce Amphitheater area during shuttle hours.

DRIVING THE PARKS

During the summer, patience is the key to driving in Utah's national parks. Roads are often crowded with slow-moving RVs, and traffic jams are not uncommon.

If you're traveling on back roads, especially in the Grand Staircase-Escalante area, make sure you have plenty of gas, even if it means paying top dollar at a small-town gas pump.

Summer heat in the desert puts an extra strain on both cars and drivers. It's worth double-checking your vehicle's cooling system, engine oil, transmission fluid, fan belts, and tires to make sure they are in top condition. Carry several gallons of water in case of a breakdown or radiator trouble. Never leave children or pets in a parked car during warm weather; temperatures inside can cause fatal heatstroke in minutes.

At times the desert has too much water, when late-summer storms frequently flood low spots in the road. Wait for the water level to subside before crossing. Dust storms can completely block visibility but tend to be short-lived. During such storms, pull completely off the road, stop, and turn off your lights so as not to confuse other drivers. Radio stations carry frequent weather updates when weather hazards exist.

If stranded, stay with your vehicle unless you're positive of where to go for help, then leave a note explaining your route and departure time. Airplanes can easily spot a stranded car (tie a piece of cloth to your antenna), but a person walking is more difficult to see. It's best to carry emergency supplies: blankets or sleeping bags, a first-aid kit, tools, jumper cables, a shovel, traction mats or chains, a flashlight, rain gear, water, food, and a can opener.

Maps

The Utah Department of Transportation prints and distributes a free, regularly updated map of Utah. Ask for it when you call for information or when you stop at a visitor information office. Benchmark Maps' *Utah Road and Recreation Atlas* is loaded with beautiful maps, recreation information, and global positioning system (GPS) grids. If you're planning on extensive backcountry exploration, be sure to ask locally about conditions.

If you're looking for USGS topo maps, you can download them for free at www.topozone.com.

Off-Road Driving

Here are some tips for safely traversing the backcountry in a vehicle (preferably one with four-wheel drive):

- Drive slowly enough to choose a safe path and avoid obstacles such as rocks or giant potholes, but keep up enough speed to propel yourself through sand or mud.

- Keep an eye on the route ahead of you. If there are obstacles, stop, get out of your vehicle, and survey the situation.

- Reduce the tire pressure if you're driving across sand.

- Drive directly up or down the fall line of a slope. Cutting across diagonally may seem less frightening, but it puts you in a position to slide or roll over.

If you really want to learn to drive your 4WD rig, consider signing up for a class.

Charging Your Electric Car

Electric vehicle (EV) charging stations are present in some areas of Southern Utah, but

Visitor Information

General tourism literature and maps are available from the Utah Travel Council (Council Hall/Capitol Hill, Salt Lake City, UT 84114-7420, tel. 801/538-1030, fax 801/538-1399, www.utah.com). Call or write in advance of your visit to obtain maps and brochures from the parks.

Arches National Park
P.O. Box 907
Moab, UT 84532-0907
435/719-2299
www.nps.gov/arch

Bryce Canyon National Park
P.O. Box 640201
Bryce Canyon, UT 84764-0201
435/834-5322
www.nps.gov/brca

Canyonlands National Park
2282 SW Resource Blvd.
Moab, UT 84532-3298
435/719-2100
www.nps.gov/cany

Capitol Reef National Park
HC 70 Box 15
Torrey, UT 84775-9602
435/425-3791
www.nps.gov/care

Grand Staircase, Kaiparowits Plateau, and Escalante Canyons Units
669 S. U.S. 89A
Kanab, UT 84741
435/644-1200
www.ut.blm.gov/monument

Zion National Park
Springdale, UT 84767-1099
435/772-3256
www.nps.gov/zion

if you plan to explore far-flung destinations, a little preplanning is in order. EV charging stations are available at St. George, Cedar City, Springdale, the visitors center at Zion

National Park, Ruby's Inn (near Bryce Canyon National Park), Green River, St. George, Kanab, Moab, Blanding, and Page, Arizona. That leaves big areas of southeast Utah with no EV charging services.

SHUTTLES

Both Zion and Bryce National Parks offer shuttle bus service during peak seasons along their primary entrance roads to reduce traffic and vehicular impact on the parks. In Zion, shuttles pick up visitors at various points around Springdale and take them to the park gate, where another shuttle runs park visitors up Zion Canyon Road, stopping at trailheads, scenic overlooks, and Zion Lodge. Essentially, private cars are no longer allowed on Zion Canyon Road during peak season. (Registered overnight guests at Zion Lodge can drive their own vehicles to the hotel.)

In Bryce, the shuttle bus picks up visitors at the park gate and drives the length of the main parkway, making stops at all the major trailheads and vista points in addition to campgrounds, Ruby's Inn, and the Bryce Canyon Lodge. Using the shuttle bus is not required in Bryce, unless your vehicle is 20 feet (6 m) or longer and you're visiting the Bryce Amphitheater, although it is highly recommended.

TOURS

Bus tours of the Southern Utah national parks, often in conjunction with Grand Canyon National Park, are available from several regional tour companies. Southern Utah Scenic Tours (435/656-1504 or 888/404-8687, http://utahscenictours.com) offers multiday scenic and thematic tours of the Southwest, including the Utah national parks.

Road Scholar (800/454-5768, www.roadscholar.org) operates programs out of St. George, including a bus tour of Southern Utah and northern Arizona's national parks and monuments. These trips are geared toward older adults (this is the organization formerly known as Elderhostel) and involve a bit of easy hiking.

For a truly unusual bus tour, consider the **Adventure Bus** (375 S. Main St., Moab, 909/633-7225 or 888/737-5263, www. adventurebus.com), a bus that's had most of its seats removed to make lounge and sleeping areas. Guests live on the bus (some meals are provided) as it makes tours of Utah and other Southwest hot spots.

Recreation

Utah's national parks are home to epic landscapes—red-rock canyons, towering arches, and needles of sandstone that are best explored by foot, by bike, or on the water. Hikers will find a variety of trails, ranging from paved all-abilities paths to remote backcountry tracks. Rafts and jet boats out of Moab provide another means to explore rugged canyons otherwise inaccessible to all but the hardiest trekkers. The sheer rock cliff faces and promontories in the parks provide abundant challenges to experienced rock climbers; be certain to check park regulations before climbing, however, as restrictions may apply.

HIKING

Utah's national parks offer lots of opportunities for hikers and backcountry enthusiasts interested in exploring the scenery on foot. Each of the parks has a variety of well-maintained hiking trails, ranging from easy strolls to multiday backcountry treks. In fact, much of the Needles and Maze Districts in Canyonlands and the most compelling parts of Capitol Reef and Zion are accessible only by foot; visits to remote Ancestral Puebloan ruins and petroglyphs are among the rewards for the long-distance hiker.

One popular activity is canyoneering—exploring mazelike slot canyons. Hundreds of feet deep but sometimes only wide enough for a hiker to squeeze through, these canyons are located across Southern Utah, with some great ones near Escalante and in the Paria River area. You'll need to be fit to explore these regions—and watch the weather carefully for flash floods.

CAMPING

All of Utah's national parks have campgrounds, with each park keeping at least one campground open year-round. Some campgrounds are first come, first served; **reservations** (877/444-6777, www. recreation.gov, reservation fee $9 online, $10 phone) are accepted seasonally at Zion's Watchman Campground, Bryce's Sunset Campground, Capitol Reef's Fruita Campground, and Arches' Devils Garden Campground. During the summer and on holiday weekends during the spring and fall, it's best to arrive at the park early in the day and select a campsite immediately. Don't expect to find hookups or showers at National Park Service campgrounds. For these comforts, look just outside the park entrance, where you'll generally find at least one full-service commercial campground.

Backcountry Camping

Backcountry campers in national parks must stop by the park visitors center for a backcountry permit. Backcountry camping may be limited to specific sites in order to spread people out a bit; if so, a park ranger will consult with you and assign you a campground.

Before heading into the backcountry, check with a ranger about weather, water sources, fire danger, trail conditions, and regulations. Backpacking stores are also good sources of information. Here are some tips for traveling safely and respectfully in the backcountry:

• Tell rangers or other reliable people where you are going and when you expect to return; they'll alert rescuers if you go missing.

The America the Beautiful Pass

The U.S. government has revamped its park pass system, inaugurating a new set of annual passes that are the result of a cooperative effort between the National Park Service, the U.S. Forest Service, the U.S. Fish and Wildlife Service, the Bureau of Land Management, and the Bureau of Reclamation.

The basic pass is called the **America the Beautiful—National Parks and Federal Recreational Lands Pass** (valid for 1 year from date of purchase, $80 plus a $5 processing and handling fee), which is available to the general public and provides access to, and use of, federal recreation sites that charge an entrance or standard amenity fee. Passes can be obtained in person at a park; by calling 888/ASK-USGS (888/275-8747, ext. 1); or at http://store.usgs.gov/pass.

U.S. citizens or permanent residents age 62 or older can purchase a lifetime version of the America the Beautiful pass for $80. This pass can only be obtained in person at a park. The Senior Pass provides free access to federal parks and recreational areas, plus a 50 percent discount on some fees, such as camping, swimming, boat launch, and specialized interpretive services.

Both passes are good for the cardholder plus three adults (children 15 and under are free). The pass is nontransferable and generally does not cover or reduce special recreation permit fees or fees charged by park concessionaires.

U.S. citizens or permanent residents with permanent disabilities are eligible for a free lifetime America the Beautiful Access Pass. Documentation such as a statement from a licensed physician, the Veterans Administration, or Social Security is required to obtain this pass, which can only be obtained in person at a park. Like the Senior Pass, the Access Pass provides free access to federal parks and recreational areas, plus a 50 percent discount on some fees, such as camping, swimming, boat launch, and specialized interpretive services. Free annual passes are also available to members of the U.S. military and their families.

Volunteers who have amassed 250 service hours with one of the participating federal agencies are eligible for a free one-year pass, which is available through their supervisor.

- Travel in small groups for the best experience (group size may also be regulated).

- Avoid stepping on—or camping on—fragile cryptobiotic soils.

- Use a portable stove to avoid leaving fire scars.

- Resist the temptation to shortcut switchbacks; this causes erosion and can be dangerous.

- Avoid digging tent trenches or cutting vegetation.

- Help preserve old Native American and other historic ruins.

- Camp at least 300 feet (91 m) away from springs, creeks, and trails. Camp at least 0.25 mile (0.4 km) from a lone water source to avoid scaring away wildlife and livestock.

- Avoid camping in washes at any time; be alert to thunderstorms.

- Take care not to throw or kick rocks off trails—someone might be below you.

- Don't drink water directly from streams or lakes, no matter how clean the water appears; it may contain the parasitic protozoan *Giardia lamblia*, which causes giardiasis. Boiling water for several minutes will kill giardia as well as most other bacterial or viral pathogens. Chemical treatments and water filters usually work too, although they're not as reliable as boiling (giardia spends part of its life in a hard shell that protects it from most chemicals).

- Bathe and wash dishes away from lakes, streams, and springs. Use biodegradable soap, and scatter your wash water.

- Bring a trowel for personal sanitation. Dig 6-8 inches deep and cover your waste; in some areas, you'll be required to carry portable human waste disposal systems.

- Pack out all your trash, including toilet paper and feminine hygiene items.
- Bring plenty of feed for your horses and mules.
- Leave dogs at home; they're not permitted on national park trails.
- If you realize you're lost, find shelter. If you're sure of a way to civilization and plan to walk out, leave a note with your departure time and planned route.
- Visit the Leave No Trace website (www.lnt.org) for more details on responsible backcountry travel.

CLIMBING

Most visitors to Utah's national parks enjoy spotting rock climbers scaling canyon walls and sandstone pillars, but for a few, the whole reason to visit Southern Utah is to climb. These folks need a climbing guide, either the classic *Desert Rock* by Eric Bjørnstad or *Rock Climbing Utah* by Stewart M. Green.

Prospective climbers should take note: Just because you're the star of the local rock gym, don't think that climbing Zion's high, exposed big walls or Canyonlands' remote sandstone towers is going to be simple. Sandstone poses its own set of challenges; it weakens when wet, so it's wise to avoid climbing in damp areas or after rain. The Entrada sandstone in Arches is particularly tough to climb.

Climbers in the national parks should take care to use clean climbing techniques. Approach climbs via established trails to prevent further erosion of slopes. Camp in park campgrounds or, on multiday climbs, get a backcountry permit. Because white chalk leaves unsightly marks on canyon walls, add red pigment to your chalk. Do not disturb vegetation growing in cracks along your route. Tube or bag human waste and carry it out. Remove all old worn rope and equipment, but do not remove fixed pins. Make sure your climb is adequately protected by visually inspecting any preexisting bolts or fixed pins. It is illegal to use a power drill to place bolts.

Never climb directly above trails, where hikers may be hit by dislodged rocks.

In Canyonlands, even stricter regulations are in place. Here, no new climbing hardware may be left in a fixed location; protection may not be placed with the use of a hammer except to replace existing belay and rappel anchors and bolts on established routes (or for emergency self-rescue); and unsafe slings must be replaced with earth-colored slings.

Plan to climb in the spring or fall. During the summer, the walls become extremely hot. Some climbing areas may be closed during the spring to protect nesting raptors. Check at the visitors centers for current closures.

4WD EXPLORATION

Utah's national parks are all blessed with fine paved roads—but if you have a high-clearance vehicle, you should explore some of the back roads of Southern Utah. The following roads are either graded dirt or gravel, often with a bit of paved road to begin with, and in dry conditions they are passable by most passenger vehicles, including cars. You'll travel with less concern if you have a higher clearance vehicle (if you're renting, get an SUV); always check in locally to make sure that roads are open and passable. By getting off the highway, you'll leave behind 99 percent of the crowds and have some of Utah's most amazing scenery to yourself.

From Escalante or Boulder, **Hell's Backbone Road** climbs up through alpine forests to 9,200 feet (2,800 m) before dropping down onto a one-lane bridge that vaults across a chasm between two precipitous canyons. Bring a camera—and some Xanax.

Handy **Notom-Bullfrog Road** links the northern reaches of Capitol Reef National Park with Lake Powell and other sites in remote southeastern Utah. Best of all, you'll get a feel for the Waterpocket Fold, the formation that makes up most of Capitol Reef, but that travelers who stick to paved Highway 24 don't really experience. Time your trip right, and you can cross Lake Powell on Utah's only public car ferry.

Burr Trail, a former cattle route, departs from Boulder to skirt the northern canyons of the Escalante River system, ending near the Waterpocket Fold in Capitol Reef National Park, which it descends in an amazing series of switchbacks—dropping 800 feet (244 m) in less than 1 mile (1.6 km). Good brakes are a plus.

Wet weather frequently closes Cottonwood Canyon Road, but it's one of the most scenic in the Kaiparowits National Monument if for no other reason than it's the access road for wonderful Kodachrome Basin and Grosvenor Arch. Continue south to U.S. 89 for excellent canyon hiking and visits to vintage movie sets.

Follow Hole-in-the-Rock Road to its end to parallel the route of intrepid Mormon pioneers and to catch a peek at Lake Powell, or simply use this well-maintained gravel road to access the amazing slot canyons of the Escalante River system (at least check out the Devils Garden).

Travel Tips

Southern Utah may seem a remote, uninhabited, and even hostile destination, but it sees hundreds of thousands of travelers each year and has sufficient facilities to ensure that visitors have a pleasant vacation. Before you visit, here are a few tips to ensure that your Utah vacation goes well.

INTERNATIONAL VISITORS
Entering the United States

Citizens of Canada must provide a passport to enter the United States, but a visa is not required for Canadian citizens.

Citizens of 28 other countries can enter the United States under a reciprocal visa-waiver program. These citizens can enter for up to 90 days for tourism or business with a valid passport, and no visa is required. These countries include most of Western Europe plus Japan, Australia, New Zealand, and Singapore. For a full list of reciprocal visa-waiver countries (along with other late-breaking news for travelers to the United States), check out http://travel.state.gov. Visitors on this program who arrive by sea or air must show round-trip tickets out of the United States dated within 90 days, and they must present proof of financial solvency (credit cards are usually sufficient). If citizens of these countries are staying longer than 90 days, they must apply for and present a visa.

Citizens of countries not covered by the reciprocal visa-waiver program are required to present both a valid passport and a visa to enter the United States. These are obtained from U.S. embassies and consulates. These travelers are also required to offer proof of financial solvency and show a round-trip ticket out of the United States dated within the timeline of the visa.

Once in the United States, foreign visitors can travel freely among states without restrictions.

Customs

U.S. Customs allows each person over the age of 21 to bring one liter of liquor and 200 cigarettes into the country duty-free. Non-U.S. citizens can bring in $100 worth of gifts without paying duty. If you are carrying more than $10,000 in cash or traveler's checks, you are required to declare it.

Money and Currency Exchange

Except in Salt Lake City, there are few opportunities to exchange foreign currency or traveler's checks in non-U.S. funds at Utah banks or exchanges. Traveler's checks in U.S. dollars are accepted at face value in most businesses without additional transaction fees.

By far the best way to keep yourself in cash is by using bank, debit, or cash cards at ATMs

Coronavirus in Utah and the National Parks

At the time of writing, Utah was managing the effects of the coronavirus, with the situation constantly evolving. Most, if not all, destinations required that **face masks** be worn in enclosed spaces and **social distancing** was encouraged. As Utah's Department of Health monitors COVID-19 cases and transmission through the state, phased guidelines may change locally, so check the websites below regularly. The National Park Service also emphasizes the importance of park visitors wearing masks.

Now more than ever, Moon encourages its readers to be courteous and ethical in their travel. We ask travelers to be respectful to residents, and mindful of the evolving situation in their chosen destination when planning their trip.

BEFORE YOU GO

- Check relevant websites (listed below) for **updated local restrictions** and the overall health status of the destination.

- If you plan to fly, check with your **airline** and the **local health authorities** for updated recommendation requirements.

- Check the websites of any venues you wish to patronize to confirm that they're open, if their hours have been adjusted, and to learn about any specific visitation requirements, such as mandatory **reservations.**

- Pack **hand sanitizer, a thermometer,** and plenty of **face masks.** Road trippers may want to bring a **cooler** to limit the number of stops along their route.

- Assess the risk of entering **crowded spaces,** joining **tours,** and taking **public transit.**

- Expect **general disruptions.** Events may be postponed or cancelled. Some tours and venues may require reservations, enforce limits on the number of guests, or operate during different hours than the ones listed. Some may be closed entirely.

RESOURCES

Monitor the following websites to keep track of the evolving COVID-19 situation in Utah:

- **Utah Health Department** (https://coronavirus.utah.gov)

- **Utah State Travel Bureau** (https://www.visitutah.com/plan-your-trip/covid-19)

- **National Park Service** (https://www.nps.gov/planyourvisit/alerts.htm)

(automated teller machines). Not only does withdrawing funds from your own home account save on fees, but you also often get a better rate of exchange. Nearly every town in Utah has an ATM. Most ATMs at banks require a small fee to dispense cash. Most grocery stores allow you to use a debit or cash card to purchase food, with the option of adding a cash withdrawal. These transactions are free to the withdrawer.

Credit cards are accepted nearly everywhere in Utah. The most common are Visa and MasterCard. American Express, Diners Club, and Discover are also used, although these aren't as ubiquitous

Electricity

As in all of the United States, electricity is 110 volts, 60 hertz. Plugs have either two flat prongs or two flat prongs plus one round prong. Older homes and hotels may only have two-prong outlets. If you're traveling with computers or appliances that have three-prong plugs, ask your hotel or motel manager for an adapter. You may need to buy a three-prong adapter, but the cost is small.

ACCESS FOR TRAVELERS WITH DISABILITIES

Travelers with disabilities will find Utah progressive when it comes to accessibility. All of the parks, except the former Grand Staircase-Escalante National Monument, have all-abilities trails and services. All five national parks have reasonably good facilities for visitors with limited mobility. Visitors centers are all accessible, and at least a couple of trails in each park are paved or smooth enough for wheelchair users to navigate with some assistance. Each park has a few accessible campsites.

Most hotels also offer some form of barrier-free lodging. It's best to call ahead and inquire what these accommodations are, however, because these services can vary quite a bit from one establishment to another.

Because the Grand Staircase, Kaiparowits Plateau, and Escalante Canyons units are almost entirely undeveloped, trails are generally inaccessible to wheelchair users.

Accessibility information for each park can also be found on the National Parks Service website (www.nps.gov).

TRAVELING WITH CHILDREN

The parks of Southern Utah are filled with dramatic vistas and exciting recreation. The parks provide lots of opportunities for adventures, whether it's rafting the Colorado River or hiking to ancient Ancestral Puebloan ruins, and most children will have the time of their young lives in Utah.

Utah is a family-vacation type of place, and no special planning is required to make a national park holiday exciting for children. Children do receive discounts on a number of things, ranging from motel rooms (where they often stay for free, but inquire about age restrictions, which vary) to museum admissions. One exception to this family-friendly rule is B&Bs, which frequently don't allow children at all.

Utah law requires all children age four or younger to be restrained in a child safety seat. Child seats can be rented from car-rental agencies—ask when making a car reservation.

SENIOR TRAVELERS

The parks and Utah in general are hospitable for senior travelers. The National Parks and Federal Recreational Lands Senior Pass is a lifetime pass for U.S. citizens or permanent residents age 62 or over. The pass provides access to, and use of, federal parks and recreation sites that charge an entrance fee or standard amenity. The pass admits the pass holder and passengers in a noncommercial vehicle at per-vehicle fee areas, not to exceed four adults. The pass costs $80 and can only be obtained in person at a park. There is a similar discount program at Utah state parks.

LGBTQ TRAVELERS

Utah is not the most enlightened place in the world when it comes to equality issues, but that shouldn't be an issue for travelers to the national parks. Needless to say, a little discretion is a good idea in most public situations, and don't expect to find much of a gay scene anywhere in southeastern Utah. Moab is notably more progressive than anywhere else in this part of the state, but there are no gay bars or gathering places.

PETS

Unless you really have no other option, it's best not to bring your dog (or cat, or bird, or ferret) along on a national park vacation. Although pets are allowed in national parks, they aren't permitted on the trails. This limits you and your dog to leashed walks along the roads, around campground loops, and in parking areas. During much of the year, it's far too hot to leave an animal in a parked car.

In Zion, private cars are prohibited on the scenic canyon drive, and no pets are allowed on the shuttle buses that drive this route. Pet boarding is available just outside

Zion at the **Doggy Dude Ranch** (800 E. Main St, Rockville, 435/772-3105, www. doggyduderanch.com).

Several pet boarding services are available in Moab:

- **Karen's Canine Campground** (2781 S. Roberts Rd., 435/259-7922, https:// karensk9campground.wordpress.com)

- **Moab Veterinary Clinic** (4575 Spanish Valley Dr., 435/259-8710, http:// moabvetclinic.com)

- When in Moab, visit the **Moab Bark Park** (300 S. 100 E.), a fenced off-leash dog park.

CONDUCT AND CUSTOMS
Alcohol and Nightlife

Observant Mormons don't drink alcoholic beverages and **Utah's liquor laws** can seem confusing to outsiders. Changes to Utah's once prohibitive rules have made it easier to buy and consume alcohol. Note that it's no longer necessary to be a member of a private club in order to consume alcohol in a bar—no more buying a temporary membership or signing in on someone else's membership just to enjoy a drink. Several different kinds of establishments are licensed to sell alcoholic beverages:

Taverns, which include brewpubs, can sell only 3.2 percent beer (beer that is 3.2 percent alcohol by volume). Taverns can't sell wine, which is classed as hard liquor in Utah. Stronger beer is available in Utah, but only in bottles, and this beer is also regulated as hard liquor. You don't need to purchase food to have a beer in a tavern. With the exception of brewpubs, taverns are usually fairly derelict and not especially cheery places to hang out.

Licensed restaurants are able to sell beer, wine, and hard liquor, but only with food orders. In many parts of Utah, you'll need to specifically ask for a drink or the drink menu to begin the process. In Salt Lake City, Moab, and Park City, most restaurants have liquor licenses. In small towns, few eating establishments offer alcohol.

Cocktail bars, lounges, live music

Say It Right!

The following place names are easy to mispronounce. Say it like a local!

- Duchesne: du-SHANE
- Ephraim: EE-from
- Hurricane: HUR-ken
- Kanab: kuh-NAB
- Lehi: LEE-high
- Manti: MAN-tie
- Moab: Moe-AB
- Monticello: mon-ta-SELL-o
- Nephi: NEE-fi
- Panguitch: PAN-gwich
- Tooele: too-WILL-uh
- Uinta: you-IN-tuh
- Weber: WEE-ber

Escalante poses an unusual problem. Utahans from northern parts of the state pronounce the name of the town and the famous river canyons as es-ka-LAN-tay; citizens of the town, however, pronounce it without the final long *e*, as es-ka-LANT.

venues, and nightclubs, which once operated on the private-club system, can now serve alcohol without asking for membership. However, some continue the income flow by demanding a cover charge for entry. Depending on which county you are in, you may still be required to order some food to have a drink.

Nearly all towns will have a state-owned **liquor store;** Blanding is the exception. They can be difficult to find. 3.2 percent beer is available in most grocery stores and gas station minimarts. Many travelers find that carrying a bottle of your favorite beverage to your room is the easiest way to enjoy an evening drink. The state drinking age is 21.

If going out for drinks and nightclubbing is part of your idea of entertainment, you'll find that only Moab offers much in the way of nightspots. Outside Moab, many restaurants in Southern Utah don't serve alcohol.

Smoking

Smoking is taboo for observant Mormons, and smoking is prohibited in almost all public places. You're also not allowed to smoke on church grounds. Obviously, take care when smoking in national parks and pick up your own butts. Besides the risk of fire, there's nothing that ruins a natural experience more than windblown piles of cigarette filters.

Small-Town Utah

If you've never traveled in Utah before, you may find that Utahans don't initially seem as welcoming and outgoing as people in other Western states. In many smaller towns, visitors from outside the community are a relatively new phenomenon, and not everyone in the state is anxious to have their towns turned into tourism or recreational meccas. Mormons are very family- and community-oriented, and if certain individuals initially seem insular and uninterested in travelers, don't take it as unfriendliness.

Mormons are also orderly and socially conservative people. Brash displays of rudeness or use of foul language in public will not make you popular.

Health and Safety

There's nothing inherently dangerous about Utah's national parks, though a few precautions can help minimize what risks do exist. For the most part, using common sense about the dangers of extreme temperatures, remote backcountry exploration, and encounters with wildlife will ensure a safe and healthy trip.

HEAT AND WATER

Southern Utah in summer is a very hot place. Be sure to use sunscreen, or else you risk having an uncomfortable vacation. Wearing a wide-brimmed hat and good sunglasses, with full UV protection, can shield you from the sun's harmful effects. Heat exhaustion can also be a problem if you're hiking in the hot sun. In midsummer, try to get an early start if you're hiking in full sun. If you're out during the heat of the afternoon, look for a shady spot and rest until the sun begins to drop.

Drink steadily throughout the day, whether you are thirsty or not, rather than gulping huge amounts of water once you feel thirsty. For hikers, one of the best ways to drink enough is to carry water in a hydration pack (the two top brands are CamelBak and Platypus). These collapsible plastic bladders come with a hose and a mouthpiece, so you can carry your water in your pack, threading the hose out the top of the pack and over your shoulder, which keeps the mouthpiece handy for frequent sips of water. One easy way to tell if you're getting enough to drink is to monitor your urine output. If you're only urinating a couple of times a day, and the color and odor of your urine are both strong, it's time to start drinking more water.

HYPOTHERMIA

Don't think that just because you're in the Utah desert that you're immune to hypothermia. This lowering of the body's temperature below 95°F causes disorientation, uncontrollable shivering, slurred speech, and drowsiness. The victim may not even realize what's wrong. Unless corrective action is taken immediately, hypothermia can lead to death. Hikers should therefore travel with companions and always carry wind and rain protection. Space blankets are lightweight and cheap and offer protection against the cold in emergencies. Remember that temperatures can plummet rapidly in Utah's dry climate—a drop of 40 degrees between day and night is common. Be especially careful at high elevations, where sunshine can quickly change into freezing rain or a blizzard. Simply falling into a mountain stream can also lead to hypothermia and death unless proper action is taken. If you're cold and tired, don't waste time: Seek shelter and build a fire, change into dry clothes, and drink warm liquids. If a victim isn't fully conscious, warm him or her by skin-to-skin contact in a sleeping bag. Try to keep the victim awake and offer plenty of warm liquids.

GIARDIA

Giardia lamblia is a protozoan that has become common in even the remotest mountain streams. It is carried in animal or human waste that is deposited or washed into the water. When ingested, it begins reproducing, causing intense cramping and diarrhea in the host; this can become serious and may require medical attention.

No matter how clear a stream looks, it's best to assume that it is contaminated and to take precautions against giardia by filtering, boiling, or treating water with chemicals before drinking it. A high-quality filter will remove giardia and a host of other things you don't want to be drinking. (Spend a bit extra for one that removes particles down to one micrometer in size.) It's also effective to simply boil your water; two to five minutes at a rolling boil will kill giardia even in the cyst stage. Because water boils at a lower temperature as elevation increases, increase the boiling time to 15 minutes if you're at 9,000 feet (2,743 m). Two drops of bleach left in a quart of water for 30 minutes will remove most giardia, although some microorganisms are resistant to chemicals.

HANTAVIRUS

Hantavirus is an infectious disease agent that was first isolated during the Korean War and then discovered in the Americas in 1993 by a task force of scientists in New Mexico. This disease agent occurs naturally throughout most of North and South America, especially in dry desert conditions. The infectious agent is airborne, and in the absence of prompt medical attention, its infections are usually fatal. This disease is called hantavirus pulmonary syndrome (HPS). It can affect anyone, but given some fundamental knowledge, it can also easily be prevented.

The natural host of the hantavirus appears to be rodents, especially mice and rats. The virus is not usually transmitted directly from rodents to humans; rather, the rodents shed hantavirus particles in their saliva, urine, and droppings. Humans usually contract HPS by inhaling particles that are infected with the hantavirus. The virus becomes airborne when the particles dry out and get stirred into the air (especially from sweeping a floor or shaking a rug). Humans then inhale these particles, which leads to the infection.

HPS is not considered a highly infectious disease, so people usually contract HPS from long-term exposure. Because transmission usually occurs through inhalation, it is easiest for a human being to contract hantavirus within a contained environment, where the virus-infected particles are not thoroughly dispersed. Being in a cabin or barn where rodents can be found poses elevated risks for contracting the infection.

Simply traveling to a place where the hantavirus is known to occur is not considered a risk factor. Camping, hiking, and other outdoor activities also pose low risk, especially if steps are taken to reduce rodent contact. If you happen to stay in a rodent-infested cabin, thoroughly wet any droppings and dead rodents with a chlorine bleach solution (one cup of bleach per gallon of water) and let them stand for a few minutes before cleaning them up. Be sure to wear rubber gloves for this task, and double-bag your garbage.

The first symptoms of HPS can occur anywhere between five days and three weeks after infection. They almost always include fever, fatigue, aching muscles (usually in the back, shoulders, or thighs), and other flu-like symptoms. Other early symptoms may include headaches, dizziness, chills, and abdominal discomfort such as vomiting, nausea, or diarrhea. These symptoms are shortly followed by intense coughing and shortness of breath. If you have these symptoms, seek medical help immediately. Untreated infections of hantavirus are almost always fatal.

THINGS THAT BITE OR STING

Although travelers in Utah's national parks are not going to get attacked by a grizzly bear, and encounters with mountain lions are rare, there are a few animals to watch out for. Snakes, scorpions, and spiders are all present in considerable numbers, and there are a few key things to know about dealing with this phobia-inducing trio.

Snakes

Rattlesnakes, including the particularly venomous midget faded rattlesnake, are present throughout Southern Utah. The midget faded snakes live in Arches and Canyonlands, where they frequent burrows and rock crevices and are mostly active at night. Even though their venom is toxic, full venom injections are relatively uncommon, and, like all rattlesnakes, they pose little threat unless they're provoked.

If you see a rattlesnake, observe it at a safe distance. Be careful where you put your hands when canyoneering or scrambling—it's not a good idea to reach above your head and blindly plant your hands on a sunny rock ledge. Hikers should wear sturdy boots to minimize the chance that a snake's fangs will reach the skin if a bite occurs. Do not walk barefoot outside after dark, as this is when snakes hunt for prey.

First aid for rattlesnake bites is full of conflicting ideas: to suck or not to suck; to apply a constricting bandage or not; to take time treating in the field versus rushing to the hospital. Most people who receive medical treatment after being bitten by a rattlesnake live to tell the story. Prompt administration of antivenin is the most important treatment, and the most important aspect of first aid is to arrange transportation of the victim to a hospital as quickly as possible.

Scorpions

A scorpion's sting isn't as painful as you'd expect (it's about like a bee sting), and the venom is insufficient to cause any real harm. Still, it's not what you'd call pleasant, and experienced desert campers know to shake out their boots every morning, as scorpions and spiders are attracted to warm, moist, dark places.

Spiders

Tarantulas and black widow spiders are present across much of the Colorado Plateau. Believe it or not, a tarantula's bite does not poison humans; the enzymes secreted when they bite turn the insides of frogs, lizards, and insects to a soft mush, allowing the tarantula to suck the guts from its prey. Another interesting tarantula fact: While males live about as long as you'd expect a spider to live, female tarantulas can live for up to 25 years. Females do sometimes eat the males, which may account for some of this disparity in longevity.

Black widow spiders, on the other hand, have a toxic bite. Although the bite is usually painless, it delivers a potent neurotoxin, which quickly causes pain, nausea, and vomiting. It is important to seek immediate treatment for a black widow bite; although few people actually die from these bites, recovery is helped along considerably by antivenin.

Resources

Suggested Reading

ARCHAEOLOGY

Childs, Craig. *House of Rain: Tracking a Vanished Civilization across the American Southwest*. New York: Back Bay Books, 2008. Only part of this book deals with Utah, but it's a great read about the Ancestral Puebloans.

Jones, Kevin T., and Miller, Layne. Standing on the Walls of Time: Ancient Art of Utah's Cliffs and Canyons. Salt Lake City: University of Utah Press, 2019. With sumptuous photos, this book looks at the artistry of Utah's rock art; written by the former Utah state archeologist.

Lister, Robert, and Florence Lister. *Those Who Came Before*. Tucson: Southwest Parks and Monuments, 1993. A well-illustrated guide to the history, artifacts, and ruins of prehistoric Southwestern people. The author also describes parks and monuments containing archaeological sites.

Simms, Steven R. *Traces of Fremont: Society and Rock Art in Ancient Utah*. Salt Lake City: University of Utah Press and Price, UT: College of Eastern Utah Prehistoric Museum, 2010. Great photos accompany the text in this look into Fremont culture.

MAPS AND GUIDEBOOKS

Benchmark Maps. *Utah Road & Recreation Atlas*. Medford, OR: Benchmark Maps, 2017. Shaded relief maps emphasize landforms, and recreational information is abundant. Use the atlas to locate campgrounds, back roads, and major trailheads, although there's not enough detail to rely on it for hiking.

Huegel, Tony. *Utah Byways: 65 of Utah's Best Backcountry Drives*. Berkeley, CA: Wilderness Press, 2006. If you're looking for off-highway adventure, this is your guide. The spiral-bound book includes detailed directions, human and natural history, outstanding photography, full-page maps for each of the 65 routes, and an extensive how-to chapter for beginners.

HISTORY AND CURRENT EVENTS

Dellenbaugh, Frederick S. *A Canyon Voyage: The Narrative of the Second Powell Expedition*. Tucson: University of Arizona Press, 2017. A well-written account of John Wesley Powell's second expedition down the Green and Colorado Rivers, 1871-1872. The members took the first Grand Canyon photographs and obtained much valuable scientific knowledge.

Stegner, Wallace. *Beyond the Hundredth Meridian: John Wesley Powell and the Second Opening of the West*. New York: Penguin Books, reprinted 1992 (first published in 1954). Stegner's book tells the story of Powell's wild rides down the Colorado River, then goes on to point out why the United States should have listened to what Powell had to say about the U.S. Southwest.

MEMOIRS

Abbey, Edward. *Desert Solitaire*. New York: Ballantine Books, 1991. A meditation on the red-rock canyon country of Utah. Abbey brings his fiery prose to the service of the American outback, while excoriating the commercialization of the West.

Childs, Craig. *The Secret Knowledge of Water*. Boston: Back Bay Books, 2001. Childs looks for water in the desert, and finds plenty of it.

Zwinger, Ann. *Run, River, Run: A Naturalist's Journey down One of the Great Rivers of the American West*. Tucson: University of Arizona Press, 1984. An excellent description of the author's experiences along the Green River, from its source in the Wind River Range of Wyoming to the Colorado River in southeastern Utah. The author weaves geology, Native American ruins, plants, wildlife, and her personal feelings into the text and drawings.

NATURAL SCIENCES

Chronic, Lucy, and Felicie Williams. *Roadside Geology of Utah*. Missoula, MT: Mountain Press Publishing, 2014. This layperson's guide tells the story of the state's fascinating geology as seen by following major roadways.

Fagan, Damian. *Canyon Country Wildflowers*. Helena, MT: Falcon Publishing, 2012. A comprehensive field guide to the diverse flora of the Four Corners area.

Fagan, Damian, and David Williams. *A Naturalist's Guide to the White Rim Trail*. Seattle: Wingate Ink, 2007. Take your time to explore nature on the White Rim Trail.

Williams, David, and Gloria Brown. *A Naturalist's Guide to Canyon Country*. Helena, MT: Falcon Publishing, 2020. If you want to buy just one field guide, this is the one to get. It's well written, beautifully illustrated, and a delight to use.

OUTDOOR ACTIVITIES

Allen, Steve. *Canyoneering 3*. Salt Lake City: University of Utah Press, 1997. Provides excellent, detailed descriptions of a variety of hikes in the Grand Staircase-Escalante area, ranging from day hikes to multiday treks.

Crowell, David. *Mountain Biking Moab*. Helena, MT: Falcon Guides, 2019. A guide to the many trails around Moab, from the most popular to the little explored, in a handy size—small enough to take on the bike with you.

Day, David. *Utah's Favorite Hiking Trails*. Provo, UT: Rincon Publishing, 2002. Good simple maps and detailed descriptions of trails all over the state, including many in Southern Utah's national parks and monuments.

Green, Stewart M. *Rock Climbing Utah*. Helena, MT: Falcon Publishing, 2012. Good detail on climbs in all of Utah's national parks, including many line drawings and photos with climbing routes highlighted.

Kelsey, Michael R. *Canyon Hiking Guide to the Colorado Plateau*. Provo, UT: Brigham Distributing, 2018. One of the best guides to hiking in southeastern Utah's canyon country. Geologic cross sections show the formations you'll be walking through.

Lambrechtse, Rudi. *Hiking the Escalante*. Salt Lake City: University of Utah Press, 2016. "A wilderness guide to an exciting land of buttes, arches, alcoves, amphitheaters, and deep canyons," this introduction to history, geology, and natural history of the Escalante region in Southern Utah contains descriptions and trailhead information for 42 hiking destinations.

Molvar, Erik. *Best Easy Day Hikes Zion and Bryce Canyon National Parks*. Helena, MT: Falcon Publishing, 2014. Features concise descriptions and easy-to-follow maps for

22 easily manageable hikes in two of Utah's most popular national parks.

Schneider, Bill. *Best Easy Day Hikes Canyonlands and Arches.* Helena, MT: Falcon Publishing, 2017. Twenty hikes in this popular vacation area, geared to travelers who are short on time or aren't able to explore the canyons on more difficult trails.

Sjogren, Morgan. *The Best Bears Ears National Monument Hikes.* Golden, CO: Colorado Mountain Club, 2018. Hikes range from easy strolls suitable for families children to extended adventures into remote corners of this now-dismantled but still explorable national monument.

Tanner, J. D., and Emily Ressler-Tanner. *Best Easy Day Hikes Grand Staircase-Escalante and the Glen Canyon Region.* Helena, MT: Falcon Publishing, 2018. Features 19 hikes in south-central Utah's canyon country, including Paria Canyon.

Wells, Charles A., and Shelly Mayer. *Guide to Moab, UT Backroads & 4-Wheel Drive Trails.* Monument, CO: Funtreks, 2016. Good descriptions and GPS waypoints for Moab-area four-wheelers.

Witt, Greg. *50 Best Hikes in Utah's National Parks.* Birmingham, AL: Wilderness Press, 2014. A veteran hiking guide shares his favorite routes in Utah's five national parks.

Internet Resources

The American Southwest
www.americansouthwest.net/utah
This online Utah guide provides an overview of national parks, national recreation areas, and some state parks.

Desert USA
www.desertusa.com
Desert USA's Utah section discusses places to visit and what plants and animals you might meet there. Here's the best part of this site: You can find out what's in bloom at www.desertusa.com/wildflo/nv.html.

Greater Zion
https://greaterzion.com
The southwestern Utah city of St. George is the focus of this site, which also covers some of the smaller communities outside Zion National Park.

Moab Area Travel Council
http://discovermoab.com
Upcoming events, mountain bike trails, local restaurants and lodging, and outfitters are all easy to find at this comprehensive site.

National Park Service
www.nps.gov
The National Park Service offers pages for all its parks at this site. Trail conditions, maps, accessible features, and other helpful information are included. You can also enter this address followed by a slash and the first two letters of the first two words of the place (first four letters if there's just a one-word name); for example, www.nps.gov/brca takes you to Bryce Canyon National Park and www.nps.gov/zion leads to Zion National Park.

Recreation.gov
www.recreation.gov
If a campground is operated by the federal government, this is the place to make a reservation. You can expect to pay close to $10 for this convenience.

Reserve America
www.reserveamerica.com
Use this website to reserve campsites in state campgrounds. It costs a few extra bucks to reserve a campsite, but compare that with the cost of being skunked out of a site and having to resort to a motel room.

State of Utah
www.utah.gov
The official State of Utah website has information on travel, agencies, programs, and what the legislature is up to.

U.S. Forest Service
www.fs.fed.us/r4
Utah falls within U.S. Forest Service Region 4. The Manti-La Sal National Forest (www.fs.fed.us/r4/mantilasal) is in southeast Utah around Moab and Monticello.

Utah Mountain Biking
www.utahmountainbiking.com
Details mountain biking routes listed in this book as well as other local trails.

Utah State Parks
http://stateparks.utah.gov
The Utah State Parks site offers details on the large park system, including links to reserve campsites.

Utah Travel Council
https://utah.com
The Utah Travel Council is a one-stop shop for all sorts of information on Utah. It takes you around the state to sights, activities, events, and maps, and offers links to local tourism offices. The accommodations listings are the most up-to-date source for current room rates and options.

Zion Park
www.zionpark.com
This site will point you to information on Springdale and the area surrounding Zion National Park, with links to lodging and restaurant sites.

Index

MOON ZION & BRYCE

Avalon Travel
Hachette Book Group
1700 Fourth Street
Berkeley, CA 94710, USA
www.moon.com

Editor: Diana Smith
Acquiring Editor: Nikki Ioakimedes
Copy Editor: Rachael Sablik
Graphics and Production Coordinator: Rue Flaherty
Cover Design: Kimberly Glyder Design
Interior Design: Domini Dragoone
Moon Logo: Tim McGrath
Map Editor: Mike Morgenfeld
Cartographer: John Culp
Indexer: Greg Jewett

ISBN-13: 978-1-64049-473-2

Printing History
1st Edition — 2003
9th Edition — September 2021
5 4 3 2 1

Front cover photo: Bryce Canyon National Park © Matt Champlin / Getty Images
Back cover photo: Virgin River narrows, Zion National Park © Pancaketom | Dreamstime.com

Printed in Malaysia for Imago

MAP SYMBOLS

═══	Expressway	○	City/Town	✈	Airport	⛳	Golf Course
───	Primary Road	◉	State Capital	✈	Airfield	🅿	Parking Area
───	Secondary Road	⊛	National Capital	▲	Mountain	▰	Archaeological Site
═ ═ ═	Unpaved Road	◎	Highlight	✦	Unique Natural Feature	⛪	Church
─ ─ ─	Trail	★	Point of Interest			⛽	Gas Station
··········	Ferry	•	Accommodation	🌿	Waterfall	◯	Glacier
▬▬▬	Railroad	▼	Restaurant/Bar	⯅	Park		Mangrove
═══	Pedestrian Walkway	▪	Other Location	TH	Trailhead		Reef
▨▨▨	Stairs	Λ	Campground	⛷	Skiing Area		Swamp

CONVERSION TABLES

°C = (°F - 32) / 1.8
°F = (°C x 1.8) + 32
1 inch = 2.54 centimeters (cm)
1 foot = 0.304 meters (m)
1 yard = 0.914 meters
1 mile = 1.6093 kilometers (km)
1 km = 0.6214 miles
1 fathom = 1.8288 m
1 chain = 20.1168 m
1 furlong = 201.168 m
1 acre = 0.4047 hectares
1 sq km = 100 hectares
1 sq mile = 2.59 square km
1 ounce = 28.35 grams
1 pound = 0.4536 kilograms
1 short ton = 0.90718 metric ton
1 short ton = 2,000 pounds
1 long ton = 1.016 metric tons
1 long ton = 2,240 pounds
1 metric ton = 1,000 kilograms
1 quart = 0.94635 liters
1 US gallon = 3.7854 liters
1 Imperial gallon = 4.5459 liters
1 nautical mile = 1.852 km

°FAHRENHEIT / °CELSIUS

°FAHRENHEIT	°CELSIUS	
230	110	
220	100	WATER BOILS
210		
200	90	
190		
180	80	
170		
160	70	
150		
140	60	
130		
120	50	
110		
100	40	
90		
80	30	
70		
60	20	
50	10	
40		
30	0	WATER FREEZES
20		
10	-10	
0		
-10	-20	
-20	-30	
-30		
-40	-40	

Get inspired for your next adventure

Follow **@moonguides** on Instagram or subscribe to our newsletter at **moon.com**

#TravelWithMoon

MORE ROAD TRIP GUIDES FROM MOON

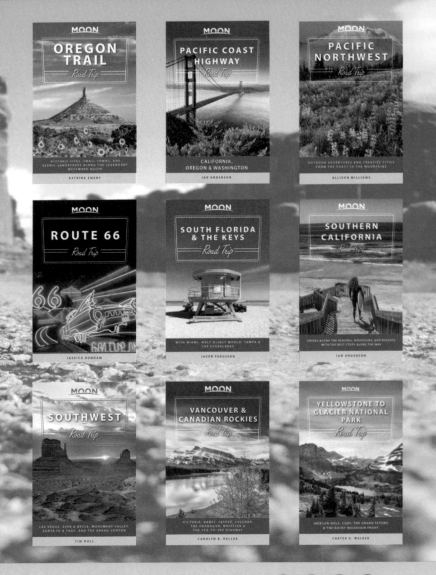

MOON
OREGON TRAIL
Road Trip

HISTORIC SITES, SMALL TOWNS, AND SCENIC LANDSCAPES ALONG THE LEGENDARY WESTWARD ROUTE

KATRINA EMERY

MOON
PACIFIC COAST HIGHWAY
Road Trip

CALIFORNIA, OREGON & WASHINGTON

IAN ANDERSON

MOON
PACIFIC NORTHWEST
Road Trip

OUTDOOR ADVENTURES AND CREATIVE CITIES FROM THE COAST TO THE MOUNTAINS

ALLISON WILLIAMS

MOON
ROUTE 66
Road Trip

JESSICA DUNHAM

MOON
SOUTH FLORIDA & THE KEYS
Road Trip

WITH MIAMI, WALT DISNEY WORLD, TAMPA & THE EVERGLADES

JASON FERGUSON

MOON
SOUTHERN CALIFORNIA
Road Trip

DRIVES ALONG THE BEACHES, MOUNTAINS, AND DESERTS WITH THE BEST STOPS ALONG THE WAY

IAN ANDERSON

MOON
SOUTHWEST
Road Trip

LAS VEGAS, ZION & BRYCE, MONUMENT VALLEY, SANTA FE & TAOS, AND THE GRAND CANYON

TIM HULL

MOON
VANCOUVER & CANADIAN ROCKIES
Road Trip

VICTORIA, BANFF, JASPER, CALGARY, THE OKANAGAN, WHISTLER & THE SEA-TO-SKY HIGHWAY

CAROLYN B. HELLER

MOON
YELLOWSTONE TO GLACIER NATIONAL PARK
Road Trip

JACKSON HOLE, CODY, THE GRAND TETONS & THE ROCKY MOUNTAIN FRONT

CARTER G. WALKER

MOON.COM | @MOONGUIDES

In these books:

Coverage of gateway cities and towns

Suggested itineraries from one day to multiple weeks

Advice on where to stay (or camp) in and around the parks

MOON

GREAT SMOKY MOUNTAINS
NATIONAL PARK

HIKING · CAMPING
SCENIC DRIVES

JASON FRYE

MOON

JOSHUA TREE
& PALM SPRINGS

MOON

YELLOWSTONE
& GRAND TETON

HIKE, CAMP,
SEE WILDLIFE

BECKY LOMAX

MOON

YOSEMITE
SEQUOIA &
KINGS CANYON

ANN MARIE BROWN

MOON

ZION &
BRYCE

W. C. McRAE JUDY JEWELL

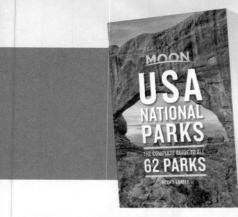

USA NATIONAL PARKS

THE COMPLETE GUIDE TO ALL 62 PARKS

BECKY LOMAX

Craft a personalized journey through the top National Parks in the U.S. and Canada with Moon!

ACADIA NATIONAL PARK
SEASIDE TOWNS · FALL FOLIAGE
CYCLING & PADDLING

ARCHES & CANYONLANDS NATIONAL PARKS

BANFF NATIONAL PARK
HIKE · CAMP
SEE WILDLIFE

DEATH VALLEY NATIONAL PARK

GLACIER NATIONAL PARK
HIKING · CAMPING
LAKES & PEAKS

GRAND CANYON
HIKE · CAMP
RAFT THE COLORADO RIVER

MOUNT RUSHMORE & THE BLACK HILLS

ROCKY MOUNTAIN NATIONAL PARK
HIKE · CAMP
SEE WILDLIFE

SEQUOIA & KINGS CANYON
HIKING · CAMPING
WATERFALLS & BIG TREES

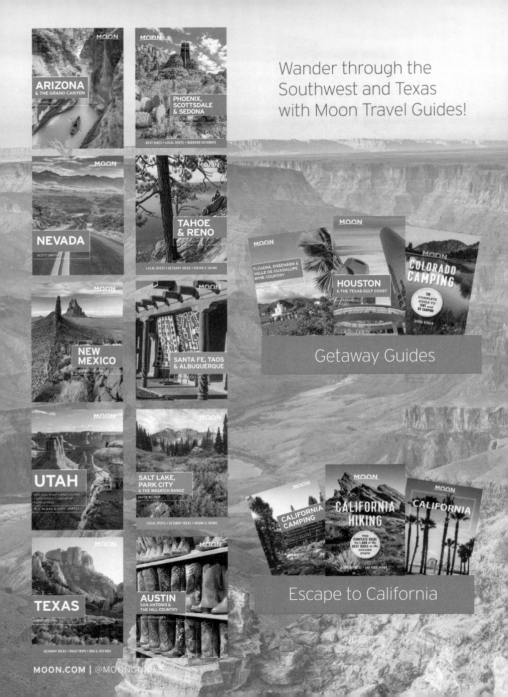

Wander through the
Southwest and Texas
with Moon Travel Guides!

Getaway Guides

Escape to California

Photo Credits

Title page photo: Mary Orr; page 2 © Bill McRae; page 3 © Bill McRae; page 10 © (top left) Bill McRae; (top right) Bill McRae; (bottom) Yobro10| Dreamstime.com; page 11 © (top) Bill McRae; (bottom left) Bill McRae; (bottom right) Bill McRae; page 12 © (top) Colin Young | Dreamstime.com; page 13 © (top) Jennifer Snarski; (bottom left) Bill McRae; (bottom right) Bill McRae; page 14 © Zhiwei Zhou | Dreamstime.com; page 16 © (top) Salvatore Conte| Dreamstime.com; (bottom) Kwiktor| Dreamstime.com; page 17 © (top) Galyna Andrushko| Dreamstime.com; (bottom) Bill McRae; page 19 © (top) Adogslifephoto | Dreamstime. com; (bottom) Lightphoto | Dreamstime.com; page 20 © NPS Neal Herber; page 21 © (top) Hpbfotos| Dreamstime.com; (bottom) Cynthia Mccrary| Dreamstime.com; page 24 © (top) Nora Fisher-Campbell; page 27 © (bottom) Bill McRae; page 30 © Lukasz Kielas| Dreamstime.com; Judy Jewell; page 31 © (top) Judy Jewell; page 33 © (top) Kevin Hutson| Dreamstime.com; page 34 © (bottom) Mikhail Dudarev| Dreamstime. com; page 37 © (bottom) Judy Jewell; page 40 © Paul Levy; page 41 © (top left) Bill McRae; (top right) Bill McRae; page 46 © (top left) Bill McRae; (bottom) Alaskaphoto | Dreamstime.com; page 49 © (top) Judy Jewell; (bottom) Paul Levy; page 50 © Stefano Caccia | Dreamstime.com; page 55 © Paul Levy; page 57 © Judy Jewell; page 63 © (top left) Judy Jewell; (top right) Jennifer Snarski; (bottom) Bill McRae; page 65 © Paul Levy; page 69 © (top left) Yobro10 | Dreamstime.com; (top right) Gelyngfjell | Dreamstime.com; (bottom) 4girlsmomma | Dreamstime.com; page 74 © (top left) Bill McRae; (top right) Bill McRae; (bottom) Michael Gordon | Dreamstime.com; page 80 © (top) Judy Jewell; (bottom) Jennifer Snarski; page 88 © (top) Judy Jewell; (bottom) Judy Jewell; page 91 © Mary Orr; page 92 © (top left) Bill McRae; (top right) Judy Jewell; page 97 © (top left) Bill McRae; (top right) Judy Jewell; (bottom) Paul Levy; page 98 © Mary Orr; page 103 © Jennifer Snarski; page 104 © Judy Jewell; page 106 © Songquan Deng | Dreamstime.com; page 109 © Judy Jewell; page 115 © (top) Judy Jewell; (bottom) Mary Orr; page 120 © Mary Orr; page 121 © (top left) Jennifer Snarski; (top right) Bill McRae; page 125 © Bill McRae; page 129 © (top left) Paul Levy; (top right) Bill McRae; (bottom) Colin Young | Dreamstime.com; page 133 © (top) Bill McRae; (left middle) Judy Jewell; (right middle) Paul Levy; (bottom) Judy Jewell; page 145 © (top) Paul Levy; (bottom) Jennifer Snarski; page 151 © (top) Bill McRae; (left middle) Bill McRae; (right middle) Bill McRae; (bottom) Bill McRae; page 161 © (top) Judy Jewell; (bottom) Bill McRae; page 163 © Mary Orr; page 164 © (top left) Bill McRae; (top right) Judy Jewell; page 169 © (top) Judy Jewell; (right middle) Judy Jewell; (bottom) Bill McRae; page 172 © Judy Jewell; page 179 © (top) Mary Orr; (bottom) Nora Fisher-Campbell; page 180 © Mary Orr; page 181 © Bill McRae; page 186 © Mary Orr; page 187 © (top left) Bill McRae; (top right) Nora Fisher-Campbell; page 195 © (top left) Bill McRae; (top right) Judy Jewell; (bottom) Bill McRae; page 197 © Jason Finn | Dreamstime.com; page 199 © Bill McRae; page 200 © Bill McRae; page 205 © (top) Judy Jewell; (left middle) Bill McRae; (right middle) Nora Fisher-Campbell; (bottom) Judy Jewell; page 211 © (top) Judy Jewell; (bottom) Judy Jewell; page 212 © Mary Orr; page 222 © (top) Bill McRae; (bottom) Bill McRae; page 225 © Mary Orr; page 226 © (top left) Bill McRae; (top right) Judy Jewell; page 231 © (top left) Bill McRae; (top right) Judy Jewell; (bottom) Judy Jewell; page 239 © (top left) Paul Levy; (top right) Judy Jewell; (bottom) Paul Levy; page 242 © Sandra Foyt| Dreamstime.com; page 244 © Bill McRae; page 245 © (top left) Paul Levy; (top right) Judy Jewell; page 249 © Judy Jewell; page 251 © (top left) Judy Jewell; (top right) Nora Fisher-Campbell; (bottom) Bill McRae; page 255 © Bill McRae; page 258 © Bill McRae; page 260 © (top left) Paul Levy; (top right) Paul Levy; (bottom left) Paul Levy; (bottom right) Prochasson Frederic | Dreamstime. com; page 267 © (top) Georgia Evans | Dreamstime.com; (bottom) Christina Felschen | Dreamstime.com; page 269 © Bill McRae; page 277 © (top) Judy Jewell; (bottom) Bill McRae; page 280 © Bill McRae; page 281 © (top left) Judy Jewell; (top right) Paul Levy; page 286 © (top) Bill McRae; (left middle) Bill McRae; (right middle) Bill McRae; (bottom) Bill McRae; page 290 © Paul Levy; page 294 © Bill McRae; page 297 © (top) Bill McRae; (left middle) Paul Levy; (right middle) Bill McRae; (bottom) Paul Levy; page 301 © (top left) Judy Jewell; (top right) Kojihirano | Dreamstime.com; (bottom) Intst | Dreamstime.com; page 309 © (top left) Nora Fisher-Campbell; (top right) Paul Levy; (bottom) Bill McRae; page 311 © Bill McRae; page 327 © Paul Levy.

List of Maps